COPTIC IN TWENTY LESSONS

COPTIC IN 20 LESSONS

Introduction to Sahidic Coptic
With Exercises & Vocabularies

Bentley Layton

PEETERS
Leuven – Paris – Dudley
2007

Library of Congress Cataloging-in-Publication Data

Layton, Bentley
  Coptic in 20 lessons: introduction to Sahidic Coptic with exercises &
vocabularies / Bentley Layton
  p. cm. -
Includes index
ISBN 90-429-1810-1 (alk. paper)
1. Coptic language -- Grammar -- Textbooks. 2. Sahidic dialect -- Grammar --
Textbooks.

PJ2035.L39 2006
493/.2522 -- dc.22   2006047412

© 2006 – Peeters – Bondgenotenlaan 153 – 3000 Leuven

D. 2006/0602/98
ISBN-10   90-429-1810-1
ISBN-13   978-90-429-1810-8

Contents

FOREWORD

THIS book will quickly teach you all the basic patterns of Coptic, mainly at the level of phrases and sentences. It contains drills to help you gain fluency as well as translation exercises, both from Coptic to English and from English to Coptic. A vocabulary list is given at the end of most lessons. If you memorize these lists thoroughly, you will know all the words that occur more than fifty times in the Sahidic Coptic New Testament[1]. In order to read Coptic it is absolutely essential to memorize these lists. Once you have finished learning the contents of this book, you will be ready to read the Gospel of Mark in Coptic[2]. The first three chapters of Mark are included in this book, with vocabulary glosses. Ordinarily one academic year should be enough time to complete both the grammar and all sixteen chapters of the Gospel.

The book can be used in the classroom or to teach yourself Coptic.

The vocabulary lists include common Greek equivalents for *Egyptian* Coptic words, based on the Coptic translation of the New Testament. (For more information, consult the *Concordance du nouveau testament sahidique*[3]). In the vocabularies, *Greco-Coptic* words are starred (*).

Bold face numbers occurring within the text—for example in the phrase "double vowel (9)" on page 8—make cross-reference to section numbers of the grammar. Some information of an advanced level is provided in boxes.

A very inclusive Reference List of Coptic Forms is provided for your convenience

---

[1] To instructors of elementary Coptic, I recommend giving a vocabulary quiz whenever a lesson is finished, perhaps ten words from Coptic to English and ten more from English to Coptic.

[2] Easiest to read will be Horner's text in normal classical spelling: [George Horner, ed.] *The Coptic Version of the New Testament in the Southern Dialect Otherwise Called Sahidic and Thebaic* (Osnabrück: Zeller, 1969 reprint of 1911 edition) vol. 1, pp. 352–639. Students interested in early, non-standardized Coptic may wish instead to study Quecke's edition of an early Barcelona manuscript: Hans Quecke, ed., *Das Markusevangelium saïdisch: Text der Handschrift PPalau Rib. Inv.-Nr. 182 mit den Varianten der Handschrift M 569* (Barcelona: Papyrologia Castroctaviana, 1972), distributed by Biblical Institute Press (Rome). Quecke's introduction includes a detailed discussion of the spelling of the manuscript.

[3] In 5 vols. (Corpus Scriptorum Christianorum Orientalium, Subsidia; Louvain: CSCO). *Les mots d'origine grecque,* by L.-Th. Lefort (Subsidia 1; 1964); *Les mots autochtones,* 3 vols., by Michel Wilmet (Subsidia 11, 13, 15; 1957, 1958, 1959); *Index copte et grec-copte,* by René Draguet (Subsidia 16; 1960).

in the back matter of this book. You should use this list whenever you have trouble identifying a form, or difficulty making sense of a passage. You will also find a Subject Index, which lists all the topics discussed in this book.

You may want to pursue some grammatical topics in greater detail and to read a wide selection of real examples taken from the Coptic literature. This information can be found in Bentley Layton, *A Coptic Grammar* (ISBN 3-447-04833-6; 2d edition, Wiesbaden: Harrassowitz, 2004; www.harrassowitz-verlag.de), to which I have provided references throughout the present book, using the siglum "CG" followed by paragraph number. You can get more practice reading Coptic by using the chrestomathy and vocabulary printed at the end of that work. You should purchase a copy of W.E. Crum, *A Coptic Dictionary* (Oxford: Clarendon, 1939 and various reprints) and start learning its contents once you've finished this grammar, or even before.

I am extremely grateful to Dr. Sofía Torallas Tovar for obtaining the photograph reproduced in lesson one; to Dr. Alberto Nodar for photographing it; and to the Archivo General de la Compañía de Jesús en Catalunya (Barcelona) for permission to reproduce it here. Several colleagues who have taught Coptic from a draft of this book kindly sent me corrections and suggestions, and to them I am also very grateful: David Brakke, Paul Dilley, and Colleen Manassa.

Good luck! I hope you enjoy Coptic!

Yale University, New Haven (Connecticut)

LESSON 1

COPTIC. THE ALPHABET.
REGULAR REPLACEMENTS.
SIMPLIFICATIONS. ABBREVIATIONS.

1. COPTIC is the final stage of the indigenous language of Egypt as it was written in the Nile Valley, the Egyptian Delta, and the Oases about AD 300–1000. It is the direct descendent of Ancient Egyptian, which was once written in the hieroglyphic, hieratic, and Demotic writing systems. Philologists treat Egyptian as a language group unto itself; it has some affinities with Semitic and various African languages. Coptic Egyptian flourished in Egypt until about AD 1000, by which time it had been replaced by Arabic as the language of daily life in Egypt. Unlike the notation of all previous stages of Egyptian (stretching back to before 3000 BC) Coptic was written in an alphabet, based on Greek. The Coptic writing system must have been standardized by the Christian religious establishment in the third century AD. Coptic comprised a number of dialects, of which *Sahidic* (centered perhaps in Shmoun-Hermopolis-Al Ashmunein) had the greatest literary importance and the widest use in the Nile valley. Almost all native Coptic literature was composed in Sahidic, between AD 325–800[5]. Sahidic is the dialect taught in this grammar. Because the climate of Egypt is especially favorable for the preservation of antiquities—desert conditions prevail south of Cairo, as one goes up the Nile Valley—an astonishing number of very early Coptic manuscripts have been discovered, dating from AD 300 onwards, and the number continues to grow. The book as we know it (the codex format) was invented in Egypt, and these earliest Coptic manuscripts are the earliest known examples of the book.

Coptic literature, which survives in a number of dialects, comprises both original works and translations from the Greek and was mostly intended for use in the non-Greek churches and monasteries of Egypt. It includes several translations of the Bible made from Greek starting about AD 300, which are a very early indirect attestation of the Greek text and a direct indication of an Egyptian (perhaps Alexandrian) understanding of what it meant: the Coptic versions are of great importance to mod-

---

[5] The liturgy of the present day Coptic Orthodox Church in Egypt is written in a mixture of Arabic, Greek, and Bohairic Coptic, the ancient dialect of the Delta and the great monasteries of the Wadi Natrun. Coptic is no longer a living language.

ern scholars of Biblical textual criticism. In antiquity, the Bible text in Coptic was the foundation on which Coptic literary style was erected. Organized, coenobitic Christian monasticism began in Egypt, and the writings of the early monastic founders—Pachomius, Theodore, Horsiese, Shenoute, Besa (all of them Copts)— give us precious and unique documentation of daily life in the monastery and the ideology of coenobitic asceticism. This is especially true in the case of Shenoute, the leader of a monastic federation from AD 385–465, whose Coptic writings (spanning seventy years) survive in great quantity; Shenoute is the most prolific native Coptic author and its first real stylist. Also extant are business documents and personal letters, concerning both monastic and secular life.

Because the survival of early Coptic manuscripts was dictated more by climate than by theological orthodoxy, a very wide selection of apocryphal and heretical works has also survived. Most famous among these are the fourth-century Nag Hammadi manuscripts, which are of paramount importance for the study of ancient Gnosticism; it is not clear who read and paid for the copying of these manuscripts. Coptic Manichean texts are also of great interest for the Western branch of Mani's world religion; not only scriptural works but also everyday letters of Manichean Copts have been discovered. Most Nag Hammadi and Manichean texts are not written in the pure classical Sahidic dialect and so require some additional study once classical Sahidic has been mastered. Native Egyptian (pre-Christian) religion continued to find literary expression in Coptic, in a corpus somewhat prejudicially labelled Coptic magic. Other ecclesiastical literature includes all the apparatus needed to operate Coptic Orthodox churches and monasteries: lectionaries, hymnals, missals, books of hours, homilies and antiphons for the feasts of saints and martyrs, canon law, monastic rules and biographies, sayings of desert father and mothers, etc. On the other hand, *not* represented in Coptic are corpora of systematic theology by the great fathers of the church, verse by verse Biblical commentary, secular works of science, education, belles lettres, and the like: for these, Egyptians would have turned to the Greek originals (or even Syriac), and later to their Arabic counterparts. [CG 1–6]

2. Coptic vocabulary comes from two sources. *Egyptian Coptic words,* as well as the grammatical structure, are from the indigenous language of the Nile Valley. *Greco-Coptic words* were adopted from Greek, especially after the Macedonian conquest of Egypt (332 BC), which imposed upon the Egyptians a Greek-speaking government based in Alexandria. Greek was also the administrative language of the Roman and Byzantine province of Egypt and was gradually replaced by Arabic after AD 642. About one fourth of the Sahidic Coptic New Testament word list is Greco-Coptic. [CG 7]

3. The authoritative dictionary is W. E. Crum, *A Coptic Dictionary* (1939 and reprints); it contains only Egyptian-Coptic words. Greco-Coptic vocabulary must be looked up in the standard Greek dictionaries: H. G. Liddell, R. Scott, and H. S. Jones, *A Greek-English Lexicon* (1939 with reprints and later revisions);

W. F. Arndt, W. Bauer, and F. W. Danker, *A Greek-English Lexicon of the New Testament and Other Early Christian Literature* (2000, and earlier editions); G. W. H. Lampe, *A Patristic Greek Lexicon* (1968).

THE ALPHABET

4. The Coptic alphabet is the twenty-four Greek letters written in rounded form (thus ε c ω), to which are added six additional letters taken from Egyptian (Demotic script): ϣ ϥ ϩ ϫ ϭ ϯ. Approximate pronunciations of these thirty letters are given in table 1. In ancient manuscripts there is no space between words, as you can see in the photograph below. Coptic has no question mark to distinguish questions from affirmations. [CG 8]

TABLE 1
PRONUNCIATION OF THE ALPHABET

		Pronunciation		Modern Name			Pronunciation		Modern Name
ⲁ		a		Alpha	ⲡ,	ⲡ̄	p	ᵉp	Pi
ⲃ,	ⲃ̄	b	ᵉb	Beta	ⲣ,	ⲣ̄	r	ᵉr	Rho
ⲅ,	ⲅ̄	g	ᵉg	Gamma	ⲥ,	ⲥ̄	s	ᵉs	Sigma
ⲇ		d		Delta	ⲧ,	ⲧ̄	t	ᵉt	Tau
ⲉ		e		Epsilon	ⲩ		w	u	Upsilon
ⲍ		z		Zeta	ⲫ		ph		Phi
ⲏ		ā[1]		Eta	ⲭ		kh		Chi
ⲑ		th		Theta	ⲯ,	ⲯ̄	ps	ᵉps	Psi
ⲓ		y	i	Iota	ⲱ		ō[3]		Omega
ⲕ,	ⲕ̄	k	ᵉk	Kappa	ϣ,	ϣ̄	š[4]	ᵉš	Shai
ⲗ,	ⲗ̄	l	ᵉl	Lambda	ϥ,	ϥ̄	f	ᵉf	Fai
ⲙ,	ⲙ̄	m	ᵉm	Mu	ϩ,	ϩ̄	h	ᵉh	Hore(h)
ⲛ,	ⲛ̄	n	ᵉn	Nu	ϫ,	ϫ̄	č[5]	ᵉč	Djandja
ⲝ,	ⲝ̄	ks	ᵉks	Xi	ϭ,	ϭ̄	kʸ	ᵉkʸ	Kyima
ⲟ,		o[2]		Omicron	ϯ		ty	ti	Ti

NOTES: [1]ā is pronounced "AY," as in *ate*.   [2]Be sure to make a difference between ⲁ and o: ⲁ like "hat" and o like "hot."   [3]ω like "old."   [4]As in *ship*.   [5]As in *church*.

Five count as vowels (ⲁ ⲉ ⲏ o ⲱ) and the remaining twenty-five are either consonants or combinations of letters.

Almost every consonant has two possible pronunciations, depending on where it appears. [CG 35]

    i. A non-syllabic pronunciation, e.g. *b* or *k* (cf. Greek β and κ).

      ⲃ as in ⲃⲱ bō, and in ϩⲱⲃ hōb

      ⲕ as in ⲕⲱⲧ kōt, and in ⲣⲱⲕ rōk

ΤΑΡΧΗΜΠΕΥ
ΑΓΓΕΛΙΟΝ ΝΝΙϹ
ΠΕΧ̅Ϲ ΚΑΤΑ
ΠΕΤϹΗϨ ϨΖΝΗ
ϹΑΙΑϹ ΠΕΠΡΟ
ΦΗΤΗϹ· ΧΕ ΕΙϹ
ϨΗΗΤΕ Ϯ·ΝΑ
ΧΕΥ ΠΑΑΓΓΕ
ΛΟϹ ϨΙΘΗ ΜΜΟ
ΝΥϹΚ ΤΕ ΤΕΚ
ϨΙΗ ΠΕΧΡΟΟΥ
ΜΠΕΤΩϢ ΕΒΟ
ΚΟΛ ϨΝ ΤΕΡΗ
ΜΟϹ ΧΕ ϹΟΥ
ϮΝ ΤΕϨΙΗ ΜΠ
ΧΟΕΙϹ ΝΤΕΤΝ
ϹΟΥΤ ΝΝΕϤ
ΜΟΙΤ·
ΑϤϢϢ ΠΕ ΛΕ
Ν ϨΙ ΩϨΑΝΝΗϹ
ΕϤϮ ΚΑΠ Ϯ
ϹΜΑ ΜΗ ΧΑΙϹ
ΕϤΚΗΡΥϹϹΕ

ΝΟΥΚΑΠ ΠΙϹΜΑ
ΜΜΕΤΑΝΟΙΑ
ΕΠΚΩ ΕΒΟΛ Ν
ΝΝΟΒΕ· ΑΥϢ
ΑϹΚΩ Κ ΝΑΥ
ΕΒΟΛ ϬΙ ΠΙ·
ΧΩΡΑ ΤΗΡϹ Ν
Ϯ ΟΥΔΑΙΑ ΝΜ
ΝΑ ΘΙΕΡΟϹΟ
ΛΥΜΑ ΤΗΡΟΥ
ΑΥΧΙ ΚΑΠ ΠΙ·
ϹΜΑ ΝΤΟΟΤϤ
ϨΜ ΠΙΟΡΔΑΝΗϹ
ΠΕΡΟ ΕΥΕϨΟ
ΜΟΛΟΓΙΝ ΝΝΕΥ
ΝΟΒΕ· ΑΥϢ ΙΩ
ϨΑΝΝΗϹ ΝΕ ΡϨ
ϨΕΝϤϢΝ ϬΑ
ΜΟΥΧ ΤΟΙ ΩϤ
ϢϤϨΡΕ ΟΥ ΜΟΧ
Ν ϢΑΑΡ ΜΗ Ρ
ΕΤΕϤϮ ΠΙ·
ΕϤΟΥΕ ΜΑϢ ΧΕ

ii. A syllabic pronunciation, with an insignificant resonant sound (ᵉ, ⁱ, or the like) *just before* the letter, e.g. *ᵉb* or *ᵉk*. The syllabic pronunciation helps to form a syllable. Letters with a syllabic pronunciation are often written with a superlinear stroke above them[6]. Thus

ā (or simply в) = ᵉb, ⁱb, etc., as in тв̄во tᵉb-bo

к̄ (or simply к) = ᵉk, ⁱk, etc., as in тк̄то tᵉk-to

The syllabic pronunciations of the consonants ı and ɣ are *i* ("EE") and *u* ("OO"); these are *not* marked with the superlinear stroke.

Position of the superlinear stroke. Some Coptic scribes write the stroke directly above a letter that has a syllabic reading, i.e. above a single letter. This "single-stroke system" is used in the present book: cωτм̄. Other Coptic scribes write a longer stroke, connecting all (or some) of the letters in any syllable formed by a letter with syllabic reading, cωτ̄м: this is the "connective-stroke system." Both systems are ancient, and in both systems the stroke is sometimes shifted slightly to the right. The letters в λ м n p are more persistently marked than any others. [CG 38]

---

5. The trema (diaeresis) symbol (¨) is sometimes written over ı or ɣ, with no apparent meaning: ï, ÿ: мωÿcнc. Likewise, the circumflex (⌢) is sometimes written over a single letter or connects a pair of letters, again with no apparent meaning: p̂, êı. [CG 12]

---

[6] The superlinear stroke is optional. It is written most often above the sonorant consonants в λ м n and p.

(Facing page) *Gospel of Mark* 1:1–1:6. P. Palau Ribes inv. 182 in the Archivo General of the Compañía de Jesús en Catalunya, Barcelona. Parchment. Written in a regular uncial script without word division; dated to AD 400–450 by H. Quecke. © Archivo General de la Compañía de Jesús en Catalunya, reproduced by permission. Photo by Alberto Nodar. Scale 1:1. In the photograph, note the title мλρкоc centered in the upper margin; to the right is the page number ā = 1. In the left column, 5 lines from the bottom, is a straight paragraphos sign (above λqϣωпелε), marking the end of the prologue to Mark. Note the use of connective superlinear strokes (2̄n, n̄тетn̄) [many of the strokes are very faint]; tremas (cλïλc "Isaiah," моïт, хλïе); and a few raised points to conclude sections of text (left column фнтнc•, моïт•; right column n̄nове•, nове•, етеq†пе•). In the left column at the end of line 9, the letter к is written small and "stacked" over о to prevent the word м̄мок from running too far into the margin. The left margin of each column is justified; but note that the letters т, ф, and † are aligned on their central upright strokes.

6. A modern American scholar's rapid writing of the Coptic letters

ⲁ Ⲃ Ⲅ Ⲇ Ⲉ Ⲍ Ⲏ Ⲑ Ⲓ Ï Ⲕ Ⲗ Ⲙ Ⲛ Ⲝ Ⲟ Ⲡ ⲣ Ⲥ
Ⲧ Ⲩ Ⲫ Ⲭ Ⲯ Ⲱ ⳉ ϥ ⳅ Ⳉ ⳍ ⲋ ϯ   Ⲛ̄ Ⲙ̄Ⲛ̄Ⲧ

7. *Ambiguities in the Alphabet.*

When you learn to play a new game, you first have to listen carefully to some abstract rules before you start to play. The same is true at this point in lesson one. The following, abstract-sounding information is dull but basic; but once you start reading Coptic aloud and doing exercises it will become second nature. Actually as languages go, it's not particularly complicated.

(*a*) *Monograms.* The alphabet is slightly redundant, for six characters (the "monograms") each represent a pair of other letters found in the alphabet. Their use is a matter of spelling convention, which must be learned word by word. [CG 13]

> ⲑ represents ⲧ + ϩ. E.g. ⲑⲉ *(t^e he)* = the way
> ⳃ represents ⲕ + ⲥ. E.g. ⳃⲟⲩⲣ *(k^e sur)* = ring
> ⲫ represents ⲡ + ϩ. E.g. ⲫⲓⲗⲓⲡⲡⲟⲥ *(p^e hi lip pos)* = Philip
> ⲭ represents ⲕ + ϩ. E.g. ⲭⲁⲣⲓⲥ *(k^e ha ris)* = grace
> ⲯ represents ⲡ + ⲥ. E.g. ⲯⲩⲭⲏ *(p^e suk hē)* = soul
> ϯ represents ⲧ + ⲓ. E.g. ϯⲙⲉ *(ti me)* = village

Note: pronounce *th, ph,* and *kh* as *t + h, p + h,* and *k + h.*

For purposes of grammatical rules, the monogram characters count as two letters.

ⲑ is also spelled as ⲧϩ, ⳃ as ⲕⲥ, ⲫ as ⲡϩ, ⲭ as ⲕϩ, ⲯ as ⲡⲥ, ϯ as ⲧⲓ, depending on the word. ⳃ, ⲫ, ⲭ, and ⲯ mostly occur in Greco-Coptic words.

(*b*) *Digrams.* There are two ways to represent *y* (and its syllabic reading *i*)—both ⲓ and ⲉⲓ, according to spelling convention. Also, there are two ways to represent *w* (and its syllabic reading *u*)—both ⲩ and ⲟⲩ. [CG 15–16] Thus:

> ⲓ = *y* or *i*
> ⲉⲓ = *y* or *i*
> ⲩ = *w* or *u*
> ⲟⲩ = *w* or *u*

The pairs ⲉⲓ and ⲟⲩ are "digrams": two characters in place of one letter.

NOTE: The spellings ï, ⲉ̂ⲓ, ⲩ̈, and ⲟ̂ⲩ also occur, without any obvious distinction in meaning. [CG 11–12]

For readers, the results are somewhat ambiguous:

$\epsilon\iota$ could represent either *y* or *i,* or else *ey* (ϵ + ι)

oγ could represent either *w* or *u,* or else *ow* (o + γ)

Some spelling conventions [CG 16]

(1) Conventional spellings of *y/i* according to three word types:

    a. ⲡⲁⲓ, ⲡⲁⲓ̈, ⲡⲁⲉⲓ, or ⲡⲁⲉ̂ⲓ (fluctuation)

       ⲁⲓ, ⲁⲓ̈, ⲁⲉⲓ, or ⲁⲉ̂ⲓ (fluctuation)

    b. ϭⲓ, ⲝⲓⲥⲉ, ⲥϩⲓⲙⲉ, ϩⲓⲏ, ⲛⲓⲙ (simple)

    c. ⲉⲓⲛⲉ, ⲉⲓⲱⲣⲙ̄ (digram)

(2) Conventional spellings of *w/u:*

    a. Simple, after ⲁ, ⲉ, ⲏ, ⲁ-, and ⲉ-: ⲛⲁⲩ, ⲙⲁⲁⲩ, ⲛⲉⲩ-, ⲙⲉⲉⲩⲉ, ⲥⲛⲏⲩ, ⲁ-ⲩϣⲉ-
       ⲗⲉⲉⲧ ϣⲱⲡⲉ

    b. Simple, after double vowel oo manifesting glottal stop (**9**): ⲝⲟⲟ-ⲩ

    c. Otherwise, digram: ⲙⲟⲟⲩ, ⲛⲟⲩ, ϩⲱⲟⲩ, ⲉⲓⲉⲣⲱⲟⲩ, ⲟⲩϣⲏ, ϣⲟⲩⲟ, ϣⲟⲩ-
       ϣⲟⲩ

---

8. *Bound groups; the meaning of hyphen (–).* The smallest, basic units of grammatical or dictionary meaning are by definition called 'morphs'. (Or call them 'words' if you like.) You should carefully note which morphs (words) end with a hyphen and which do not, and learn this feature as part of the morph. (These hyphens are not part of the ancient writing system; they have been added only by modern linguists and are not used in text editions.) Coptic morphs group themselves into an uninterruptible string until they reach a morph that has no hyphen at the end.

    ϩⲛ̄–ⲧⲉ–ϩⲟⲩⲉⲓⲧⲉ *h^entehwite* = In the beginning

Such a string of morphs is a called a *bound group.* Bound groups are arranged in various grammatical patterns to make intelligible phrases and sentences. These patterns, and their permissible constituents, are the subject matter of grammar. [CG 27–29]

For example, the opening sentence of the Gospel of John contains three bound groups:

    ϩⲛ̄–ⲧⲉ–ϩⲟⲩⲉⲓⲧⲉ ⲛⲉ–ϥ–ϣⲟⲟⲡ ⲛ̄ϭⲓ–ⲡ–ϣⲁⲝⲉ
    In-the-beginning past tense marker-He-exists subject marker-the-Word
    = In the beginning was the Word

Some groups consist of only one morph:

    ⲁⲩⲱ ⲛⲉ–ⲩ–ⲛⲟⲩⲧⲉ ⲡⲉ ⲡ–ϣⲁⲝⲉ
    And past tense marker-a-god is the-Word
    = And the Word was God

7

Note carefully that the hyphen does *not* mark the end of a syllable: it should not be pronounced. Thus the bound group ⲡ–ϣⲁϫⲉ should be pronounced in two syllables, *pša je* or even *ᵉpša je*, etc. (The exact pronunciation of syllables in a non-living language like Coptic is impossible to know.)

9. *Double vowel* mostly stands for vowel + glottal stop consonant (a catch in the throat so that the flow of breath is briefly interrupted). The technical notation for a glottal stop is an apostrophe. [CG 36]

ⲙⲁⲁⲩ (mother) = *ma'u*
ⲙⲉⲉⲩⲉ (think) = *me'we*
ⲧⲏⲏⲃⲉ (finger) = *tā'be*
ⲉⲧⲟⲟⲧ–ⲥ̄ (to her) = *eto't ᵉs*
ⲧⲱⲱⲃⲉ (mud brick) = *tō'be*

But the sequence ⲟⲟⲩ is ambiguous, for in some words it = *o'u* (ϫⲟⲟ–ⲩ = say them) while in others it = *ow* (ϫⲟ–ⲟⲩ = sow them).

10. *Stress accent.* Within each bound group the main stress (tonic) accent probably fell on the last or next to last syllable of the group. If this syllable occurs in an Egyptian Coptic morph and if it contains the letter ⲏ, ⲟ, or ⲱ, or a double vowel (**9**) the stress accent probably fell on that sound. (But many bound groups do not contain these letters, or else they end with a Greco-Coptic morph: in such cases, more complicated theories are required.) [CG 32]

SOME REGULAR REPLACEMENTS

11. ⲙ̄– *Instead of* ⲛ̄–.

  i. The morphs spelled ⲛ̄– (in all their meanings) [CG 21]

    ⲛ̄– = to, for
    ⲛ̄– = of
    ⲛ̄– = the (plur.)

  become ⲙ̄– before ⲡ or non-syllabic ⲙ (i.e. ⲙ without superlinear stroke). Thus

    ⲛ̄– + ⲡⲉⲧⲣⲟⲥ becomes ⲙ̄–ⲡⲉⲧⲣⲟⲥ = to Peter
    ⲛ̄– + ⲡ–ⲉⲓⲱⲧ becomes ⲙ̄–ⲡ–ⲉⲓⲱⲧ = of the father
    ⲛ̄– + ⲙⲁⲁⲩ   becomes ⲙ̄–ⲙⲁⲁⲩ = the mothers

  ii. ⲛ̄– = to, for, of, becomes ⲙ̄– also before ψ and φ.

    ⲛ̄– + ψⲩⲭⲏ ⲛⲓⲙ   becomes ⲙ̄–ψⲩⲭⲏ ⲛⲓⲙ = to *or* of every soul
    ⲛ̄– + φⲓⲗⲟⲥⲟφⲟⲥ ⲛⲓⲙ becomes ⲙ̄–φⲓⲗⲟⲥⲟφⲟⲥ ⲛⲓⲙ = to *or* of every philosopher

iii. The preposition ϩⲛ̅– (= in) becomes ϩⲙ̅– before ⲡ, or non-syllabic ⲙ, or ⲯ, or
ⲫ. Thus

ϩⲛ̅– + ⲡ–ⲏⲓ̈   becomes ϩⲙ̅–ⲡ–ⲏⲓ̈ = in the house

ϩⲛ̅– + ⲯⲩⲭⲏ ⲛⲓⲙ becomes ϩⲙ̅–ⲯⲩⲭⲏ ⲛⲓⲙ = in every soul

Final ⲛ̅– of the prenominal state of compound prepositions (55) is normally
replaced by ⲙ̅– before a following ⲡ, ⲯ, ⲫ, or non-syllabic ⲙ. Thus ⲉⲧⲛ̅– but
ⲉⲧⲙ̅–ⲡ–ⲉⲓⲱⲧ = to the father, ⲉⲧⲙ̅–ⲯⲩⲭⲏ ⲛⲓⲙ = to every soul; ⲉⲝⲛ̅– but
ⲉⲝⲙ̅–ⲡ–ⲕⲟⲥⲙⲟⲥ = upon the world, ⲉⲝⲙ̅–ⲙⲁⲣⲧⲩⲣⲟⲥ ⲥⲛⲁⲩ = upon two martyrs. [CG 21]

---

12. ⲙⲟⲩ *and* ⲛⲟⲩ *Instead of* ⲙⲱ *and* ⲛⲱ.

Whenever the vowel *ō* forms a syllable with a preceding ⲙ or ⲛ, it is spelled as ⲟⲩ.
[CG 20] E.g. in the paradigm

ⲡⲱ= "(the) one belonging to" (57)

ⲧⲱ=

ⲛⲟⲩ= (instead of nō)

13. ⲙⲛ̅ⲧ *Instead of* ⲙⲧ̅.

Whenever *mt* forms a syllable, it is spelled as ⲙⲛ̅ⲧ. E.g. ⲟⲩⲟⲙ= "eat" + –ⲧ "me"
is written ⲟⲩⲟⲙⲛ̅ⲧ = eat me. [CG 26]

14. ⲣ *and* ⲣ̅ *Instead of* ⲕ *or* ⲕ̅.

Whenever *k* or syllabic *ᵉk* forms a syllable with preceding ⲛ̅ or ⲛ it is spelled as ⲣ or
ⲣ̅, optionally. [CG 23] Thus

ⲛ̅– + –ⲕ– = ⲛ̅ⲣ *ᵉng*

ⲛ– + –ⲕ̅– = ⲛⲣ̅ *nᵉg*

SOME SCRIBAL SIMPLIFICATIONS

15. Scribes sometimes simplify ⲁⲁⲁ to ⲁⲁ, ⲉⲉ to ⲉ, and ⲟⲩⲟⲩ to ⲟⲩ. [CG 24] Thus

ⲛⲁ–ⲁⲁ–ϥ "will do it" can be written as ⲛⲁⲁϥ

ⲁⲛⲟⲕ ⲡⲉ–ⲉⲧⲉ– "It is I who ... " as ⲁⲛⲟⲕ ⲡⲉⲧⲉ–

ⲟⲩ–ⲟⲩⲏⲏⲃ "a priest" as ⲟⲩⲏⲏⲃ

16. Scribes often omit the one-letter morph ⲉ– before a morph beginning ⲃ̅, ⲗ̅, ⲙ̅,
ⲛ̅, or ⲣ̅. Thus ⲉ–ⲙ̅ⲡ–ϥ̅–ⲥⲱⲧⲡ̅ *without his having chosen* is also written simply
ⲙ̅ⲡϥ̅ⲥⲱⲧⲡ̅. [CG 25]

NOMINA SACRA ABBREVIATIONS

17. A small set of sacred words are almost always abbreviated and marked with a superlinear stroke, e.g. ī̄c πεx̄c̄ (= ιнcoγc πεxριcτoc) Jesus Christ. You will encounter them in printed editions as well as manuscripts. [CG 41]

ᾱᾱᾱ = ᴅᴀγειᴀ David (in Old Testament books)

θιᴧнм̄, θιнм̄ etc. = τϩιερογcᴀᴧнм Jerusalem

ιн̄ᴧ = ιcρᴀнᴧ Israel

ī̄c, ιн̄c = ιнcoγc (i) Jesus, (ii) Joshua

c̄ρō̄c = cτᴀγροc cross

c̄ρōγ̄ = cτᴀγρογ crucify

x̄c̄, x̄ρ̄c̄ = (i) xριcτoc Christ, (ii) xρнcτoc excellent

EXERCISES 1

A. *Carefully write the letters of the Coptic alphabet in alphabetical order, three times. Study minutely the photograph above of a fifth-century manuscript to see how the letters are formed. A magnifying glass may be helpful.*

B. *Write in Coptic letters. Consult box "Some Spelling Conventions" (above) for the spellings of* i *and* w.

ba	ia	ka	la	ma	na	pa	ra	sa	ta	wa	ša	fa	ha	ja	kʸa
be	ie	ke	le	me	ne	pe	re	se	te	we	še	fe	he	je	kʸe
bā	iā	kā	lā	mā	nā	pā	rā	sā	tā	wā	šā	fā	hā	jā	kʸā
bi	ii	ki	li	mi	ni	pi	ri	si	ti	wi	ši	fi	hi	ji	kʸi
bo	io	ko	lo	mo	no	po	ro	so	to	wo	šo	fo	ho	jo	kʸo
bu	iu	ku	lu	mu	nu	pu	ru	su	tu	wu	šu	fu	hu	ju	kʸu
bō	iō	kō	lō	mō	nō	pō	rō	sō	tō	wō	šō	fō	hō	jō	kʸō

C. *Read aloud the following words. (Hint: underlined syllables receive the stress accent; you should be able to figure out the others* **10**.)

a. ϣᴀ, ϣo, ϣω, ϣoγ-, ϣι, вᴀᴧ, воᴧ, вωᴧ, внᴧ, вᾱᴧε, вp̄ρε, вn̄nε, в̄ϣε, в̄ϣ-, ϣв̄-, ϣωв, ϣιвε, ϣoγϣoγ, ϣιnε, ϣικε. b. ϣнρε, ϣεερε, ϣᴀρε-, ϣωπε, ϣωnε, ϣιπε, <u>ϣι</u>nε, ϣooπ, ϣп̄-, ϣ̄-, ϣϣε, ϣбoм,

ⲕⲁⲙ, ϭⲟⲙ, ⲕⲓⲙ, ϭⲓⲛ, ⲕⲓⲧⲉ, ϭⲓⲛⲉ, ⲥⲓⲛⲉ, ϣⲓⲛⲉ, ⲥⲙⲓⲛⲉ, ϣⲙⲓⲛ. c. ⲥⲟⲗⲥⲗ̄,
ⲧⲟⲃⲧⲃ̄, ϩⲉ, ϩⲁ, ϩⲟ, ϩⲱ, ϩⲓ, ϩⲟⲕϩⲕ̄, ϭⲉ, ϭⲱ, ϭⲟⲙϭⲙ̄, †, ⲧⲟ, ⲧⲟⲛⲧⲛ̄, ϫⲟ, ϫⲱ,
ϫⲓ. d. ϫⲟⲟⲥ, ϫⲱϫ, ϣⲟⲣϣⲣ̄, ϭⲟϫϭⲝ̄, ⲕⲟⲥⲕⲥ̄, ⲡⲟⲧⲡⲧ̄, ϣⲟϥϣϥ̄, ⲧⲁϩⲧϩ̄,
ⲛ̄-, ⲛ̄ⲛ̄-, ⲙ̄ⲡⲏⲩⲉ, ⲛ̄ⲙⲡⲏⲩⲉ, ⲕⲏⲙⲉ, ⲛ̄ⲕⲏⲙⲉ, ϩⲛ̄ⲕⲏⲙⲉ, ⲣⲙ̄ⲛⲕⲏⲙⲉ,
ⲙⲛ̄ⲧⲣⲙ̄ⲛⲕⲏⲙⲉ, ⲧⲙⲛ̄ⲧⲣⲙ̄ⲛⲕⲏⲙⲉ, ⲛ̄ⲧⲙⲛ̄ⲧⲣⲙ̄ⲛⲕⲏⲙⲉ. e. ⲧϩⲓⲙⲉ, ⲑⲓⲙⲉ,
ⲡⲣⲱⲙⲉ, ⲡⲁⲓ, ⲡⲁⲉⲓ, ⲡⲏⲓ, ⲡϩⲟ, ⲫⲟ, ϥⲡⲱⲧ, ⲥⲙⲉ, ⲥⲕⲱ, ⲕⲉⲓⲙⲉ, †ⲉⲓⲙⲉ,
†ⲥⲱ, †ⲙⲉ, †ⲟⲩⲇⲁⲓⲁ. f. ⲥⲃ̄ⲃⲉ, ⲥⲱⲃⲉ, ⲥⲁⲃⲏ, ⲥⲁⲃⲉⲉⲩⲉ, ⲛ̄ⲑⲉ, ⲙ̄ⲙⲏⲛⲉ,
ⲣ̄ⲡⲏⲩⲉ, ⲗ̄ϩⲏⲙ, ⲟⲩⲱϣ, ⲟⲩϣⲏ, ⲟⲩⲟⲉⲓϣ, ⲟⲩⲱⲛϣ, ⲱⲱ, ⲁⲁϥ, ⲉⲓⲣⲉ, ⲉⲓⲛⲉ,
ⲉⲓⲙⲉ, ⲉⲓϣⲉ. g. ⲁⲛ, ⲟⲛ, ⲟⲩⲛ, ⲟⲩⲛ̄-, ϩⲛ̄-, ϩⲉⲛ-, ϩⲱⲛ, ϩⲏⲛ, ⲥⲁⲛ-, ⲥⲟⲛ,
ⲉϣ-, ⲁϣ, ⲱϣ, ⲱ̄-, ⲡⲉⲧⲉϣϣⲉ, ⲉⲡⲉⲧⲉϣϣⲉ, ⲛ̄ⲟⲩⲡⲉⲧⲉϣϣⲉ. h. ⲙⲁⲁⲩ,
ⲗⲁⲁⲩ, ⲙⲉⲉⲩⲉ, ⲥⲉⲉⲡⲉ, ⲧⲏⲏⲃⲉ, ⲙⲏⲛϣⲉ, ⲉⲧⲟⲟⲧⲥ̄, ϫⲟⲟⲥ, ⲛⲟⲩⲟⲩ,
ⲧⲱⲱⲃⲉ, ϩⲱⲱⲧ. i. ⲫⲓⲗⲟⲥⲟⲫⲟⲥ, ⲫⲟⲛⲟⲥ, ⲑⲁⲗⲁⲥⲥⲁ, ⲑⲗⲓⲃⲉ, ⲫⲑⲟⲛⲟⲥ,
ϫⲁⲓⲣⲉ, ϫⲁⲣⲓⲥ, ⲯⲁⲗⲗⲉⲓ, ⲭⲣⲓⲥⲧⲟⲥ, ⲡⲣⲱⲙⲉ, ⲧⲉⲥϩⲓⲙⲉ, ⲡⲉⲓⲱⲧ, ⲧⲙⲁⲁⲩ,
ⲡⲥⲟⲛ, ⲧⲥⲱⲛⲉ, ⲡϣⲏⲣⲉ, ⲧϣⲉⲉⲣⲉ.

D. Working with another person, take dictation from this list, writing each word as you hear it.

E. Practice reading aloud the following text (the Lord's Prayer, Luke 11:2–4).

1 ⲡⲉⲛⲉⲓⲱⲧ ⲉⲧϩⲛ̄ⲙ̄ⲡⲏⲩⲉ
  ⲙⲁⲣⲉⲡⲉⲕⲣⲁⲛ ⲟⲩⲟⲡ
  ⲙⲁⲣⲉⲧⲉⲕⲙⲛ̄ⲧⲉⲣⲟ ⲉⲓ
  ⲙⲁⲣⲉⲡⲉⲕⲟⲩⲱϣ ϣⲱⲡⲉ
5 ⲡⲉⲛⲟⲉⲓⲕ ⲉⲧⲛⲏⲩ
  ⲧⲁⲁϥ ⲛⲁⲛ ⲙ̄ⲙⲏⲛⲉ
  ⲕⲁⲛⲉⲛⲛⲟⲃⲉ ⲛⲁⲛ ⲉⲃⲟⲗ
  ⲕⲁⲓⲅⲁⲣ ⲁⲛⲟⲛ
  ⲧⲛ̄ⲕⲱ ⲉⲃⲟⲗ ⲛ̄ⲟⲩⲟⲛ ⲛⲓⲙ
10 ⲉⲧⲉⲟⲩⲛ̄ⲧⲁⲛ ⲉⲣⲟϥ
  ⲁⲩⲱ ⲙ̄ⲡⲣ̄ϫⲓⲧⲛ̄
  ⲉϩⲟⲩⲛ ⲉⲡⲓⲣⲁⲥⲙⲟⲥ

Here is the same text grammatically divided into morphs. Read it aloud exactly the same way (do not try to pronounce the hyphens between morphs).

ⲡⲉⲛ–ⲉⲓⲱⲧ ⲉⲧ^ø–ϩⲛ̄–ⲙ̄–ⲡⲏⲩⲉ	Our-father who-(is)-in-the-heavens
ⲙⲁⲣⲉ–ⲡⲉⲕ–ⲣⲁⲛ ⲟⲩⲟⲡ	Let-your-name be(come)-holy
ⲙⲁⲣⲉ–ⲧⲉⲕ–ⲙⲛ̄ⲧ–ⲉⲣⲟ ⲉⲓ	Let-your-quality-of-king come
ⲙⲁⲣⲉ–ⲡⲉⲕ–ⲟⲩⲱϣ ϣⲱⲡⲉ	Let-your-wish happen
ⲡⲉⲛ–ⲟⲉⲓⲕ ⲉⲧ^ø–ⲛⲏⲩ	Our-bread which-(is)-coming
ⲧⲁⲁ–ϥ ⲛⲁ–ⲛ ⲙ̄ⲙⲏⲛⲉ	Give-it to-us daily

ⲕⲁ–ⲛⲉⲛ–ⲛⲟⲃⲉ ⲛⲁ–ⲛ ⲉⲃⲟⲗ	Put-our-sins for us away
ⲕⲁⲓⲅⲁⲣ ⲁⲛⲟⲛ	For we
ⲧⲛ̄–ⲕⲱ ⲉⲃⲟⲗ ⲛ̄–ⲟⲩⲟⲛ ⲛⲓⲙ	We-put away (direct object)-everyone
ⲉⲧⲉ–ⲟⲩⲛⲧⲁ–ⲛ ⲉⲣⲟ–ϥ	Such-that-have-we (anything) against-him
ⲁⲩⲱ ⲙ̄ⲡ̄ⲣ̄–ϫⲓⲧ–ⲛ̄	And do-not-take-us
ⲉϩⲟⲩⲛ ⲉ–⁰ⲡⲓⲣⲁⲥⲙⲟⲥ	In to-temptation(s)

F. *Read aloud the following personal names.* ⲓⲏⲥⲟⲩⲥ, ⲙⲁⲣⲓⲁ, ⲙⲁⲑⲑⲁⲓⲟⲥ, ⲙⲁⲣⲕⲟⲥ, ⲗⲟⲩⲕⲁⲥ, ⲓⲱϩⲁⲛⲛⲏⲥ, ⲡⲁⲩⲗⲟⲥ, ⲡⲉⲧⲣⲟⲥ, ⲁⲛⲧⲱⲛⲓⲟⲥ, ⲙⲁⲕⲁⲣ-ⲓⲟⲥ, ⲡⲁϩⲱⲙ, ϩⲱⲣⲥⲓⲏⲥⲉ, ⲡϭⲱⲗ, ϣⲉⲛⲟⲩⲧⲉ, ⲁⲑⲁⲛⲁⲥⲓⲟⲥ, ⲕⲩⲣⲓⲗⲗⲟⲥ.

G. *Looking ahead to lesson 2, pronounce the following.* ⲡⲣⲱⲙⲉ, ⲡϩⲟⲟⲩⲧ, ⲫⲟⲟⲩⲧ, ⲧⲉⲥϩⲓⲙⲉ, ⲛⲉϩⲓⲟⲙⲉ, ⲡⲉⲓⲱⲧ, ⲛ̄ⲉⲓⲟⲧⲉ, ⲧⲙⲁⲁⲩ, ⲛ̄ⲥⲟⲛ, ⲛⲉⲥⲛⲏⲩ, ⲧⲥⲱⲛⲉ, ⲡϣⲏⲣⲉ, ⲧϣⲉⲉⲣⲉ, ⲡϣⲏⲣⲉ ϣⲏⲙ, ⲧϣⲉⲉⲣⲉ ϣⲏⲙ, ⲡϩⲁⲓ̈, ⲧϩⲓⲙⲉ, ⲑⲓⲙⲉ, ⲡⲉϣⲃⲏⲣ, ⲧⲉϣⲃⲉⲉⲣ, ⲡϩⲉⲑⲛⲟⲥ, ⲫⲉⲑⲛⲟⲥ, ⲡⲗⲁⲟⲥ, ⲡⲭⲟⲉⲓⲥ, ⲡϩⲙ̄ϩⲁⲗ, ⲧϩⲙ̄ϩⲁⲗ, ⲑⲙ̄ϩⲁⲗ, ⲧϭⲟⲙ, ⲡⲉⲟⲟⲩ, ⲡⲧⲁⲉⲓⲟ, ⲡⲣ̄ⲣⲟ, ⲡⲣ̄ⲣⲱⲟⲩ, ⲧⲙⲛ̄ⲧⲣ̄ⲣⲟ, ⲙ̄ⲙⲛ̄ⲧⲣ̄ⲣⲱⲟⲩ.

H. *Copy out some (or all) of the text in the photograph above, which is part of a fifth-century Gospel of Mark.*

LESSON 2

ARTICLES AND WHAT THEY EXPRESS. NOUN. PROPER NOUN. OMISSION OF ARTICLE. ARTICLE PHRASE. *'AND', 'OR',* AND *'OF'.*

18. Coptic distinguishes

two *numbers:* singular, plural

two *grammatical genders:* masculine, feminine

two kinds of *determination* **21***:* indefinite ("a, some"), definite ("the")

These distinctions are expressed in pronouns

Indefinite Pronoun

oyλ *wa* = one, someone (sing. masc.)
oyєι *wi* = one, someone (sing. fem.)
ϩoєιnє *hoyne* = some (plur.)

Definite (Demonstrative) Pronoun

πλϊ = this one, this (sing. masc.)
τλϊ = this one, this (sing. fem.)
nλϊ = these (plur.)

and in articles

Indefinite Article

oy– = a (sing.)
ϩєn– = [some][7] (plur.)

Definite Article

π– = the (def. sing. masc.)
τ– = the (def. sing. fem.)
n̄– or n– = the (def. plur.)
(Also πє–, τє–, nє– **22.**)

---

[7] ϩєn– [some]: In English we often express the indefinite plural by omitting the article before a plural noun: a house (sing.), *houses* (plur.).

Definite (Demonstrative) Article

пеï– = this (def. sing. masc.)
теï– = this (def. sing. fem.)
неï– = these (def. plur.)

Note that gender is not expressed in the plural, nor in the indefinite singular article
оу–. [CG 42]

19. *Gender.* Every noun has a gender, either masculine or feminine. Gender is not
expressed by the form of the noun but can be seen when the noun has a definite singular article. [CG 46, 105–6]

п–оуоеіn *pwoin* The light   т–ме *tme* The truth

You should memorize each noun together with its def. sing. article ("п–р͞ммао the
rich man").

The gender of a noun is also expressed when any of the following cross-refers to
it; 2d and 3d person sing. personal morphs, gendered cardinal numbers **45**.
The gender of nouns denoting people (and proper names) corresponds to sex.

п–еіωт *pyôt* (masc.) = the father
т–мааγ *tma'u* (fem.) = the mother
п–ка2 *pkah* (masc.) = the land
т–ме *tme* (fem.) = the truth

Greek masculine and feminine nouns keep their same genders in Coptic; Greek
neuters are masculine in Coptic.

п–лаос *plaos* (masc.) = the people ὁ λάος
т–сар͞ξ *tsar^eks* (fem.) = the flesh ἡ σάρξ
п–сωма *psôma* (masc.) = the body τὸ σῶμα

Every verbal infinitive **66** can be used as a masc. noun.

ωn2̄ (infinitive) = to live, п–ωn2̄ *pōn^eh* (masc. noun) = life

Otherwise the gender of nouns is unpredictable.

A few nouns occur in formal pairs expressing biological sex: р̄ро, р̄рω =
emperor, empress; соn, сωне = brother, sister; etc. A very few nouns can be
used with either masc. or fem. article: п.хоеіс, т.хоеіс = the lord, the lady;
п2̄м2ал, т2̄м2ал = the male servant, the female servant. [CG 107]

14

20. *Number.* For nouns, the distinction of singular/plural is primarily expressed by the article.

ογ–ρωμε = a man, ϩεν–ρωμε = men *or* some men
π–ρωμε = the man, N̄–ρωμε = the men

But about one hundred nouns also have a *special plural form,* whose use is optional. [CG 108(b)]

π–con = the brother
N̄–con = the brothers
ne–cnhy = the brothers

The difference in usage between the two plurals is hard to perceive.

Collective nouns (naming a collection of individuals, e.g. π–мннϣє = the crowd, т–πολιc = the city) take a singular article but are plural in meaning and can optionally be referred to by plural personal pronouns. E.g. т–πολιc тнρ–c αγ–cωoγϩ = As for the (sing.) whole city, they (plur.) gathered. [CG 108(a)]

---

21. *Determination* ("a" versus "the") can be illustrated by three contrasts in meaning between the indefinite and definite articles. [CG 45]

(*a*) Unknown versus known

   i. ογ– *Indefinite:* unknown to the listener but known to the speaker, as at the beginning of a story.

     There was a man (ογ–ρωμε) *who had two sons* ... (Luke 15:11)

   ii. π– *Definite:* known or anticipated by both listener and speaker.

     A cloud (ογ–κλοoλε) came . . . And a voice came out of *the cloud* (тє–κλοoλε) (Luke 9:34–35)
     πє–πνєγμα єт⁰–oγααβ The Holy Spirit
     т–мN̄т–єρo N̄– ... The kingdom of . . .

(*b*) Individual versus class

   i. ογ– *Indef.:* one or more limited instances of a class.

     ογ–ρωμε = a man   ϩεν–ρωμε = some men
     ογ–мooγ = some water
     ογ–єooγ = glory (on one particular occasion)
     ογ–νoγβ = some gold or a golden coin
     ογ–oєικ = a loaf of bread or some bread

ii. ⲡ– *Def.:* the class name of an entity.

ⲡ–ⲙⲟⲟⲩ = water (as such)   ⲡ–ⲡⲟⲛⲏⲣⲟⲛ = evil (as such)
ⲡ–ⲥⲟⲫⲟⲥ = a wise person (as a type)
ⲛ̄–ⲣⲱⲙⲉ = humankind   ⲡ–ⲛⲟⲩⲃ = gold

Or the name of a unique entity.

ⲧ–ⲡⲉ = the sky   ⲡⲉ–ϩⲟⲟⲩ = daytime

(*c*) Ordinary versus typical

i. ⲟⲩ– *Indef.:* an ordinary instance.

ⲛ̄–ⲑⲉ ⲛ̄–ⲟⲩ–ϣⲏⲣⲉ = like a child

ii. ⲡ– *Def.:* the most typical instance.

ⲡ–ⲛⲟⲙⲟⲥ = the Law   ⲡ–ⲛⲟⲩⲧⲉ = God

Note that the Coptic use of "a" and "the" does not exactly correspond to English usage!

Composite noun formation. Gendered prefixes forming composite nouns are the following. [CG 109]

ⲃⲱ–ⲛ̄– (fem.), species of tree or vine: ϫⲟⲉⲓⲧ = olive, ⲃⲱ–ⲛ̄–ϫⲟⲉⲓⲧ = olive tree.

ⲉⲓⲉⲡ– (fem.), artifacts: ⲛⲟⲩⲃ = gold, ⲉⲓⲉⲡ–ⲛⲟⲩⲃ = goldwork.

ⲙⲁ–ⲛ̄– (masc.), 'place of': ⲉⲗⲟⲟⲗⲉ = vine, ⲙⲁ–ⲛ̄–ⲉⲗⲟⲟⲗⲉ = vineyard.

ⲙⲛ̄ⲧ– (fem.), denoting abstracts. ⲛⲟⲩⲧⲉ = God, ⲙⲛ̄ⲧ–ⲛⲟⲩⲧⲉ = divinity.

ⲡⲉⲧ– (masc.), one who is . . . : ϩⲟⲟⲩ = be evil, ⲡ–ⲡⲉⲧ–ϩⲟⲟⲩ = the evil one.

ⲥⲁ–ⲛ̄– (masc.), maker or dealer: ϫⲏϭⲉ = purple dye, ⲥⲁ–ⲛ̄–ϫⲏϭⲉ = seller of purple goods.

ⲟⲩⲛ̄–, ⲟⲩⲛ̄–ⲛ̄–, ⲣⲉ– (masc.), arithmetical fractions. ϣⲟⲙⲛ̄ⲧ = three, ⲟⲩⲛ̄–ϣⲟⲙⲛ̄ⲧ = one third.

ϣⲟⲩ– (masc. only?), one who is worthy of . . . : ⲙⲉⲣⲓⲧ–ϥ̄ = love him, ϣⲟⲩ–ⲙⲉⲣⲓⲧ–ϥ̄ = worthy of being loved.

ϩⲁⲙ–, ϩⲁⲙ–ⲛ̄– (masc.), types of artisan: ϣⲉ = wood, ϩⲁⲙ–ⲛ̄–ϣⲉ = carpenter.

ϩⲟⲩⲉ–, ϩⲟⲩⲟ– (masc.), excess of, excessive, greater: ⲥϩⲁⲓ̈ = learning, ϩⲟⲩⲉ–ⲥϩⲁⲓ̈ = excessive learning.

ϭⲓⲛ– (fem.), nouns referring to action. ⲟⲩⲱⲙ = eating, ϭⲓⲛ–ⲟⲩⲱⲙ = diet, foodstuff.

---

22. *Alternative forms of the simple articles.*

(*a*) The indefinite singular article ⲟⲩ– is replaced by ⲩ– after the morphs ⲁ– or ⲉ–. [CG 50] ⲁ-ⲩ-ⲇⲟⲅⲙⲁ ⲉⲓ ⲉⲃⲟⲗ = a decree (ⲟⲩ-ⲇⲟⲅⲙⲁ) went out

ⲉ-ⲩ-ϩⲓⲉⲓⲧ = into a pit (ⲟⲩ-ϩⲓⲉⲓⲧ)

(b) The simple definite article ⲡ-, ⲧ-, ⲛ̅- is replaced [CG 52] by the long definite article

ⲡⲉ-, ⲧⲉ-, ⲛⲉ- = the

i. Before nouns beginning with two consonants, the second of which would not have a superlinear stroke.

ⲡⲉ-ⲡⲣⲉⲥⲃⲩⲧⲉⲣⲟⲥ = the elder, the priest

ⲧⲉ-ⲭⲁⲣⲓⲥ [te-<u>kh</u>aris] = the gift

ⲛⲉ-ⲡⲣⲟⲫⲏⲧⲏⲥ = the prophets

ii. Before nouns beginning with a syllabic consonant

ⲣ̅ⲡⲉ = temple, ⲡⲉ-ⲣⲡⲉ = the temple

(and the syllabic consonant loses its superlinear stroke).

iii. Before ϩⲟⲟⲩ (masc.) = day and ⲣⲟⲙⲡⲉ (fem.) = year.

(c) If ⲛⲉ- is not required, then the def. plur. ⲛ̅- is replaced by ⲙ̅- before ⲡ or non-syllabic ⲙ.

ⲙ̅-ⲡⲟⲛⲏⲣⲟⲛ = the evil ones, ⲙ̅-ⲙⲁⲁⲩ = the mothers

PROPER NOUNS

23. Proper nouns—names of persons, places, months, etc.—mostly occur without any article and are largely used like a definite pronoun or definite article phrase. [CG 126–36] Each proper noun has a gender. Thus

ⲓⲱϩⲁⲛⲛⲏⲥ (masc.) John is treated like ⲡⲁⲓ̈ or ⲡⲣⲱⲙⲉ

ⲙⲁⲣⲓⲁ (fem.) Mary   is treated like ⲧⲁⲓ̈ or ⲧⲉⲥϩⲓⲙⲉ

The special grammar of proper nouns [CG 129]

1. They are modified by apposition rather than the attributive construction **36**. E.g. ⲁⲃⲉⲗ ⲡⲁⲓⲕⲁⲓⲟⲥ = Abel the just.
2. A proper noun in apposition to an indefinite or demonstrative term must be introduced by ⲭⲉ-. E.g. ⲟⲩⲁ ⲭⲉ-ⲥⲓⲙⲱⲛ = a certain person named Simon.
3. Proper nouns do not appear as predicate of a 1st or 2d person nominal sentence **32** (I am, you are); other constructions are used instead.
4. When a proper noun comes before a 1st or 2d person subject it is preceded by ⲁⲛⲟⲕ (ⲛ̅ⲧⲟⲕ etc.). E.g. ⲁⲛⲟⲕ ⲡⲁⲩⲗⲟⲥ ⲁⲓ̈-ⲥϩⲁⲓ̈ = I, Paul, have written.
5. A repeated proper noun calls attention to the speaker. E.g. ⲁⲃⲣⲁϩⲁⲙ ⲁⲃⲣⲁϩⲁⲙ = Abraham, Abraham!

But some place names always occur with a sing. def. article:

ⲧ–ⲅⲁⲗⲓⲗⲁⲓⲁ = Galilee

ⲡ–ⲓⲥⲣⲁⲏⲗ (abbreviated ⲡⲓ̅ⲏ̅ⲗ) = Israel

ⲑⲓⲉⲣⲟⲩⲥⲁⲗⲏⲙ (abbreviated ⲑ̅ⲗ̅ⲏ̅ⲙ̅) Jerusalem

OMISSION OF ARTICLE

24. Omission of article (where otherwise the indef. or def. article could occur) enables a speaker to be non-committal about gender, number, and determination. [CG 47–48] There is no single equivalent in English; often several English translations are implied, as illustrated below. Omission of the article typically occurs:

(*a*) *To provide general meaning in a compound expression.*

ⲧ̄–ⲃⲁⲡⲧⲓⲥⲙⲁ = give-baptism/give-baptisms, i.e. to baptize

(*b*) *To predicate a characteristic of someone or something.*

They took them *captive* (ⲁⲓⲭⲙⲁⲗⲱⲧⲏⲥ)
God sent him as *ruler* (ⲁⲣⲭⲱⲛ)
Make yourself *rich* (ⲣⲙ̄ⲙⲁⲟ)

(*c*) *In generalizations.*

ⲙ̄ⲙⲛ̄ⲧⲉ–ⲡⲣⲟⲫⲏⲧⲏⲥ ⲧⲁⲉⲓⲟ = No prophets have (No prophet has, A prophet does not have, Prophets do not have) honors (honor, any honor)

ⲡⲣⲟⲫⲏⲧⲏⲥ = prophet, prophets, any prophet
ⲧⲁⲉⲓⲟ = honors, honor, any honor

(*d*) *In negative expressions.*

ⲁⲭⲛ̄–ⲫⲟⲃⲟⲥ = fearlessly (without fear, fears)
ⲙ̄ⲡⲛ̄–ϣⲓⲛⲉ ⲛ̄ⲥⲁ–ⲉⲟⲟⲩ We did not seek honors (honor, any honor)

(*e*) *In comparisons and distributive ideas.*

ϩⲱⲥ–ⲡⲣⲟⲫⲏⲧⲏⲥ As a prophet
ⲕⲁⲧⲁ–ϣⲁ At every feast (at the feast, feast by feast, at feasttime).

Omission of article is also non-committal about gender. Thus cross-references to a feminine noun without article can be made by the sing. masculine personal morph ϥ, since masculine is the general (non-committal) gender. E.g. ⲁⲅⲁⲡⲏ ⲉ–ⲛⲁⲁⲁ–ϥ ⲉ–ⲧⲁⲓ̈ = greater love than this. [CG 48]

---

25. *"Zero article"; the symbol* ⁰. [CG 47] In grammatical analysis an omitted article (where otherwise the indef. or def. article could occur) is called a '*zero article*' (meaningful absence of article) and will be notated by a superior zero ($^{\emptyset}$), e.g. ϯ-$^{\emptyset}$ⲃⲁⲡⲧⲓⲥⲙⲁ = baptize, ⲁⲭⲛ̄-$^{\emptyset}$ⲫⲟⲃⲟⲥ = fearlessly, ⲙ̄ⲙⲛ̄ⲧⲉ-$^{\emptyset}$ⲡⲣⲟⲫⲏⲧⲏⲥ $^{\emptyset}$ⲧⲁⲉⲓⲟ = No prophets have honors etc. **103(i).**

THE ARTICLE PHRASE

26. The combination of article + noun, including the zero article, is called the *article phrase*. [CG 43] Definite and indefinite pronouns such as ⲡⲁⲓ̈ or ⲟⲩⲁ, proper nouns, and certain other items are interchangeable with article phrases in grammar. [CG 141–51]

'AND', 'OR', AND 'OF'

27. *Expressions for* 'And' *before an article phrase etc.* [CG 145]

(*a*) ⲍⲓ- = *and*, used before absence of article (zero article).

$^{\emptyset}$ⲙⲁⲉⲓⲛ ⲍⲓ-$^{\emptyset}$ϣⲡⲏⲣⲉ = signs and wonders
$^{\emptyset}$ⲍⲟⲟⲩⲧ ⲍⲓ-$^{\emptyset}$ⲥⲍⲓⲙⲉ = males and females

(*b*) ⲙⲛ̄- = *and*, used before an indefinite or definite article, and before an indefinite or definite pronoun.

ⲍⲉⲛ-ⲙⲁⲉⲓⲛ ⲙⲛ̄-ⲍⲉⲛ-ϣⲡⲏⲣⲉ = signs and wonders
ⲙ̄-ⲙⲁⲉⲓⲛ ⲙⲛ̄-ⲛⲉ-ϣⲡⲏⲣⲉ = the signs and the wonders
ⲛⲉⲓ̈-ⲙⲁⲉⲓⲛ ⲙⲛ̄-ⲛⲉⲓ̈-ϣⲡⲏⲣⲉ = these signs and these wonders

(*c*) ⲁⲩⲱ = *and*, used under both of these conditions.

ⲡⲉ-ⲥⲙⲟⲩ ⲙⲛ̄-ⲡ-ⲉⲟⲟⲩ ⲙⲛ̄-ⲧ-ⲥⲟⲫⲓⲁ <u>ⲁⲩⲱ</u> ⲧ-ⲉⲩⲭⲁⲣⲓⲥⲧⲓⲁ = glory and honor and wisdom and thanksgiving
$^{\emptyset}$ⲙⲁⲉⲓⲛ ⲁⲩⲱ $^{\emptyset}$ϣⲡⲏⲣⲉ = signs and wonders
ⲍⲉⲛ-ⲙⲁⲉⲓⲛ ⲁⲩⲱ ⲍⲉⲛ-ϣⲡⲏⲣⲉ = signs and wonders
ⲛⲉⲓ̈-ⲙⲁⲉⲓⲛ ⲁⲩⲱ ⲛⲉⲓ̈-ϣⲡⲏⲣⲉ = these signs and these wonders

(*d*) ⲛⲙ̄ⲙⲁ= completed by a personal suffix (to be studied in **51–52**) = *and*.

ⲡⲁⲩⲗⲟⲥ ⲛⲙ̄ⲙⲁ-ⲛ = Paul and us

28. *Expressions for* 'Or' *before an Article Phrase etc.* [CG 145]

ⲏ = and, or
ⲉⲓⲧⲉ . . . ⲉⲓⲧⲉ = either . . . or
ⲭⲛ̄- = or else, or (exclusive)
ⲟⲩⲁⲉ = nor
ⲟⲩⲧⲉ . . . ⲟⲩⲧⲉ = neither . . . nor
negation + ⲁⲗⲗⲁ = not . . . but rather

For example, ⲡ–ⲛⲟⲙⲟⲥ ⲏ ⲛⲉ–ⲡⲣⲟⲫⲏⲧⲏⲥ = the law and the prophets, ⲃⲁⲣⲁⲃⲃⲁⲥ ⲝⲛ̄–ⲓ̄ⲥ̄ Barabbas or Jesus, ⲟⲩⲧⲉ ⁰ϩⲟⲟⲩⲧ ⲟⲩⲧⲉ ⁰ⲥϩⲓⲙⲉ = neither male nor female.

29. *Expressions for 'Of' before an Article Phrase etc.*

(*a*) Ordinarily, *'Of'* (a very general kind of relationship) is expressed by ⲛ̄– (ⲙ̄– before ⲡ, ⲯ, ⲫ, or non-syllabic ⲙ). [CG 147]

ⲧ–ⲙⲁⲁⲩ ⲛ̄–ⲓ̄ⲥ̄ (i.e. ⲛ̄–ⲓⲏⲥⲟⲩⲥ) = the mother of Jesus, Jesus' mother

ⲡ–ⲏⲓ̈ ⲛ̄–ⲟⲩⲡⲣⲟⲫⲏⲧⲏⲥ = the house of a prophet, a certain prophet's house

ϩⲉⲛ–ϣⲏⲣⲉ ⲛ̄–ⲧⲉⲓ̈–ⲥϩⲓⲙⲉ = children of this woman, some of this woman's children

ϩⲉⲛ–ϣⲏⲣⲉ ⲛ̄–ⲧ–ϩⲙ̄ϩⲁⲗ = children of the maidservant, some of the maidservant's children

ⲡ–ⲏⲓ̈ ⲙ̄–ⲡ–ⲭⲟⲉⲓⲥ = the house of the Lord, the Lord's house

ⲡ–ⲭⲟⲉⲓⲥ ⲙ̄–ⲡ–ⲏⲓ̈ = the lord of the house, the house's owner

ⲡ–ⲭⲟⲉⲓⲥ ⲙ̄–ⲡ–ⲉⲟⲟⲩ ⲙⲛ̄–ⲡ–ⲧⲁⲉⲓⲟ = the Lord of glory and honor

ⲧ–ϭⲟⲙ ⲙ̄–ⲡⲉⲟⲟⲩ ⲛ̄–ⲧ–ⲙⲛ̄–ⲣ̄ⲣⲟ ⲙ̄–ⲡ–ⲭⲟⲉⲓⲥ = the power of the glory of the kingdom of the Lord

(*b*) ⲛ̄ⲧⲉ– *'Of'* [CG 148] can be optionally used to express appurtenance—the natural relation of part to whole, component to system, offspring to source. It is fairly rare.

ⲙ̄–ⲙⲉⲗⲟⲥ ⲛ̄ⲧⲉ–ⲡ–ⲥⲱⲙⲁ = the parts of the body

ⲟⲩ–ⲡⲟⲗⲓⲥ ⲛ̄ⲧⲉ–ⲧ–ⲅⲁⲗⲓⲗⲁⲓⲁ = a city of Galilee

ⲡⲉⲓ̈–ⲟⲩϫⲁⲓ̈ ⲛ̄ⲧⲉ–ⲡ–ⲛⲟⲩⲧⲉ = this salvation from God

Repetition of an article phrase signals the following.

(*a*) Definite article phrase repeated = *Each, Every, Each and every*

ⲡ-ⲣⲱⲙⲉ ⲡ-ⲣⲱⲙⲉ = Each man

ⲧ-ⲟⲩⲉⲓ ⲧ-ⲟⲩⲉⲓ = Each one, each female

ⲡ-ⲏⲓ̈ ⲡ-ⲏⲓ̈ = Each and every house

ⲛⲉⲓ̈-ⲧⲁⲉⲓⲟ ⲛⲉⲓ̈-ⲧⲁⲉⲓⲟ = These various honors, Each and every one of these honors

(*b*) Zero article phrase repeated = *One... after another...*

⁰ⲣⲱⲙⲉ ⁰ⲣⲱⲙⲉ = One person after another, Person by person

⁰ⲙⲁ ⁰ⲙⲁ = One place after another

⁰ϩⲟⲟⲩ ⁰ϩⲟⲟⲩ = Day by day

(*c*) Bare cardinal number **45** repeated = *... by...*

ⲥⲛⲁⲩ ⲥⲛⲁⲩ = Two by two

VOCABULARY 2

The family

ⲡ-ⲣⲱⲙⲉ	human being, person, man (gender not emphasized)	ἄνθρωπος, ἀνήρ
ⲡ-ϩⲟⲟⲩⲧ	male, man	ἄρσην, ἀνήρ
ⲧⲉ-ⲥϩⲓⲙⲉ, pl. ϩⲓⲟⲙⲉ	female, woman, wife	θῆλυς, γύνη
ⲡ-ⲉⲓⲱⲧ, pl. ⲉⲓⲟⲧⲉ	father, parent	πατήρ, γονεῦς
ⲧ-ⲙⲁⲁⲩ	mother	μήτηρ
ⲡ-ⲥⲟⲛ, pl. ⲥⲛⲏⲩ	brother, sibling	ἀδελφός
ⲧ-ⲥⲱⲛⲉ	sister	ἀδελφή
ⲡ-ϣⲏⲣⲉ	son, child	υἱός, τέκνον
ⲧ-ϣⲉⲉⲣⲉ	daughter	θυγάτηρ
ⲡ-ϣⲏⲣⲉ ϣⲏⲙ	child (male), baby, youth	παῖς, παῖς νήπιος
ⲧ-ϣⲉⲉⲣⲉ ϣⲏⲙ	child (female), baby, youth	παῖς, παῖς νήπιος
ⲡ-ϩⲁⲓ̈	husband	ἀνήρ
ⲧ-ϩⲓⲙⲉ, pl. ϩⲓⲟⲙⲉ	wife	γύνη
ⲡⲉ-ϣⲃⲏⲣ, pl. ϣⲃⲉⲉⲣ	friend	φίλος
ⲡ-ⲏⲓ̈	house, building	οἶκος
ⲡ-ⲣⲟ	door, entrance, mouth	θύρα, στόμα
*ⲡ-ϩⲉⲑⲛⲟⲥᵃ	nation, people	
*ⲡ-ⲗⲁⲟⲥ	people	

Authority, power

ⲡ-ϫⲟⲉⲓⲥ	master, lord	κύριος
ⲧ-ϫⲟⲉⲓⲥ	mistress, lady	κύρια
ⲡ-ϩⲙ̄ϩⲁⲗ	servant, slave (male)	δοῦλος
ⲧ-ϩⲙ̄ϩⲁⲗ	servant, slave (female)	δούλη, παιδίσκη
ⲧ-ϭⲟⲙ	power, capacity, strength	δύναμις
ⲧ-ϩⲟⲧⲉ	fear	φόβος
ⲡ-ⲉⲟⲟⲩ	glory, honor	δόξα
ⲡ-ⲧⲁⲉⲓⲟ	honor	τιμή
ⲡ-ⲣ̄ⲣⲟ, pl. ⲣ̄ⲣⲱⲟⲩ	king, emperor	βασιλεῦς
ⲧ-ⲙⲛ̄ⲧ-ⲣ̄ⲣⲟ (ⲧ-ⲙⲛ̄ⲧ-ⲉⲣⲟ), pl. ⲙⲛ̄ⲧ-ⲣ̄ⲣⲱⲟⲩ (ⲙⲛ̄ⲧⲉⲣⲱⲟⲩ)	kingdom, empire	βασιλεία

Other

ⲡ–, ⲧ–, ⲛ̄–	the (**18**)
ⲡⲉ–, ⲧⲉ–, ⲛⲉ–	the (**22**)
ⲡⲁⲓ̈, ⲧⲁⲓ̈, ⲛⲁⲓ̈	this one, these (**18**)
ⲡⲉⲓ̈–, ⲧⲉⲓ̈–, ⲛⲉⲓ̈–	this . . . , these . . . (demonstrative article, used like ⲡ–, ⲧ–, ⲛ–) (**18**)
ⲟⲩ– (or ⲩ– **22**), ϩⲉⲛ–	a, some, *plural often untranslated* (**18**)
ⲟⲩⲁ, ⲟⲩⲉⲓ, ϩⲟⲉⲓⲛⲉ	one, someone, some (**18**)
ⲛ̄– or ⲙ̄–	of (**29**)
ⲛ̄ⲧⲉ–	of (**29**)
ⲁⲩⲱ	and (**27**)
ϩⲓ–	and (**27**)
ⲙⲛ̄–	and (**27**)

ᵃGreco-Coptic words are starred (*) in the vocabulary lists. Note that some Greek words that begin with a smooth breathing, such as ἔθνος *ethnos,* have come into Coptic with initial ϩ: ϩⲉⲑⲛⲟⲥ *hethnos.* Thus ϩⲉⲗⲡⲓⲥ (ἐλπίς), ϩⲁⲙⲏⲛ (ἀμήν), etc.

EXERCISES 2

Translate each item, giving alternate translations where possible[8].

A. a. ⲡⲁⲓ̈. ⲟⲩⲁ. ⲡ–ⲭⲟⲉⲓⲥ. ⲟⲩ–ⲭⲟⲉⲓⲥ. ⲧ–ϭⲟⲙ. ⲟⲩ–ϭⲟⲙ. b. ϩⲉⲛ–ϭⲟⲙ. ϩⲉⲛ–ⲉⲟⲟⲩ ⲙⲛ̄–ϩⲉⲛ–ⲧⲁⲉⲓⲟ. ϩⲉⲛ–ⲉⲟⲟⲩ ⲁⲩⲱ ϩⲉⲛ–ⲧⲁⲉⲓⲟ. ⲡ–ⲉⲟⲟⲩ ⲙⲛ̄–ⲡ–ⲧⲁⲉⲓⲟ. c. ⁰ⲉⲟⲟⲩ ϩⲓ–⁰ⲧⲁⲉⲓⲟ. ⁰ⲥⲟⲛ ϩⲓ–⁰ⲥⲱⲛⲉ. ⲡⲁⲓ̈ ⲙⲛ̄–ⲛⲁⲓ̈. ⲧⲉⲓ̈–ⲥϩⲓⲙⲉ ⲙⲛ̄–ⲡⲁⲓ̈. d. ⲟⲩⲉⲓ. ⲛⲉⲓ̈–ⲉⲓⲟⲧⲉ. ϩⲟⲉⲓⲛⲉ. ⲛ̄–ⲉⲓⲱⲧ. ⲛ̄–ⲉⲓⲟⲧⲉ. ⲛⲉⲓ̈–ⲉⲓⲱⲧ. e. ⲡⲉ–ϣⲃⲏⲣ. ⲛⲉ–ϣⲃⲏⲣ. ⲛⲉ–ϣⲃⲉⲉⲣ. ⲙ̄–ⲙⲛ̄ⲧ–ⲣ̄ⲣⲟ. ⲙ̄–ⲙⲁⲁⲩ. ⲧⲉⲓ̈–ⲙⲁⲁⲩ. f. ⲡ–ϩⲁⲓ̈ ⲙⲛ̄–ⲑⲓⲙⲉ. ⲟⲩ–ϣⲏⲣⲉ ϣⲏⲙ ⲁⲩⲱ ⲟⲩ–ϣⲉⲉⲣⲉ ϣⲏⲙ. ⁰ⲉⲟⲟⲩ ⲁⲩⲱ ⁰ⲧⲁⲉⲓⲟ. ⁰ϩⲟⲟⲩⲧ ϩⲓ–⁰ⲥϩⲓⲙⲉ. g. ⲡⲉ–ⲥⲣ̄ⲟⲥ ⲛ̄–ⲓ̄ⲥ̄ ⲡⲉ–ⲭⲥ̄.

B. Translate into Coptic. *a.* Man and woman. *b.* Husband and wife. *c.* Men and women. *d.* The women. *e.* The brothers. *f.* The mothers. *g.* (Any) man (*or* men) and (any) woman (*or* women). *h.* These men and these women. *i.* A friend. *j.* Friends. *k.* The friends. *l.* The kingdoms. *m.* These kingdoms. *n.* The servants. *o.* Some servants. *p.* Honor and glory. *q.* A son and a daughter. *r.* Sons and daughters. *s.* Either a son or a daughter.

C. Translate. a. ⲡ–ⲗⲁⲟⲥ ⲙ̄–ⲡ–ⲭⲟⲉⲓⲥ. ⲡ–ⲭⲟⲉⲓⲥ ⲙ̄–ⲡ–ⲗⲁⲟⲥ. b. ⲡ–ⲉⲟⲟⲩ ⲛ̄–ⲧⲉ–ⲥϩⲓⲙⲉ. ⲧ–ϩⲙ̄ϩⲁⲗ ⲙ̄–ⲡ–ⲣ̄ⲣⲟ. ⲡ–ϩⲙ̄ϩⲁⲗ ⲛ̄–ⲛⲉ–ⲣ̄ⲣⲱⲟⲩ. c. ⲛ̄–ϣⲏⲣⲉ ⲛ̄–ⲧⲉⲓ̈–ⲥϩⲓⲙⲉ. d. ⲛⲉ–ϣⲃⲏⲣ ⲛ̄–ⲧ–ⲙⲛ̄ⲧ–ⲣ̄ⲣⲟ ⲙ̄–ⲡ–ⲭⲟⲉⲓⲥ. e. ⲛ̄–ϭⲟⲙ ⲛ̄ⲧⲉ–ⲡ–ⲭⲟⲉⲓⲥ. f. ⲡ–ϣⲏⲣⲉ ⲙ̄–ⲡ–ⲣⲱⲙⲉ. g. ⲧ–ϭⲟⲙ ⲛ̄ⲧⲉ–ⲡⲉⲓ̈–ⲗⲁⲟⲥ. h. ⲡ–ⲗⲁⲟⲥ ⲛ̄–ⲧⲉⲓ̈–ϭⲟⲙ.

D. Translate into Coptic. *a.* The father of this nation. *b.* John's father. *c.* The house of Mary. *d.* Mary's house. *e.* John and Mary's house. *f.* The nation of these women and the power of the emperor. *g.* (Any/Some) servants of this man. *h.* The lord's friends. *i.* The slave's sister. *j.* Some men of this kingdom. *k.* Male and female. *l.* The fear of the Lord. *m.* The door of this house.

---

[8] Although you may write out the exercises, it's very important to practice until you can do them without looking at written notes.

LESSON 3

POSSESSIVE ARTICLE.
SIMPLE NOMINAL SENTENCE.

---

30. *The possessive article* follows the pattern ⲡ–ⲧ–ⲛ that was seen in the simple definite article. [CG 54]

	sg. masc.	sg. fem.	pl.
my	ⲡⲁ–	ⲧⲁ–	ⲛⲁ–
your (sing. masc.)	ⲡⲉⲕ–	ⲧⲉⲕ–	ⲛⲉⲕ–
your (sing. fem.)	ⲡⲟⲩ–	ⲧⲟⲩ–	ⲛⲟⲩ–
his	ⲡⲉϥ–	ⲧⲉϥ–	ⲛⲉϥ–
her	ⲡⲉⲥ–	ⲧⲉⲥ–	ⲛⲉⲥ–
our	ⲡⲉⲛ–	ⲧⲉⲛ–	ⲛⲉⲛ–
your (pl.)	ⲡⲉⲧⲛ̄–	ⲧⲉⲧⲛ̄–	ⲛⲉⲧⲛ̄–
their	ⲡⲉⲩ–	ⲧⲉⲩ–	ⲛⲉⲩ–

Thus with ⲉⲓⲱⲧ (masc.) = father, ⲙⲁⲁⲩ (fem.) = mother, and ϩⲓ̈ = house:

my	ⲡⲁ–ⲉⲓⲱⲧ	ⲧⲁ–ⲙⲁⲁⲩ	ⲛⲁ–ϩⲓ̈
your (sing. masc.)	ⲡⲉⲕ–ⲉⲓⲱⲧ	ⲧⲉⲕ–ⲙⲁⲁⲩ	ⲛⲉⲕ–ϩⲓ̈
your (sing. fem.)	ⲡⲟⲩ–ⲉⲓⲱⲧ	ⲧⲟⲩ–ⲙⲁⲁⲩ	ⲛⲟⲩ–ϩⲓ̈
his	ⲡⲉϥ–ⲉⲓⲱⲧ	ⲧⲉϥ–ⲙⲁⲁⲩ	ⲛⲉϥ–ϩⲓ̈
her	ⲡⲉⲥ–ⲉⲓⲱⲧ	ⲧⲉⲥ–ⲙⲁⲁⲩ	ⲛⲉⲥ–ϩⲓ̈
our	ⲡⲉⲛ–ⲉⲓⲱⲧ	ⲧⲉⲛ–ⲙⲁⲁⲩ	ⲛⲉⲛ–ϩⲓ̈
your (pl.)	ⲡⲉⲧⲛ̄–ⲉⲓⲱⲧ	ⲧⲉⲧⲛ̄–ⲙⲁⲁⲩ	ⲛⲉⲧⲛ̄–ϩⲓ̈
their	ⲡⲉⲩ–ⲉⲓⲱⲧ	ⲧⲉⲩ–ⲙⲁⲁⲩ	ⲛⲉⲩ–ϩⲓ̈

The initial letters ⲡ, ⲧ, ⲛ express definite determination and the number/gender of the following noun. The personal marks ⲁ, ⲉⲕ, ⲟⲩ, ⲉϥ, ⲉⲥ, ⲉⲛ, ⲉⲧⲛ̄, ⲉⲩ express the person, number, and gender of the possessor:

ⲡ–ⲁ–ⲉⲓⲱⲧ = the + of-me + father = my father.
ⲡ–ⲉⲥ–ⲉⲓⲱⲧ = the + of-her + father = her father.
ⲧ–ⲉⲕ–ⲙⲁⲁⲩ = the + of-you [sing. masc.] + mother = your mother.
ⲡ–ⲟⲩ–ⲉⲓⲱⲧ = your (sing. fem.) father.
ⲧ–ⲟⲩ–ⲙⲁⲁⲩ = your (sing. fem.) mother.
ⲛ–ⲁ–ϩⲓ̈ = my houses.

ⲡⲁ–ⲉⲓⲱⲧ my father, ⲧⲁ–ⲥϩⲓⲙⲉ my wife, ⲛⲁ–ⲥⲛⲏⲩ my brothers, ⲛⲉϥ–ⲥⲛⲏⲩ his brothers, ⲛⲉⲧⲛ̄–ⲥⲛⲏⲩ your (pl.) brothers, ⲡⲟⲩ–ⲏⲓ̈ your (sing. fem.) house, ⲡⲉⲕ–ⲏⲓ̈ your (sing. masc.) house, ⲡⲉⲧⲛ̄–ⲏⲓ̈ your (pl.) house, ⲛⲉⲕ–ϣⲉⲉⲣⲉ ϣⲏⲙ your (sing. masc.) female children, etc.

> Since the possessive article expresses definite meaning like ⲡ–, ⲧ–, ⲛ̄–, indefinite meaning plus possessor must be expressed as ⲟⲩ–ⲏⲓ̈ ⲛ̄ⲧⲁ–ϥ, "a house of his," ⲟⲩ–ⲏⲓ ⲛ̄ⲧⲉ–ⲡⲛⲟⲩⲧⲉ "a house of God's." ⲛ̄ⲧⲉ–/ⲛ̄ⲧⲁ= is declined like a preposition (lesson 7). [CG 61]

THE SIMPLE NOMINAL SENTENCE

31. Minimally, Coptic nominal sentences consist of a pronoun as subject and an article phrase as predicate.

ⲁⲛⲅ̄–|ⲟⲩ–ϥⲛ̄ⲧ = I am a worm (I a-worm)
subject + predicate

ⲟⲩ–ϥⲛ̄ⲧ | ⲡⲉ = He is a worm (a-worm he)
predicate + subject

ⲁⲛⲅ̄–|ⲟⲩ–ⲡⲣⲟⲫⲏⲧⲏⲥ = I am a prophet (I a-prophet)
subject + predicate

ⲟⲩ–ⲡⲣⲟⲫⲏⲧⲏⲥ | ⲡⲉ = he is a prophet (a-prophet he)
predicate + subject

> *Subject and predicate.* By definition, the subject presents (or reminds the reader of) the topic that is being discussed; it is familiar, or at least presupposed, information. The predicate states new information about the subject. You should bear in mind that, in the broader view, the term predicate does *not* necessarily mean 'verbal part of the sentence'. Rather we may conveniently say that the subject is the topic of conversation and the predicate is the comment that is made about it—and that languages differ in the ways they connect the topic and the comment. [CG 247]

Note that the Coptic nominal sentence does not contain a verb. In this, Coptic is different from our familiar Indo-European languages, which employ a copula verb *to be* (être, sein, εἶναι, esse, etc.) to connect subject and predicate. Indeed, in translating a Coptic nominal sentence into English we always *add* the English copula verb: "I *am* a prophet" (Coptic: I-a prophet), for Coptic has none. [CG 252]

32. The simplest nominal sentence has only two components. [CG 252, 263–67]

i. A personal subject pronoun as subject (I, you, he, etc.)
ii. An article phrase or other eligible item as predicate (a prophet, prophets, the prophet of God, this one, John, etc.)

The *personal subject pronouns* are

ⲁⲛⲅ̄– . . .	= I
ⲛ̄ⲧⲕ̄– . . .	= you (sing. masc.)
ⲛ̄ⲧⲉ– . . .	= you (sing. fem.)
. . . ⲡⲉ	= he, it
. . . ⲧⲉ	= she, it
ⲁⲛ– or ⲁⲛⲟⲛ– . . .	= we
ⲛ̄ⲧⲉⲧⲛ̄– . . .	= you (pl.)
. . . ⲛⲉ	= they

and

. . . ⲡⲉ [invariable] it (impersonal)[9]

Thus

ⲁⲛⲅ̄–ⲟⲩ–ⲡⲣⲟⲫⲏⲧⲏⲥ = I am a prophet
ⲛ̄ⲧⲕ̄–ⲟⲩ–ⲡⲣⲟⲫⲏⲧⲏⲥ = you (sing. masc.) are a prophet
ⲛ̄ⲧⲉ–ⲟⲩ–ⲡⲣⲟⲫⲏⲧⲏⲥ = you (sing. fem.) are a prophet
ⲟⲩ–ⲡⲣⲟⲫⲏⲧⲏⲥ ⲡⲉ = he is a prophet
ⲟⲩ–ⲡⲣⲟⲫⲏⲧⲏⲥ ⲧⲉ = she is a prophet

ⲁⲛ–ϩⲉⲛ–ⲡⲣⲟⲫⲏⲧⲏⲥ or ⲁⲛⲟⲛ–ϩⲉⲛ–ⲡⲣⲟⲫⲏⲧⲏⲥ = we are prophets
ⲛ̄ⲧⲉⲧⲛ̄–ϩⲉⲛ–ⲡⲣⲟⲫⲏⲧⲏⲥ = you (pl.) are prophets
ϩⲉⲛ–ⲡⲣⲟⲫⲏⲧⲏⲥ ⲛⲉ = they are prophets

Into this paradigm we can insert any appropriate article phrase, pronoun, or other eligible item as the predicate.

ⲁⲛⲅ̄–ⲟⲩ–ϩⲙ̄ϩⲁⲗ	ⲁⲛ–ϩⲉⲛ–ⲙⲛ̄ⲧⲣⲉ
ⲛ̄ⲧⲕ̄–ⲡ–ⲣ̄ⲣⲟ	ⲛ̄ⲧⲉⲧⲛ̄–ⲛⲉ–ⲡⲣⲟⲡⲟⲫⲏⲧⲏⲥ
ⲛ̄ⲧⲉ–ⲧ–ⲙⲁⲁⲩ	
ⲡⲉⲥ–ⲥⲟⲛ ⲡⲉ	ⲛⲁⲓ̈ ⲛⲉ
ⲙⲁⲣⲓⲁ ⲧⲉ	

Literal translations:

I-a-servant	we-(some)-witnesses
you-the king	you-the-prophets
you-the-mother	

---

[9] Sometimes ⲡⲉ corresponds to the expletive pronoun, "*It* is I who am the light of the world"; "*It* is winter."

her-brother he   these they
Maria she

I.e. "I am a servant, you are the king, you are the mother, he is her brother, she is Mary, we are witnesses, you are the prophets, they are these (they are the following)."

33. Obviously two different patterns are united in the nominal sentence. (*a*) The 1st or 2d person subject pronoun (ⲁⲛⲅ̄– etc.) always comes first, immediately followed by the predicate. (*b*) The 3d person subject pronoun (ⲡⲉ, ⲧⲉ, ⲛⲉ) always comes after the predicate, and is connected more loosely.

    (*a*) ⲁⲛⲅ̄– . . .
    (*b*) . . . ⲡⲉ

Note carefully where a hyphen (–) does and does not occur. When two words, e.g. the predicate and subject (ⲡⲉⲡⲣⲟⲫⲏⲧⲏⲥ ⲡⲉ), are *not* connected by a hyphen we call this an *open group,* and it can be interrupted by another word or phrase, such as a connective particle or an '*Of*' construction.

    ⲟⲩ–ⲥ̄ϩⲓⲙⲉ ⲅⲁⲣ ⲧⲉ = For (γάρ), she is a woman
    ⲧ–ⲙⲁⲁⲩ ⲛ̄–ⲓⲱϩⲁⲛⲛⲏⲥ ⲧⲉ = She is the mother of John

and

    ⲧ–ⲙⲁⲁⲩ ⲧⲉ ⲛ̄–ⲓⲱϩⲁⲛⲛⲏⲥ = She is the mother of John

But where subject and predicate are connected by a hyphen they form a *bound group* **8** and cannot be interrupted.

    ⲁⲛⲅ̄–ⲟⲩ–ⲥ̄ϩⲓⲙⲉ ⲅⲁⲣ = For, I am a woman
    ⲛ̄ⲧⲉ–ⲧ–ⲙⲁⲁⲩ ⲁⲉ ⲛ̄–ⲓⲱϩⲁⲛⲛⲏⲥ = And you are the mother of John

---

Restrictions on the predicate. The following may *not* occur as predicate with a 1st and 2d person subject pronoun: noun with absence of article, demonstrative, proper noun, and cardinal number or other specifier (except ⲟⲩⲁ meaning 'such a one' and ⲛⲓⲙ 'who?'). But the predicate with a 3d person subject pronoun is not restricted. [CG 259]

---

34. *Negation.* Nominal sentences are negatived by inserting ⲁⲛ after the predicate. With 1st and 2d person subject pronoun:

    ⲁⲛⲅ̄–ⲟⲩ–ⲥ̄ϩⲓⲙⲉ ⲁⲛ = I am not a woman
    ⲁⲛⲅ̄–ⲟⲩ–ⲥ̄ϩⲓⲙⲉ ⲅⲁⲣ ⲁⲛ = For, I am not a woman
    ⲛ̄ⲧⲉ–ⲧ–ⲙⲁⲁⲩ ⲁⲛ = You are not the mother
    ⲛ̄ⲧⲉ–ⲧ–ⲙⲁⲁⲩ ⲁⲛ ⲛ̄–ⲓⲱϩⲁⲛⲛⲏⲥ = You are not John's mother

ⲚⲦⲈ–Ⲧ–ⲘⲀⲀⲨ Ⲛ̄–ⲒⲰⳞⲀⲚⲚⲎⲤ ⲀⲚ = You are not John's mother

In the simple 3d person pattern, ⲀⲚ always comes between the predicate and ⲡⲉ/ⲧⲉ/ⲛⲉ.

ⲞⲨ–ⲤⳞⲒⲘⲈ ⲀⲚ ⲦⲈ = She is not a woman
ⲞⲨ–ⲤⳞⲒⲘⲈ ⲅⲁⲣ ⲀⲚ ⲦⲈ = For, she is not a woman
Ⲧ–ⲘⲀⲀⲨ ⲀⲚ ⲦⲈ = She is not the mother
Ⲧ–ⲘⲀⲀⲨ Ⲛ̄–ⲒⲰⳞⲀⲚⲚⲎⲤ ⲀⲚ ⲦⲈ = She is not John's mother
Ⲧ–ⲘⲀⲀⲨ ⲀⲚ Ⲛ̄–ⲒⲰⳞⲀⲚⲚⲎⲤ ⲦⲈ = She is not John's mother

Sometimes the negative prefix Ⲛ̄– (Ⲙ̄– before ⲡ or non-syllabic ⲙ) is also used. In the 1st and 2d person pattern, Ⲛ̄– is prefixed (optionally) to the subject pronoun ⲀⲚⲒ̄– (etc.): (Ⲛ̄–) . . . ⲀⲚ.

Ⲛ̄–ⲀⲚⲒ̄–ⲞⲨ–ⲤⳞⲒⲘⲈ Ⲁ̲Ⲛ̲ = I am not a woman

In the 3d person pattern, Ⲛ̄– is prefixed (optionally) to the predicate:

Ⲛ̄–ⲞⲨ–ⲤⳞⲒⲘⲈ Ⲁ̲Ⲛ̲ ⲦⲈ = She is not a woman

Optional negative Ⲛ̄– occurs more frequently in the 3d person pattern.

Long spellings of the 1st and 2d person subject pronouns:

ⲀⲚⲞⲔ–   = ⲀⲚⲒ̄–
Ⲛ̄ⲦⲞⲔ–   = Ⲛ̄ⲦⲔ̄–
Ⲛ̄ⲦⲞ–   = Ⲛ̄ⲦⲈ–
ⲀⲚⲞⲚ–   = ⲀⲚ–
Ⲛ̄ⲦⲰⲦⲚ̄– = Ⲛ̄ⲦⲈⲦⲚ̄–

Of these, ⲀⲚⲞⲚ– is especially common (perhaps the usual form).

VOCABULARY 3

Authority, power (continued)

ⲡ-ⲣⲙ̄ⲙⲁⲟ	rich person (man or woman)	πλούσιος
ⲡ-ϩⲁⲡ	judgement	κρίμα, κρίσις
*ⲡ-ⲁⲡⲟⲥⲧⲟⲗⲟⲥ	apostle	
*ⲧ-ⲉⲝⲟⲩⲥⲓⲁ	authority, ability	
*ⲡⲉ-ⲑⲣⲟⲛⲟⲥ	throne	
*ⲡⲉ-ⲡⲣⲉⲥⲃⲩⲧⲉⲣⲟⲥ	elder, (Christian) priest	

Daily life

ⲡ-ⲟⲉⲓⲕ	bread, loaf	ἄρτος, ψωμίον
ⲡ-ⲙⲟⲟⲩ, pl. ⲙⲟⲩⲉⲓⲟⲟⲩⲉ	water	ὕδωρ
ⲡ-ⲱⲛⲉ	stone	λίθος
ⲡ-ϫⲟⲓ̈, pl. ⲉϫⲏⲩ	boat	πλοῖον
ⲡ-ⲕⲱϩⲧ̄	fire	πῦρ
*ⲧ-ⲡⲟⲗⲓⲥ	city, polis	
*ⲡ-ⲕⲁⲣⲡⲟⲥ	fruit, crop, profit	

Religion, ethics

ⲡ-ⲛⲟⲩⲧⲉ	god; God (always ⲡ-ⲛⲟⲩⲧⲉ)	θεός
ⲓⲏⲥⲟⲩⲥ (abbrev. ⲓ̄ⲥ̄ or ⲓ̄ⲏ̄ⲥ̄, 17)	Jesus	
*ⲡⲉ-ⲭⲣⲓⲥⲧⲟⲥ (abbrev. ⲡⲉ-ⲭ̄ⲥ̄ or ⲡⲉ-ⲭ̄ⲣ̄ⲥ̄)	Christ, anointed	
*ⲡ-ⲁⲅⲅⲉⲗⲟⲥ	angel	
ⲡ-ⲛⲟⲃⲉ	sin	ἁμαρτία
*ⲡ-ⲃⲁⲡⲧⲓⲥⲙⲁ	baptism	
ⲡ-ⲟⲩϫⲁⲓ̈	salvation, health	σωτηρία
ⲡ-ⲱⲛϩ̄	life	ζωή
ⲡ-ⲙⲟⲩ	death	θάνατος
*ⲡ-ⲇⲁⲓⲙⲟⲛⲓⲟⲛ	demon	
ⲧ-ⲙⲉ	truth	ἀλήθεια
ⲡ-ⲟⲩⲁ	blasphemy	βλασφημία
ⲡ-ⲟⲩⲟⲉⲓⲛ	light	φῶς
ⲡ-ⲕⲁⲕⲉ	darkness	σκοτία, σκότος

п-мⲛ̄ⲧⲣⲉ	witness	μάρτυς
ⲧ-мⲛ̄ⲧ-мⲛ̄ⲧⲣⲉ	testimony	μαρτυρία
ⲡⲉ-ⲣⲡⲉ, pl. ⲣ̄ⲡⲏⲩⲉ	temple	ἱερόν, ναός
*ⲡ-ⲁⲣⲭⲓⲉⲣⲉⲩⲥ	high priest	
*ⲡ-ⲥⲁⲃⲃⲁⲧⲟⲛ	Sabbath	
*ⲧ-ⲥⲩⲛⲁⲅⲱⲅⲏ	synagogue	
*ⲡ-ⲇⲓⲕⲁⲓⲟⲥ	just person, righteous person (man or woman)	
*ⲡⲉ-ⲡⲣⲟⲫⲏⲧⲏⲥ	prophet	

Optional: Learn the gendered prefixes forming composite nouns (above, box).

EXERCISES 3

A. Translate. a. ⲡⲁ-ϩⲁⲡ. b. ⲧⲁ-ⲉϩⲟⲩⲥⲓⲁ. c. ⲡⲉⲥ-ϩⲁⲡ. d. ⲧⲉϥ-ⲉϩⲟⲩⲥⲓⲁ. e. ⲡⲉⲕ-ϩⲁⲡ. f. ⲧⲉⲕ-ⲉϩⲟⲩⲥⲓⲁ. g. ⲛⲉⲩ-ϩⲁⲡ. h. ⲛⲉⲕ-ϩⲁⲡ. i. ⲛⲟⲩ-ϩⲁⲡ. j. ⲛⲉⲥ-ϩⲁⲡ. k. ⲛⲉϥ-ϩⲁⲡ. l. ⲧⲉⲩ-ⲉϩⲟⲩⲥⲓⲁ. m. ⲧⲉⲕ-ⲉϩⲟⲩⲥⲓⲁ. n. ⲛⲉⲕ-ⲉϩⲟⲩⲥⲓⲁ. o. ⲛⲟⲩ-ⲉϩⲟⲩⲥⲓⲁ. p. ⲧⲟⲩ-ⲉϩⲟⲩⲥⲓⲁ. q. ⲧⲉⲩ-ⲉϩⲟⲩⲥⲓⲁ. ⲅ. ⲛⲉⲥ-ⲉϩⲟⲩⲥⲓⲁ. s. ⲟⲩ-ⲉϩⲟⲩⲥⲓⲁ. t. ⲛⲉϥ-ⲉϩⲟⲩⲥⲓⲁ. u. ⲧ-ⲉϩⲟⲩⲥⲓⲁ. v. ⲡ-ϩⲁⲡ.

B. Translate rapidly into Coptic.

(*a*) My boat, your (pl.) boat, your (sing. masc.) boats, your (sing. fem.) boats, your (sing. fem.) boat, her boat, his boat, our boat, our boats.

(*b*) My testimony, your (pl.) testimony, your (sing. masc.) testimonies, your (sing. fem.) testimonies, your (sing. fem.) testimony, her testimony, his testimony, our testimony, our testimonies.

(*c*) My sister's house, her sister's house, his sister's house, their sister's house, his sisters' house, their sisters' house, your (pl.) sisters' house, your (pl.) sister's house, our sister's house, our sisters' house, your (sing. masc.) sisters' house, your (sing. fem.) sister's house.

(*d*) The judgement of God. God's judgement. Our sins and God's judgement. The kingdom of God and the power of salvation. The water of life. The waters of life. The authority of the apostles. The temple of Jerusalem.

C. Translate into Coptic. a. I am the light and the truth. *b.* I am God's witness. *c.* You are God's witnesses. *d.* She is the servant of the rich man.

e. He is a just person. *f.* It is the fire of God's judgement. *g.* You are a just woman. *h.* You are a rich man. *i.* It is the fruit of death.

D. Translate into Coptic. a. I am not the light and the truth. *b.* I am not God's witness. *c.* You are not God's witnesses. *d.* She is not the servant of the rich man. *e.* He is not a just person. *f.* It is not the fire of God's judgement. *g.* You are not a just woman. *h.* You are not a rich man. *i.* It is not the fruit of death.

E. Translate. a. ⲡ–ⲟⲉⲓⲕ ⲛ̄–ⲧ–ⲙⲉ ⲡⲉ. b. ϩⲉⲛ–ⲟⲩⲁ ⲛⲉ. c. ⲁⲛⲟⲛ–ϩⲉⲛ–ϩⲙ̄ϩⲁⲗ ⲙ̄–ⲡ–ⲛⲟⲩⲧⲉ. d. ⲛ̄ⲧⲉⲧⲛ̄–ⲡ–ⲗⲁⲟⲥ ⲛ̄–ⲧ–ⲙⲉ. e. ⲧⲉⲛ–ⲡⲟⲗⲓⲥ ⲧⲉ. f. ⲛ̄ⲧⲕ̄–ⲟⲩ–ⲣⲙ̄ⲙⲁⲟ. g. ⲛ̄ⲧⲉ–ⲟⲩ–ⲇⲓⲕⲁⲓⲟⲥ. h. ⲡⲉϥ–ⲑⲣⲟⲛⲟⲥ ⲡⲉ. i. ϩⲉⲛ–ⲱⲛⲉ ⲛⲉ ⲛ̄–ⲧ–ⲙⲛ̄ⲧ–ⲙⲛ̄ⲧⲣⲉ. j. ⲁⲛⲟⲕ–ⲟⲩ–ⲡⲣⲉⲥⲃⲩⲧⲉⲣⲟⲥ. k. ⲁⲛⲅ̄–ⲧ–ϩⲙ̄ϩⲁⲗ ⲙ̄–ⲡ–ⲭⲟⲉⲓⲥ.

F. Form the negative of each sentence in (E), giving alternate forms where possible.

G. Translate. a. ⲓ̄ⲥ ⲡⲉ–ⲭ̄ⲥ̄. b. ⲓ̄ⲥ ⲡⲉ ⲡⲉ–ⲭ̄ⲥ̄. c. ⲡ–ⲁⲅⲅⲉⲗⲟⲥ ⲙ̄–ⲡ–ⲱⲛϩ̄. d. ⲡ–ⲃⲁⲡⲧⲓⲥⲙⲁ ⲙ̄–ⲡ–ⲟⲩⲭⲁⲓ̈. e. ⲡ–ⲁⲣⲭⲓⲉⲣⲉⲩⲥ ⲙ̄–ⲡⲉⲓ̈–ⲣ̄ⲡⲉ. f. ⲡ–ⲭⲟⲓ̈ ⲙ̄–ⲡ–ⲁⲡⲟⲥⲧⲟⲗⲟⲥ. g. ⲡ–ⲙⲟⲟⲩ ⲙⲛ̄–ⲡ–ⲕⲱϩⲧ̄. h. ⲡ–ⲕⲁⲕⲉ ⲙ̄–ⲡ–ⲇⲁⲓⲙⲟⲛⲓⲟⲛ ⲡⲉ ⲡ–ⲕⲁⲣⲡⲟⲥ ⲙ̄–ⲡ–ⲛⲟⲃⲉ. i. ⲟⲩ–ⲟⲩⲟⲉⲓⲛ ⲙ̄–ⲡ–ⲥⲁⲃⲃⲁⲧⲟⲛ ⲡⲉ ⲡ–ⲛⲟⲙⲟⲥ ⲁⲩⲱ ⲛⲉ–ⲡⲣⲟⲫⲏⲧⲏⲥ.

LESSON 4

ADJECTIVE. ATTRIBUTIVE CONSTRUCTION. ADJECTIVAL PREDICATE.

35. Adjectives[10] [CG 113–17] are not particular about gender: each adjective occurs freely with both ⲡ– and ⲧ–. There are two main classes:

(*a*) Greco-Coptic adjectives (a huge list—potentially *all* Greek adjectives). Those of the Greek -ος declension come into Coptic as word pairs ending in –ⲟⲥ and –ⲟⲛ to distinguish animate versus inanimate. This is a very large class of Coptic words.

ⲡ–ⲡⲟⲛ ⲏ ⲣ<u>ⲟⲥ</u> = the wicked one (man) ⎫
ⲧ–ⲡⲟⲛ ⲏ ⲣ<u>ⲟⲥ</u> = the wicked one (woman) ⎬ animate
ⲡ–ⲡⲟⲛ ⲏ ⲣ<u>ⲟⲛ</u> = the wicked one (thing) ⎭ inanimate

Note that the –ⲟⲥ ending is both masculine and feminine in Coptic (unlike Greek): ⲡ–ⲡⲟⲛ ⲏ ⲣⲟⲥ, ⲧ–ⲡⲟⲛ ⲏ ⲣⲟⲥ.

(*b*) Egyptian-Coptic adjectives (about twenty in number), some of which have optional feminine and/or plural forms.

ⲁⲥ = old
ⲃⲣ̄ⲣⲉ = new
ⲉⲃⲓ ⲏ ⲛ = wretched
ⲕⲟⲩ ï = small
ⲕⲁⲙⲉ = black
ⲙⲉⲣ ⲓ ⲧ, pl. ⲙⲉⲣⲁⲧⲉ = beloved
ⲛⲟ ϭ = big
ⲥⲁⲃⲉ, fem. ⲥⲁⲃⲏ, pl. ⲥⲁⲃⲉⲉ ⲩ = prudent, wise
ⲥⲁⲉ ⲓ ⲉ = beautiful
ⲥⲱⲧⲡ̄ = excellent
ϣ ⲏ ⲙ, fem. ϣ ⲏ ⲙⲉ = small
ϣ ⲙ̄ⲙⲟ, fem. ϣ ⲙ̄ⲙⲱ = foreign
ϣⲟ ⲣ ⲡ̄, fem. ϣⲟ ⲣ ⲡⲉ = first
ϩⲁⲉ, fem. ϩⲁⲏ, pl. ϩⲁⲉⲉ ⲩ = last
ϩ ⲁ ⲕ = sober, prudent
ϩ ⲏ ⲕⲉ = poor

---

[10] Called "genderless common nouns" in *CG*.

ϩⲁⲗⲟ, fem. ϩⲗⲗⲱ, pl. ϩⲗⲗⲟⲓ = old
ϩⲟⲩⲉⲓⲧ, fem. ϩⲟⲩⲉⲓⲧⲉ, pl. ϩⲟⲩⲁⲧⲉ = first, original
ⲭⲱⲱⲣⲉ = strong
ⲭⲁⲭⲉ, pl. ⲭⲓⲭⲉⲉⲩ(ⲉ) = hostile

All Coptic adjectives can also be used as nouns: ⲡ–ⲡⲟⲛⲏⲣⲟⲥ = the wicked man, ⲧ–ⲡⲟⲛⲏⲣⲟⲥ = the wicked woman, ⲡ–ⲉⲃⲓⲏⲛ = the wretch, ⲡ–ⲭⲁⲭⲉ = the enemy, ⲧ–ϩⲏⲕⲉ = the poor woman, etc.

Composite adjective formation. Prefixes forming composite adjectives (i.e. without a particular gender) are the following. [CG 118–21, 123–25]

ⲁⲧ– = privative, 'not having, unable to': ⲉⲓⲱⲧ = father, ⲁⲧ–ⲉⲓⲱⲧ = father-less

ⲣⲙ̄– or ⲣⲙ̄ⲛ̄– = 'person related to': ⲕⲏⲙⲉ = Egypt, ⲣⲙ̄ⲛ̄–ⲕⲏⲙⲉ = Egyptian

ⲣⲉϥ– agential, ' . . .-ing, doing . . . ': ⲣ̄–ⲛⲟⲃⲉ = to sin, ⲣⲉϥ–ⲣ̄–ⲛⲟⲃⲉ = sinner

---

36. The attributive construction enables an adjective *or noun* to modify an article phrase. [CG 96–103] The modifier follows the article phrase, linked by ⲛ̄– (ⲙ̄– before ⲡ or non-syllabic ⲙ):

ⲡ–ⲅⲉⲛⲟⲥ ⲙ̄–ⲡⲟⲛⲏⲣⲟⲥ the *wicked* race
                 (adjective)
ⲡ–ⲅⲉⲛⲟⲥ ⲛ̄–ⲃⲣ̄ⲣⲉ the *new* race
                 (adjective)
ⲡ–ⲅⲉⲛⲟⲥ ⲛ̄–ⲣⲱⲙⲉ the *human* race
                 (noun)

If, and only if, the modifier is an adjective (such as ⲡⲟⲛⲏⲣⲟⲥ or ⲃⲣ̄ⲣⲉ), the construction can also be inverted, so that the modifier precedes its target of modification. This construction is fairly common, particularly with certain adjectives. It expresses a special nuance.

ⲡ–ⲡⲟⲛⲏⲣⲟⲥ ⲛ̄–ⲅⲉⲛⲟⲥ the *wicked* race (inverted word order)

By the use of the attributive construction the number of modifiers is vastly increased beyond the words listed in **35**, since all "nouns" as well as all "adjectives" can be modifiers. Thanks to this construction, every noun can express an adjectival meaning as well as a substantial one. Thus

ⲛ̄–ⲣⲱⲙⲉ = human
ⲛ̄–ⲟⲩⲟⲉⲓⲛ = luminous

 N̄–con = fraternal

etc. etc.

Several attributive constructions can modify a single article phrase; they can be optionally connected by ⲁⲩⲱ "and."

ⲟⲩ–ⲣⲱⲙⲉ ⲛ̄–ϫⲁϫⲉ ⲙ̄–ⲡⲟⲛⲏⲣⲟⲥ = a wicked, hostile man

ⲡ–ⲣ̄ⲣⲟ ⲛ̄–ⲥⲁⲃⲉ ⲁⲩⲱ ⲛ̄–ϭⲟⲙ = the powerful, wise emperor

37. The adjectives ϣⲏⲙ = small, ⲕⲟⲩⲓ̈ = small, and ⲛⲟϭ = big can be placed immediately after the target of modification *without* the presence of ⲛ̄–. This is the usual construction of ϣⲏⲙ. [CG 101]

ϣⲏⲣⲉ ϣⲏⲙ = little boy, ϣⲉⲉⲣⲉ ϣⲏⲙ = little girl

ADJECTIVAL PREDICATES IN THE NOMINAL SENTENCE

38. "Adjectival" predicates in the nominal sentence are normally formulated with an indefinite article (ⲟⲩ–, ϩⲉⲛ–), which is not translated into English when it has adjectival meaning. [CG 292(b)]

ⲁⲛⲅ̄–ⲟⲩ–ⲡⲟⲛⲏⲣⲟⲥ = I am wicked (ⲟⲩ–ⲡⲟⲛⲏⲣⲟⲥ)

ⲁⲛⲅ̄–ⲟⲩ–ⲉⲃⲓⲏⲛ = I am wretched (ⲟⲩ–ⲉⲃⲓⲏⲛ)

ⲁⲛ–ϩⲉⲛ–ⲡⲟⲛⲏⲣⲟⲥ = we are wicked (ϩⲉⲛ–ⲡⲟⲛⲏⲣⲟⲥ)

ⲟⲩ–ϫⲱⲱⲣⲉ ⲧⲉ = she (or it) is strong (ⲟⲩ–ϫⲱⲱⲣⲉ)

ϩⲉⲛ–ⲥⲁⲃⲉ ⲛⲉ or ϩⲉⲛ–ⲥⲁⲃⲉⲉⲩ ⲛⲉ = they are prudent (ϩⲉⲛ–ⲥⲁⲃⲉ)

ϩⲉⲛ–ⲇⲓⲕⲁⲓⲟⲥ ⲛⲉ = they are righteous (ϩⲉⲛ–ⲇⲓⲕⲁⲓⲟⲥ)

Note that nouns, too, are used as "adjectival" predicates in the nominal sentence, formulated in just the same way (ⲟⲩ–, ϩⲉⲛ–). So with the noun ⲛⲟⲩⲧⲉ = god:

ⲁⲛⲅ̄–ⲟⲩ–ⲛⲟⲩⲧⲉ = I am divine   ⲟⲩ–ⲛⲟⲩⲧⲉ ⲧⲉ = she is divine

ⲟⲩ–ⲛⲟⲩⲧⲉ ⲡⲉ = he is divine   ϩⲉⲛ–ⲛⲟⲩⲧⲉ ⲛⲉ = they are divine

Such predicates are ambiguous, since they might also be interpreted as referring to entities.

ⲁⲛⲅ̄–ⲟⲩ–ⲛⲟⲩⲧⲉ = I am a god

ⲟⲩ–ⲛⲟⲩⲧⲉ ⲡⲉ = he is a god

ⲟⲩ–ⲛⲟⲩⲧⲉ ⲧⲉ = she is a god(ess)

ϩⲉⲛ–ⲛⲟⲩⲧⲉ ⲛⲉ = they are gods

Similarly

ⲟⲩ–ⲟⲩⲟⲉⲓⲛ ⲡⲉ = he/it is luminous = he/it is a light

ⲟⲩ–ⲣⲱⲙⲉ ⲡⲉ = he/it is human = he/it is a person

etc.

34

VOCABULARY 4

Egyptian Coptic adjectives

ⲁⲥ	old	παλαιός
ⲃⲣ̄ⲣⲉ	new	καινός
ⲉⲃⲓⲏⲛ	wretched	ἐλεεινός
ⲕⲟⲩⲓ̈	small, insignificant	μικρός
ⲕⲁⲙⲉ	black	μέλας
ⲙⲉⲣⲓⲧ, pl. ⲙⲉⲣⲁⲧⲉ	beloved	ἀγαπητός
ⲛⲟϭ	big	μέγας
ⲥⲁⲃⲉ, fem. ⲥⲁⲃⲏ, pl. ⲥⲁⲃⲉⲉⲩ	wise	φρόνιμος
ⲥⲁⲉⲓⲉ	beautiful	εὔμορφος
ⲥⲱⲧⲡ̄	excellent, elect	ἐκλεκτός
ϣⲏⲙ, fem. ϣⲏⲙⲉ	small	ὀλίγος
ϣⲙ̄ⲙⲟ, fem. ϣⲙ̄ⲙⲱ	foreign	ξένος
ϣⲟⲣⲡ̄, fem. ϣⲟⲣⲡⲉ	first	πρῶτος
ϩⲁⲉ, fem. ϩⲁⲏ, pl. ϩⲁⲉⲉⲩ	last	ἔσχατος
ϩⲁⲕ	sober, prudent	ἐπιεικής
ϩⲏⲕⲉ	poor	πτωχός
ϩⲁ̄ⲗⲟ, fem. ϩⲁ̄ⲗⲱ, pl. ϩⲁ̄ⲗⲟⲓ	old	πρεσβύτης
ϩⲟⲩⲉⲓⲧ, fem. ϩⲟⲩⲉⲓⲧⲉ, pl. ϩⲟⲩⲁⲧⲉ	first, original	ἄρχαιος, πρῶτος
ϫⲱⲱⲣⲉ	strong	ἰσχυρός
ϫⲁϫⲉ, pl. ϫⲓϫⲉⲉⲩ(ⲉ)	hostile, enemy	ἐχθρός

Greco-Coptic adjectives

*ⲁⲛⲟⲙⲟⲥ, ⲁⲛⲟⲙⲟⲛ	lawless	
*ⲁⲥⲉⲃⲏⲥ	impious	
*ⲇⲓⲕⲁⲓⲟⲥ, ⲇⲓⲕⲁⲓⲟⲛ	just, righteous	
*ⲉⲗⲁⲭⲓⲥⲧⲟⲥ, ⲉⲗⲁⲭⲓⲥⲧⲟⲛ	insignificant	
*ⲡⲟⲛⲏⲣⲟⲥ, ⲡⲟⲛⲏⲣⲟⲛ	wicked	
*ⲥⲁⲣⲕⲓⲕⲟⲥ, ⲥⲁⲣⲕⲓⲕⲟⲛ	fleshly, carnal	

More nouns: Religion, ethics (continued)

*ⲧ–ⲇⲓⲕⲁⲓⲟⲥⲩⲛⲏ	righteousness
*ⲧ–ⲉⲓⲣⲏⲛⲏ	peace
*ⲧⲉ–ⲯⲩⲭⲏ	soul
*ⲧ–ⲉⲕⲕⲗⲏⲥⲓⲁ	church
*ⲡ–ⲉⲩⲁⲅⲅⲉⲗⲓⲟⲛ	gospel

EXERCISES 4

A. Translate, giving alternate translations where possible. a. ⲧ-ⲙⲛ̄ⲧ-ⲙⲛ̄ⲧⲣⲉ ⲛ̄-ⲥⲁⲣⲕⲓⲕⲟⲛ. b. ⲡⲉ-ⲣⲡⲉ ⲛ̄-ⲛⲟϭ. ⲡ-ⲛⲟϭ ⲛ̄-ⲣ̄ⲡⲉ. c. ⲡ-ⲡⲟⲛⲏ-ⲣⲟⲥ ⲛ̄-ⲁⲡⲟⲥⲧⲟⲗⲟⲥ. ϩⲉⲛ-ⲛⲟⲃⲉ ⲙ̄-ⲙⲟⲩ. d. ⲡⲉⲓ̈-ⲣ̄ⲣⲟ ⲛ̄-ⲉⲟⲟⲩ. ⲡⲁ-ⲙⲉⲣⲓⲧ ⲛ̄-ⲭⲟⲉⲓⲥ. ⲧⲁ-ⲙⲉⲣⲓⲧ ⲛ̄-ⲭⲟⲉⲓⲥ. e. ⲡ-ϩⲗ̄ⲗⲟ. ⲧ-ϩⲗ̄ⲗⲱ. ⲧ-ϩⲗ̄ⲗⲟ. ⲧⲉ-ⲥϩⲓⲙⲉ ⲛ̄-ϩⲗ̄ⲗⲱ. ⲧⲉ-ⲥϩⲓⲙⲉ ⲛ̄-ϩⲗ̄ⲗⲟ. f. ⲧⲉⲛ-ⲥⲱⲛⲉ ⲛ̄-ϩⲁⲕ ⲛ̄-ⲉⲗⲁⲭⲓⲥⲧⲟⲥ. ⲟⲩ-ⲣⲱⲙⲉ ⲛ̄-ⲭⲱⲱⲣⲉ. g. ⲟⲩ-ⲣⲱⲙⲉ ⲛ̄-ϭⲟⲙ ⲁⲩⲱ ⲛ̄-ⲇⲓⲕⲁⲓⲟⲥ. ⲧ-ⲉϫⲟⲩⲥⲓⲁ ⲛ̄-ⲛⲟⲩⲧⲉ. ⲧ-ϭⲟⲙ ⲛ̄-ⲛⲟⲩⲧⲉ ⲛ̄-ⲛⲟϭ.

B. Translate into Coptic. a. The big house. The large woman. The large kingdoms. b. The huge house. The gigantic woman. The great kingdoms. c. Paternal authority. Maternal authority. Fraternal authority. Friendly authority. d. Paternal power. Maternal honor. Fraternal judgement. A friendly judgement. e. A wise and just emperor. Wise and just emperors. f. These beautiful cities. An insignificant manservant. An insignificant maidservant.

C. Translate. a. ⲁⲛⲅ̄-ⲑⲙ̄ϩⲁⲗ ⲙ̄-ⲡ-ⲭⲟⲉⲓⲥ. ⲛ̄ⲧⲉ-ⲧ-ϩⲙ̄ϩⲁⲗ ⲙ̄-ⲡⲁ-ⲭⲟⲉⲓⲥ. b. ⲛ̄ⲧⲕ̄-ⲡ-ⲣ̄ⲣⲟ ⲙ̄-ⲡ-ⲉⲟⲟⲩ. ⲛ̄ⲧⲉⲧⲛ̄-ⲛⲉⲛ-ⲣ̄ⲣⲱⲟⲩ ⲛ̄-ⲇⲓⲕⲁⲓⲟⲥ. c. ⲁⲛⲅ̄-ⲟⲩ-ⲉⲗⲁⲭⲓⲥⲧⲟⲥ. ⲛ̄ⲧⲉⲧⲛ̄-ϩⲉⲛ-ⲉⲗⲁⲭⲓⲥⲧⲟⲥ ⲁⲛ. ⲛ̄-ⲁⲛ-ϩⲉⲛ-ⲥⲁⲃⲉⲉⲩ ⲁⲛ. d. ⲁⲛ-ϩⲉⲛ-ⲣⲱⲙⲉ ⲛ̄-ⲕⲟⲩⲓ̈ ⲛ̄-ⲉⲗⲁⲭⲓⲥⲧⲟⲥ. e. ⲁⲛⲅ̄-ⲟⲩ-ⲥϩⲓⲙⲉ ⲛ̄-ϩⲗ̄ⲗⲱ ⲛ̄-ⲁⲛⲟⲙⲟⲥ. f. ⲛ̄ⲧⲉ-ⲟⲩ-ⲁⲛⲟⲙⲟⲥ ⲁⲛ, ⲛ̄ⲧⲉ-ⲟⲩ-ⲙⲉⲣⲓⲧ ⲛ̄-ⲥⲱⲛⲉ ⲙ̄-ⲡⲉⲛ-ⲭⲟⲉⲓⲥ.

D. Translate. a. ⲟⲩ-ϩⲏⲕⲉ ⲡⲉ. ⲟⲩ-ϩⲏⲕⲉ ⲧⲉ. b. ϩⲉⲛ-ⲣⲱⲙⲉ ⲛ̄-ⲁⲛⲟⲙⲟⲥ ⲛ̄-ⲭⲁⲭⲉ ⲛⲉ ⲛ̄ⲧⲉ-ⲧⲉⲕ-ⲡⲟⲗⲓⲥ. c. ⲛ̄-ϩⲉⲛ-ⲣⲱⲙⲉ ⲛ̄-ⲁⲛⲟⲙⲟⲥ ⲛ̄-ⲭⲁⲭⲉ ⲁⲛ ⲛⲉ ⲛ̄ⲧⲉ-ⲧⲉⲕ-ⲡⲟⲗⲓⲥ. d. ⲟⲩ-ⲛⲟⲃⲉ ⲛ̄-ⲃⲣ̄ⲣⲉ ⲡⲉ. ⲛ̄-ⲟⲩ-ⲛⲟⲃⲉ ⲁⲛ ⲛ̄-ⲃⲣ̄ⲣⲉ ⲡⲉ. ⲛ̄-ⲟⲩ-ⲛⲟⲃⲉ ⲛ̄-ⲃⲣ̄ⲣⲉ ⲁⲛ ⲡⲉ. e. ⲧ-ⲙⲛ̄ⲧ-ⲉⲣⲟ ⲙ̄-ⲡ-ⲕⲁⲕⲉ ⲧⲉ. ⲧ-ⲙⲛ̄ⲧ-ⲉⲣⲟ ⲛ̄-ⲕⲁⲕⲉ ⲧⲉ. ⲧ-ⲙⲛ̄ⲧ-ⲉⲣⲟ ⲧⲉ ⲛ̄-ⲕⲁⲕⲉ. f. ⲧ-ⲙⲛ̄ⲧ-ⲉⲣⲟ ⲁⲛ ⲧⲉ ⲛ̄-ⲕⲁⲕⲉ. ⲛ̄-ⲧ-ⲙⲛ̄ⲧ-ⲉⲣⲟ ⲁⲛ ⲧⲉ ⲛ̄-ⲕⲁⲕⲉ. g. ⲛⲉⲛ-ⲉϫⲏⲩ ⲛⲉ. ⲛⲉⲛ-ⲭⲟⲓ̈ ⲛⲉ.

E. Translate into Coptic, giving alternate translations where possible. a. I am impious and wicked. b. You are strong. c. She is foreign. d. They are wise. e. We are beautiful. f. I am beautiful and black. g. He is wretched. h. I am not impious and wicked. i. You are not strong. j. She is not foreign. k. They are not wise. l. I am not beautiful and black. m. He is not wretched.

LESSON 5

NOMINAL SENTENCES WITH THREE MEMBERS.

39. If ογ–προφнтнс πε means He is a prophet ("A-prophet he") then how do we make a nominal sentence whose *subject* is an article phrase, pronoun, or proper noun—such as, *My father* is a prophet? One Coptic solution is to say: *My father, he is a prophet* ("My-father, a-prophet he"). [CG 272]

> πλ–ειωτ ογ–προφнтнс πε = My father is a prophet
> πλϊ ογ–προφнтнс πε = This one is a prophet
> мωγснс ογ–προφнтнс πε = Moses is a prophet

In such a sentence we can call the initial component (πλ–ειωτ, πλϊ, мωγснс) an *extraposition*—literally, one that has been "put outside" of a simple form of sentence pattern such as ογ–προφнтнс πε.

> мωγснс | ογ–προφнтнс πε = Moses is a prophet

Extraposition is a typical way of speaking in Coptic, and we shall see that all kinds of sentences can be equipped with an extraposition, or even with several.

When the extraposited subject differs in number and/or gender from the predicate, the selection of πε, τε, or ne is unpredictable, sometimes having the number and/or gender of the subject, often that of the predicate, and rarely having the form of πε agreeing with neither.

---

40. *Extrapositions can also have the form of* independent personal pronouns. [CG 77]

	sing.		pl.	
1st	λnοκ = I, me		λnοn = we, us	
2d masc.	n̄τοκ = you		n̄τωτn̄ = you	
2d fem.	n̄το = you			
3d masc.	n̄τοq = he, him		n̄τοογ = they, them	
3d fem.	n̄τοc = she, her			

Note that these pronouns do not end in a hyphen.

This opens up the possibility of the extraposition of the 1st and 2d person subject [CG 264]

ⲁⲛⲟⲕ ⲇⲉ | ⲁⲛⲅ̄-ⲟⲩ-ϧⲛ̄ⲧ. ⲁⲛⲅ̄-ⲟⲩ-ⲣⲱⲙⲉ ⲁⲛ.
As for me, I am a worm, I am not a man
ⲛ̄ⲧⲱⲧⲛ̄ | ⲛ̄ⲧⲉⲧⲛ̄-ⲛⲁ-ϣⲃⲉⲉⲣ
As for you, you are My friends

as well as extraposition of a 3d person subject [CG 272]

ⲛ̄ⲧⲟϥ ⲅⲁⲣ ⲁⲩⲱ ⲡⲉϥ-ⲉⲓⲱⲧ | ⲟⲩⲁ ⲛⲉ
As for Him and His father, they are one

The extraposition of personal pronouns typically occurs when two persons or objects are being compared: "As for me (ⲁⲛⲟⲕ), I am a worm; but as for you (ⲛ̄ⲧⲟⲕ), you are a . . . "

41. *Negation* is exactly as in the simple, two-member nominal sentence patterns **34.** [CG 272]

Extraposition | (ⲛ̄-) Predicate ⲁⲛ ⲡⲉ

ⲁⲛ is inserted between the predicate and ⲡⲉ/ⲧⲉ/ⲛⲉ. Negative ⲛ̄- is optionally prefixed to the predicate. ⲛ̄- is optional, ⲁⲛ is always required.

ⲡⲁ-ⲉⲓⲱⲧ ⲛ̄-ⲟⲩ-ⲡⲣⲟⲫⲏⲧⲏⲥ ⲁⲛ ⲡⲉ
ⲡⲁ-ⲉⲓⲱⲧ ⲟⲩ-ⲡⲣⲟⲫⲏⲧⲏⲥ ⲁⲛ ⲡⲉ

ⲡⲁⲓ̈ ⲛ̄-ⲟⲩ-ⲡⲣⲟⲫⲏⲧⲏⲥ ⲁⲛ ⲡⲉ
ⲡⲁⲓ̈ ⲟⲩ-ⲡⲣⲟⲫⲏⲧⲏⲥ ⲁⲛ ⲡⲉ

ⲙⲱⲩⲥⲏⲥ ⲛ̄-ⲟⲩ-ⲡⲣⲟⲫⲏⲧⲏⲥ ⲁⲛ ⲡⲉ
ⲙⲱⲩⲥⲏⲥ ⲟⲩ-ⲡⲣⲟⲫⲏⲧⲏⲥ ⲁⲛ ⲡⲉ

ⲁⲛⲟⲕ ⲛ̄-ⲁⲛⲅ̄-ⲟⲩ-ⲣ̄ⲣⲟ ⲁⲛ
ⲁⲛⲟⲕ ⲁⲛⲅ̄-ⲟⲩ-ⲣ̄ⲣⲟ ⲁⲛ

ⲛ̄ⲧⲟⲕ ⲛ̄-ⲛ̄ⲧⲕ̄-ⲡⲁ-ϫⲟⲉⲓⲥ ⲁⲛ
ⲛ̄ⲧⲟⲕ ⲛ̄ⲧⲕ̄-ⲡⲁ-ϫⲟⲉⲓⲥ ⲁⲛ

ⲛ̄ⲧⲟϥ ⲙ̄-ⲡ-ⲣ̄ⲣⲟ ⲁⲛ ⲡⲉ
ⲛ̄ⲧⲟϥ ⲡ-ⲣ̄ⲣⲟ ⲁⲛ ⲡⲉ

"My father is not a prophet. This man is not a prophet. Moses is not a prophet. As for me, I am not a king. As for you, you are not my lord. As for him, he is not the king."

The Three Member Nominal Sentence with Central ⲡⲉ.

42. Very often, nominal sentences have the form of two components connected by central ⲡⲉ, ⲧⲉ, or ⲛⲉ. [CG 275, 277]

article phrase   ⲡⲉ   article phrase
ⲡⲉϥ-ⲉⲓⲱⲧ   ⲡⲉ   ⲡ-ⲣ̄ⲣⲟ

This kind of sentence brings the two components together into a complete statement, but does not signal which is subject and which is predicate. Such sentences are ambiguous, and can be interpreted in two different ways according to what best suits the argument of the text. Here are two interpretations of the same sentence:

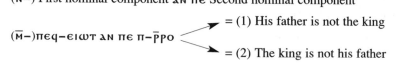

ⲡⲉϥ-ⲉⲓⲱⲧ ⲡⲉ ⲡ-ⲣ̄ⲣⲟ
= (1) His father is the king
= (2) The king is his father

Both are normal interpretations of this sentence.

The article phrases that occur in this pattern can be built upon all kinds of articles (definite, indefinite, and zero article). Pronouns, proper nouns, and independent pronouns can occur in place of article phrases (as can prepositional phrases **49** expressing relationship, and specifiers **43**). [CG 268 (end)]

Negation. ⲁⲛ is inserted before ⲡⲉ. Optionally, ⲛ̄- is prefixed to the first component.

(ⲛ̄-) First nominal component ⲁⲛ ⲡⲉ Second nominal component

(ⲙ̄-)ⲡⲉϥ-ⲉⲓⲱⲧ ⲁⲛ ⲡⲉ ⲡ-ⲣ̄ⲣⲟ
= (1) His father is not the king
= (2) The king is not his father

The many *sub-varieties of the nominal sentence* are described in CG 252, from which (p. 200) the following list is adapted.

1. ⲁⲛⲅ̄–ⲟⲩⲡⲣⲟⲫⲏⲧⲏⲥ = I am a prophet.
2. ⲁⲛⲟⲕ ⲁⲛⲅ̄–ⲟⲩⲡⲣⲟⲫⲏⲧⲏⲥ = As for me, I am a prophet.
3. ⲡϣⲱⲙ ⲡⲉ = It's summer.
4. ⲡⲉⲛⲛⲟⲩⲧⲉ ⲡⲉ = He is our God.
5. ⲛⲉⲓ̈ⲣⲱⲙⲉ ϩⲉⲛⲓⲟⲩⲁⲁⲓ ⲛⲉ = These men are Jews.
5a. ⲡⲓⲥⲁⲧⲁⲛⲁⲥ ⲡⲓⲥⲁⲧⲁⲛⲁⲥ ⲟⲛ ⲡⲉ = Satan is always the same.
5b. ⲛ̄ⲥⲟⲃⲧ̄ ⲇⲉ ⲛ̄ⲧⲟⲟⲩ ⲛ̄ⲧⲟⲟⲩ ⲟⲛ ⲡⲉ = Walls are always the same.
6. ⲧⲁⲅⲁⲡⲏ ⲡⲉ ⲡⲛⲟⲩⲧⲉ = God is love. Love is God.
6a. ⲁⲛⲟⲕ ⲡⲉ ⲡⲟⲩⲟⲉⲓⲛ ⲙ̄–ⲡⲕⲟⲥⲙⲟⲥ = It is *I* who am the light of the world.
7. ⲡⲉⲓ̈ⲁⲡⲟⲧ ⲡⲉ ⲧⲁⲓⲁⲑⲏⲕⲏ ⲙ̄–ⲃⲣ̄ⲣⲉ = This cup is the new covenant.
7a. ⲁⲛⲟⲕ ⲡⲉ ⲅⲁⲃⲣⲓⲏⲗ = I am Gabriel. [predicate is a proper name]
8. ⲡⲕⲟⲩⲓ ⲛ̄ϩⲏⲧ–ⲑⲏⲩⲧⲛ̄ ⲧⲏⲣ–ⲧⲛ̄ ⲡⲁⲓ̈ ⲡⲉ ⲡⲛⲟϭ = The one who is least among all of you is the great one.
9. ⲁⲛⲟⲕ ⲡⲉ = It is I/It's me.
10. ⲁⲛⲟⲕ ⲡⲉ = I am he/I am such.
11. ⲁⲛⲟⲕ ⲡⲉ = I am someone important.
12. ⲁⲗⲗⲁ ⲛⲉϥⲙⲁⲑⲏⲧⲏⲥ ⲛⲉ = Rather, it was His disciples (who were doing so) [continuing a cleft sentence].

VOCABULARY 5

Religion, ethics (continued)

ⲡ-ⲣⲁϣⲉ	joy	χαρά
ⲡⲉ-ϩⲙⲟⲧ	gift	χάρισμα, χάρις
*ⲧ-ⲁⲅⲁⲡⲏ	love	
*ⲧⲉ-ⲭⲁⲣⲓⲥ	divine grace, favor	
ⲡ-ⲥⲟⲡⲥ̄	entreaty, consolation	δέησις, παράκλη-σις
ⲡ-ⲙⲁⲉⲓⲛ	sign	σημεῖον
ⲧⲉ-ϣⲡⲏⲣⲉ	omen, wonder, miracle	τέρας, θαυμαστόν
ⲡ-ⲡⲉⲧⲛⲁⲛⲟⲩϥ	good (that which is good)	τὸ ἀγαθόν
ⲡ-ⲡⲉⲑⲟⲟⲩ	evil (that which is evil)	τὸ πονηρόν
*ⲡⲉ-ⲅⲣⲁⲙⲙⲁⲧⲉⲩⲥ	scribe	
ⲡ-ⲥⲁϩ	teacher	διδάσκαλος
*ⲡ-ⲙⲁⲑⲏⲧⲏⲥ	disciple, student	
ⲧⲉ-ⲥⲃⲱ, pl. ⲥⲃⲟⲟⲩⲉ	teaching (that which is taught)	διδαχή
ⲡ-ⲥⲟⲟⲩⲛ	acquaintance, knowledge	γνῶσις
*ⲧⲉ-ⲅⲣⲁⲫⲏ	scripture	
*ⲡ-ⲛⲟⲙⲟⲥ	law	
*ⲧ-ⲉⲛⲧⲟⲗⲏ	commandment	
*ⲧ-ⲡⲓⲥⲧⲓⲥ	faith	
*ⲡ-ⲡⲓⲥⲧⲟⲥ (adjective)	faithful	
*ⲡⲉ-ⲡⲛⲉⲩⲙⲁ (abbrev. ⲡⲉ-ⲡ̄ⲛ̄ⲁ̄)	spirit	

Time

ⲡⲉ-ϩⲟⲟⲩ	day	ἡμέρα
ⲧⲉ-ⲩϣⲏ (ⲟⲩϣⲏ)	night	νύξ
ⲧⲉ-ⲩⲛⲟⲩ (ⲟⲩⲛⲟⲩ)	hour, moment	ὥρα
ⲧⲉ-ⲣⲟⲙⲡⲉ	year	ἔτος, ἐνιαυτός
ⲡⲉ-ⲩⲟⲉⲓϣ (ⲟⲩⲟⲉⲓϣ)	occasion, time	καιρός, χρόνος

Other

ⲡ-ⲙⲏⲏϣⲉ	crowd, multitude	ὄχλος, πλῆθος

Postpositive connective words[a]

*ⲅⲁⲣ	for	
*ⲇⲉ	and, but, now	
*ⲙⲉⲛ	now, to be sure[b] . . .	
ⲟⲛ	once again, additionally, back	πάλιν once again, καί additionally
ϭⲉ	then, therefore, any more	οὖν, δέ

---

[a]As in Greek these particles can never stand first in a sentence and tend to appear in, or compete for, the second available position. In Coptic they appear after the first or second bound group **33**: ⲡ–ⲥⲟⲛ ⲅⲁⲣ ⲛ̄–ⲓⲱϩⲁⲛⲛⲏⲥ = For, the brother of John . . . ; ⲁⲛⲅ̄–ⲟⲩ–ϥⲛ̄ⲧ ϭⲉ ⲁⲛ = Thus, I am not a worm.

[b]In classical Greek a clause containing μέν is normally followed by a clause containing δέ. This is not so in Coptic.

EXERCISES 5

A. *Translate, giving alternate translations where possible.* a. ⲧⲉⲕ–ⲥⲃⲱ
ⲟⲩ–ⲡⲉⲧⲛⲁⲛⲟⲩϥ ⲧⲉ. b. ⲛⲉⲓ–ⲙⲁⲉⲓⲛ ϩⲉⲛ–ⲙⲉ ⲛⲉ. c. ⲧⲟⲩ–ⲡⲓⲥⲧⲓⲥ
ⲟⲩ–ⲛⲟϭ ⲧⲉ. d. ⲡⲉ–ⲡ̄ⲛ̄ⲁ̄ ⲙ̄–ⲡ–ⲛⲟⲩⲧⲉ ⲟⲩ–ⲭⲱⲱⲣⲉ ⲡⲉ. e. ⲡⲁⲓ ⲡⲉ
ⲡ–ⲙⲁⲉⲓⲛ. f. ⲡ–ⲣⲁϣⲉ ⲙ̄–ⲡ–ⲥⲁϩ ⲡⲉ ⲧ–ϭⲟⲙ ⲙ̄–ⲡⲉϥ–ⲙⲁⲑⲏⲧⲏⲥ. g. ⲡ–ⲛⲟⲙⲟⲥ ⲛ̄–ⲧⲉ–ⲭⲁⲣⲓⲥ ⲡⲉ ⲡ–ⲥⲟⲟⲩⲛ ⲙ̄–ⲡ–ⲡⲉⲑⲟⲟⲩ ⲙⲛ̄–ⲡ–ⲡⲉⲧⲛⲁⲛⲟⲩϥ.
h. ⲡⲉ–ϩⲟⲟⲩ ⲙ̄–ⲡ–ⲥⲟⲡⲥ̄ ⲡⲉ ⲟⲩ–ⲟⲩⲟⲉⲓϣ ⲛ̄–ⲟⲩ–ⲣⲁϣⲉ. i. ⲧⲉⲛ–ⲭⲟⲉⲓⲥ
ⲧⲉ ⲧ–ⲙⲁⲁⲩ ⲙ̄–ⲡ–ⲛⲟⲩⲧⲉ. j. ⲛ̄ⲧⲟⲕ ⲛ̄ⲧⲕ̄–ⲡⲁ–ⲭⲟⲉⲓⲥ ⲁⲩⲱ ⲡⲁ–ⲛⲟⲩⲧⲉ.
k. ⲁⲛⲟⲕ ⲁⲛⲅ̄–ⲑⲙ̄ϩⲁⲗ ⲙ̄–ⲡⲁ–ⲭⲟⲉⲓⲥ. l. ⲛ̄ⲧⲱⲧⲛ̄ ⲛ̄ⲧⲉⲧⲛ̄–ⲛⲁ–ⲥⲛⲏⲩ.
m. ⲛ̄ⲧⲱⲧⲛ̄ ⲛ̄ⲧⲉⲧⲛ̄–ⲛⲁ–ⲥⲟⲛ. n. ⲛ̄ⲧⲟⲟⲩ ϩⲉⲛ–ⲇⲓⲕⲁⲓⲟⲥ ⲛ̄–ⲛⲟϭ ⲛⲉ.
o. ⲛ̄ⲧⲟⲟⲩ ϩⲉⲛ–ⲇⲓⲕⲁⲓⲟⲥ ⲛⲉ ⲛ̄–ⲛⲟϭ.

B. *Form the negation of each sentence in (1), giving alternate forms where
possible, and translate.*

C. *Translate (cf.* **35** *[b]).* a. ⲟⲩ–ⲥⲃⲱ ⲛ̄–ⲃ̄ⲣ̄ⲣⲉ. ⲡ–ⲛⲟⲙⲟⲥ ⲛ̄–ⲁⲥ. b. ⲟⲩ–
ⲥⲁϩ ⲛ̄–ⲉⲃⲓⲏⲛ. ⲡ–ⲕⲟⲩⲓ̈ ⲙ̄–ⲙⲁⲑⲏⲧⲏⲥ ⲙ̄–ⲙⲉⲣⲓⲧ. ⲡⲙⲉⲣⲓⲧ ⲙ̄–ⲙⲁⲑⲏⲧⲏⲥ
ϣⲏⲙ. c. ϩⲉⲛ–ϩⲟⲟⲩ ⲛ̄–ⲥⲁⲉⲓⲉ. ⲧⲉ–ϩⲟⲩⲉⲓⲧⲉ ⲛ̄–ⲣⲟⲙⲡⲉ. ⲧ–ϩⲁⲏ ⲛ̄–ⲣⲟⲙⲡⲉ. ⲑⲁⲏ ⲛ̄–ⲣⲟⲙⲡⲉ. d. ⲟⲩ–ⲡⲛⲉⲩⲙⲁ ⲛ̄–ⲭⲁⲭⲉ. ⲟⲩ–ⲡⲓⲥⲧⲓⲥ ⲛ̄–ⲭⲱⲱⲣⲉ.
ⲡ–ⲥⲟⲟⲩⲛ ⲛ̄–ϩⲁⲕ. e. ⲡ–ⲃ̄ⲣ̄ⲣⲉ. ϩⲉⲛ–ⲉⲃⲓⲏⲛ. ⲧ–ⲕⲟⲩⲓ̈. ⲡ–ⲕⲟⲩⲓ̈. f. ⲛ̄–ⲕⲟⲩⲓ̈.
ϩⲉⲛ–ⲥⲁⲉⲓⲉ. ⲧⲉ–ϩⲟⲩⲉⲓⲧⲉ. ⲡⲉ–ϩⲟⲩⲉⲓⲧ. ⲑⲁⲏ. g. ⲛ̄–ⲭⲁⲭⲉ. ⲟⲩ–ϩⲁⲕ.
ⲧ–ϣⲟⲣⲡⲉ ⲛ̄–ⲉⲕⲕⲗⲏⲥⲓⲁ. h. ⲡ–ⲛⲟϭ ⲛ̄–ⲉⲩⲁⲅⲅⲉⲗⲓⲟⲛ ⲁⲩⲱ ⲡ–ⲉⲩⲁⲅⲅⲉⲗⲓⲟⲛ ϣⲏⲙ. i. ⲧⲉ–ⲯⲩⲭⲏ ⲙ̄–ⲡ–ⲇⲓⲕⲁⲓⲟⲥ ⲟⲩ–ⲉⲓⲣⲏⲛⲏ ⲧⲉ ⲙⲛ̄–ⲟⲩⲇⲓ-
ⲕⲁⲓⲟⲥⲩⲛⲏ.

D. *Translate into Coptic, giving alternate translations where possible.*
a. The year of the Lord is the joy of his people. *b.* The moment of grace is
not an insignificant thing. *c.* The law of God is the joy of this nation. *d.* For
your part, you are not the least of the apostles. *e.* As for them, they are a great
crowd of witnesses.

LESSON 6

SPECIFIERS.
CARDINAL AND ORDINAL NUMBERS.

---

43. The following six *specifiers*

ⲟⲩⲏⲣ = how many? how much?
ⲛⲓⲙ = who? which (person)?
ⲟⲩ = what? what kind of (thing)?
ⲁϣ = which one? which?
ϩⲁϩ = many
ⲗⲁⲁⲩ = any at all, any

can be used alone as pronouns

ⲛⲓⲙ = who?   ϩⲁϩ = many

or can specify a noun or adjective in the *specifier construction*

specifier ⲛ̄– noun/adjective

ⲛⲓⲙ ⲛ̄–ⲣⲱⲙⲉ   = which person?
ϩⲁϩ ⲛ̄–ⲣⲱⲙⲉ   = many people

No article is required, since the specifier is in place of the article.

ϩⲁϩ ⲛ̄–ⲣⲱⲙⲉ = many men
ⲛⲓⲙ ⲛ̄–ⲣⲱⲙⲉ = which man?
ⲗⲁⲁⲩ ⲛ̄–ⲣⲱⲙⲉ = any man

Specifier constructions are mostly used where a noun with indefinite article or zero article is permissible. [CG 63–64, 72–73]

44. In a few expressions, the indefinite article ⲟⲩ–/ϩⲉⲛ– or the article ⲕⲉ– 'another' **61** can be used with ⲟⲩ, ⲁϣ, and ⲗⲁⲁⲩ. [CG 74]

ϩⲉⲛ–ⲟⲩ ⲛⲉ = What sort of thing (some-what) are they?
ⲟⲩ–ⲗⲁⲁⲩ ⲡⲉ = It is insignificant (an-anything)
ⲕⲉ–ⲗⲁⲁⲩ ⲛ̄–ⲣⲱⲙⲉ = Any other man (another-any-man)

So with ϩⲉ and ⲙⲓⲛⲉ = kind, sort, type. [CG 111(b), 301]

ⲟⲩ-ⲁϣ ⲛ̄-ϩⲉ ⲡⲉ = What kind (a-which kind) is he?

answered by

ⲟⲩ-ⲧⲉⲓ̈-ϩⲉ or ⲟⲩ-ⲧⲉⲓ̈-ⲙⲓⲛⲉ ⲡⲉ = He is of this kind, such, like this (plural ϩⲉⲛ-ⲧⲉⲓ̈-ϩⲉ etc.)

45. The *cardinal numbers* also belong to the specifier class. [CG 66–70] They are used both alone like pronouns

ⲥⲛⲁⲩ ⲏ ϣⲟⲙⲛ̄ⲧ = two or three (people, things)

and in the specifier construction, specifying a noun.

ϣⲟⲙⲛ̄ⲧ ⲛ̄-ⲣⲱⲙⲉ = three men
ϣⲟⲙⲧⲉ ⲛ̄-ⲥϩⲓⲙⲉ = three women

The numbers from one to ten and certain others occur in pairs, expressing masculine and feminine gender[11], and the appropriate form is selected according to the gender of the noun to which the number refers. Letters of the alphabet, marked with a super-linear stroke, are used for the corresponding numerals as shown in the following table.

CARDINAL NUMBERS FROM ONE TO TEN

		masc.	fem.
ⲁ̄	one	ⲟⲩⲁ	ⲟⲩⲉⲓ
ⲃ̄	two	ⲥⲛⲁⲩ	ⲥⲛ̄ⲧⲉ
ⲅ̄	three	ϣⲟⲙⲛ̄ⲧ	ϣⲟⲙⲧⲉ
ⲇ̄	four	ϥⲧⲟⲟⲩ	ϥⲧⲟ or ϥⲧⲟⲉ
ⲉ̄	five	ϯⲟⲩ	ϯ or ϯⲉ
ⲋ̄	six	ⲥⲟⲟⲩ	ⲥⲟ or ⲥⲟⲉ
ⲍ̄	seven	ⲥⲁϣϥ̄	ⲥⲁϣϥⲉ
ⲏ̄	eight	ϣⲙⲟⲩⲛ	ϣⲙⲟⲩⲛⲉ
ⲑ̄	nine	ⲯⲓⲥ	ⲯⲓⲧⲉ
ⲓ̄	ten	ⲙⲏⲧ	ⲙⲏⲧⲉ

Cardinal numbers above ten, if not round numbers (twenty, thirty, etc.), are compounds consisting of a prefixal component (teens, twenties, thirties, etc.) and a final component (-one, -two, -three). E.g. ⲭⲟⲩⲧ-ϣⲟⲙⲧⲉ (twenty + three) = twenty-three, ⲙⲛ̄ⲧ-ϣⲟⲙⲧⲉ (ten + three) = thirteen.

---

[11] The numbers twenty and thirty and all those above ten whose last digit is 1, 2, 8, or 9 occur in masculine/feminine pairs.

		Round Numbers	Prefixal Components
ⲓ̄	ten	masc. ⲙⲏⲧ, fem. ⲙⲏⲧⲉ	ⲙⲛ̄ⲧ–
ⲕ̄	twenty	ϫⲟⲩⲱⲧ, fem. ϫⲟⲩⲱⲧⲉ	ϫⲟⲩⲧ–
ⲗ̄	thirty	ⲙⲁⲁⲃ, fem. ⲙⲁⲁⲃⲉ	ⲙⲁⲃ–
ⲙ̄	forty	ϩⲙⲉ	ϩⲙⲉ– (ϩⲙⲉⲧ– before ⲁϥⲧⲉ and ⲁⲥⲉ)
ⲛ̄	fifty	ⲧⲁⲉⲓⲟⲩ	ⲧⲁⲉⲓⲟⲩ–
ⲝ̄	sixty	ⲥⲉ	ⲥⲉ– (ⲥⲉⲧ– before ⲁϥⲧⲉ and ⲁⲥⲉ)
ⲟ̄	seventy	ϣϥⲉ	ϣϥⲉ–
ⲡ̄	eighty	ϩⲙⲉⲛⲉ	ϩⲙⲉⲛⲉ– (ϩⲙⲉⲛⲉⲧ– before ⲁϥⲧⲉ and ⲁⲥⲉ)
ϥ̄	ninety	ⲡⲥⲧⲁⲓⲟⲩ	ⲡⲥⲧⲁⲓⲟⲩ–

TERMINAL COMPONENTS

. . . ⲁ̄	. . . -one	masc. –ⲟⲩⲉ, fem. –ⲟⲩⲉⲓ
. . . ⲃ̄	. . . -two	masc. –ⲥⲛⲟⲟⲩⲥ, fem. –ⲥⲛⲟⲟⲩⲥⲉ
. . . ⲅ̄	. . . -three	–ϣⲟⲙⲧⲉ
. . . ⲇ̄	. . . -four	–ⲁϥⲧⲉ
. . . ⲉ̄	. . . -five	–ⲧⲏ (but –ⲏ after ⲙⲛ̄ⲧ– and ϫⲟⲩⲧ–)
. . . ⲋ̄	. . . -six	–ⲁⲥⲉ
. . . ⲍ̄	. . . -seven	–ⲥⲁϣϥⲉ
. . . ⲏ̄	. . . -eight	masc. –ϣⲙⲏⲛ, fem. –ϣⲙⲏⲛⲉ
. . . ⲑ̄	. . . -nine	masc. –ⲯⲓⲥ, fem. –ⲯⲓⲧⲉ

Hundreds: ⲣ̄ (100) ϣⲉ, ⲥ̄ (200) ϣⲏⲧ, ⲧ̄ (300) ϣⲙⲛ̄ⲧ–ϣⲉ, ⲩ̄– (400) ϥⲧⲟⲟⲩ ⲛ̄–ϣⲉ or ϥⲧⲉⲩ–ϣⲉ, ϥ̄ (500), ⲭ̄ (600), ⲯ̄ (700), ⲱ̄ (800), ⳁ̄ (900).

Thousands: ⲁ̿ (1,000) ϣⲟ, ⲃ̿ (2,000) ϣⲟ ⲥⲛⲁⲩ, ⲅ̿ (3,000) ϣⲟⲙⲛ̄ⲧ ⲛ̄–ϣⲟ or ϣⲙⲛ̄ⲧ–ϣⲟ, ⲇ̿ (4,000) ϥⲧⲟⲟⲩ ⲛ̄–ϣⲟ or ϥⲧⲉⲩ–ϣⲟ, etc.

Ten thousand: ⲧⲃⲁ is a noun of masculine gender.

Complex numbers go from highest to lowest: ⲙⲛ̄ⲧ–ⲥⲛⲟⲟⲩⲥ ⲛ̄–ϣⲉ ⲙⲛ̄–ⲥⲉ (ten-and-two hundreds and sixty) = ⲁ̿ⲥ̄ⲝ̄ 1,260. The use of ⲙⲛ̄– "and" in the spelled-out form is optional.

46. As with the other specifiers no article is required since the cardinal number replaces the article. [CG 66]

ϣⲟⲙⲛ̄ⲧ ⲛ̄–ⲣⲱⲙⲉ = three men
ϣⲟⲙⲧⲉ ⲛ̄–ⲥϩⲓⲙⲉ = three women

But cardinal numbers are also compatible with the *singular* definite article ⲡ–/ⲧ– (only the singular!), though their meaning (from "two" on up) is plural. (The plural definite article is *not* used with the numbers.)

ⲡ–ϣⲟⲙⲛ̅ⲧ = the three
ⲡⲉϥ–ϣⲟⲙⲛ̅ⲧ ⲙ̅–ⲙⲁⲑⲏⲧⲏⲥ = his three disciples
ⲧ–ϣⲟⲙⲧⲉ ⲛ̅–ⲥ̅ϩⲓⲙⲉ = the three women

In addition, cardinals can be used with the article ⲕⲉ– "another" (**61**)

ⲕⲉ–ϣⲟⲙⲛ̅ⲧ = another three, three more
ⲕⲉ–ϣⲟⲙⲛ̅ⲧ ⲛ̅–ⲣⲱⲙⲉ = another three men, three more men

The special plural forms of nouns **20** do not occur with the cardinal numbers.

---

47. *One* and *Two* do not usually occur in the specifier construction. [CG 70]

(*a*) *One* is usually expressed by the indefinite article ⲟⲩ–.

(*b*) *Two* (masc. ⲥⲛⲁⲩ, fem. ⲥⲛ̅ⲧⲉ) usually follows the noun it quantifies, as a separate item.

ⲣⲱⲙⲉ ⲥⲛⲁⲩ = two men   ⲥϩⲓⲙⲉ ⲥⲛ̅ⲧⲉ = two women
ⲡ–ⲣⲱⲙⲉ ⲥⲛⲁⲩ = the two men   ⲧⲉ–ⲥϩⲓⲙⲉ ⲥⲛ̅ⲧⲉ = the two women

(Compare the construction of ϣⲏⲙ **37**.)

ORDINAL NUMBERS

48. Ordinals ("second, third, fourth" etc.) are produced by prefixing ⲙⲉϩ– to any cardinal number from *Two* up. [CG 123] (*First* is expressed by the adjective ϣⲟⲣⲡ̅, ϣⲟⲣⲡⲉ.) ⲙⲉϩ– appears with both ⲡ– and ⲧ–. It is used just like an adjective (lesson 4). If the cardinal number has masculine and feminine forms, the appropriate gender is selected. ⲡ–ⲙⲉϩ–ⲥⲛⲁⲩ = the second man, the second one. ⲧ–ⲙⲉϩ–ⲥⲛ̅ⲧⲉ = the second woman, the second one. ⲡ–ⲙⲉϩ–ϣⲟⲙⲛ̅ⲧ ⲛ̅–ⲉⲩⲁⲅⲅⲉⲗⲓⲟⲛ = the third gospel. ⲧ–ⲙⲉϩ–ϣⲟⲙⲧⲉ ⲛ̅–ⲥϩⲓⲙⲉ = the third woman. ⲡⲁ–ⲙⲉϩ–ϩⲙⲉ ⲛ̅–ϩⲟⲟⲩ ⲙⲛ̅–ⲧⲁ–ⲙⲉϩ–ϩⲙⲉ ⲛ̅–ⲟⲩϣⲏ = my fortieth day and my fortieth night.

VOCABULARY 6

Learn the six specifiers in **43**.

Learn the cardinal numbers from one *to* ten *and round numbers from* twenty *to* ninety **45**.

Geography

ⲡ–ⲙⲁ	place	τόπος
ⲧ–ⲡⲉ, pl. ⲡⲏⲩⲉ	sky, heaven	οὐρανός
ⲡ–ⲉⲥⲏⲧ	bottom, ground	κάτω
ⲡ–ⲕⲁ2	earth, terra firma	γῆ
*ⲑⲁⲗⲁⲥⲥⲁ, 2ⲁⲗⲁⲥⲥⲁ	sea	
ⲧⲉ–2ⲓⲏ, pl. 2ⲓⲟⲟⲩⲉ	road, path, way	ὁδός
ⲧ–ⲙⲏⲧⲉ	midst, middle	μέσος
ⲡ–ⲧⲟⲟⲩ, pl. ⲧⲟⲩⲉⲓⲏ	mountain, valley wall of Nile	ὄρος
ⲡⲉ–ⲕⲣⲟ	shore, bank (of river etc.)	αἰγιαλός, γῆ
*ⲡ–ⲕⲟⲥⲙⲟⲥ	world, universe	

The human being

ⲡ–ⲣⲁⲛ	name	ὄνομα
*ⲡ–ⲥⲱⲙⲁ	body	
*ⲧ–ⲥⲁⲣⳅ	flesh	
ⲡⲉ–ⲥⲛⲟϥ	blood	αἷμα
ⲡ–ⲙⲉⲉⲩⲉ	thought	διάνοια etc.
ⲡ–2ⲏⲧ	heart, mind	καρδία
ⲧⲉ–ⲥⲙⲏ	voice	φωνή
ⲧ–ⲁⲡⲉ, pl. ⲁⲡⲏⲩⲉ	head	κεφαλή
ⲡ–ⲃⲁⲗ	eye	ὀφθαλμός
ⲡ–2ⲟ	face	πρόσωπον
ⲧ–ϭⲓⳈ	hand	χείρ
ⲧ–ⲟⲩⲛⲁⲙ	right, right hand	δεξιός, ἡ δεξιά
ⲧⲉ–2ⲃⲟⲩⲣ	left, left hand	εὐώνυμος
ⲧ–ⲟⲩⲉⲣⲏⲧⲉ	foot, leg	ποῦς

Classification (mostly occuring in adverbial expressions)[a]

ⲧ–2ⲉ (ⲑⲉ)	manner, way
ⲧ–ⲙⲓⲛⲉ	sort, quality, manner

---

[a]E.g. ⲛ̄–ⲧⲉⲓ̈–2ⲉ = thus; ⲛ̄ⲑⲉ ⲛ̄– = like, even as; ⲛ̄–ⲧⲉϥ–2ⲉ = like him.

EXERCISES 6

A. Translate. a. ⲁϣ ⲙ̄-ⲙⲁ. ⲡⲉⲓ̈-ⲙⲁ. b. ⲁϣ ⲛ̄-ⲕⲁϩ. ⲡⲉⲩ-ⲕⲁϩ. c. ⲛⲓⲙ ⲛ̄-ⲣⲱⲙⲉ ⲡⲉ. ⲡ-ⲣ̄ⲣⲟ ⲛ̄-ⲧ-ⲡⲉ ⲡⲉ. ⲡ-ⲣ̄ⲣⲟ ⲡⲉ ⲛ̄-ⲧ-ⲡⲉ. d. ⲛ̄ⲧⲉ-ⲟⲩ-ⲟⲩ (44). ⲁⲛⲅ̄-ⲧⲉ-ⲥⲙⲏ ⲙ̄-ⲡ-ⲭⲟⲉⲓⲥ. e. ⲟⲩⲏⲣ ⲛ̄-ϩⲓⲏ. ϩⲓⲏ ⲥⲛ̄ⲧⲉ. ⲟⲩⲏⲣ ⲛ̄-ⲧⲟⲟⲩ. ϣⲟⲙⲛ̄ⲧ ⲛ̄-ⲧⲟⲟⲩ. f. ⲟⲩⲏⲣ ⲛ̄-ⲥϩⲓⲙⲉ. ϣⲟⲙⲧⲉ ⲛ̄-ⲥϩⲓⲙⲉ. ϩⲁϩ ⲛ̄-ⲣⲁⲛ. ⲗⲁⲁⲩ ⲛ̄-ⲣⲁⲛ. g. ⲟⲩ ⲙ̄-ⲡⲉⲑⲟⲟⲩ. ⲧⲉⲓ̈-ⲙⲓⲛⲉ ⲙ̄-ⲡⲉⲑⲟⲟⲩ. h. ⲛⲁ-ⲙⲉⲉⲩⲉ ϩⲉⲛ-ⲗⲁⲁⲩ (44) ⲛⲉ. ⲛⲁ-ⲙⲉⲉⲩⲉ ⲛ̄-ϩⲉⲛ-ⲗⲁⲁⲩ ⲁⲛ ⲛⲉ. ⲛⲁ-ⲙⲉⲉⲩⲉ ⲛⲉ ϩⲉⲛ-ⲗⲁⲁⲩ. i. ⲙⲛ̄ⲧ-ⲥⲛⲟⲟⲩⲥ ⲛ̄-ⲁⲡⲟⲥⲧⲟⲗⲟⲥ. ⲡ-ⲙⲛ̄ⲧ-ⲥⲛⲟⲟⲩⲥ ⲛ̄-ⲁⲡⲟⲥⲧⲟⲗⲟⲥ. ⲡⲉϥ-ⲙⲛ̄ⲧ-ⲥⲛⲟⲟⲩⲥ ⲛ̄-ⲁⲡⲟⲥⲧⲟⲗⲟⲥ. j. ⲡ-ϣⲟⲙⲛ̄ⲧ ⲛ̄-ϩⲟ ⲙ̄-ⲡ-ⲛⲟⲩⲧⲉ. ⲧⲉⲓ̈-ⲙⲓⲛⲉ ⲛ̄-ⲥⲁⲣⲝ̄. k. ⲧ-ⲙⲏⲧⲉ ⲛ̄-ⲛⲉ-ϩⲓⲟⲟⲩⲉ. ⲡ-ⲉⲥⲏⲧ ⲛ̄-ⲧⲉ-ⲑⲁⲗⲁⲥⲥⲁ.

B. Translate into Coptic. *a.* Eleven apostles of the Lord. The Lord's eleven apostles. *b.* Three women. The three women. *c.* My two hands. Your two eyes. *d.* How many men? Two men. How many girls? Two girls. *e.* The midst of the seventy-two nations. *f.* Its head, its feet, and its eyes. *g.* The two mountains are his feet, the two worlds are his eyes, his right hand is the sea, and his left hand is its shore. *h.* This is the Lord's body and blood. *i.* His heart is a heart of stone. *j.* Who is the head of this faith?

C. Translate. a. ϣⲟⲙⲛ̄ⲧ. ⲡ-ϣⲟⲙⲛ̄ⲧ. b. ϥⲧⲟⲟⲩ. ⲕⲉ-ϥⲧⲟⲟⲩ. ⲡ-ⲕⲉ-ϥⲧⲟⲟⲩ. ⲡⲉⲓ̈-ϥⲧⲟⲟⲩ. ⲡⲉⲓ̈-ⲕⲉ-ϥⲧⲟⲟⲩ. c. ⲡⲉϥ-ⲕⲉ-ⲥⲁϣϥ̄ ⲛ̄-ⲏⲓ̈. ⲕⲉ-ⲥⲁϣϥ̄ ⲛ̄-ⲏⲓ̈. ⲡⲉϥ-ⲕⲉ-ⲥⲁϣϥⲉ ⲛ̄-ⲥϩⲓⲙⲉ. ⲕⲉ-ⲥⲁϣϥⲉ ⲛ̄-ⲥϩⲓⲙⲉ. d. ⲙⲛ̄ⲧ-ⲟⲩⲉ. e. ϩⲙⲉⲛⲉⲧ-ⲁϥⲧⲉ. f. ⲙⲛ̄ⲧⲏ. g. ϥⲧⲟⲟⲩ-ϣⲉ ⲙⲁⲁⲃ. h. ⲙⲛ̄ⲧ-ⲥⲛⲟⲟⲩⲥ ⲛ̄-ϣⲉ ⲙⲛ̄-ⲥⲉ. i. ⲕⲁϩ ⲥⲛⲁⲩ. j. ⲁⲡⲉ ⲥⲛ̄ⲧⲉ. k. ⲧⲉϥ-ⲛⲟϭ ⲛ̄-ⲁⲡⲉ ⲥⲛ̄ⲧⲉ. l. ⲡⲙⲉϩ-ⲙⲁⲁⲃ. m. ⲧⲙⲉϩ-ⲧⲁⲉⲓⲟⲩ. n. ⲡⲙⲉϩ-ⲙⲛ̄ⲧ-ⲡⲥⲛⲟⲟⲩⲥ ⲛ̄-ⲁⲡⲟⲥⲧⲟⲗⲟⲥ. o. ⲧⲙⲉϩ-ϯⲟⲩ ⲛ̄-ϩⲁ̄ⲗⲱ ⲛ̄-ⲛⲟϭ.

D. Translate rapidly, giving both masculine and feminine forms. One. Six. Eight. Two. Nine. Four. Ten. Eleven. Twenty-two. Thirty-three. Forty-four. Fifty-five. The sixty-sixth. The seventy-seventh. The eighty-eighth. The ninety-ninth. One hundred ten.

LESSON 7

PREPOSITION. PERSONAL SUFFIXES. POSSESSED NOUN. COMPOUND PREPOSITION. COMBINATIVE ADVERB.

49. This lesson mostly concerns the formation of prepositions. [CG 200–202] Coptic has many prepositions (well over a hundred), but fortunately you don't have to learn them all at once. The most common ones will be given in vocabulary lists spread out over several lessons, so you can memorize these a few at a time. For reference, a list of simple prepositions is given in a box later in this lesson. For compound prepositions, cf. **55**.

50. Almost all prepositions appear in a pair of *states*, e.g. ϵ-, ϵⲣⲟⲝ = to, into, for, against, in comparison to. [CG 30, 200] These are

   i. The *prenominal state* (ϵ-), which must be completed by an article phrase, pronoun, etc. ϵ-ⲧ-ⲡⲟⲗⲓⲥ = against the city, ϵ-ⲑⲓⲉⲣⲟⲩⲥⲁⲗⲏⲙ = into Jerusalem, ϵ-ⲡⲁⲓ̈ = against this one.

   ii. The *prepersonal state* (ϵⲣⲟⲝ), which must be completed by a personal suffix. ϵⲣⲟ-ϥ = against him/it, ϵⲣⲟ-ⲥ = against her/it.

In dictionaries, all prepersonal states are written with a slanted double hyphen (ⲝ), and prenominal states with a single hyphen (–). Prenominal and prepersonal states will return again and again as we study other kinds of morphs, so it's important to stop now and be sure you understand what they are.

In learning prepositions, be sure to memorize the pair of states along with the meaning ("ϵ-, ϵⲣⲟⲝ to, into, for, against, in comparison to"). Simple prepositions are filed under the prenominal, thus ϵ-, ϵⲣⲟⲝ is filed under ϵ-.

51. The inflection of the prepersonal states requires a bit of learning. Most prepositions are inflected like one of the following five paradigms. You should now memorize these paradigms thoroughly. This is your main task in the present lesson.

FIVE MODEL PREPOSITIONS

	Final Letter of Prepersonal State				
	ⲁ⸗	ⲟ⸗	ⲱ⸗	ⲧ⸗	ⲱⲱ⸗
	ⲛⲁ⸗ 'to', 'for'	ⲉⲣⲟ⸗ 'to'	ⲉⲝⲱ⸗ 'upon'	ⲛ̄ϩⲏⲧ⸗ 'in'	ϩⲓⲱⲱ⸗ 'on'
1st sing.	ⲛⲁⲓ̈	ⲉⲣⲟⲓ̈	ⲉⲝⲱⲓ̈	ⲛ̄ϩⲏⲧⲧ̄ or ⲛ̄ϩⲏⲧ	ϩⲓⲱⲱⲧ
2d sing. masc.	ⲛⲁⲕ	ⲉⲣⲟⲕ	ⲉⲝⲱⲕ	ⲛ̄ϩⲏⲧⲕ̄	ϩⲓⲱⲱⲕ
2d sing. fem.	ⲛⲉ (sic)	ⲉⲣⲟ	ⲉⲝⲱ	ⲛ̄ϩⲏⲧⲉ	ϩⲓⲱⲱⲧⲉ
3d sing. masc.	ⲛⲁϥ	ⲉⲣⲟϥ	ⲉⲝⲱϥ	ⲛ̄ϩⲏⲧϥ̄	ϩⲓⲱⲱϥ
3d sing. fem.	ⲛⲁⲥ	ⲉⲣⲟⲥ	ⲉⲝⲱⲥ	ⲛ̄ϩⲏⲧⲥ̄	ϩⲓⲱⲱⲥ
1st pl.	ⲛⲁⲛ	ⲉⲣⲟⲛ	ⲉⲝⲱⲛ	ⲛ̄ϩⲏⲧⲛ̄	ϩⲓⲱⲱⲛ
2d pl.	ⲛⲏⲧⲛ̄	ⲉⲣⲱⲧⲛ̄	ⲉⲝⲱⲧⲛ̄	ⲛ̄ϩⲏⲧ–ⲧⲏⲩⲧⲛ̄	ϩⲓⲱⲧ–ⲧⲏⲩⲧⲛ̄
3d pl.	ⲛⲁⲩ	ⲉⲣⲟⲟⲩ	ⲉⲝⲱⲟⲩ	ⲛ̄ϩⲏⲧⲟⲩ	ϩⲓⲱⲟⲩ

Pay special attention to the 1st sing., 2d sing. fem., and 2d pl., which differ according to the ending of the prepersonal state.

1st sing.	ⲛⲁ–ⲓ̈	ⲉⲣⲟ–ⲓ̈	ⲉⲝⲱ–ⲓ̈	ⲛ̄ϩⲏⲧ–ⲧ̄ or ⲛ̄ϩⲏⲧ	ϩⲓⲱⲱ–ⲧ
2d sing. fem.	ⲛⲉ–⁰	ⲉⲣⲟ–⁰	ⲉⲝⲱ–⁰	ⲛ̄ϩⲏⲧ–ⲉ	ϩⲓⲱⲱ–ⲧⲉ
2d pl.	ⲛⲏ–ⲧⲛ̄	ⲉⲣⲱ–ⲧⲛ̄	ⲉⲝⲱ–ⲧⲛ̄	ⲛ̄ϩⲏⲧ–ⲧⲏⲩⲧⲛ̄	ϩⲓⲱⲧ–ⲧⲏⲩⲧⲛ̄

52. *Personal suffixes.* As you can see, a regular set of personal suffixes is attached to the prepositions. If you memorize the five paradigms given above, you'll be in good shape for the moment. But here for reference is a table showing all the alter-

THE PERSONAL SUFFIXES

Person	Final Letter of the Prepersonal State				
	Single Vowel	Consonant + ⲃ ⲗ ⲙ ⲛ ⲣ	Final ⲧ	Other Consonant	Double Vowel
Sing.					
1st	ⲓ̈	ⲉⲧ	⁰ or ⲧ̄	ⲧ̄, ⲧ	ⲧ
2d masc.	ⲕ	ⲉⲕ	ⲕ̄ or ⲕ	ⲕ̄, ⲕ, ⲣ̄ .	ⲕ
2d fem.	⁰	ⲉ	ⲉ	ⲉ	ⲧⲉ
3d masc.	ϥ	ⲉϥ	ϥ̄ or ϥ	ϥ̄ or ϥ	ϥ
3d fem.	ⲥ	ⲉⲥ	ⲥ̄ or ⲥ	ⲥ̄ or ⲥ	ⲥ
Pl.					
1st	ⲛ	ⲛ̄ or ⲉⲛ	ⲛ̄	ⲛ̄	ⲛ
2d	ⲧⲛ̄[a] or ⲧⲏⲩⲧⲛ̄[b]	ⲧⲏⲩⲧⲛ̄[b]	ⲧⲏⲩⲧⲛ̄[c]	ⲧⲏⲩⲧⲛ̄[b]	ⲧⲏⲩⲧⲛ̄[d]
3d	(ⲟ)ⲩ	ⲟⲩ	ⲟⲩ	ⲟⲩ	(ⲟ)ⲩ

NOTES: [a]ⲧⲛ̄ is suffixed to the prepersonal form　[b]ⲧⲏⲩⲧⲛ̄ is suffixed to the prenominal form
[c]ⲧⲏⲩⲧⲛ̄ is suffixed to either the prepersonal or the prenominal form, according to each particular word
[d]ⲧⲏⲩⲧⲛ̄ is suffixed to the prenominal form. Note that ϩⲓⲱⲱ⸗ is slightly irregular

nations of the personal suffixes. [CG 85] You will find this table useful again as we study other kinds of morphs (such as verbs combined with a personal direct object).

There are some unpredictable differences and variations in the formation of the 2d plur. when the stem ends in т. See CG 85 (table 6, notes).

The Simple Prepositions

ⲁⲛⲧⲓ- (ἀντί) instead of
ⲁⲝⲛ̄-, ⲁⲝⲛ̄ⲧ⸗ without (also spelled ⲉⲝⲛ̄-, ⲉⲝⲱ⸗)
ⲉ-, ⲉⲣⲟ⸗ to, for, against, in comparison to
ⲉⲧⲃⲉ-, ⲉⲧⲃⲏⲏⲧ⸗ because of, concerning
ⲕⲁⲧⲁ-, ⲕⲁⲧⲁⲣⲟ⸗ (κατά) according to, like, by
ⲙ̄ⲙⲁϩ- in the presence of (a god) [rare]
ⲙⲛ̄-, ⲛⲙ̄ⲙⲁ⸗ with, and (also ⲛⲙ̄-)
ⲛ̄-, ⲙ̄ⲙⲟ⸗ of, out of, from, related to; also, mark of direct object, untranslatable
ⲛ̄-, ⲛⲁ⸗ to, for
ⲛ̄ⲥⲁ-, ⲛ̄ⲥⲱ⸗ behind, after
ⲛ̄ϭⲓ- mark of postponed subject, untranslatable
(ⲛ̄)ⲛⲁϩⲣⲛ̄-, (ⲛ̄)ⲛⲁϩⲣⲁ⸗ in the presence of, before, in relation to
ⲡⲁⲣⲁ-, ⲡⲁⲣⲁⲣⲟ⸗ (παρά) contrary to, in comparison with, beyond, more than
ⲡⲣⲟⲥ-, ⲡⲣⲟⲥⲣⲟ⸗ (πρός) in accordance with, for; than
ⲟⲩⲃⲉ-, ⲟⲩⲃⲏ⸗ opposite, towards, against
ⲟⲩⲧⲉ-, ⲟⲩⲧⲱ⸗ between, among
ⲭⲱⲣⲓⲥ- (χωρίς) without, apart from
ϣⲁ-, ϣⲁⲣⲟ⸗ to, toward
ϩⲁ-, ϩⲁⲣⲟ⸗ under, from, in respect of, on behalf of
ϩⲓ-, ϩⲓⲱⲱ⸗ on, at, in
ϩⲛ̄-, ⲛ̄ϩⲏⲧ⸗ in, at, on, from
ϩⲁⲣⲓϩⲁⲣⲟ⸗ apart, on my (your, etc.) own
ϩⲱⲥ- (ὡς) like, as if
ⲝⲓⲛ- since (time, place)

53. Two personal suffixes with a single preposition are connected by ⲛⲙ̄ⲙⲁ⸗ "and" (cf. 27 [b]), which is declined like ⲛⲁ⸗. [CG 201] E.g. ⲛⲁ-ⲛ ⲛⲙ̄ⲙⲏ-ⲧⲛ̄ = For us and you. ⲉⲣⲟ-ⲓ ⲛⲙ̄ⲙⲁ-ϥ = Against me and him. ⲛ̄ϩⲏⲧ-ⲉ ⲛⲙ̄ⲙⲁ-ⲓ = Within you and me. Similarly, an additional article phrase or pronoun can be connected by ⲙⲛ̄-. E.g. ⲛⲁ-ⲛ ⲙⲛ̄-ⲡⲉⲛ-ⲗⲁⲟⲥ = For us and our people. ⲉⲣⲟ-ⲓ ⲙⲛ̄-ⲡⲁ-ⲉⲓⲱⲧ = Against me and my father.

POSSESSED NOUNS

54. Possessed nouns are a small group (about twenty) whose possessor must be suffixed. Possessed nouns play a central role in the formation of compound prepositions, and that is why they are described in this lesson.

ⲣⲛ̄–ⲡⲣⲱⲙⲉ mouth of the man, the man's mouth
ⲣⲱ–ϥ mouth of him, his mouth

Like simple prepositions, they occur in two states: prenominal and prepersonal. [CG 138–40]

Here are some examples of possessed nouns. Please note that there are two possible formations of the prenominal state.

Prenominals		Prepersonal	
ⲡⲛ̄–	ⲣⲱ–ϥ ⲛ̄–	ⲣⲱ⸗	= mouth of
——	ⲣⲁⲧ–ϥ ⲛ̄–	ⲣⲁⲧ⸗	= foot/feet of
ⲧⲛ̄–, ⲧⲉ–	ⲧⲟⲟⲧ–ϥ ⲛ̄–	ⲧⲟⲟⲧ⸗	= hand(s) of
——	ϩⲏⲧ–ϥ ⲛ̄–	ϩⲏⲧ⸗	= fore part(s) of
——	ϩⲏⲧ–ϥ ⲛ̄–	ϩⲏⲧ⸗	= belly, womb (of)
ϩⲣⲛ̄–, ϩⲛ̄–	ϩⲣⲁ–ϥ ⲛ̄–	ϩⲣⲁ⸗	= face of
——	ϩⲧⲏ–ϥ ⲛ̄–	ϩⲧⲏ⸗	= tip of
ϫⲛ̄–	ϫⲱ–ϥ ⲛ̄–	ϫⲱ⸗	= head of

Possessed nouns are peculiar. They never have an article, and they cannot be modified by an attributive or specifier construction. They are mostly used *as a component* to form compounds, especially compound prepositions **55**.

Possessed nouns descend from earlier Egyptian names for parts of the body, but in Coptic their meanings have become abstract. Coptic mostly uses them to express relationship, in an abstract way. To literally speak of parts of the body, Coptic uses a different set of ordinary nouns.

	Literal (parts of the body)	Abstract Relationship (in compound preposition)
'foot/leg'	ⲧ–ⲟⲩⲉⲣⲏⲧⲉ	ⲣⲁⲧ⸗
'hand'	ⲧ–ϭⲓϫ	ⲧⲟⲟⲧ⸗
'mouth'	ⲧ–ⲧⲁⲡⲣⲟ	ⲣⲱ⸗

Thus, for example, the ordinary nouns ϭⲓϫ and ⲧⲁⲡⲣⲟ are used literally: 'your hand' = ⲧⲉⲕ–ϭⲓϫ, 'your mouth' = ⲧⲉⲕ–ⲧⲁⲡⲣⲟ; but components in compound prepositions are expressed by ⲧⲟⲟⲧ⸗ and ⲣⲱ⸗: 'give the book to you' = ⲉⲧⲟⲟⲧ–ⲕ (to-hand-of-you), while 'serve the food to you' = ϩⲁⲣⲱ–ⲕ (under-mouth-of-you).

For a list of all the possessed nouns, see box at the end of this lesson.

55. *Compound prepositions.* Coptic has more than a hundred compound prepositions, which are based on nouns. They are composed of a simple preposition + a noun (often a possessed noun 54) + either a hyphen (– and ꞊) or ⲛ̄– 'of'. Compound prepositions are formed in three ways:

i. *Simple preposition + possessed noun,* ⲉ–ⲡⲛ̄–, ⲉ–ⲡⲱ꞊ = to, upon ("towards mouth of"). Thus ϩⲁ–ⲉⲓⲁⲧ꞊ before ("under eyes of"); ⲉ–ⲧⲛ̄–, ⲉ–ⲧⲟⲟⲧ꞊ to ("towards hand of"); ⲉ–ⲭⲛ̄–, ⲉ–ⲭⲱ꞊ upon ("towards head of").

ii. *Simple preposition + def. article + noun + 'Of' construction,* ϩⲓ–ⲧ–ⲟⲩⲛⲁⲙ ⲛ̄–, ϩⲓ–ⲧⲉϥ–ⲟⲩⲛⲁⲙ = at the right of, at his right ("on the right hand of"). Thus ⲙ̄–ⲡⲃⲟⲗ ⲛ̄– outside of ("in the exterior of"); ⲉ–ⲡⲙⲁ ⲛ̄– in place of ("towards the place of"); ⲉ–ⲡⲥⲁ ⲛ̄– to ("towards the side of").

iii. *Simple preposition + ᵉnoun (or ⲡⲓ–noun) + ⲛ̄–/ⲙ̄ⲙⲟ꞊,* e.g. ⲉ–ᵉⲡⲁϩⲟⲩ ⲛ̄–/ⲙ̄ⲙⲟ꞊ = behind ("towards rear end of"). Thus ϩⲓ–ᵉⲑⲏ ⲛ̄–/ⲙ̄ⲙⲟ꞊ = before ("on prow of"); ϩⲓ–ᵉⲟⲩⲛⲁⲙ ⲛ̄–/ⲙ̄ⲙⲟ꞊ at the right of ("on right hand of"); ⲙ̄–ⲡⲓⲥⲁ ⲛ̄–/ⲙ̄ⲙⲟ꞊ beyond ("in the farther side of").

[A full list of compound prepositions is given in CG 208–213.]

COMBINATIVE ADVERBS

56. Combinative adverbs combine with prepositions, adverbs, and verbs to produce new meanings. [CG 206–7] For example, the preposition ϩⲛ̄– (= in) also combines with the adverb ⲉⲃⲟⲗ and changes its meaning

ϩⲛ̄–, ⲛ̄ϩⲏⲧ꞊ = in
ⲉⲃⲟⲗ ϩⲛ̄–, ⲉⲃⲟⲗ ⲛ̄ϩⲏⲧ꞊ = from

There are eleven combinative adverbs.

i. *Inside:* ⲉϩⲟⲩⲛ, ⲛ̄ϩⲟⲩⲛ, ϣⲁϩⲟⲩⲛ

ii. *Outside:* ⲉⲃⲟⲗ

iii. *Top-or-bottom:* ⲉϩⲣⲁⲓ̈, ⲛ̄ϩⲣⲁⲓ̈, ϣⲁϩⲣⲁⲓ̈

iv. *Bottom:* ⲉⲡⲉⲥⲏⲧ

v. *Front:* ⲉⲑⲏ

vi. *Rear:* ⲉⲡⲁϩⲟⲩ

vii. *Emotional orientation:* ⲛ̄ϩⲏⲧ

Since these adverbs have meaning only in combination with something else, it is not possible to define them exactly. The first four combine with prepositions and to some extent verbs, the last three with verbs only.

ϩⲛ̄- = in, ⲉⲃⲟⲗ ϩⲛ̄- = from
ⲕⲱ = put, ⲕⲱ ⲉⲃⲟⲗ = forgive
ϩⲉ ⲉ- = find, ϩⲉ ⲉⲡⲉⲥⲏⲧ ⲉ- = fall down into
ⲙ̄ⲕⲁϩ = feel physical pain, ⲙ̄ⲕⲁϩ ⲛ̄ϩⲏⲧ = feel distressed

Reference list of all the possessed nouns (**54**), *with references to Crum's* Coptic Dictionary

Prenominals		Prepersonal	
———	ⲁⲛⲁ-ϥ ⲛ̄-	ⲁⲛⲁ⸗	will of (Crum p. 11*a*)
———	ⲁⲡϩⲭ(ⲛ)-ϥ̄ ⲛ̄-	ⲁⲡϩⲭ(ⲛ)⸗	end of (16*b*)
ⲃⲁ̄-, ⲃⲁ̄ⲛ-	ⲃⲁ̄ⲗⲁ-ϥ ⲛ̄-	ⲃⲁ̄ⲗⲁ⸗	outside of (33*b*)
ⲉⲓⲉⲣ-, ⲉⲓⲁⲛ̄-	ⲉⲓⲁⲧ-ϥ̄ ⲛ̄-	ⲉⲓⲁⲧ⸗	eye(s) of (73*b*)
———	ⲕⲟⲩⲛ(ⲧ)-ϥ̄ ⲛ̄-	ⲕⲟⲩⲛ(ⲧ)⸗, ⲕⲟⲩⲟⲩⲛ⸗	bosom of (111*b*)
———	ⲗⲓⲕⲧ-ϥ̄ ⲛ̄-	ⲗⲓⲕⲧ⸗	covering of (140*a*)
ⲡⲛ̄-	ⲣⲱ-ϥ ⲛ̄-	ⲣⲱ⸗	mouth of (288*a*)
ⲣⲉⲛ-	ⲣⲛ̄ⲧ-ϥ̄ ⲛ̄-	ⲣⲛ̄ⲧ⸗	name of (297*b*)
———	ⲣⲁⲧ-ϥ̄ ⲛ̄-	ⲣⲁⲧ⸗	foot/feet of (302*b*)
———	ⲥⲟⲩⲛ̄ⲧ-ϥ̄ ⲛ̄-	ⲥⲟⲩⲛ̄ⲧ⸗	value of (369*b*)
ⲧⲛ̄-, ⲧⲉ-	ⲧⲟⲟⲧ-ϥ̄ ⲛ̄-	ⲧⲟⲟⲧ⸗	hand(s) of (425*a*)
ⲧⲟⲩⲛ̄-	ⲧⲟⲩⲱ-ϥ ⲛ̄-	ⲧⲟⲩⲱ⸗	bosom of (444*b*)
———	ϣⲁⲛⲧ-ϥ̄ ⲛ̄-	ϣⲁⲛⲧ⸗	nose of (543*b*)
———	ϩⲏⲧ-ϥ̄ ⲛ̄-	ϩⲏⲧ⸗	fore part(s) of (640*b*)
———	ϩⲏⲧ-ϥ̄ ⲛ̄-	ϩⲏⲧ⸗	belly, womb (of) (642*b*)
ϩⲣⲛ̄-, ϩⲛ̄-	ϩⲣⲁ-ϥ ⲛ̄-	ϩⲣⲁ⸗	face of (646*b*)
ϩⲣⲟⲩⲛ̄-	ϩⲣⲁ-ϥ ⲛ̄-	ϩⲣⲁ⸗	voice of (704*b*)
(ϩ)ⲧⲉ-, (ϩ)ⲧⲛ̄-	ϩⲧⲏ-ϥ ⲛ̄-	ϩⲧⲏ⸗	heart of (714*a*)
———	ϩⲧⲏ-ϥ ⲛ̄-	ϩⲧⲏ⸗	tip of (718*a*)
ⲭⲛ̄-	ⲭⲱ-ϥ ⲛ̄-	ⲭⲱ⸗	head of (756*a*)

VOCABULARY 7

More nouns

ⲡ-ϩⲱⲃ, pl. ϩⲃⲏⲩⲉ	thing, product; deed, matter	ἔργον
ⲡⲉ-ⲛⲕⲁ	material thing, possession	κτῆμα, ὑπάρχον
ⲡ-ϣⲁϫⲉ	utterance, word	λαλία, λόγος

Prepositions

ϩⲛ̄- (also ⲛ̄-), ⲛ̄ϩⲏⲧ⸗	in, at, on, from, by means of	ἐν κτλ.
ⲛ̄-, ⲙ̄ⲙⲟ⸗	of, out of, from, related to	(marker of direct object)
ⲛ̄-, ⲛⲁ⸗	to, for	Greek dative
ⲉ-, ⲉⲣⲟ⸗	to, for, against, in comparison to	εἰς κτλ.
ⲙⲛ̄-, ⲛⲙ̄ⲙⲁ⸗	with; and (27)	μετά, σύν, κτλ.
ⲁⲭⲛ̄-, ⲁⲭⲛ̄ⲧ⸗	without	χωρίς, α- privative
ⲉⲭⲛ̄-, ⲉⲭⲱ⸗	upon, over; for, on account of; against; to; in addition to, after	ἐπί
ϩⲓ-, ϩⲓⲱⲱ⸗	on, at, in; and (27); concerning; from; at the time of	ἐπί
ⲉⲧⲃⲉ-, ⲉⲧⲃⲏⲏⲧ⸗	because of, concerning	διά
*ⲕⲁⲧⲁ-, ⲕⲁⲧⲁⲣⲟ⸗	according to, like, by	κατά accus.
*ϩⲱⲥ-	like, as if	ὡς
ⲉⲃⲟⲗ ϩⲛ̄-, ⲉⲃⲟⲗ ⲛ̄ϩⲏⲧ⸗	from, out of, as a result of	ἐκ κτλ.
ⲉϩⲟⲩⲛ ⲉ-, ⲉϩⲟⲩⲛ ⲉⲣⲟ⸗	into, into the interior of	εἰς κτλ.
ⲉϩⲟⲩⲛ ϩⲛ̄- or ⲉϩⲟⲩⲛ ⲉϩⲣⲛ̄- 54, ⲉϩⲟⲩⲛ ⲉϩⲣⲁ⸗	in toward, before	εἰς κτλ.
ϩⲣⲁⲓ ϩⲛ̄-, ϩⲣⲁⲓ ⲛ̄ϩⲏⲧ⸗	in, up in, down in	ἐν κτλ.
ⲙ̄ⲡⲉ-ⲙⲧⲟ ⲉⲃⲟⲗ ⲛ̄-, ⲙ̄ⲡⲉϥ-ⲙⲧⲟ ⲉⲃⲟⲗ (any possessive article can occur in place of ⲡⲉϥ-)	in the presence of, before	ἐνώπιον

Adverbs

ⲙ̄ⲙⲁⲩ	there	ἐκεῖ
ⲙ̄ⲡⲉⲓ̈ⲙⲁ i.e. ⲙ̄–ⲡⲉⲓ̈–ⲙⲁ	here	ὧδε
ⲉⲃⲟⲗ ϩⲙ̄–ⲡⲉⲓ̈–ⲙⲁ	hence, from here	ἐντεῦθεν
ⲉ–ⲡⲉⲓ̈–ⲙⲁ	hither, to here	ὧδε
ϩⲙ̄–ⲡ–ⲙⲁ ⲉⲧⲙ̄ⲙⲁⲩ	there	ἐκεῖ
ⲉⲃⲟⲗ ϩⲙ̄–ⲡ–ⲙⲁ ⲉⲧⲙ̄–ⲙⲁⲩ	thence, from there	ἐκεῖθεν
ⲉ–ⲡ–ⲙⲁ ⲉⲧⲙ̄ⲙⲁⲩ	thither, to there	ἐκεῖ
ⲉⲡⲙⲁ ⲛ̄– i.e. ⲉ–ⲡ–ⲙⲁ ⲛ̄–	in place of, instead of	ἀντί
ϩⲙ̄–ⲙⲁ ⲛⲓⲙ	everywhere	πανταχοῦ
ⲧⲱⲛ	where? whence, from where?	ποῦ, πόθεν
ⲉⲃⲟⲗ ⲧⲱⲛ	whence, from where?	πόθεν

Conjunctions

*ⲁⲗⲗⲁ	but, but rather, yet, nonetheless	ἀλλά
*ⲏ	or, and, and/or (inclusive)	ἤ
ⲭⲛ̄– (or ⲭⲉⲛ– or ⲭⲉ–)	or, or else (restrictive)	ἤ

Expressions based on ϩⲟⲩⲟ

ⲡⲉ–ϩⲟⲩⲟ	abundance, greater part	περίσσον
ⲉ–ⲡⲉ–ϩⲟⲩⲟ	greatly, much	πολλά, πολύ
ⲉϩⲟⲩⲉ–, ⲉϩⲟⲩⲉⲣⲟ⸗ (i.e. ⲉ–ϩⲟⲩⲟ ⲉ–/ ⲉⲣⲟ⸗)	rather than, more than	μᾶλλον ἤ
ⲛ̄ϩⲟⲩⲟ	all the more, more than ever	μᾶλλον, μάλιστα

EXERCISES 7

A. *Practice reciting rapidly in Coptic the full paradigm (with all eight personal suffixes) of the following prepositions, giving the English meanings as you go.* ⲛⲁ= for, ⲛⲙ̄ⲙⲁ= with, ⲉⲡⲟⲩⲛ ⲉϩⲣⲁ= in towards, ⲉⲣⲟ= against, ⲙ̄ⲙⲟ= of, ⲉϩⲟⲩⲛ ⲉⲣⲟ= into, ⲉⲭⲱ= upon, ⲛ̄ϩⲏⲧ= in, ⲁⲭⲛ̄ⲧ= without, ⲉⲧⲃⲏⲏⲧ= because of, ϩⲣⲁⲓ̈ ⲛ̄ϩⲏⲧ= above/below in, ⲉⲃⲟⲗ ⲛ̄ϩⲏⲧ= from, ϩⲓⲱⲱ= on.

Practice reciting each paradigm backwards (3d pl., 2d pl., 1st pl., 3d sing. fem., etc.).

B. *Practice translating rapidly until you are fluent.* ⲛⲁ-ⲓ̈, ⲛⲙ̄ⲙⲉ-⁰, ϩⲓⲱⲱ-ϥ, ⲉϩⲟⲩⲛ ⲉϩⲣⲁ-ⲥ, ⲉⲣⲱ-ⲧⲛ̄, ⲙ̄ⲙⲟ-ⲓ̈, ⲉϩⲟⲩⲛ ⲉⲣⲟ-ⲕ, ⲉⲭⲱ-ϥ, ⲛ̄ϩⲏⲧ-ⲛ̄, ⲁⲭⲛ̄ⲧ-ⲟⲩ, ⲉⲧⲃⲏⲏⲧ-⁰, ϩⲣⲁⲓ̈ ⲛ̄ϩⲏⲧ-ⲉ, ⲉⲃⲟⲗ ⲛ̄ϩⲏⲧ-ⲥ̄, ⲛⲏ-ⲧⲛ̄, ⲛⲙ̄ⲙⲁ-ⲓ̈, ϩⲓⲱⲱ-ⲕ, ⲉϩⲟⲩⲛ ⲉϩⲣⲉ-⁰, ⲉⲣⲟ-ⲥ, ⲙ̄ⲙⲱ-ⲧⲛ̄, ⲉϩⲟⲩⲛ ⲉⲣⲟ-ⲟⲩ, ⲉⲭⲱ-ⲕ, ⲛ̄ϩⲏⲧ-ϥ̄, ⲁⲭⲛ̄ⲧ-ⲛ̄, ⲉⲧⲃⲏⲏⲧ-ⲟⲩ, ϩⲣⲁⲓ̈ ⲛ̄ϩⲏⲧ-⁰, ⲉⲃⲟⲗ ⲛ̄ϩⲏⲧ-ⲕ̄, ⲛⲁ-ϥ, ⲛⲙ̄ⲙⲏ-ⲧⲛ̄, ϩⲓⲱ-ⲟⲩ, ⲉϩⲟⲩⲛ ⲉϩⲣⲁ-ⲩ, ⲉⲣⲟ-ⲕ, ⲙ̄ⲙⲟ-ϥ, ⲉϩⲟⲩⲛ ⲉⲣⲱ-ⲧⲛ̄, ⲉⲭⲱ-ⲟⲩ, ⲛ̄ϩⲏⲧ-ⲕ̄, ⲁⲭⲛ̄ⲧ-ϥ̄, ⲉⲧⲃⲉ-ⲑⲏⲩⲧⲛ̄, ϩⲣⲁⲓ̈ ⲛ̄ϩⲏⲧ-ⲟⲩ.

C. *Practice translating rapidly into Coptic until you are fluent. a.* For you (sing. masc.). With him. On her. In towards us. Against them. Of you (sing. masc.). *b.* Into you (sing. fem.). Upon us. In you (pl.). Without me. Because of you (sing. masc.). *c.* Above/Below in him. From us. For them. With you (sing. masc.). On you (sing. fem.) *d.* In towards him. Against us. Of them. Into me. Upon you (sing. fem.). *e.* In us. Without you (pl.). Because of me. Above/Below in you (sing. masc.). From you (sing. fem.). *f.* For her. With them. On me. In towards me. Against you (sing. fem.). Of us. *g.* Into them. Upon me. In you (sing. fem.). Without us. Because of them. Above/Below in you (pl.).

D. *Translate. a.* ⲙ̄-ⲡⲁ-ⲙ̄ⲧⲟ ⲉⲃⲟⲗ. ⲙ̄-ⲡⲉⲩ-ⲙ̄ⲧⲟ ⲉⲃⲟⲗ. *b.* ϩⲱⲥ-⁰ϣⲏⲣⲉ. ⲕⲁⲧⲁ-ⲧⲉϥ-ϩⲉ. *c.* ϩⲛ̄-ⲧⲉ-ⲩϣⲏ. ⲉ-ⲧ-ⲡⲟⲗⲓⲥ. ⲙⲛ̄-ⲛⲉϥ-ϣⲃⲉⲉⲣ. *d.* ⲁⲭⲛ̄-⁰ⲙⲟⲟⲩ ϩⲓ-⁰ⲟⲉⲓⲕ. ⲉⲭⲙ̄-ⲡ-ⲕⲁϩ. ϩⲓ-ⲧⲉ-ϩⲓⲏ. *e.* ⲉⲧⲃⲉ-ⲧⲉϥ-ⲁⲅⲁⲡⲏ. *f.* ⲉⲃⲟⲗ ϩⲙ̄-ⲡⲉⲓ̈-ⲙⲁ. ⲉ-ⲡⲉⲓ̈-ⲙⲁ. ϩⲙ̄-ⲙⲁ ⲛⲓⲙ. *g.* ⲉⲡⲙⲁ ⲙ̄-ⲡⲉϥ-ⲗⲁⲟⲥ. ⲉϩⲟⲩⲉ-ⲡⲉϥ-ⲗⲁⲟⲥ. ⲉⲡⲉϩⲟⲩⲟ. *h.* ⁰ϩⲟⲟⲩⲧ ⲏ ⁰ⲥϩⲓⲙⲉ. ⲛ̄-ϩⲟⲟⲩⲧ ⲭⲛ̄-ⲛⲉ-ϩⲓⲟⲙⲉ.

LESSON 8

POSSESSIVE PRONOUN.
SURVEY OF ARTICLES AND PRONOUNS.

---

57. You have already learned how to form nominal sentence predicates of

i. Identity

Who are they? ΝΙΜ ΝΕ
They are *my brothers* ΝΑ–ϹΝΗΥ ΝΕ

ii. Description **44**

Of what sort is he? ΟΥ–ΑϢ Ν̄–ϨΕ ΠΕ
He is *true* ΟΥ–ΜΕ ΠΕ
He is *like this, of this sort* ΟΥ–ΤΕΪ–ΜΙΝΕ ΠΕ

Next we shall study how to form nominal sentence predicates of

iii. Ownership (being owned)[12] [CG 296]

Whose is it? ΠΑ–ΝΙΜ ΠΕ
It is *John's* ΠΑ–ΙⲰϨΑΝΝΗϹ ΠΕ
It is *mine* ΠⲰ–Ϊ ΠΕ

For this, Coptic uses the *possessive pronoun* [CG 54]

ΠΑ–, ΤΑ–, ΝΑ–[13]
ΠⲰ⸗, ΤⲰ⸗, ΝΟΥ⸗   (the) one(s) of . . . , belonging to . . .

The ΠΑ– set must be completed by an article phrase or equivalent; the ΠⲰ⸗ set must be completed by a personal suffix **52**.

ΠΑ–Π–ⲭΟΕΙϹ ΠΕ Π–ΚΑϨ = the earth is *the Lord's*
ΤⲰ–Κ ΤΕ Τ–ϬΟΜ ΜΝ̄–Π–ΕΟΟΥ = *Yours* (sing. masc.) is the power and the glory
Ν̄ΤΕΤΝ̄–ΠⲰ–ΤΝ̄ ΑΝ = you (pl.) are not *your own* (you-are ones-who-belong-to-you not)

---

[12] "Ownership" is here meant in the vaguest possible way, like the *'Of'* construction, described in **29**.
[13] It is important to distinguish ΠΑ– "the one of . . . " from the 1st person possessive article **30** ΠΑ– "my . . . "

ⲛⲟⲩ-ⲕ ⲛⲟⲩ-ï ⲛⲉ = *Thine* are *Mine* (ones-who-belong-to-you are ones-who-belong-to-me)

ⲁⲛ̄ⲅ-ⲡⲁ-ⲡⲁⲩⲗⲟⲥ I *belong to Paul*

Full paradigm of ⲡⲱ⸗, ⲧⲱ⸗, ⲛⲟⲩ⸗ with personal suffixes (ⲡⲱ⸗ and ⲧⲱ⸗ follow the pattern of ⲉⲝⲱ⸗ "upon").

	masc.	fem.	pl.
mine	ⲡⲱ-ï	ⲧⲱ-ï	ⲛⲟⲩ-ï
yours (sing. masc.)	ⲡⲱ-ⲕ	ⲧⲱ-ⲕ	ⲛⲟⲩ-ⲕ
yours (sing. fem.)	ⲡⲱ-⁰	ⲧⲱ-⁰	ⲛⲟⲩ-⁰
his	ⲡⲱ-ϥ	ⲧⲱ-ϥ	ⲛⲟⲩ-ϥ
hers	ⲡⲱ-ⲥ	ⲧⲱ-ⲥ	ⲛⲟⲩ-ⲥ
ours	ⲡⲱ-ⲛ	ⲧⲱ-ⲛ	ⲛⲟⲩ-ⲛ
yours (pl.)	ⲡⲱ-ⲧⲛ̄	ⲧⲱ-ⲧⲛ̄	ⲛⲟⲩ-ⲧⲛ̄
theirs	ⲡⲱ-ⲟⲩ	ⲧⲱ-ⲟⲩ	ⲛⲟⲩ-ⲟⲩ

Compare the possessive article:

my	ⲡⲁ-ⲉⲓⲱⲧ	ⲧⲁ-ⲙⲁⲁⲩ	ⲛⲁ-ⲥⲛⲏⲩ
your (sing. masc.)	ⲡⲉⲕ-ⲉⲓⲱⲧ	ⲧⲉⲕ-ⲙⲁⲁⲩ	ⲛⲉⲕ-ⲥⲛⲏⲩ
your (sing. fem.)	ⲡⲟⲩ-ⲉⲓⲱⲧ	ⲧⲟⲩ-ⲙⲁⲁⲩ	ⲛⲟⲩ-ⲥⲛⲏⲩ
his	ⲡⲉϥ-ⲉⲓⲱⲧ	ⲧⲉϥ-ⲙⲁⲁⲩ	ⲛⲉϥ-ⲥⲛⲏⲩ
her	ⲡⲉⲥ-ⲉⲓⲱⲧ	ⲧⲉⲥ-ⲙⲁⲁⲩ	ⲛⲉⲥ-ⲥⲛⲏⲩ
our	ⲡⲉⲛ-ⲉⲓⲱⲧ	ⲧⲉⲛ-ⲙⲁⲁⲩ	ⲛⲉⲛ-ⲥⲛⲏⲩ
your	ⲡⲉⲧⲛ̄-ⲉⲓⲱⲧ	ⲧⲉⲧⲛ̄-ⲙⲁⲁⲩ	ⲛⲉⲧⲛ̄-ⲥⲛⲏⲩ
their	ⲡⲉⲩ-ⲉⲓⲱⲧ	ⲧⲉⲩ-ⲙⲁⲁⲩ	ⲛⲉⲩ-ⲥⲛⲏⲩ

The possessive pronoun follows the pattern ⲡ–ⲧ–ⲛ of the simple definite article. The initial letters ⲡ, ⲧ, ⲛ express the number/gender of the person or thing spoken about. The personal suffixes **52** (ⲓ, ⲕ, ⁰, ϥ, ⲥ, ⲛ, ⲧⲛ̄, ⲟⲩ) express the person, number, and gender of the possessor.

ⲡⲱ-ï   = (the) [sing. masc.] one belonging to + me = mine
ⲧⲱ-ⲕ   = (the) [sing. fem.] one belonging to + you [sing. masc.] = yours
ⲡⲱ-⁰   = (the) [sing. masc.] one belonging to + you [sing. fem.] = yours
ⲛⲟⲩ-⁰ = (the) [pl.] ones belonging to you = yours
ⲡⲱ-ⲟⲩ = theirs, ⲛⲟⲩ-ⲟⲩ = theirs, etc.

58. ⲡⲁ-, ⲡⲱ⸗ is also used pronominally, always looking back to a preceding (possessive) article phrase:

ⲡⲁ-ⲡⲛⲉⲩⲙⲁ ⲙⲛ̄-ⲡⲱ-ⲧⲛ̄ = my spirit and *yours*
ⲡⲉϥ-ⲉⲟⲟⲩ ⲙⲛ̄-ⲡⲁ-ⲡⲉϥ-ⲉⲓⲱⲧ = His glory and *that of His Father*

59. Finally, two more kinds of nominal sentence predicate must be learned, namely, predicates of

iv. Source, origin, and agential cause [CG 302]

> *Whence* is it? *From where* does it come? oy-eⲃoⲗ ⲧⲱⲛ ⲡⲉ
> It is from God oy-eⲃoⲗ ϩ︦ⲙ-ⲡ-ⲛoyⲧe ⲡⲉ

For this, Coptic uses the indefinite article oy-/ϩeⲛ- expanded by the prepositions eⲃoⲗ ϩⲛ︦-, eⲃoⲗ ⲛ︦-, or (for agential cause) eⲃoⲗ ϩⲓⲧⲛ︦- = from.

> ⲛ︦ⲧeⲧⲛ︦-ϩeⲛ-eⲃoⲗ ϩ︦ⲙ-ⲡeï-ⲕocⲙoc = you are of (from) this world
> ⲡⲁï oy-eⲃoⲗ ⲙ︦ⲙo-oy ⲡe = this one is one of them
> ⲁⲛⲅ︦-oy-eⲃoⲗ ⲁⲛ ϩ︦ⲙ-ⲡeï-ⲕocⲙoc = I am not of (from) this world
> ⲧeï-ⲛoϭ ⲛ︦-ⲇⲱⲣeⲁ oy-eⲃoⲗ ϩⲓⲧⲙ︦-ⲡ-ⲛoyⲧe ⲧe = this great gift is from God

v. Relationship (time; location measured 'from' or 'towards'; and manner) [CG 298]

> *For how long is it? How long will it endure?* ϣⲁ-oyⲏⲣ ⲡe
> It is *eternal* (unto-eternity) ϣⲁ-eⲛeϩ ⲡe or oy-ϣⲁ-eⲛeϩ ⲡe

For this Coptic uses the appropriate preposition either with or without the indefinite article oy-/ϩeⲛ-.

> ϩeⲛ-ϣⲁ-eⲛeϩ ⲛe = they are *eternal* (some-instances-of-unto-eternity
> oy-ⲡⲣoc-⁰oyoeⲓϣ ⲡe = it is *temporary* (an-instance-of-in-relation-to-time)
> ⲡeϥ-ⲣooyϣ ⲡe eⲧⲃe-ⲛ︦-ϩⲏⲕe = his care is *for the poor*
> e-ⲡ-ⲝⲓⲛⲝⲏ ⲧe = it is *in vain* (unto-the-uselessness)

SURVEY OF ARTICLES AND PRONOUNS

60. Below are listed all the articles based on ⲡ-ⲧ-ⲛ, together with their corresponding pronouns. [CG 42–60]

ⲡ-, ⲧ-, ⲛ︦- (lesson 1) = the
No corresponding pronoun

ⲡⲁ- (ⲡeⲕ-, etc.) **30** = my (your, etc.)
ⲡⲱ⸗, ⲧⲱ⸗, ⲛoy⸗ **57** (iii)–**58** = mine (yours, etc.)

ⲡⲕe-, ⲧⲕe- ⲛ︦ⲕe- = the other (the second, the contrasting)
ⲡⲕe, ⲧⲕeⲧ, ⲛ︦ⲕooye = the other

ⲡⲓ-, ϯ-, ⲛⲓ- = the, that, this (expressing either emotional involvement[14] or remoteness in place or time)
ⲡⲏ, ⲧⲏ, ⲛⲏ = he, it, that one, this one

---

[14] E.g. with vices, virtues, angels, demons, etc.

ⲡⲉⲓ̈-, ⲧⲉⲓ̈-, ⲛⲉⲓ̈- = this, the following, the previously mentioned **18**

ⲡⲁⲓ̈, ⲧⲁⲓ̈, ⲛⲁⲓ̈ = this, he, it, the following, the preceding **18**

ⲡ-/ⲧ-/ⲛ̄- . . . ⲉⲧⲙ̄ⲙⲁⲩ that (over there), the previously mentioned; **130** (ⲡ-ⲏⲓ̈
ⲉⲧⲙ̄ⲙⲁⲩ = that house, ⲧⲉ-ϩⲓⲏ ⲉⲧⲙ̄ⲙⲁⲩ = that road)

ⲡⲉⲧⲙ̄ⲙⲁⲩ, ⲧⲉⲧⲙ̄ⲙⲁⲩ, ⲛⲉⲧⲙ̄ⲙⲁⲩ = that, he, she, they, it **130**

61. Articles and corresponding pronouns like ⲟⲩ-, ϩⲉⲛ-:

ⲟⲩ-, ϩⲉⲛ- (lesson 1) = a, some, —[15] **18**

ⲟⲩⲁ, ⲟⲩⲉⲓ, ϩⲟⲉⲓⲛⲉ = one, a certain one, some, certain ones **18**

ⲕⲉ-[16], ϩⲉⲛⲕⲉ- = another (a second, a contrasting)

ϭⲉ, ⲕⲉⲧ (ⲕⲉⲧⲉ sing. fem.), ϩⲉⲛⲕⲟⲟⲩⲉ = another (a second, a contrasting)

62. Other articles and corresponding pronouns:

∅ = the zero article, cf. **25, 26**

ⲟⲩⲟⲛ = Untranslatable pronoun, used as a filler in certain constructions

. . . ⲛⲓⲙ = any, every, all

ⲟⲩⲟⲛ ⲛⲓⲙ = any, each, all

Note that ⲛⲓⲙ follows its noun, as a separate item (like ⲥⲛⲁⲩ 'two' **47**)[17].

---

[15] ϩⲉⲛ- [some]: In English we often express the indef. plur. by omitting the article before a plural noun: a house (sing.), *houses* (plur.).

[16] Note carefully that the combination ⲟⲩ-ⲕⲉ- does not occur.

[17] Caution: this word is not the same as interrogative ⲛⲓⲙ = 'who?' **43**.

VOCABULARY 8

Learn all the articles **60–62**.

More prepositions

⳿ⲁ-, ⳿ⲁⲡⲟ꞊	under, at, from, in respect of, on behalf of	ὑπό, ὑπέρ, περί
ϣⲁ-, ϣⲁⲡⲟ꞊	to, toward (esp. people)	πρός, εἰς, ἕως
ⲙⲛ̄ⲛⲥⲁ-, ⲙⲛ̄ⲛⲥⲱ꞊	after (temporal)	μετά
ⲭⲓⲛ-	from . . . onwards, since	ἀπό
(ⲛ̄)ⲛⲁϩⲣⲛ̄-, (ⲛ̄)ⲛⲁϩⲣⲁ꞊	in the presence of, before, in the opinion of, compared with	πρός

Prepositions based on ⲧⲛ̄-, ⲧⲟⲟⲧ꞊ *(hand-of)*

ϩⲓⲧⲛ̄-, ϩⲓⲧⲟⲟⲧ꞊	through, by, from	ἀπό, διά
ⲉⲃⲟⲗ ϩⲓⲧⲛ̄-, ⲉⲃⲟⲗ ϩⲓⲧⲟⲟⲧ꞊	through, by, from	ἀπό, διά
ⲛ̄ⲧⲛ̄-, ⲛ̄ⲧⲟⲟⲧ꞊	in, by, with, beside, from	ἀπό, παρά
ⲉⲧⲛ̄-, ⲉⲧⲟⲟⲧ꞊	to	Greek dative
ϩⲁⲧⲛ̄-, ϩⲁⲧⲟⲟⲧ꞊	beside, with	πρός

Preposition based on ⲭⲛ̄-, ⲭⲱ꞊ *(head-of)*

ϩⲓⲭⲛ̄-, ϩⲓⲭⲱ꞊	upon, over, in, on, at, beside; for, through, from upon	ἐπί

More adverbs

ⲉⲛⲉϩ	ever (as in "not *ever*")	(οὐδέ)ποτε
ⲛ̄ϣⲟⲣⲡ	first of all, formerly	πρῶτον
ⲧⲉⲛⲟⲩ	now	νῦν
ⲛ̄ⲧⲉⲩⲛⲟⲩ	suddenly, immediately	εὐθύς, εὐθέως
ⲭⲓⲛ-ⲛ̄ϣⲟⲣⲡ	from the first	ἀπ᾽ ἀρχῆς
ⲭⲓⲛ-ⲧⲉⲛⲟⲩ	from now on	νῦν, ἄρτι, ἤδη
ϣⲁ-ⲉⲛⲉϩ	forever	εἰς τὸν αἰῶνα

Conjunction

ⲛ̄ⲥⲁ-	except	εἰ μή

EXERCISES 8

A. Practice translating rapidly into Coptic until you are fluent.

My deed and yours (sing. masc.). Cf. **58**.
His deed and yours (sing. fem.).
Her deed and yours (pl.).
Our deeds and theirs.
Our deeds and yours (pl.).
Your (sing. masc.) deed and his.
Your (sing. masc.) hand and his.
Our hands and his.
His hands and ours.
His wife and mine.
Her husband and mine.

B. Translate. a. ⲡⲕⲉ-ⲕⲟⲥⲙⲟⲥ. ⲧⲕⲉ-ⲡⲉ. ⲛ̄ⲕⲉ-ⲍⲓⲟⲟⲩⲉ. b. ⲡⲓ-ⲛⲟϭ
ⲛ̄-ⲣⲁϣⲉ. ϯ-ⲥⲍⲓⲙⲉ. ⲧ-ⲡⲟⲗⲓⲥ ⲉⲧⲙ̄ⲙⲁⲩ. c. ⲛ̄-ϣⲏⲣⲉ ϣⲏⲙ ⲉⲧⲙ̄ⲙⲁⲩ.
ⲡ-ⲙⲁ ⲉⲧⲙ̄ⲙⲁⲩ. d. ⲕⲉ-ⲍⲓⲏ. ⲍⲉⲛⲕⲉ-ⲍⲓⲟⲟⲩⲉ. ⲍⲓⲏ ⲛⲓⲙ. e. ⲡⲟⲗⲓⲥ ⲛⲓⲙ.
ϣⲏⲣⲉ ϣⲏⲙ ⲛⲓⲙ. ⲥⲍⲓⲙⲉ ⲛⲓⲙ. ⲕⲟⲥⲙⲟⲥ ⲛⲓⲙ. f. ⲕⲉ-ⲥⲛⲁⲩ ⲛ̄-ⲁⲡⲟⲥⲧⲟⲗⲟⲥ.
ⲁⲡⲟⲥⲧⲟⲗⲟⲥ ⲥⲛⲁⲩ. ⲡ-ⲁⲡⲟⲥⲧⲟⲗⲟⲥ ⲥⲛⲁⲩ. g. ⲕⲉ-ⲕⲟⲥⲙⲟⲥ. ⲕⲉ-ⲟⲩⲁ. ϭⲉ.
ⲕⲉⲧ. h. ⲟⲩⲟⲛ ⲛⲓⲙ. ⲡⲏ. ⲡⲁⲓ̈. ⲡⲉⲧⲙ̄ⲙⲁⲩ. ⲛⲉⲧⲙ̄ⲙⲁⲩ.

C. Translate into Coptic. a. The other law. *b.* Some other places. *c.* Another
day. *d.* Every day. *e.* Every place. *f.* That place. *g.* Those places. *h.* Those
days. *i.* These days. *j.* The other days. *k.* Some other days. *l.* From that place.
m. To that place. *n.* In that place.

D. Translate. a. ⲧⲱ-ϥ ⲧⲉ ⲧ-ϭⲟⲙ, ⲡⲱ-ϥ ⲡⲉ ⲡ-ⲉⲟⲟⲩ, ⲁⲩⲱ ⲡⲱ-ϥ
ⲡⲉ ⲡ-ⲧⲁⲉⲓⲟ. b. ⲡⲁ-ⲡ-ⲛⲟⲩⲧⲉ ⲡⲉ ⲡ-ⲕⲁⲍ. ⲡ-ⲕⲁⲍ ⲡⲁ-ⲡ-ⲛⲟⲩⲧⲉ ⲡⲉ.
c. ⲛⲁ-ⲡⲉⲓ̈-ⲣⲱⲙⲉ ⲛⲉ ⲛ̄-ϣⲏⲣⲉ ⲉⲧⲙ̄ⲙⲁⲩ. d. ⲟⲩ-ⲉⲃⲟⲗ ⲍⲓⲧⲙ̄-ⲡ-ⲣⲱⲙⲉ
ⲡⲉ ⲡ-ⲛⲟⲃⲉ, ⲁⲗⲗⲁ ⲟⲩ-ⲉⲃⲟⲗ ⲍⲓⲧⲙ̄-ⲡ-ⲛⲟⲩⲧⲉ ⲧⲉ ⲧⲉ-ⲭⲁⲣⲓⲥ. e. ⲛⲉⲓ̈-
ⲣⲱⲙⲉ ⲍⲉⲛ-ⲉⲃⲟⲗ ⲧⲱⲛ ⲛⲉ. ⲍⲉⲛ-ⲉⲃⲟⲗ ⲧⲱⲛ ⲛⲉ ⲛⲉⲓ̈-ⲣⲱⲙⲉ.

E. Translate into Coptic, giving alternate translations where possible.
a. This nation is mine. *b.* That house is not yours (sing. masc.), it is Mary's.
c. These houses are not yours (sing. masc.). *d.* You (pl.) do not belong to this
nation. *e.* Where does this nation come from (**59** [iv])? *f.* Where are you

(sing. fem.) from? *g.* I am not from this world. *h.* I do not belong to this world. *i.* I am God's. *j.* I am from God.

F. Translate. a. ⲉⲃⲟⲗ ϩⲓⲧⲛ̄–ⲟⲩ–ⲁⲅⲅⲉⲗⲟⲥ. b. ⲛ̄ⲧⲙ̄–ⲡ–ⲁⲣⲭⲓⲉⲣⲉⲩⲥ. c. ⲉⲃⲟⲗ ϩⲓⲧⲟⲟⲧ–ⲟⲩ. d. ⲉⲧⲙ̄–ⲡⲉ–ⲅⲣⲁⲙⲙⲁⲧⲉⲩⲥ. e. ϩⲁⲧⲟⲟⲧ–ⲥ. f. ϩⲁⲧⲛ̄–ⲧⲁ–ϩⲓⲙⲉ. g. ϩⲁ–ⲡⲉϥ–ⲗⲁⲟⲥ. h. ϣⲁ–ⲡⲉ–ⲡⲣⲟⲫⲏⲧⲏⲥ. i. ϣⲁⲣⲟ–ϥ. j. ⲙⲛ̄ⲛ̄ⲥⲁ–ⲟⲩϣⲏ ⲥⲛ̄ⲧⲉ. k. ϫⲓⲛ–ⲧⲉⲛⲟⲩ. l. ⲛ̄ⲛⲁϩⲣⲙ̄–ⲡⲉ–ⲭ̄ⲥ̄. m. ⲉϫⲙ̄–ⲡⲧⲟⲟⲩ. n. ⲉϫⲱ–ⲛ. o. ϩⲓⲧⲛ̄–ⲙ̄–ⲙⲟⲩⲉⲓⲟⲟⲩⲉ.

LESSON 9

DURATIVE SENTENCE. INFINITIVE AND STATIVE. ADJECTIVAL MEANING. COMPARATIVE AND SUPERLATIVE. DIRECT OBJECT. ADDITIONAL PREDICATE AFTER A DIRECT OBJECT. INGRESSIVE.

Hereafter in this book, prefixed articles (ⲡ–, ⲟⲩ–, ⲡⲉϥ– etc.) will no longer be set off by a hyphen. You can now expect to find ⲡⲣⲱⲙⲉ, ⲟⲩⲣⲱⲙⲉ, ⲧⲁⲙⲁⲁⲩ, ⲡⲉⲓ̈ⲗⲁⲟⲥ, etc.

THE DURATIVE SENTENCE

63. The durative sentence consists of subject + predicate, always in that order. There are three types of durative sentence, which can be recognized by the kind of subject that occurs. [CG 305–24]

    i. A *definite subject:* def. article phrase or its equivalent (ⲡⲣⲱⲙⲉ, ⲡⲁⲓ̈, ⲙⲁⲣⲓⲁ, etc.).

    ⲡⲣⲱⲙⲉ ⲃⲱⲗ = the man is releasing *or* releases

    ii. A *personal subject prefix* of the durative sentence.

    ϥ–ⲃⲱⲗ = he is releasing *or* releases

The Personal Subject Prefixes

ϯ–	ⲧⲛ̄–	I (am)	we (are)
ⲕ–	ⲧⲉⲧⲛ̄–	you (are)	you (are)
ⲧⲉ–		you (are)	
ϥ–	ⲥⲉ–	he (is)	they (are)
ⲥ–		she (is)	

    iii. A *non-definite subject* (ⲟⲩⲣⲱⲙⲉ, ⲟⲩⲁ, ⁰ⲣⲱⲙⲉ, ⲗⲁⲁⲩ, ⲗⲁⲁⲩ ⲛ̄–ⲣⲱⲙⲉ etc.) must be preceded by

    ⲟⲩⲛ̄– *there is*
    ⲙⲛ̄– or ⲙ̄ⲙⲛ̄– *there is no(t)*, or
    ⲉⲓⲥ– *behold*

Thus:

ⲟⲩⲛ̄-ⲟⲩⲣⲱⲙⲉ ⲃⲱⲗ = a man is releasing *or* releases
ⲉⲓⲥ-ⲟⲩⲣⲱⲙⲉ ⲃⲱⲗ = behold, a man is releasing *or* releases
ⲙⲛ̄-ⲗⲁⲁⲩ ⲃⲱⲗ = no one is (there is not any) releasing *or* no one releases

(ⲉⲓⲥ- *behold* also occurs with definite subject. [CG 479])

With each of these subjects, four kinds of predicate can occur interchangeably. The predicate follows the subject.

THE FOUR INTERCHANGEABLE PREDICATES OF THE DURATIVE SENTENCE

(*a*) An *infinitive* form of the verb (see **66**). ⲃⲱⲗ = is releasing, releases

(*b*) A *stative* form of the verb (see **66**). ⲃⲏⲗ = is free (describing a static condition after the action of releasing has ended).

(*c*) A *prepositional phrase or adverb* expressing situation[18].

(*d*) The future auxiliary ⲛⲁ- *will . . . , is going to . . .* completed by an infinitive. ⲛⲁ-ⲃⲱⲗ = will release, is going to release.

The four kinds of predicate and the three types of subject combine into twelve possible sentence forms (4 × 3).

Predicate = infinitive
1. ⲡⲁϫⲟⲉⲓⲥ ⲃⲱⲗ = My master is releasing *or* releases
2. ϥ-ⲃⲱⲗ = He is releasing *or* releases
3. ⲟⲩⲛ̄-$^{\emptyset}$ⲣⲱⲙⲉ ⲃⲱⲗ = People are releasing *or* release

Predicate = stative
4. ⲡⲉⲓ̈ⲗⲁⲟⲥ ⲃⲏⲗ = This nation is free
5. ϥ-ⲃⲏⲗ = It is free
6. ⲟⲩⲛ̄-$^{\emptyset}$ⲗⲁⲟⲥ ⲃⲏⲗ = Some nations are free

Predicate = prepositional phrase or adverb expressing situation
7. ⲡϫⲟⲉⲓⲥ ϩⲙ̄-ⲡⲉϥⲏⲓ̈ = The lord is in his house
8. ϥ-ϩⲙ̄-ⲡⲉϥⲏⲓ̈ = He is in his house
9. ⲟⲩⲛ̄-$^{\emptyset}$ⲣⲱⲙⲉ ϩⲙ̄-ⲡⲉϥⲏⲓ̈ = There are people in his house

[18] Examples of situational prepositions: ⲉϫⲛ̄- upon, ⲙⲛ̄- with, ⲛ̄ⲧⲛ̄- in, by, ⲛⲁϩⲣⲛ̄- in the presence of, ⲟⲩⲃⲉ- opposite, ϩⲁ- under, ϩⲓ- on, ϩⲛ̄- in, ϩⲣⲁⲓ̈ ϩⲛ̄- in, ϩⲁⲣⲱ⸗ beneath, ϩⲁⲣⲁⲧ⸗ beneath, ϩⲓϫⲛ̄- upon, ϩⲣⲁⲓ̈ ϩⲓϫⲛ̄- upon. Situational adverbs include ⲙ̄ⲙⲁⲩ is there, ⲙ̄ⲡⲟⲟⲩ (is) today, falls on today's date; ⲧⲱⲛ (is) where?, where is?; ⲧⲁⲓ̈ (is) here (only in the phrase ⲉⲧ-ⲧⲁⲓ̈ = which is here).

Predicate = future auxiliary ⲛⲁ– completed by infinitive

    10. ⲡⲁϫⲟⲉⲓⲥ ⲛⲁ–ⲃⲱⲗ = My master is going to release *or* will release

    11. ϥ–ⲛⲁ–ⲃⲱⲗ = He is going to release *or* will release

    12. ⲟⲩⲛ̄–⁰ⲣⲱⲙⲉ ⲛⲁ–ⲃⲱⲗ = People are going to release *or* will release

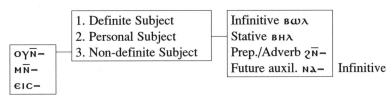

These predicates are "durative" in the sense that they express an enduring, ongoing, or general action, process, or state; or an imminently anticipated action or process.

64. There are two forms of negation.

(*a*) Negation with *definite or personal subject* [CG 317–18] is

        (ⲛ̄–) Subject (def./personal) + Predicate ⲁⲛ

Negative ⲁⲛ comes after the predicate and is always required; negative ⲛ̄– (ⲙ̄– before ⲡ or non-syllabic ⲙ) is optional, and is prefixed to the subject.

    ⲙ̄–ⲡⲁϫⲟⲉⲓⲥ ⲃⲱⲗ ⲁⲛ = My master is not releasing *or* does not release

    ⲛ̄–ϥ–ⲃⲱⲗ ⲁⲛ = He is not releasing *or* does not release

    ⲙ̄–ⲡⲉⲓ̈ⲗⲁⲟⲥ ⲃⲏⲗ ⲁⲛ = This nation is not free

    ⲛ̄–ϥ–ⲃⲏⲗ ⲁⲛ = It is not free

    ⲙ̄–ⲡⲭⲟⲉⲓⲥ ϩⲙ̄–ⲡⲉϥⲏⲓ̈ ⲁⲛ = The lord is not in his house

    ⲛ̄–ϥ–ϩⲙ̄–ⲡⲉϥⲏⲓ̈ ⲁⲛ = He is not in his house

    ⲙ̄–ⲡⲁϫⲟⲉⲓⲥ ⲛⲁ–ⲃⲱⲗ ⲁⲛ = My master is not going to release *or* will not release

    ⲛ̄–ϥ–ⲛⲁ–ⲃⲱⲗ ⲁⲛ = He is not going to release *or* will not release

(And all the above without ⲛ̄–.)

(*b*) Negation with non-definite subject [CG 322] is

        ⲙⲛ̄– Subject + Predicate

Here ⲙⲛ̄– or ⲙ̄ⲙⲛ̄– appears in place of ⲟⲩⲛ̄– and ⲉⲓⲥ–.

    ⲙⲛ̄–⁰ⲣⲱⲙⲉ ⲃⲱⲗ = No one is releasing *or* releases, People are not releasing *or* do not release, etc.

    ⲙⲛ̄–⁰ⲗⲁⲟⲥ ⲃⲏⲗ = No nations are free

    ⲙⲛ̄–⁰ⲣⲱⲙⲉ ϩⲙ̄–ⲡⲉϥⲏⲓ̈ = There are no people in his house, No one is in his house, etc.

    ⲙⲛ̄–⁰ⲣⲱⲙⲉ ⲛⲁ–ⲃⲱⲗ = No people are going to release *or* will release, No one is going to release *or* will release, People are not going to release *or* will not release, etc.

65. Personal subject prefixes with ⲛⲁ– future:

ϯ–ⲛⲁ–   ⲧⲛ̄–ⲛⲁ–
ⲕ–ⲛⲁ–   ⲧⲉⲧⲛⲁ– (sic)
ⲧⲉ–ⲛⲁ–
ϥ–ⲛⲁ–   ⲥⲉ–ⲛⲁ–
ⲥ–ⲛⲁ–

THE VERB: INFINITIVE AND STATIVE

66. Two important forms of the verb have already been mentioned in this lesson—the infinitive and the stative, and you will now begin learning about each of these.

Infinitives [CG 159–60] express action (ⲃⲱⲗ = release), process (ⲙⲟⲩ = die), or acquisition of a quality (ⲟⲩⲃⲁϣ = become white).

The corresponding *statives* [CG 162, 168] describe the enduring state of a subject after the action or process or quality is achieved: thus statives ⲃⲏⲗ = free, ⲙⲟⲟⲩⲧ = dead, ⲟⲩⲟⲃⲱ̄ = white. The stative can only be used in durative sentences. Not every verb has both forms; many infinitives have no stative, and a few statives have no infinitive. In the dictionary verbs are filed under the infinitive form (ⲃⲱⲗ) and statives are marked with an elevated obelus symbol (ⲃⲏⲗ†).

67. Any infinitive can also be used as a masculine noun, which expresses either the action of the infinitive or its result or both. [CG 105(c)] Thus infinitive ϫⲡⲟ = to bear, to give birth to, masc. noun ϫⲡⲟ = birth, offspring; infin. ϯ = to give, masc. noun ϯ = charity; infin. ⲉⲓ ⲉⲃⲟⲗ = come forth, masc. noun ⲉⲓ ⲉⲃⲟⲗ = exodus; etc. In fact you have already learned a few infinitives as nouns in the vocabularies leading up to this lesson. They are:

ⲙⲟⲩ, to die
ⲙⲉⲉⲩⲉ, to think
ⲣⲁϣⲉ, to rejoice
ⲥⲟⲡⲥ̄, to entreat, console
ⲥⲟⲟⲩⲛ, to become acquainted with, know
ⲧⲁⲉⲓⲟ, to honor
ⲟⲩϫⲁⲓ̈, to become healthy, safe, saved
ⲱⲛ̄ϩ, to live
ϣⲁϫⲉ, to speak

The verbal meaning can be negatived by the prefix ⲧⲙ̄– = not. Thus ⲡ–ⲧⲙ̄–ϯ = the act of not giving; not to give. [CG 161]

68. Greco-Coptic verbs have only an infinitive, which takes a form resembling the Greek active imperative singular. This is very close to the Greek verbal stem.

ⲡⲓⲥⲧⲉⲅⲉ = believe, ⲃⲁⲡⲧⲓⲍⲉ = baptize, ⲙⲉⲧⲁⲛⲟⲉⲓ = repent, ⲡⲁⲣⲁⲇⲓⲇⲟⲩ = betray, ⲁⲣⲛⲁ = deny. [CG 191–92]

69. List of Common Egyptian-Coptic Infinitives That Have a Stative

(*a*) *Action (transitive verbs).*

ⲃⲱⲗ	release, interpret	= λύειν
ⲃⲏⲗ†	free (after release), interpreted	= λύεσθαι
ⲃⲱⲗ ⲉⲃⲟⲗ	destroy, dissolve	= λύειν
ⲃⲏⲗ† ⲉⲃⲟⲗ	ruined	= λύεσθαι
ⲉⲓⲣⲉ	make, do	= ποιεῖν
ⲟ†	be (ⲟ† ⲛ̄-)	= εἶναι
ⲕⲱ	put	= ἐφιέναι, τιθέναι
ⲕⲏ†	be, lie	= κεῖσθαι
ⲕⲱ ⲉⲃⲟⲗ	forgive, release	= ἀπολύειν, ἀφιέναι
ⲕⲏ† ⲉⲃⲟⲗ	forgiven	= ἀφίεσθαι
ⲕⲱⲧ	build, build up	= οἰκοδομεῖν
ⲕⲏⲧ†	built up, situated	= οἰκοδομεῖσθαι
ⲙⲟⲩⲣ	bind	= δεῖν
ⲙⲏⲣ†	bound, under arrest	= δεῖσθαι, δέσμιος
ⲙⲟⲩϩ	fill	= πιμπλάναι, πληροῦν
ⲙⲉϩ†	full	= γέμειν, μεστὸς
ⲙ̄ⲧⲟⲛ	cause to rest, refresh	= ἐπαναπαύειν
ⲙⲟⲧⲛ̄†	easy, restful, refreshed	= εὔκοπος
ⲛⲟⲩϫⲉ	throw, cast	= βάλλειν
ⲛⲏϫ†	lie, recline	= ἀνακεῖσθαι
ⲡⲱϣ	divide	= κλᾶν
ⲡⲏϣ†	(be) split	= μερίζεσθαι
ⲥⲟⲃⲧⲉ	prepare	= ἑτοιμάζειν
ⲥⲃ̄ⲧⲱⲧ†	ready	= ἕτοιμος
ⲥⲙⲟⲩ	bless	= εὐλογεῖν
ⲥⲙⲁⲙⲁⲁⲧ†	blessed, happy	= εὐλογητὸς, εὐλογεῖσθαι
ⲥⲱⲧⲡ̄	choose	= ἐκλέγεσθαι
ⲥⲟⲧⲡ̄†	elect, chosen	= ἐκλεκτός
ⲥⲱⲟⲩϩ	gather	= συνάγειν
ⲥⲟⲟⲩϩ†	assembled	= συνάγεσθαι, συνέρχεσθαι
ⲥϩⲁⲓ̈	write	= γράφειν
ⲥⲏϩ†	scripture, written	= γεγράφεσθαι

ⲧ	give, give back	=	(ἀπο)διδόναι
ⲧⲟ†	fated, put	=	ἔξεστιν
ⲧⲃ̄ⲃⲟ	purify	=	καθαρίζειν
ⲧⲃ̄ⲃⲏⲩ†	pure	=	καθαρὸς
ⲧⲁⲉⲓⲟ	to honor	=	τιμᾶν
ⲧⲁⲉⲓⲏⲩ†	glorious, honored	=	ἔντιμος, δοξάζεσθαι
ⲧⲁⲕⲟ	ruin	=	ἀπολλύναι
ⲧⲁⲕⲏⲩⲧ†	corrupt	=	διαφθείρεσθαι
ⲧⲁⲗⲟ	take up, mount, board	=	ἀναλαμβάνειν
ⲧⲁⲗⲏⲩ†	seated, on board	=	καθῆσθαι
ⲧⲱ2ⲙ̄	invite	=	καλεῖν
ⲧⲁ2ⲙ̄†	invited, invitee	=	κλητὸς, καλεῖσθαι
ⲧⲁⲭⲣⲟ	make firm	=	στηρίζειν
ⲧⲁⲭⲣⲏⲩ†	solid	=	βέβαιος
ⲟⲩⲱⲛ	make open	=	ἀνοίγειν
ⲟⲩⲏⲛ†	open	=	ἀνοίγεσθαι
ⲟⲩⲱⲛ2̄ ⲉⲃⲟⲗ	reveal	=	φανεροῦν
ⲟⲩⲟⲛ2̄† ⲉⲃⲟⲗ	manifest, clear	=	φανερὸς, φαντάζεσθαι
ⲟⲩⲱ2	lay upon, occupy	=	προστιθέναι, κατοικεῖν
ⲟⲩⲏ2†	rest, inhabit	=	μένειν, κατοικεῖν
ⲟⲩⲝⲁⲓ̄	become healthy, saved	=	σῴζεσθαι
ⲟⲩⲟⲝ†	healthy, saved, safe	=	ὑγιὴς
ⲱⲡ	calculate, consider	=	λογίζεσθαι
ⲏⲡ†	reckoned	=	ἀριθμεῖσθαι
ϣⲱⲡ	receive, buy	=	δέχεσθαι, ἀγοράζειν
ϣⲏⲡ†	accepted, acceptable	=	δεκτός
ϣⲱⲱⲧ	cut off, sacrifice, lack	=	ἐκκόπτειν, θύειν, ὑστερεῖν
ϣⲁⲁⲧ†	fall short, be lacking	=	ὑστερεῖν
ϣⲧⲟⲣⲧⲣ̄	disturb	=	ταράσσεσθαι
ϣⲧⲣ̄ⲧⲱⲣ†	disturbed	=	θορυβεῖσθαι
2ⲱⲡ	hide	=	κρύπτειν
2ⲏⲡ†	secret	=	κρυπτός
ⲭⲟ	sow	=	σπείρειν
ⲭⲏⲩ†	sown with seed	=	σπόριος
ⲭⲱⲕ ⲉⲃⲟⲗ	fill	=	πληροῦν
ⲭⲏⲕ† ⲉⲃⲟⲗ	full	=	πλήρης, πληροῦσθαι

| ϫιce | raise up | = ὑψοῦν |
| ϫoce† | high | = ὑψηλός |

(b) Process.

eιβe	become thirsty	= διψᾶν
oβe†	thirsty	= διψᾶν
moy	die (become dead)	= ἀποθνήσκειν
mooyt†	dead	= νεκρός
ωνⲁϩ	live, become alive	= ζῆν
oνⲁϩ†	alive	= ζῆν
ϣωπe	become, come into existence	= γίνεσθαι
ϣooπ†	be, dwell, exist	= εἶναι
ϩιce	become tired, labor	= κοπιᾶν
ϩoce†	tired	= κοπιᾶν

(c) Acquisition of a quality.

oyβaϣ	become white	= λευκὸς γίνεσθαι
oyoβⲱ†	white	= λευκός
ϣooye	become dry	= ξηραίνεσθαι
ϣoyωoy†	dry	= ξηρός
ϩωn eϩoyn	draw near	= ἐγγίζειν
ϩηn† eϩoyn	near	= ἐγγύς
no infinitive		
ϩooy†	bad, evil	= πονηρός

All these verbs occur more than fifty times in the New Testament and must be learned thoroughly.

70. *Adjectival meaning of statives.* Many statives have the meaning of English adjectives, as the list in **69** well demonstrates (is full, is easy, is ready, is happy, is pure, is glorious, is corrupt, is solid, is dead, is white, is dry, etc.). In fact Coptic has several different ways to express adjectival meaning:

(a) The adjective as such **35**.

ϩaπ ⲙ̄-πoнн poc = *wicked* judgement
oyπoнн poc πe = It is *wicked*
ϥ-o ⲙ̄-⁰πoнн poc = It is *wicked* **82**

(b) The noun in certain constructions.

ϩaπ ⲛ̄-noyτe = *divine* judgement **36**
oynoyτe πe = It is *divine* **38**
ϥ-o ⲛ̄-⁰noyτe = It is *divine* **82**

73

(c) The stative in a durative sentence **66**.

ϥ-ⲙⲉϩ = It is *full*

(d) Later on (**101**) you will learn a fourth way, called the verboid.

ⲛⲁⲛⲟⲩ-ϥ = It is good

In **130** you will learn how a stative or verboid, attached by a relative converter, can modify a noun:

ⲧⲡⲟⲗⲓⲥ ⲉⲧ$^{\emptyset}$-ⲟⲩⲁⲁⲃ = the holy city (the-city that-is-holy)
ⲧⲉⲥϩⲓⲙⲉ ⲉⲧ-ⲛⲁⲛⲟⲩ-ⲥ = the good woman (the-woman who-is-good)

---

71. The *comparative* of adjectival meaning [CG 95] is expressed by adding an appropriate preposition of comparison such as ⲉ-, ⲉⲣⲟ= *than* or by the simple definite article in a context that makes things clear.

ⲡⲕⲟⲩⲓ̈ ⲉⲣⲟ-ϥ = the one who is *lesser* than he (small with regard to him)
ⲁϣ ⲡⲉ ⲡⲛⲟϭ. ⲡⲛⲟⲩⲃ ⲡⲉ ⲭⲛ̄-ⲡⲉⲣⲡⲉ ⲡⲉ = Which is *greater?* Is it gold or is it the temple?
ⲧⲉⲧⲛ̄-ϣⲟⲃⲉ ⲉ-ϩⲁϩ = You are *more valuable* (stative) than many

The *superlative* is expressed by a possessive article (ⲡⲉⲩ-, ⲧⲉⲩ-, ⲛⲉⲩ) or by the simple definite article in a context that makes things clear.

ⲡⲉⲩⲛⲟϭ = the *greatest* of them [their-great-one]
ⲁϣ ⲡⲉ ⲡⲛⲟϭ ⲛ̄ϩⲏⲧ-ⲟⲩ = Which is the *greatest* among them?
ⲡϩⲗ̄ⲗⲟ = the *Eldest* (administrative title in monastery)

72. *Direct objects.* [CG 166] The infinitive of verbs of action-being-done-to-some-one (called *transitive verbs*) can be followed by an expression of the receiver or goal of the action, which we call a *direct object* of the verb. With very many infinitives, the signal of a direct object is the preposition ⲛ̄-, ⲙ̄ⲙⲟ=.

ϥ-ⲃⲱⲗ ⲙ̄ⲙⲟ-ⲥ = he releases *her*
ϥ-ⲃⲱⲗ ⲙ̄ⲙⲟ-ⲟⲩ ⲉⲃⲟⲗ = he destroys *them*
ϯ-ⲛⲁ-ⲉⲓⲣⲉ ⲛ̄-ⲛⲁⲓ̈ = I shall do *these things*
ϥ-ⲕⲱ ⲉⲃⲟⲗ ⲙ̄-ⲡⲉϥⲥⲟⲛ = he forgives *his brother*
ϯ-ⲕⲱ ⲙ̄ⲙⲟ-ϥ ⲉⲃⲟⲗ = I forgive *him*

But for some infinitives, the signal of direct object is a some other preposition.

ϥ-ϣⲓⲛⲉ ⲛ̄ⲥⲁ-ⲡⲉⲓ̈ⲣⲱⲙⲉ = he is seeking this man
ϯ-ϣⲓⲛⲉ ⲛ̄ⲥⲱ-ϥ = I am seeking him

ⲥⲉ-ⲛⲁⲩ ⲉ-ⲧⲡⲟⲗⲓⲥ = they see the city
ⲕ-ⲛⲁⲩ ⲉⲣⲟ-ⲥ = you see it

In negations, negative ⲁⲛ can come either before or after a direct object.

ⲛ̄-ϯ-ⲛⲁ-ⲉⲓⲡⲉ ⲁⲛ ⲛ̄-ⲛⲁⲓ̈   I shall not do these things
ⲛ̄-ϯ-ⲛⲁ-ⲉⲓⲡⲉ ⲛ̄-ⲛⲁⲓ̈ ⲁⲛ

ⲛ̄-ϯ-ⲛⲁ-ⲉⲓⲡⲉ ⲁⲛ ⲙ̄ⲙⲟ-ⲟⲩ   I shall not do them
ⲛ̄-ϯ-ⲛⲁ-ⲉⲓⲡⲉ ⲙ̄ⲙⲟ-ⲟⲩ ⲁⲛ

ⲛ̄-ϯ-ϣⲓⲛⲉ ⲁⲛ ⲛ̄ⲥⲱ-ϥ   I am not seeking him
ⲛ̄-ϯ-ϣⲓⲛⲉ ⲛ̄ⲥⲱ-ϥ ⲁⲛ

As you learn each transitive infinitive, it is important to learn which preposition(s) mark its direct object ("ⲉⲓⲡⲉ ⲛ̄-/ⲙ̄ⲙⲟ⸗ do"; "ϣⲓⲛⲉ ⲛ̄ⲥⲁ- seek"). This information will be given in subsequent vocabulary lists.

Of course, transitive infinitives can also be used without any expression of a direct object. [CG 169]

ⲥⲉ-ⲭⲱ ⲅⲁⲣ ⲁⲩⲱ ⲛ̄-ⲥⲉ-ⲉⲓⲡⲉ ⲁⲛ = They *say* and they do not *do*

Infinitives that can never occur with a direct object (ⲙⲟⲩ = die, ⲟⲩⲃⲁϣ = become white) are called *intransitives*.

73. *Additional predicate after the direct object.* Depending on the meaning of the infinitive, a direct object may be followed by an additional predication (second direct object). [CG 178] (Such are verbs meaning *make, send, consider, appoint, call, see,* etc.) The additional predication can be

i. ⲛ̄- plus noun or adjective (typically without article). ϥ-ⲉⲓⲡⲉ ⲙ̄ⲙⲟ-ⲟⲩ ⲛ̄-⁰ϩⲙ̄ϩⲁⲗ = He makes them *slaves*.

ii. Preposition or conjunction plus noun or adjective. ⲥⲉ-ⲭⲓ ⲙ̄ⲙⲟ-ϥ ϩⲱⲥ-⁰ⲡⲣⲟ-ⲫⲏⲧⲏⲥ = They hold him to be *a prophet* ("*as prophet*").

iii. Completive circumstantial, which you will learn about in lesson 15. ⲥⲉ-ⲛⲁⲩ ⲉⲣⲟ-ϥ ⲉϥ-ⲃⲏⲕ = They see him *leaving*.

74. *Ingressive meaning of transitives.* [CG 174] Finally, you should know that in principle, any transitive infinitive, without direct object, can also express the process entering into a state. This is called the "ingressive" meaning (entering-into).

ⲃⲱⲗ (release), ingressive sense = become free
ⲃⲱⲗ ⲉⲃⲟⲗ (destroy), ingr. = go to ruin
ⲕⲱⲧ (build), ingr. = get built
ⲙ̄ⲧⲟⲛ (cause to rest), ingr. = become refreshed, get rested

The ingressive meaning is common only with certain infinitives.

Construct participles (the participium coniunctum, *p.c.)* [CG 122]

A small number of Egyptian-Coptic verbs also have an adjectival form called the construct participle, which expresses general tenseless action or process, something like an English participle. Construct participles end in a hyphen, and must be completed by an article phrase, usually with zero article. Their *only* use is to form compound adjectives; they have no other purpose. The usual abbreviation is "p.c.".

ⲙⲉ to love, p.c. ⲙⲁⲓ̈- loving, ⲙⲁⲓ̈-⁰ⲛⲟⲩⲧⲉ pious (God loving), ⲙⲁⲓ̈-ϣⲙ̄ⲙⲟ hospitable (loving strangers), etc.

ⲝⲓⲥⲉ to raise, p.c. ⲝⲁⲥⲓ- raising, ⲝⲁⲥⲓ-⁰ϩⲏⲧ arrogant (mind raising)

ϩⲗⲟ6 to be(come) sweet, p.c. ϩⲁⲗϭ̄- being sweet, ϩⲁⲗϭ̄-⁰ϣⲁⲝⲉ (sweet with words)

Construct participles contain the vowel ⲁ after the first consonant of the infinitive; in some, ⲓ̈- appears at the end (ⲙⲉ to love, ⲙⲁⲓ̈- loving).

The three *verbal preextensions* are prefixed to an infinitive or a stative to alter its lexical meaning as though modified by an adverb. [CG 183]

ⲣ̄ⲡⲕⲉ- = also, additionally, moreover, even

ⲣ̄ϣ̄ⲣ̄ⲡ(ⲛ̄)- = first, before hand, previously

ⲣ̄ϩⲟⲩⲉ- more, even more, greatly

Thus: ϣⲁⲝⲉ = speak. ⲣ̄ⲡⲕⲉ-ϣⲁⲝⲉ = also speak, even speak. ⲣ̄ϣ̄ⲣ̄ⲡ(ⲛ̄)-ϣⲁⲝⲉ = speak first, previously speak. ⲣ̄ϩⲟⲩⲉ-ϣⲁⲝⲉ = speak more, speak greatly.

Verbal auxiliaries. Somewhat like the future auxiliary ⲛⲁ- **63** the following verbal auxiliaries can be conjugated as verbs and have another infinitive directly suffixed. [CG 184]

    ⲙⲉⲣⲉ- like to

    ⲟⲩⲉϣ- want to

    ⲡϩⲛ̄- for once..., succeed in...

    ⲧⲁϣⲉ- frequently, greatly

    ⲟⲩⲉϩⲙ̄- again

    ϣ- or ⲉϣ- be able to

    ⲝⲡⲓ- or ⲝⲡⲉ- have to, must

ϥ-ⲙⲉⲣⲉ-ⲟⲩⲱⲙ = He likes to eat. ϥ-ⲛⲁ-ⲝⲡⲓ-ⲉⲓ = He will have to come. ⲛ̄ⲛⲉϥ-ϣ-ⲃⲱⲕ = He shall not be able to go, *but* ⲛ̄ⲛⲉ-ϣ-ⲗⲁⲁⲩ ⲃⲱⲕ = None shall be able to go (ϣ- occurs after a personal subject such as ϥ but before a non-personal subject such as ⲗⲁⲁⲩ).

VOCABULARY 9

Learn the personal subject prefixes **63**.

Learn the matching infinitive and stative of each of the verbs listed above. Try to get to the point where if you see the infinitive you can give the stative, and if you see the stative you can give the infinitive. (We shall return to these verbs in smaller groups in succeeding vocabulary lists.)

Verbs that have a stative

ⲙⲟⲩ, ⲙⲟⲟⲩⲧ†	die (dead†)	ἀποθνῄσκειν (νε-κρός†)
ⲧⲁⲉⲓⲟ ⲛ̄-/ⲙ̄ⲙⲟ⸗, ⲧⲁⲉⲓⲏⲩ†	honor (honored†)	τιμᾶν (ἔντιμος†)
ⲟⲩⲟⲡ, ⲟⲩⲁⲁⲃ†	become holy (be holy†)	ἁγιάζεσθαι, ἅγιος
ⲟⲩⲭⲁⲓ̈, ⲟⲩⲟⲭ†	become healthy or saved (healthy†, saved†)	σῴζεσθαι (ὑγιαί-νειν†)
ⲱⲛⲁ̄, ⲟⲛⲁ̄†	become alive (alive†)	ζῆν

Verbs that have no stative

ⲙⲉⲉⲩⲉ ⲉ- or ϫⲉ-	think about *or* that	λογίζεσθαι
ⲣⲁϣⲉ ⲛ̄-/ⲙ̄ⲙⲟ⸗ or ϩⲛ̄-	rejoice at *or* in	χαίρειν
ⲥⲟⲡⲥ̄ ⲛ̄-/ⲙ̄ⲙⲟ⸗	entreat, console	παρακαλεῖν
ⲥⲟⲟⲩⲛ ⲛ̄-/ⲙ̄ⲙⲟ⸗	become acquainted with, know	γιγνώσκειν, εἰδέ-ναι
ϣⲁϫⲉ ⲛ̄-/ⲙ̄ⲙⲟ⸗ or ⲙⲛ̄-	speak, say	λαλεῖν
*ⲡⲓⲥⲧⲉⲩⲉ ⲉ-	believe	
*ⲃⲁⲡⲧⲓⲍⲉ ⲛ̄-/ⲙ̄ⲙⲟ⸗	baptize	
*ⲙⲉⲧⲁⲛⲟⲉⲓ	repent	
*ⲡⲁⲣⲁⲇⲓⲇⲟⲩ ⲛ̄-/ⲙ̄ⲙⲟ⸗	betray	
*ⲁⲣⲛⲁ ⲛ̄-/ⲙ̄ⲙⲟ⸗	deny	

EXERCISES 9

A. *Translate rapidly.* ϯ–ⲙⲉⲉⲩⲉ. ⲥⲉ–ⲙⲉⲉⲩⲉ. ⲧⲉ–ⲙⲉⲉⲩⲉ. ⲛ̄–ⲥⲉ–ⲙⲉⲉⲩⲉ ⲁⲛ. ϯ–ⲙⲉⲉⲩⲉ ⲉⲣⲟ–ϥ. ⲕ–ⲙⲉⲉⲩⲉ ⲉⲣⲟ–ï. ⲛ̄–ⲅ–ⲙⲉⲉⲩⲉ (14) ⲁⲛ ⲉⲣⲟ–ï. ⲕ–ⲙⲉⲉⲩⲉ ⲁⲛ ⲉⲣⲟ–ï. ⲙ̄–ⲡⲉïⲣⲱⲙⲉ ⲙⲉⲉⲩⲉ ⲁⲛ. ⲛ̄–ⲧⲉïⲥϩⲓⲙⲉ ⲙⲉⲉⲩⲉ ⲁⲛ. ⲛ̄–ⲛⲉⲛⲥⲛⲏⲩ ⲙⲉⲉⲩⲉ ⲁⲛ. ⲙⲛ̄–ᵉⲣⲱⲙⲉ ⲙⲉⲉⲩⲉ. ⲟⲩⲛ̄–ⲟⲩⲣⲱⲙⲉ ⲙⲉⲉⲩⲉ. ⲟⲩⲛ̄–ᵉⲣⲱⲙⲉ ⲙⲉⲉⲩⲉ. ⲉⲓⲥ–ⲟⲩⲣⲱⲙⲉ ⲙⲉⲉⲩⲉ. ⲉⲓⲥ–ⲡⲉïⲣⲱⲙⲉ ⲙⲉⲉⲩⲉ.

B. *Recite the entire paradigm (8 persons) of* ϯ–ⲣⲁϣⲉ *(I rejoice/I am rejoicing), with translation.*

Recite the paradigm in reverse order (starting with 3d pl.).

Recite the negations (two possible forms) of the paradigm, with translation.

The same, in reverse order.

C. *Translate rapidly.* ϯ–ⲧⲁⲉⲓⲟ ⲙ̄ⲙⲟ–ϥ. ⲧⲉ–ⲥⲟⲡⲥ̄ ⲙ̄ⲙⲟ–ⲛ. ⲥ–ⲥⲟⲟⲩⲛ ⲙ̄ⲙⲟ–ⲟⲩ. ⲧⲉⲧⲛ̄–ⲡⲓⲥⲧⲉⲩⲉ ⲉⲣⲟ–ï. ⲕ–ⲃⲁⲡⲧⲓⲍⲉ ⲙ̄ⲙⲟ–ⲥ. ϥ–ⲡⲁⲣⲁⲇⲓⲇⲟⲩ ⲙ̄ⲙⲟ–ᵉ. ⲧⲛ̄–ⲁⲣⲛⲁ ⲙ̄ⲙⲱ–ⲧⲛ̄. ⲥⲉ–ⲧⲁⲉⲓⲟ ⲙ̄ⲙⲟ–ⲕ. ϯ–ⲥⲟⲡⲥ̄ ⲙ̄ⲙⲟ–ϥ. ⲧⲉ–ⲥⲟⲟⲩⲛ ⲙ̄ⲙⲟ–ⲛ. ⲥ–ⲡⲓⲥⲧⲉⲩⲉ ⲉⲣⲟ–ⲟⲩ. ⲧⲉⲧⲛ̄–ⲃⲁⲡⲧⲓⲍⲉ ⲙ̄ⲙⲟ–ï. ⲕ–ⲡⲁⲣⲁⲇⲓⲇⲟⲩ ⲙ̄ⲙⲟ–ⲥ. ϥ–ⲁⲣⲛⲁ ⲙ̄ⲙⲟ–ⲥ. ⲧⲛ̄–ⲧⲁⲉⲓⲟ ⲙ̄ⲙⲱ–ⲧⲛ̄. ⲥⲉ–ⲙⲉⲉⲩⲉ ⲉⲣⲟ–ⲕ.

D. *Form the negative (four possible formulations) of each of the sentences in (C), and translate.*

E. *Translate.* a. ϯ–ⲧⲁⲉⲓⲏⲩ. ⲧⲉ–ⲟⲩⲟⲭ. ⲥ–ⲙⲟⲟⲩⲧ. ⲧⲉⲧⲛ̄–ⲟⲛϩ̄. ⲕ–ⲧⲁⲉⲓⲏⲩ. ϥ–ⲟⲩⲟⲭ. ⲧⲛ̄–ⲙⲟⲟⲩⲧ. ⲥⲉ–ⲟⲛϩ̄. ⲡϫⲟⲉⲓⲥ ⲧⲁⲉⲓⲏⲩ. b. ϯ–ⲧⲁⲉⲓⲟ. ϯ–ⲧⲁⲉⲓⲏⲩ. ⲧⲉ–ⲟⲩⲭⲁï. ⲧⲉ–ⲟⲩⲟⲭ. ⲥ–ⲛⲁ–ⲙⲟⲩ. ⲥ–ⲙⲟⲟⲩⲧ. ⲧⲉⲧⲛ̄–ⲱⲛϩ̄. ⲧⲉⲧⲛ̄–ⲟⲛϩ̄. c. ⲕ–ⲧⲁⲉⲓⲟ. ⲕ–ⲧⲁⲉⲓⲏⲩ. ϥ–ⲟⲩⲭⲁï. ϥ–ⲟⲩⲟⲭ. ⲧⲛ̄–ⲛⲁ–ⲙⲟⲩ. ⲧⲛ̄–ⲙⲟⲟⲩⲧ. ⲥⲉ–ⲱⲛϩ̄. ⲥⲉ–ⲟⲛϩ̄. d. ⲡϫⲟⲉⲓⲥ ⲧⲁⲉⲓⲟ. ⲡϫⲟⲉⲓⲥ ⲧⲁⲉⲓⲏⲩ. ϯ–ϩⲙ̄–ⲡⲉϥⲣ̄ⲡⲉ. ⲧⲉ–ⲛⲙ̄ⲙⲁ–ⲩ. ⲥ–ϩⲙ̄–ⲡⲉϥⲣ̄ⲡⲉ. ⲧⲉⲧⲛ̄–ⲛⲙ̄ⲙⲁ–ⲩ. ⲕ–ϩⲙ̄–ⲡⲉϥⲣ̄ⲡⲉ. e. ϥ–ⲛⲙ̄ⲙⲁ–ⲩ. ⲧⲛ̄–ϩⲙ̄–ⲡⲉϥⲣ̄ⲡⲉ. ⲥⲉ–ⲛⲙ̄ⲙⲁ–ⲩ. ⲡϫⲟⲉⲓⲥ ϩⲙ̄–ⲡⲉϥⲣ̄ⲡⲉ. ϯ–ⲛⲁ–ⲧⲁⲉⲓⲟ ⲙ̄ⲙⲟ–ϥ. ⲧⲉ–ⲛⲁ–ⲟⲩⲭⲁï. ϥ–ⲛⲁ–ⲟⲩⲟⲡ. f. ϥ–ⲟⲩⲁⲁⲃ. ⲥⲉ–ⲟⲩⲁⲁⲃ. ⲥⲉ–ⲟⲩⲟⲡ. ⲥ–ⲛⲁ–ⲙⲟⲩ. ⲧⲉⲧⲛⲁ–ⲱⲛϩ̄. ⲕ–ⲛⲁ–ⲧⲁⲉⲓⲟ ⲙ̄ⲙⲟ–ϥ. ϥ–ⲛⲁ–ⲟⲩⲭⲁï. ⲧⲛ̄–ⲛⲁ–ⲙⲟⲩ. ⲥⲉ–ⲛⲁ–ⲱⲛϩ̄. g. ⲡϫⲟⲉⲓⲥ ⲛⲁ–ⲧⲁⲉⲓⲟ ⲙ̄ⲙⲟ–ϥ. ϯ–ⲙⲉⲧⲁⲛⲟⲉⲓ ⲉϩⲣⲁï ⲉϫⲛ̄–ⲛⲁ–ⲛⲟⲃⲉ. ⲥⲉ–ⲙⲉⲧⲁ ⲛⲟⲉⲓ. h. ϥ–ϣⲁϫⲉ ⲙⲛ̄–ⲡⲉϥ–ⲉⲓⲱⲧ. ϥ–ϣⲁϫⲉ ⲛⲙ̄ⲙⲁ–ⲥ. ϥ–ϣⲁϫⲉ ⲙ̄ⲙⲟ–ϥ. i. ϥ–ⲧⲁⲉⲓⲏⲩ ⲉ–ⲛⲟⲩⲧⲉ ⲛⲓⲙ. ⲛ̄ⲧⲟⲟⲩ ϩⲉⲛ–ⲡⲟⲛⲏⲣⲟⲥ ⲉⲣⲟ–ⲕ ⲛⲉ.

F. *Form the negative of each of the sentences in (E), and translate.*

LESSON 10

NON-DURATIVE CONJUGATION: MAIN CLAUSE CONJUGATION BASES. *'TO BE'* IN COPTIC.

75. The non-durative verbal sentence consists of three parts:

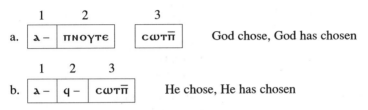

a.

| 1 | 2 | 3 |
God chose, God has chosen (for pattern a: ⲁ – ⲡⲛⲟⲩⲧⲉ | ⲥⲱⲧⲡ̄)

b.

| 1 | 2 | 3 |
He chose, He has chosen (for pattern b: ⲁ – ϥ – ⲥⲱⲧⲡ̄)

(1) A conjugation base, which has two states, such as ⲁ–, ⲁ⸗.
(2) A subject suffixed to the base.
(3) An infinitive (separated in pattern a, attached in pattern b).

The infinitive can be expanded by a direct object, various prepositional phrases, adverbs, subordinate clauses, etc. There are ten non-durative conjugation bases. Five of these form main clauses (independent sentences), and five form subordinate (dependent) clauses. [CG 325–28] You will learn the main clause bases in this lesson.

THE MAIN CLAUSE CONJUGATION BASES

76. Four of the five main clause conjugations have distinct affirmative and negative bases. The remaining one is negative only.

Past affirmative: ⲁ–, ⲁ⸗   He chose, He has chosen
Past negative: ⲙ̄ⲡⲉ–, ⲙ̄ⲡ⸗   He did not choose, He has not chosen

'Not Yet': ⲙ̄ⲡⲁⲧⲉ–, ⲙ̄ⲡⲁⲧ⸗   He has not yet chosen

Aorist affirmative: ϣⲁⲣⲉ–, ϣⲁ⸗   (tenseless)
Aorist negative: ⲙⲉⲣⲉ–, ⲙⲉ⸗   (tenseless)

Optative affirmative: ⲉⲣⲉ-, ⲉⲥⲉ-   He shall choose, He might choose
Optative negative: ⲛ̄ⲛⲉ-, ⲛ̄ⲛⲉⲥ   He shall not choose, He might not choose

Jussive affirmative: ⲙⲁⲣⲉ-, ⲙⲁⲣⲥ   Let him choose (He ought to choose)
Jussive negative: ⲙ̄ⲡⲣ̄ⲧⲣⲉ-, ⲙ̄ⲡⲣ̄ⲧⲣⲉⲥ   Let him not choose

These bases do not convey any information as to whether the action or process was ongoing (durative).

77. The Past, affirm. ⲁ-, ⲁⲥ / neg. ⲙ̄ⲡⲉ-, ⲙ̄ⲡⲥ [CG 334–35]

ⲁⲓ̈-	ⲙ̄ⲡⲓ-
ⲁⲕ-	ⲙ̄ⲡⲕ̄-
ⲁᵠ- or ⲁⲣ- or ⲁⲣⲉ-	ⲙ̄ⲡⲉ- or ⲙ̄ⲡⲣ̄-
ⲁϥ-	ⲙ̄ⲡϥ̄-
ⲁⲥ-	ⲙ̄ⲡⲥ̄-
ⲁⲛ-	ⲙ̄ⲡⲛ̄-
ⲁⲧⲉⲧⲛ̄-	ⲙ̄ⲡⲉⲧⲛ̄-
ⲁⲩ-	ⲙ̄ⲡⲟⲩ-
ⲁ-ⲡⲛⲟⲩⲧⲉ	ⲙ̄ⲡⲉ-ⲡⲛⲟⲩⲧⲉ

In English, this corresponds to both past narration (ⲁϥ-ⲃⲱⲕ = *He went*) and present-based description of the past (ⲁϥ-ⲃⲱⲕ = *He has gone*).

78. 'Not yet', ⲙ̄ⲡⲁⲧⲉ-, ⲙ̄ⲡⲁⲧⲥ [CG 336]

ⲙ̄ⲡⲁϯ-
ⲙ̄ⲡⲁⲧⲕ̄-
ⲙ̄ⲡⲁⲧⲉ-
ⲙ̄ⲡⲁⲧϥ̄-
ⲙ̄ⲡⲁⲧⲥ̄-

ⲙ̄ⲡⲁⲧⲛ̄-
ⲙ̄ⲡⲁⲧⲉⲧⲛ̄-
ⲙ̄ⲡⲁⲧⲟⲩ-

ⲙ̄ⲡⲁⲧⲉ-ⲡⲛⲟⲩⲧⲉ

A present-based description of the past in terms of what has not happened, with expectation that it will or might come to pass (*He has not yet gone*). ⲙ̄ⲡⲁⲧⲉ-ⲧⲁⲟⲩⲛⲟⲩ ⲉⲓ = My hour has not yet come.

79. The Aorist, affirm. ϣⲁⲣⲉ-, ϣⲁⲥ / neg. ⲙⲉⲣⲉ-, ⲙⲉⲥ [CG 337]

ϣⲁⲓ̈-	ⲙⲉⲓ̈-
ϣⲁⲕ-	ⲙⲉⲕ-
ϣⲁⲣⲉ-	ⲙⲉⲣⲉ-
ϣⲁϥ-	ⲙⲉϥ-
ϣⲁⲥ-	ⲙⲉⲥ-
ϣⲁⲛ-	ⲙⲉⲛ-
ϣⲁⲧⲉⲧⲛ̄-	ⲙⲉⲧⲉⲧⲛ̄-
ϣⲁⲩ-	ⲙⲉⲩ-
ϣⲁⲣⲉ-ⲡⲛⲟⲩⲧⲉ	ⲙⲉⲣⲉ-ⲡⲛⲟⲩⲧⲉ

Forms a complete sentence consisting of subject + verb, but without expressing any tense (hence *aorist* = limitless, timeless). In some situations (statements of timeless truth) tense is irrelevant. ϣⲁⲣⲉ-ⲟⲩϣⲏⲣⲉ ⲛ̄-ⲥⲟⲫⲟⲥ ⲉⲩⲫⲣⲁⲛⲉ ⲙ̄-ⲡⲉϥⲉⲓⲱⲧ = A wise son makes his father glad. But the Coptic aorist also occurs in past tense narration, as a technique of story telling. This is a distinctly Coptic device. There is nothing quite like it in English, so when you translate the Coptic aorist you may be forced to commit yourself about tense, whereas a Coptic writer was not. To the English speaker, the Coptic aorist often seems to mirror the tense (if any) of the immediate context in which it occurs.

Caution: the Coptic aorist has nothing to do with the form called aorist in Greek.

80. The Optative, affirm. ⲉⲣⲉ-, ⲉⲥⲉ- / neg. ⲛ̄ⲛⲉ-, ⲛ̄ⲛⲉⲥ [CG 338]

The prepersonal affirmative is a split base, ⲉⲥⲉ. The personal suffixes are inserted into the middle of the affirmative base.

ⲉⲓ̈ⲉ-	ⲛ̄ⲛⲁ-
ⲉⲕⲉ-	ⲛ̄ⲛⲉⲕ-
ⲉⲣⲉ-	ⲛ̄ⲛⲉ-
ⲉϥⲉ-	ⲛ̄ⲛⲉϥ-
ⲉⲥⲉ-	ⲛ̄ⲛⲉⲥ-
ⲉⲛⲉ-	ⲛ̄ⲛⲉⲛ-
ⲉⲧⲉⲧⲛⲉ-	ⲛ̄ⲛⲉⲧⲛ̄-
ⲉⲩⲉ-	ⲛ̄ⲛⲉⲩ-
ⲉⲣⲉ-ⲡⲛⲟⲩⲧⲉ	ⲛ̄ⲛⲉ-ⲡⲛⲟⲩⲧⲉ

Two main uses:

(*a*) As an independent clause, expressing an absolute future, even a command or rule or unconditional prediction (as in divine commands, monastic rules, prophetic predictions, the Ten Commandments, etc.) (*I shall go, you shall go, he shall go*). ⲉⲕⲉ-ⲧⲁⲉⲓⲉ-ⲡⲉⲕⲉⲓⲱⲧ ⲙⲛ̄-ⲧⲉⲕⲙⲁⲁⲩ = You shall honor your father and your mother. ⲛ̄ⲛⲉⲕ-ϩⲱⲧⲃ̄ = You shall not kill.

(*b*) Following ⲭⲉ- or ⲭⲉⲕⲁⲥ or ⲭⲉⲕⲁⲁⲥ to express purpose or result, *so that . . . might . . . ; so as to . . . , so that . . .* (ⲭⲉ-ⲉϥⲉ-ⲃⲱⲕ *so that he might go*). Cf. **153**.

Note: After ⲭⲉⲕⲁ(ⲁ)ⲥ the negative sometimes has the following spelling.

ⲭⲉⲕⲁ(ⲁ)ⲥ	ⲉⲛⲛⲁ-
"	ⲉⲛⲛⲉⲕ-
"	ⲉⲛⲛⲉ-
"	ⲉⲛⲛⲉϥ-
"	ⲉⲛⲛⲉⲥ-
ⲭⲉⲕⲁ(ⲁ)ⲥ	ⲉⲛⲛⲉⲛ-
"	ⲉⲛⲛⲉⲧⲛ̄-
"	ⲉⲛⲛⲉⲩ-
ⲭⲉⲕⲁ(ⲁ)ⲥ	ⲉⲛⲛⲉ-ⲡⲛⲟⲩⲧⲉ

81. The Jussive, affirm. ⲙⲁⲣⲉ-, ⲙⲁⲣ⸗ / neg. ⲙ̄ⲡⲣ̄ⲧⲣⲉ-, ⲙ̄ⲡⲣ̄ⲧⲣⲉ⸗ [CG 340]

ⲙⲁⲣⲓ-	ⲙ̄ⲡⲣ̄ⲧⲣⲁ-
——	——
ⲙⲁⲣⲉϥ-	ⲙ̄ⲡⲣ̄ⲧⲣⲉϥ-
ⲙⲁⲣⲉⲥ-	ⲙ̄ⲡⲣ̄ⲧⲣⲉⲥ-
ⲙⲁⲣⲛ̄-	ⲙ̄ⲡⲣ̄ⲧⲣⲉⲛ-
——	——
ⲙⲁⲣⲟⲩ-	ⲙ̄ⲡⲣ̄ⲧⲣⲉⲩ-
ⲙⲁⲣⲉ-ⲡⲛⲟⲩⲧⲉ	ⲙ̄ⲡⲣ̄ⲧⲣⲉ-ⲡⲛⲟⲩⲧⲉ

An exhortation or oblique command addressed to one or more 1st or 3d persons: *Let me..., Let us..., Let him/her..., Let them...* Occurs only in dialogue. There is no 2d person form, as this function is fulfilled by the imperative. ⲙⲁⲣⲉϥ-ⲣ̄-ᵠⲟⲩⲟⲉⲓⲛ ⲛ̄ϭⲓ-ⲡⲉⲧⲛ̄ⲟⲩⲟⲉⲓⲛ = Let your light shine. ⲙ̄ⲡⲣ̄ⲧⲣⲉⲛ-ⲥⲱϣ ⲛ̄-ⲧⲉⲭⲁⲣⲓⲥ = Let us not despise grace.

82. 'To Be' *in Coptic.*

(*a*) Statements about an essential, unchangeable characteristic are usually expressed by a nominal sentence or verboid (which you will learn about in lesson thirteen).

ⲡⲛⲟⲩⲧⲉ ⲟⲩⲙⲉ ⲡⲉ = God is true. ⲁⲛⲟⲕ ⲡⲉ ⲡⲟⲩⲟⲉⲓⲛ ⲙ̄-ⲡⲕⲟⲥⲙⲟⲥ = It is I who am the light of the world. ⲟⲩⲥⲁⲃⲏ ⲧⲉ = She is wise. ⲟⲩⲣ̄ⲣⲟ ⲡⲉ = He is a king/kingly in nature. ⲛⲁⲁⲁ-ϥ (verboid) = He is great. [CG 292]

(*b*) Statements about an incidental, temporary, or constructed characteristic are usually expressed by ⲟ ⲛ̄- in a durative sentence (ⲟ is the stative of ⲉⲓⲣⲉ "to make"). Note the Coptic use of zero article (⁰) after ⲛ̄-. ϯ-ⲟ ⲛ̄-⁰ⲱ̄ⲙⲙⲟ = I am a stranger. ⲥ-ⲟ ⲛ̄-⁰ⲥⲁⲃⲏ = She is wise, is acting wisely. ϥ-ⲟ ⲛ̄-⁰ⲟⲩⲟⲉⲓⲛ = It shines. ϥ-ⲟ ⲛ̄-⁰ⲣ̄ⲣⲟ = He is reigning or is (now) king. ϥ-ⲟ ⲛ̄-⁰ⲛⲟϭ = It is great. [CG 179]

(*c*) ϥ-ϣⲟⲟⲡ (stative of ϣⲱⲡⲉ "to become") = He exists. ϥ-ϣⲟⲟⲡ ⲛ̄- = He exists as...

VOCABULARY 10

Learn the conjugation (8 persons plus a prenominal state) of each of the eleven conjugation bases presented in this lesson. In the exercises below, verbs have been taken from the vocabulary of lesson nine.

EXERCISES 10

A. Recite the full paradigm (8 persons and the noun subject), with English translation, of the following. ⲁⲓ̈–ⲣⲁϣⲉ I rejoiced/I have rejoiced (ⲁ⸗). ⲙⲁⲣⲓ–ⲣⲁϣⲉ Let me rejoice (ⲙⲁⲣ⸗). ⲙ̄ⲡⲁϯ–ⲣⲁϣⲉ I have not yet rejoiced (ⲙ̄ⲡⲁⲧ⸗). ⲙ̄ⲡⲓ–ⲣⲁϣⲉ I did not rejoice/I have not rejoiced (ⲙ̄ⲡ⸗). ⲉⲓ̈ⲉ–ⲣⲁϣⲉ I shall rejoice (ⲉ⸗ⲉ–).

B. Practice translating until you are fluent. a. ⲁⲓ̈–ⲧⲁⲉⲓⲟ. ⲙ̄ⲡⲉ–ⲟⲩⲭⲁⲓ̈. b. ⲙ̄ⲡⲁⲧϥ̄–ⲱⲛⲅ̄. ϣⲁⲧⲉⲧⲛ̄–ⲙⲉⲉⲩⲉ. c. ⲙⲉⲩ–ⲣⲁϣⲉ. ⲉⲕⲉ–ⲥⲟⲡⲥ̄. d. ⲛ̄ⲛⲉϥ–ⲥⲟⲟⲩⲛ. ⲙⲁⲣⲓ–ϣⲁϫⲉ. e. ⲙ̄ⲡⲣ̄ⲧⲣⲁ–ⲡⲓⲥⲧⲉⲩⲉ. ⲁⲣⲉ–ⲃⲁⲡⲧⲓⲍⲉ. f. ⲙ̄ⲡϥ̄–ⲙⲉⲧⲁⲛⲟⲉⲓ. ⲙ̄ⲡⲁⲧⲉⲧⲛ̄–ⲁⲣⲛⲁ. g. ϣⲁⲩ–ⲧⲁⲉⲓⲟ. ⲙⲉⲕ–ⲟⲩⲭⲁⲓ̈. h. ⲉϥⲉ–ⲱⲛⲅ̄. ⲛ̄ⲛⲁ–ⲡⲁⲣⲁⲇⲓⲇⲟⲩ. i. ⲙⲁⲣⲉϥ–ⲣⲁϣⲉ. ⲙ̄ⲡⲣ̄ⲧⲣⲉⲥ–ⲥⲟⲡⲥ̄. j. ⲁⲥ–ⲥⲟⲟⲩⲛ. ⲙ̄ⲡⲉⲧⲛ̄–ϣⲁϫⲉ. k. ⲙ̄ⲡⲁⲧⲟⲩ–ⲙⲉⲉⲩⲉ. ϣⲁⲕ–ⲃⲁⲡⲧⲓⲍⲉ. l. ⲙⲉϥ–ⲙⲉⲧⲁⲛⲟⲉⲓ. ⲉⲛⲉ–ⲁⲣⲛⲁ. m. ⲛ̄ⲛⲉ–ⲧⲁⲉⲓⲟ. ⲙⲁⲣⲉⲥ–ⲙⲟⲩ. n. ⲙ̄ⲡⲣ̄ⲧⲣⲉⲩ–ⲱⲛⲅ̄. ⲁⲩ–ⲙⲉⲉⲩⲉ. o. ⲙ̄ⲡⲕ̄–ⲣⲁϣⲉ. ϣⲁϥ–ⲥⲟⲡⲥ̄. p. ⲙⲉⲛ–ⲥⲟⲟⲩⲛ. ⲉⲓ̈ⲉ–ϣⲁϫⲉ. ⲛ̄ⲛⲉ–ⲙⲉⲉⲩⲉ.

C. Translate into Coptic.
a. You (pl.) denied/have denied.
b. You (pl.) did not betray/have not betrayed.
c. You (pl.) have not yet repented.
d. You (pl.) baptize [aorist].
e. You (pl.) do not believe [aorist].

f. You (pl.) shall say.
g. You (pl.) shall not know.
h. You (sing. fem.) denied/have denied.
i. You (sing. fem.) did not betray/have not betrayed.
j. You (sing. fem.) have not yet repented.
k. You (sing. fem.) baptize [aorist].
l. You (sing. fem.) do not believe [aorist].
m. You (sing. fem.) shall say.
n. You (sing. fem.) shall not know.

D. Translate into Coptic. a. They entreated/have entreated. *b.* They did not rejoice/have not rejoiced. *c.* They have not yet thought. *d.* They live [aorist]. *e.* They do not become saved [aorist]. *f.* They shall honor. *g.* They shall not deny. *h.* Let them repent. *i.* Let them not betray.

E. Translate into Coptic. a. The man denied/has denied. *b.* The man did not betray/has not betrayed. *c.* The man has not yet repented. *d.* The man baptizes (aorist). *e.* The man does not say [aorist]. *f.* The man shall know. *g.* The man shall not entreat. *h.* Let the man rejoice. *i.* Let not the man think.

F. Translate into Coptic. a. You (sing. masc.) shall honor your father and your mother. *b.* Let us repent. *c.* Let them not baptize in this place. *d.* I have not denied the Lord. *e.* You (sing. fem.) have betrayed your God. *f.* We have not yet become saved. *g.* The wise man knows (aorist) good and evil.

G. Translate into Coptic. (For vocabulary, cf. **35***; for grammar, cf.* **82***).* *a.* God is wise. *b.* This woman is beloved. *c.* I am not a stranger to (ε–) this city. *d.* Are you hostile to this nation? *e.* Truth is beautiful.

LESSON 11

BOUND STATES OF THE INFINITIVE. DIRECT OBJECT CONSTRUCTIONS. COMPOUND INFINITIVES. IMPERATIVE. VOCATIVE.

83. Many transitive infinitives (**72**) appear in prenominal and prepersonal states (for "states" cf. **50** [CG 167]). These are called the *bound states* of the infinitive. Thus ⲧⲁⲉⲓⲟ (= honor) also appears as ⲧⲁⲉⲓⲉ- and ⲧⲁⲉⲓⲟ⸗. The bound states permit a direct object to be directly suffixed to the infinitive without the intervention of a preposition.

ⲉⲧⲉⲧⲛⲉ–ⲧⲁⲉⲓⲉ–ⲛⲉⲕⲉⲓⲟⲧⲉ = You shall honor your parents
ⲉⲧⲉⲧⲛⲉ–ⲧⲁⲉⲓⲟ–ⲟⲩ = You shall honor them

(*a*) The various combinations of infinitive plus personal pronoun (ⲧⲁⲉⲓⲟ–ⲕ = honor you) follow the same patterns as the prepositions; you should stop now and reread the table in **52**. But you will also find two verb patterns that have no parallel among the prepositions [CG 85, table]:

i. Prepersonals ending in ⲃ⸗, ⲗ⸗, ⲙ⸗, ⲛ⸗, or ⲡ⸗ combining with the personal pronoun to form a syllable (ⲥⲟⲧⲙⲉⲧ *sot* | *met*)

ⲥⲟⲧⲙ⸗ from ⲥⲱⲧⲙ̄ = hear:

ⲥⲟⲧⲙ–ⲉⲧ	ⲥⲟⲧⲙ–ⲛ̄ or ⲥⲟⲧⲙ–ⲉⲛ
ⲥⲟⲧⲙ–ⲉⲕ	ⲥⲉⲧⲙ̄–ⲑⲏⲩⲧⲛ̄
ⲥⲟⲧⲙ–ⲉ	
ⲥⲟⲧⲙ–ⲉϥ	ⲥⲟⲧⲙ–ⲟⲩ
ⲥⲟⲧⲙ–ⲉⲥ	

ii. Prepersonals ending in other consonants.

ϩⲟⲡ⸗, from ϩⲱⲡ = hide:

ϩⲟⲡ–ⲧ̄ or ϩⲟⲡ–ⲧ	ϩⲟⲡ–ⲛ̄
ϩⲟⲡ–ⲕ̄ or ϩⲟⲡ–ⲕ	ϩⲉⲡ–ⲑⲏⲩⲧⲛ̄
ϩⲟⲡ–ⲉ	
ϩⲟⲡ–ϥ̄ or ϩⲟⲡ–ϥ	ϩⲟⲡ–ⲟⲩ
ϩⲟⲡ–ⲥ̄ or ϩⲟⲡ–ⲥ	

(*b*) Alternatively, a preposition can be used to mark the direct object, as you learned in lesson 9 (**72**):

ⲉⲧⲉⲧⲛⲉ–ⲧⲁⲉⲓⲟ ⲛ̄–ⲛⲉⲕⲉⲓⲟⲧⲉ = You shall honor your parents

ⲉⲧⲉⲧⲛⲉ–ⲧⲁⲉⲓⲟ ⲙ̄ⲙⲟ–ⲟⲩ = You shall honor them

As a matter of fact, all infinitives that have bound states also allow ⲛ̄–/ⲙ̄ⲙⲟ⸗ to mark the direct object.

84. *Direct object constructions.* The use or non-use of the bound states or the preposition ⲛ̄–/ⲙ̄ⲙⲟ⸗ is governed by the Stern-Jernstedt Rule, as follows. (Infinitives that do not have bound states are not covered by this rule.) [CG 171]

i. All zero article phrases (**24–26**) *must* be directly suffixed to the prenominal state, in both durative and non-durative sentences.

ⲍ–ⲕⲁ–⁰ⲛⲟⲃⲉ ⲉⲃⲟⲗ = He forgives sins

ⲁⲍ–ⲕⲁ–⁰ⲛⲟⲃⲉ ⲉⲃⲟⲗ = He forgave sins, He has forgiven sins

ii. Otherwise, *in durative sentences the direct object must be marked by* ⲛ̄–/ⲙ̄ⲙⲟ⸗. But in non-durative conjugation, use of the bound states or ⲛ̄/ⲙ̄ⲙⲟ⸗ is optional.

ⲍ–ⲕⲱ ⲉⲃⲟⲗ ⲛ̄–ⲛⲉⲛⲛⲟⲃⲉ = He forgives our sins

ⲁⲍ–ⲕⲱ ⲉⲃⲟⲗ ⲛ̄–ⲛⲉⲛⲛⲟⲃⲉ and ⲁⲍ–ⲕⲁ–ⲛⲉⲛⲛⲟⲃⲉ ⲉⲃⲟⲗ = He forgave our sins, He has forgiven our sins

iii. An infinitive completing ⲛⲁ– (future) is non-durative[19].

ⲍ–ⲛⲁ–ⲕⲱ ⲉⲃⲟⲗ ⲛ̄–ⲛⲉⲛⲛⲟⲃⲉ and ⲍ–ⲛⲁ–ⲕⲁ–ⲛⲉⲛⲛⲟⲃⲉ ⲉⲃⲟⲗ = He will forgive our sins

Likewise, any complementary infinitive (ⲉ–⁰ⲥⲟⲧⲡ–ⲍ̄ = to choose him) or infinitive as a noun (ⲡ–ⲥⲟⲧⲡ–ⲍ̄ = the act of choosing him) is non-durative.

iv. *Exception.* Direct objects of the verb ⲟⲩⲱⲱ, ⲟⲩⲉⲱ–, ⲟⲩⲁⲱ⸗ (= want, desire, love) are always directly suffixed in all kinds of sentence, even the durative. ⲍ–ⲟⲩⲁⲱ–ⲕ̄ = he loves you.

85. Following is a list of all the common infinitives that have bound states. (For all of these, the direct object preposition is ⲛ̄–/ⲙ̄ⲙⲟ⸗.) Try to learn the contents of this table thoroughly. [CG 186–93]

---

[19] Only ⲛⲁ– itself counts as the durative predicate **63**.

LIST OF COMMON VERBS THAT HAVE
BOUND STATES OF THE INFINITIVE

1. Biconsonantal

ⲃⲱⲗ = release, interpret	ⲃⲁ̄–	ⲃⲟⲗ⸗
ⲃⲱⲗ ⲛ̄– ⲉⲃⲟⲗ = destroy, dissolve	ⲃⲁ̄– ⲉⲃⲟⲗ	ⲃⲟⲗ⸗ ⲉⲃⲟⲗ
ⲕⲱⲧ = build, build up	ⲕⲉⲧ–	ⲕⲟⲧ⸗
ⲙⲟⲩⲣ = bind	ⲙⲣ̄–, ⲙⲉⲣ–	ⲙⲟⲣ⸗
ⲙⲟⲩϩ = fill	ⲙⲉϩ–	ⲙⲁϩ⸗ (sic)
ⲡⲱϣ = divide	ⲡⲉϣ–	ⲡⲟϣ⸗
ⲟⲩⲱⲙ = eat	ⲟⲩⲉⲙ–	ⲟⲩⲟⲙ⸗
ⲟⲩⲱϣ = want, desire, love	ⲟⲩⲉϣ–	ⲟⲩⲁϣ⸗ (sic)
ⲟⲩⲱϩ = lay upon, occupy	ⲟⲩⲉϩ–	ⲟⲩⲁϩ⸗ (sic)
ⲱϣ ['ōš] = read	ⲉϣ–	ⲟϣ⸗
ϣⲱⲡ = receive, buy	ϣⲉⲡ–	ϣⲟⲡ⸗
ϩⲱⲡ = hide	ϩⲉⲡ–	ϩⲟⲡ⸗
ϫⲱⲕ ⲛ̄– ⲉⲃⲟⲗ = fill	ϫⲉⲕ– ⲉⲃⲟⲗ	ϫⲟⲕ⸗ ⲉⲃⲟⲗ

2. Biconsonantal with final ⲉ

ⲕⲱⲧⲉ = turn	ⲕⲉⲧ–	ⲕⲟⲧ⸗
ⲛⲟⲩϫⲉ = throw, cast	ⲛⲉϫ–	ⲛⲟϫ⸗

3. Triconsonantal

ⲙⲟⲩⲟⲩⲧ [mōwt **12**] = kill	ⲙⲟⲩⲧ–, ⲙⲉⲩⲧ–	ⲙⲟⲟⲩⲧ⸗
ⲥⲟⲡⲥ̄ = entreat, console	ⲥⲉⲡⲥ̄–	
ⲥⲱⲧⲡ̄ = choose	ⲥⲉⲧⲡ̄–	ⲥⲟⲧⲡ⸗
ⲥⲱⲟⲩϩ = gather	ⲥⲉⲩϩ–	ⲥⲟⲟⲩϩ⸗
ⲟⲩⲱⲛϩ̄ ⲛ̄– ⲉⲃⲟⲗ = reveal	ⲟⲩⲉⲛϩ̄– ⲉⲃⲟⲗ	ⲟⲩⲟⲛϩ⸗ ⲉⲃⲟⲗ
ϣⲱⲱⲧ [šō't **9**] = cut off, lack	ϣⲉⲧ–, ϣⲉⲉⲧ–	ϣⲁⲁⲧ⸗ (sic)

4. Triconsonantal, third consonant is ⲃ, ⲗ, ⲙ, ⲛ, *or* ⲣ

ⲥⲱⲧⲙ̄ = hear	ⲥⲉⲧⲙ̄–	ⲥⲟⲧⲙ⸗
ⲧⲱϩⲙ̄ = invite	ⲧⲉϩⲙ̄–	ⲧⲁϩⲙ⸗ (sic)

5. Initial ⲧ, final personal suffix

ⲧⲟⲩⲛⲟⲥ = awaken	ⲧⲟⲩⲛⲉⲥ–	ⲧⲟⲩⲛⲟⲥ⸗
ⲧⲛ̄ⲛⲟⲟⲩ = send (hither), bring	ⲧⲛ̄ⲛⲉⲩ–	ⲧⲛ̄ⲛⲟⲟⲩ⸗
ϫⲟⲟⲩ [ⲧϣⲟⲟⲩ] = send (away)	ϫⲉⲩ–	ϫⲟⲟⲩ⸗

6. Initial ⲧ, final ⲟ

ⲧⲃ̄ⲃⲟ = purify	ⲧⲃ̄ⲃⲉ–	ⲧⲃ̄ⲃⲟ⸗
ⲧⲁⲉⲓⲟ = honor	ⲧⲁⲉⲓⲉ–	ⲧⲁⲉⲓⲟ⸗
ⲧⲁⲕⲟ = ruin	ⲧⲁⲕⲉ–	ⲧⲁⲕⲟ⸗

ⲕⲧⲟ [for ⲧⲕⲧⲟ] reflexive = return	ⲕⲧⲉ–	ⲕⲧⲟ⸗
ⲧⲁⲗⲟ = take up, mount, board	ⲧⲁⲗⲉ–	ⲧⲁⲗⲟ⸗
ⲧⲁⲙⲟ = teach	ⲧⲁⲙⲉ–	ⲧⲁⲙⲟ⸗
ⲧⲁⲟⲩⲟ = send forth	ⲧⲁⲟⲩⲉ–	ⲧⲁⲟⲩⲟ⸗
ⲧⲁϣⲟ = make numerous, multiply	ⲧⲁϣⲉ–	ⲧⲁϣⲟ⸗
ϫⲛⲟⲩ [tšnō] = ask, interrogate	ϫⲛⲉ–	ϫⲛⲟⲩ⸗
ϫⲡⲟ [tšpo] = produce, get	ϫⲡⲉ–	ϫⲡⲟ⸗
ⲧⲁϩⲟ = seize, attain, get to	ⲧⲁϩⲉ–	ⲧⲁϩⲟ⸗
ⲧⲁϩⲟ ⲛ̄– ⲉⲣⲁⲧ⸗ reflexive = stand, make to stand	ⲧⲁϩⲉ– ⲉⲣⲁⲧ⸗	ⲧⲁϩⲟ⸗ ⲉⲣⲁⲧ⸗
ⲧⲁϫⲣⲟ = make firm, confirm	ⲧⲁϫⲣⲉ–	ⲧⲁϫⲣⲟ⸗

7. In prepersonal state the last syllable contains ⲱ

ⲙⲟⲥⲧⲉ = hate	ⲙⲉⲥⲧⲉ–	ⲙⲉⲥⲧⲱ⸗
ⲥⲟⲃⲧⲉ = prepare	ⲥⲃ̄ⲧⲉ–	ⲥⲃ̄ⲧⲱⲧ⸗
ⲥⲟⲡⲥ̄ = entreat	ⲥⲡ̄ⲥⲡ̄–	ⲥⲡ̄ⲥⲱⲡ⸗
ⲥⲟⲟⲩⲛ = know	ⲥⲟⲩⲛ̄–	ⲥⲟⲩⲱⲛ⸗
ϣⲧⲟⲣⲧⲣ̄ = disturb	ϣⲧⲣ̄ⲧⲣ̄–	ϣⲧⲣ̄ⲧⲱⲣ⸗

8. In prepersonal state final ⲧ⸗ appears

ⲉⲓⲛⲉ = bring	ⲛ̄–	ⲛ̄ⲧ⸗
ⲙⲉ = love	ⲙⲉⲣⲉ–	ⲙⲉⲣⲓⲧ⸗
ϥⲓ = take, take away, pick up	ϥⲓ–	ϥⲓⲧ⸗
ϫⲓ = take, get, receive	ϫⲓ–	ϫⲓⲧ⸗
ϫⲓⲥⲉ = raise up	ϫⲉⲥⲧ– (sic)	ϫⲁⲥⲧ⸗ (sic)

9. Prepersonal state ends with a double vowel

ⲉⲓⲣⲉ = make, do	ⲣ̄–	ⲁⲁ⸗
ⲕⲱ = put	ⲕⲁ–	ⲕⲁⲁ⸗
ⲕⲱ ⲛ̄– ⲉⲃⲟⲗ = forgive (a sin), release	ⲕⲁ– ⲉⲃⲟⲗ	ⲕⲁⲁ⸗ ⲉⲃⲟⲗ
ⲥⲱ = drink	ⲥⲉ–	ⲥⲟⲟ⸗
ϯ = give	ϯ–	ⲧⲁⲁ⸗
ϫⲱ = say	ϫⲉ–	ϫⲟⲟ⸗

10. Some others

ⲥϩⲁⲓ̈ = write	ⲥϩⲁⲓ–, ⲥⲉϩ–	ⲥϩⲁⲓ̈⸗, ⲥⲁϩ⸗ (sic)
ⲧⲱⲟⲩⲛ = raise up	ⲧⲟⲩⲛ–	ⲧⲱⲟⲩⲛ⸗
ϫⲟ = sow	ϫⲉ–	ϫⲟ⸗

86. *Compound infinitives* [CG 180] are fixed expressions

ϯ–⁰ⲃⲁⲡⲧⲓⲥⲙⲁ = baptize (give-⁰baptism)
ϫⲓ–⁰ⲃⲁⲡⲧⲓⲥⲙⲁ = be baptized (get-⁰baptism)

consisting of a zero article phrase suffixed to a prenominal state. Especially common are those built upon ⲣ̄- (= do, make, act as), ϯ- (= give, produce), and ϫⲓ- (= get, receive), though many others occur also. This is a very common kind of formation.

ϯ-⁰ⲥⲃⲱ teach (give-⁰teaching)
ⲣ̄-⁰ⲛⲟⲃⲉ to sin (do-⁰sin)
ⲣ̄-⁰ϣⲟⲣⲡ̄ precede (act-as-⁰first)
ⲧⲁϣⲉ-⁰ⲟⲉⲓϣ proclaim, evangelize (multiply-⁰cry)

Greek equivalents are often denominal verbs: ⲣ̄-⁰ϩⲙ̄ϩⲁⲗ = δουλεύειν serve (δοῦλος = ϩⲙ̄ϩⲁⲗ). ⲣ̄-⁰ϩⲟⲧⲉ = φοβεῖσθαι to fear (φόβος = ϩⲟⲧⲉ). A few compounds contain a possessed noun **54** instead of a zero article phrase: ⲧⲥⲁⲃⲉ-ⲉⲓⲁⲧ⸗ = teach (instruct-eyes-of).

Some compound infinitives are, as a whole, capable of having a direct object; the preposition used to mark such a direct object varies from one expression to another.

ϯ-⁰ⲥⲃⲱ ⲛⲁ-ϥ = teach (give-⁰lesson for) him
ⲣ̄-⁰ⲭⲣⲉⲓⲁ ⲙ̄ⲙⲟ-ϥ = need (produce-⁰need of) it
ϫⲓ-⁰ⲥⲃⲱ ⲉⲣⲟ-ϥ = learn (receive-⁰lesson about) it

Compound infinitives made from ⲣ̄- meaning "have or perform the function or characteristic of"

ⲣ̄-⁰ϩⲙ̄ϩⲁⲗ = serve
ⲣ̄-⁰ⲣ̄ⲣⲟ = reign
ⲣ̄-⁰ϫⲟⲉⲓⲥ = be master

appear in durative sentences as ⲟ† ⲛ̄- (ⲟ† is the stative corresponding to ⲣ̄-, from the verb ⲉⲓⲣⲉ)

ⲟ† ⲛ̄-⁰ϩⲙ̄ϩⲁⲗ = serve
ⲟ† ⲛ̄-⁰ⲣ̄ⲣⲟ = reign
ⲟ† ⲛ̄-⁰ϫⲟⲉⲓⲥ = be master

Some compound infinitives contain a definite or possessive article. E.g.

ⲣ̄-ⲡⲙⲉⲉⲩⲉ ⲛ̄- = remember (do-the-thinking of)
ⲣ̄-ⲡⲉϥⲙⲉⲉⲩⲉ = remember him (do-his-thinking)

THE IMPERATIVE AND VOCATIVE

87. The affirmative imperative has the same form as the infinitive (with its bound states if any). [CG 364-72] For special affirmative imperative forms, see box below.

ⲥⲟⲧⲡ̄-ⲟⲩ or ⲥⲱⲧⲡ̄ ⲙ̄ⲙⲟ-ⲟⲩ = Choose them
ⲥⲉⲧⲡ̄-ⲡⲉⲓ̈ⲗⲁⲟⲥ or ⲥⲱⲧⲡ̄ ⲙ̄-ⲡⲉⲓ̈ⲗⲁⲟⲥ = Choose this people

ⲧⲁϣⲉ-ᵠⲟⲉⲓϣ = Evangelize
ⲟⲩⲱⲙ = Eat

Negative imperatives are formed by prefixing ⲙ̄ⲡⲣ̄- (or ⲙ̄ⲡⲱⲣ ⲉ-) to the infinitive.

ⲙ̄ⲡⲣ̄-ⲥⲟⲧⲡ-ⲟⲩ or ⲙ̄ⲡⲣ̄-ⲥⲱⲧⲡ̄ ⲙ̄ⲙⲟ-ⲟⲩ = Do not choose them
ⲙ̄ⲡⲣ̄-ⲥⲉⲧⲡ̄-ⲡⲉⲓ̈ⲗⲁⲟⲥ or ⲙ̄ⲡⲣ̄-ⲥⲱⲧⲡ̄ ⲙ̄-ⲡⲉⲓ̈ⲗⲁⲟⲥ = Do not choose this people
ⲙ̄ⲡⲣ̄-ⲧⲁϣⲉ-ᵠⲟⲉⲓϣ = Do not evangelize
ⲙ̄ⲡⲣ̄-ⲟⲩⲱⲙ = Do not eat

There are *special affirmative imperatives* of ten verbs; these are used instead of the corresponding infinitive. Note that most begin with the letter ⲁ. (Their negatives are formed with ⲙ̄ⲡⲣ̄- + normal infinitive.) Here, for reference, is the full list. [CG 366]

ⲁⲗⲟ⸗ (reflexive) = cease (infinitive ⲗⲟ)
ⲁⲙⲟⲩ = come (infin. ⲉⲓ)
  ⲁⲙⲟⲩ [said to one male]
  ⲁⲙⲏ [said to one female]
  ⲁⲙⲏⲉⲓⲧⲛ̄ or ⲁⲙⲏⲉⲓⲛ [said to more than one person]
ⲁⲛⲓⲛⲉ = bring (ⲁⲛⲓ-, ⲁⲛⲓ⸗) (infin. ⲉⲓⲛⲉ)
ⲁⲛⲁⲩ = look (infin. ⲛⲁⲩ)
ⲁⲣⲓⲣⲉ = do, make (ⲁⲣⲓ-, ⲁⲣⲓ⸗) (infin. ⲉⲓⲣⲉ)
ⲁⲩ- or ⲁⲩⲉ- (ⲁⲩⲉⲓ⸗) = hand over (no infinitive)
ⲁⲟⲩⲱⲛ = open (ⲟⲩⲛ̄-) (infin. ⲟⲩⲱⲛ)
ⲁⲝⲓ- or ⲁⲝⲉ- (ⲁⲝⲓ⸗) = say (infin. ⲝⲱ)
ⲙⲁ- (but usually ϯ, ϯ-, ⲧⲁⲁ⸗) = give (infin. ϯ)
ⲙⲟ or ⲙⲱ = take (no infinitive)

For example: ⲁⲙⲟⲩ ⲉⲃⲟⲗ ϩⲙ̄-ⲡⲣⲱⲙⲉ "Come out of the man!"; ⲓ̅ⲥ̅ ⲁⲣⲓ-ⲡⲁⲙⲉⲉⲩⲉ ⲡϫⲟⲉⲓⲥ "Jesus, remember me, Lord."

ⲙⲁ- is optionally prefixed to the imperative of compound infinitives formed on ϯ- (= give) and causative verbs of the class ⲧⲁⲉⲓⲟ (initial ⲧ, final ⲟ). Thus ⲙⲁ-ϯ-ᵠⲥⲃⲱ = Teach. ⲙⲁ-ⲧⲁⲉⲓⲉ-ⲡⲉⲕⲉⲓⲱⲧ ⲙⲛ̄-ⲧⲉⲕⲙⲁⲁⲩ = Honor your father and your mother. [CG 367]

88. The *vocative* (summoning the attention of the person one is speaking to) must be expressed as a *definite* article phrase or as a personal name. ⲧⲉⲥϩⲓⲙⲉ = O woman! ⲡϫⲟⲉⲓⲥ = O Lord! ⲡⲁⲛⲟⲩⲧⲉ ⲡⲁⲛⲟⲩⲧⲉ = My God, My God! ⲙⲁⲣⲓⲁ = O Mary! [CG 137]

'Yes' and 'No' in Coptic [CG 241]

There are several ways to say 'Yes' or 'No', and Coptic speakers selected them according to the syntax and meaning of what was being affirmed or denied.

'Yes'	Syntax	Compare
ογον	Yes there is	ογν̄- **63**
εϩε	(Yes)	?
ϣο	Yes he (etc.) does	ϣⲁ= **79**
ϲε	(Yes)	?
'No'		
м̄мон	No there isn't	мⲛ̄- **63**
м̄пε	No he (etc.) didn't	м̄п= **77**
ⲛ̄ⲛо	No he (etc.) doesn't	ⲛ̄ⲛε= **80**
м̄пⲱр	Don't!	м̄пр̄- **87**

---

89. The following five verbs

ⲡⲱⲧ, ⲡⲏⲧ[†] = run
ⲉⲓ, ⲛⲏⲩ[†]   = come
ⲃⲱⲕ, ⲃⲏⲕ[†] = go
ϩⲱⲗ, ϩⲏⲗ[†] = fly
ϩⲉ, ϩⲏⲩ[†]   = fall[20]

behave in a peculiar way. When they are used in a durative sentence, only the stative can occur, and the stative expresses on-going motion. [CG 168(c)] Outside of the durative sentence, only the infinitive occurs, but with the same meaning. Thus

†-ⲃⲏⲕ I am going, I go. ⲁⲓ̈-ⲃⲱⲕ I went, I have gone
†-ϩⲏⲗ I am flying, I fly. ⲁⲓ̈-ϩⲱⲗ I flew, I have flown
†-ϩⲏⲩ I am falling, I fall. ⲁⲓ̈-ϩⲉ I fell, I have fallen

Remember these five verbs—Run, come, go, fly up, fall down.

---

[20] Also ϩⲉ ⲉ-, ϩⲏⲩ[†] ⲉ- find; ϩⲉ ⲉⲃⲟⲗ, ϩⲏⲩ[†] ⲉⲃⲟⲗ perish.

VOCABULARY 11

*Learn the five verbs described in paragraph **89** and remember their unusual usage.*

ⲡⲱⲧ, ⲡⲏⲧ†	run	τρέχειν, φεύγειν
ⲉⲓ, ⲛⲏⲩ†	come	ἔρχεσθαι
ⲃⲱⲕ, ⲃⲏⲕ†	go	πορεύεσθαι, ἀπέρχεσθαι
ⲡⲱⲗ, ⲡⲏⲗ†	fly	πεταννύναι
ⲡⲉ, ⲡⲏⲩ†	fall	πίπτειν

More verbs: Religion

ⲙⲟⲩⲣ (ⲙⲡ̄-, ⲙⲟⲣ⸗) ⲙⲏⲣ†	bind, tie	δεῖν
ⲃⲱⲗ (ⲃⲁ̄-, ⲃⲟⲗ⸗) ⲃⲏⲗ†	loosen, untie, interpret	λύειν
ⲣ̄-ᵒⲛⲟⲃⲉ	sin	ἁμαρτάνειν
ⲣⲉϥ- (masc. or fem.)	one who…, a thing which…	(deverbal nouns)
ⲣⲉϥ-ⲣ̄-ᵒⲛⲟⲃⲉ (masc., fem.)	sinner	ἁμαρτωλός
ⲕⲱ ⲉⲃⲟⲗ (ⲕⲁ-, ⲕⲁⲁ⸗) ⲕⲏ†	release, loosen; forgive	ἀφιέναι
ⲥⲙⲟⲩ ⲉ-, ⲥⲙⲁⲙⲁⲁⲧ†	praise, bless	εὐλογεῖν
ⲧⲁⲉⲓⲟ (ⲧⲁⲉⲓⲉ-, ⲧⲁⲉⲓⲟ⸗) ⲧⲁⲉⲓⲏⲩ†	honor	τιμᾶν
ⲟⲩⲱϣⲧ̄ ⲛ̄-/ⲛⲁ⸗	worship, bow before, greet	προσκυνεῖν
ⲙⲉ (ⲙⲉⲣⲉ-, ⲙⲉⲣⲓⲧ⸗)	love	ἀγαπᾶν
ϣⲗⲏⲗ	pray	προσεύχεσθαι
ⲥⲟⲡⲥ̄ (ⲥⲉⲡⲥ̄-), also ⲥⲟⲡⲥⲡ̄ (ⲥⲡ̄ⲥⲡ̄-, ⲥⲡ̄ⲥⲱⲡ⸗) ⲥⲡ̄ⲥⲱⲡ†	entreat, console	παρακαλεῖν
ⲧⲱϩⲙ̄ (ⲧⲉϩⲙ-, ⲧⲁϩⲙ⸗) ⲧⲁϩⲙ̄†	summon, invite	καλεῖν
ⲥⲱⲧⲡ̄ (ⲥⲉⲧⲡ̄-, ⲥⲟⲧⲡ⸗) ⲥⲟⲧⲡ̄†	choose	ἐκλέγεσθαι
ⲧⲃ̄ⲃⲟ (ⲧⲃ̄ⲃⲉ-, ⲧⲃ̄ⲃⲟ⸗) ⲧⲃ̄ⲃⲏⲩ†	purify	καθαρίζειν
*ⲕⲣⲓⲛⲉ ⲛ̄-/ⲙ̄ⲙⲟ⸗	judge	
ⲙ̄ⲡϣⲁ ⲛ̄-/ⲙ̄ⲙⲟ⸗	become worthy of	ἄξιος εἶναι

ⲧⲁϣⲉ-⁰ⲟⲉⲓϣ ⲛ̄-/ⲙ̄ⲙⲟ=	proclaim, preach	κηρύσσειν, εὐαγγελίζειν

Daily life (verbs)

ⲕⲱⲧ (ⲕⲉⲧ-, ⲕⲟⲧ=) ⲕⲏⲧ†	build, edify	οἰκοδομεῖν
ⲟⲩⲱⲙ (ⲟⲩⲉⲙ-, ⲟⲩⲟⲙ=)	eat	φαγεῖν
ⲥⲱ (ⲥⲉ-, ⲥⲟⲟ=)	drink	πίνειν
ϫⲟ (ϫⲉ-, ϫⲟ=) ϫⲏⲩ†	sow (seed)	σπείρειν
ⲟⲩⲱϩ (ⲟⲩⲉϩ-, ⲟⲩⲁϩ=) ⲟⲩⲏϩ†	put, lay; dwell	προστιθέναι, κατοικεῖν
ϣⲱⲱⲧ (ϣⲉⲧ-/ϣⲉⲉⲧ-, ϣⲁⲁⲧ=) ϣⲁⲁⲧ†	cut, sacrifice; (ϣⲁⲁⲧ† ⲛ̄-/ ⲙ̄ⲙⲟ=) lack	ἐκκόπτειν, ὑστερεῖν

Conjunctions

*ⲧⲟⲧⲉ	thereupon, then, next	
ϫⲉⲕⲁⲁⲥ or ϫⲉⲕⲁⲥ (+ optative)	*so that . . . might*	ἵνα
ϫⲉ- (+ optative)	*so that . . . might*	ἵνα
ϫⲉ- (+ clause, *not* optative)	because; for	ὅτι
ⲉϣϫⲉ-	supposing that, since, if	εἰ
ⲉϣⲱⲡⲉ	if (ever)	ἐάν, εἰ
*ⲟⲩⲇⲉ or *ⲟⲩⲧⲉ (the two forms are equated in Coptic)	nor; and . . . not	

Interjections

ⲉⲓⲥ-, ⲉⲓⲥϩⲏⲏⲧⲉ (and other spellings)	lo! behold! (marks a new moment in narrative)	ἰδού
*ϩⲁⲙⲏⲛ (ἀμήν)	amen, may it be	

EXERCISES 11

A. *Translate into Coptic, giving alternate translations where possible.*

a. He bound the man.
b. He released the man.
c. He purified the man.
d. He honored the man.
e. He loved the man.
f. He chose the man.
g. He will bind the man.
h. He will release the man.
i. He will purify the man.
j. He will honor the man.
k. He will love the man.
l. He will choose the man.
m. He is binding the man.
n. He is releasing the man.
o. He is purifying the man.
p. He is honoring the man.
q. He is choosing the man.

B. *Translate into Coptic using the bound state and going through all eight persons and the noun (ⲡⲣⲱⲙⲉ) as suffixed object.*

a. He bound me, He bound you, . . . etc.
b. He released me, . . .
c. He purified me, . . .
d. He honored me, . . .
e. He loved me, . . .
f. He chose me, . . .
g. He drank me, . . .

C. *Translate.* a. ⲁⲩ-ⲙⲟⲣ-ⲉⲧ [cf. **83** (*a*)(i)]. b. ⲙ̄ⲡⲟⲩ-ⲃⲟⲗ-ⲉ. c. ⲙ̄ⲡⲁⲧⲟⲩ-ⲕⲁⲁ-ⲥ. d. ⲁⲩ-ⲧⲁⲉⲓⲉ-ⲧⲏⲩⲧⲛ̄. e. ⲙ̄ⲡⲟⲩ-ⲙⲉⲣⲓⲧ-ⲟⲩ. f. ⲙ̄ⲡⲁⲧⲟⲩ-ⲥⲡ̄ⲥⲱⲡ-ⲕ̄. g. ⲁⲩ-ⲧⲁϩⲙ-ⲟⲩ. h. ⲙ̄ⲡⲟⲩ-ⲥⲟⲧⲡ-ⲛ̄. i. ⲙ̄ⲡⲁⲧⲟⲩ-ⲧⲃ̄ⲃⲟ-ï. j. ⲁⲩ-ⲕⲟⲧ-ⲉ. k. ⲙ̄ⲡⲟⲩ-ⲟⲩⲟⲙ-ⲉⲥ. l. ⲙ̄ⲡⲁⲧⲟⲩ-ϫⲟ-ⲟⲩ. m. ⲁⲩ-ⲥⲟⲟ-ⲩ. n. ⲙ̄ⲡⲟⲩ-ⲟⲩⲁϩ-ⲕ̄. o. ⲙ̄ⲡⲁⲧⲟⲩ-ϣⲁⲁⲧ-ⲛ̄. p. ⲁⲥ-ⲙⲟⲣ-ⲉⲕ. q. ⲙ̄ⲡⲥ̄-ⲃⲟⲗ-ⲉϥ. r. ⲙ̅ⲡⲁⲧⲥ̅–ⲕⲁⲁ–ⲛ. s. ⲁⲥ–ⲧⲁⲉⲓⲟ–ⲟⲩ. t. ⲙ̅ⲡⲥ̅–ⲙⲉⲣⲓⲧ–ⲧ̅. u. ⲙ̅ⲡⲁⲧⲥ̅–ⲥ̅ⲡⲥⲱⲡ–ϥ̅. v. ⲁⲥ–ⲧⲁϩⲙ–ⲛ̅. w. ⲙ̅ⲡⲥ̅–ⲧⲁϩⲙ–ⲉⲛ. x. ⲙ̅ⲡⲁⲧⲥ̅–ⲧⲃ̅ⲃⲟ–ⲕ. y. ⲁⲥ–ⲕⲟⲧ–ϥ̅. z. ⲙ̅ⲡⲥ̅–ⲟⲩⲟⲙ–ⲉⲛ. aa. ⲙ̅ⲡⲁⲧⲥ̅–ϫⲟ–ϥ. bb. ⲁⲥ–ⲥⲟⲟ–ⲧ. cc. ⲙ̅ⲡⲥ̅–ⲟⲩⲁϩ–ϥ̅. dd. ⲙ̅ⲡⲁⲧⲥ̅–ϣⲉⲧ–ⲧⲏⲩⲧⲛ̅.

D. Translate into Coptic, giving alternate translations where possible (cf. **84***).* *a*. He honors (*or* is honoring) the prophet. *b*. He honored the prophet. *c*. He will honor the prophet. *d*. He honors prophets. *e*. He honored prophets. *f*. He will honor prophets. *g*. He loves the prophet (ⲟⲩⲱϣ = love). *h*. He loved the prophet. *i*. He will love the prophet.

E. Reading selections from the New Testament.

1. ⲁϥ–ⲉⲓ ⲁϥ–ⲟⲩⲱϩ ϩⲛ̅–ⲕⲁⲫⲁⲣⲛⲁⲟⲩⲙ[21]. Matthew 4:13
2. ⲛ̅–ϥ–ⲛⲁ–ⲕⲱ ⲛⲏ–ⲧⲛ̅ ⲁⲛ ⲉⲃⲟⲗ ⲛ̅–ⲛⲉⲧⲛ̅ⲛⲟⲃⲉ. Matthew 6:15
3. ⲙ̅ⲡⲣ̅–ⲕⲣⲓⲛⲉ ϫⲉⲕⲁⲥ ⲛ̅ⲛⲉⲩ–ⲕⲣⲓⲛⲉ ⲙ̅ⲙⲱ–ⲧⲛ̅. Matthew 7:1
4. ⲟⲩⲁϣ ⲙ̅–ⲙⲓⲛⲉ ⲡⲉ ⲡⲁï. Matthew 8:27
5. ⲉⲧⲃⲉ–ⲟⲩ ⲡⲉⲧⲛ̅ⲥⲁϩ ⲟⲩⲱⲙ ⲙⲛ̅–ⲛ̅ⲣⲉϥ–ⲣ̅–$^{\emptyset}$ⲛⲟⲃⲉ. Matthew 9:11 alt.
6. ⲛ̅–ϥ–ⲙ̅ⲡϣⲁ ⲙ̅ⲙⲟ–ï ⲁⲛ. Matthew 10:37
7. ⲁⲙⲏⲉⲓⲧⲛ̅ (cf. **87** [box]) ϣⲁⲣⲟ–ï ⲟⲩⲟⲛ ⲛⲓⲙ. Matthew 11:28
8. ⲃⲱⲗ ⲉⲣⲟ–ⲛ ⲛ̅–ⲧⲡⲁⲣⲁⲃⲟⲗⲏ[22]. Matthew 13:36
9. ⲛ̅ⲛⲉϥ–ⲧⲁⲉⲓⲟ ⲙ̅–ⲡⲉϥⲉⲓⲱⲧ. Matthew 15:6
10. ⲉϩⲣⲁï ⲉϫⲛ̅–ⲧⲉïⲡⲉⲧⲣⲁ[23] ϯ–ⲛⲁ–ⲕⲱⲧ ⲛ̅–ⲧⲁⲉⲕⲕⲗⲏⲥⲓⲁ. Matthew 16:18
11. ⲡⲃⲁⲡⲧⲓⲥⲙⲁ ⲛ̅–ⲓⲱϩⲁⲛⲛⲏⲥ ⲟⲩⲉⲃⲟⲗ ⲧⲱⲛ ⲡⲉ. ⲟⲩⲉⲃⲟⲗ ϩⲛ̅–ⲧⲡⲉ ⲡⲉ ϫⲛ̅–ⲟⲩⲉⲃⲟⲗ ϩⲛ̅–ⲛ̅ⲣⲱⲙⲉ ⲡⲉ. Matthew 21:25
12. ⲉⲧⲃⲉ–ⲟⲩ ϭⲉ ⲙ̅ⲡⲉⲧⲛ̅–ⲡⲓⲥⲧⲉⲩⲉ ⲉⲣⲟ–ϥ. Matthew 21:25
13. ⲧⲟⲧⲉ ⲁϥ–ⲕⲱ ⲛⲁ–ⲩ ⲉⲃⲟⲗ ⲛ̅–ⲃⲁⲣⲁⲃⲃⲁⲥ[24]. Matthew 27:26
14. ϥ–ⲙ̅ⲡϣⲁ ⲙ̅–ⲡⲙⲟⲩ. Mark 14:64
15. ⲧⲉ–ⲥⲙⲁⲙⲁⲁⲧ ϩⲛ̅–ⲛⲉϩⲓⲟⲙⲉ. Luke 1:42 alt.
16. ⲉⲓⲥϩⲏⲏⲧⲉ ⲅⲁⲣ ϯ–ⲛⲁ–ⲧⲁϣⲉ–$^{\emptyset}$ⲟⲉⲓϣ ⲛⲏ–ⲧⲛ̅ ⲛ̅–ⲟⲩⲛⲟϭ ⲛ̅–ⲣⲁϣⲉ. Luke 2:10
17. ⲁ–ⲥⲩⲙⲉⲱⲛ[25] ⲇⲉ ⲥⲙⲟⲩ ⲉⲣⲟ–ⲟⲩ. Luke 2:34
18. ϥ–ⲙⲉ ⲅⲁⲣ ⲙ̅–ⲡⲉⲛϩⲉⲑⲛⲟⲥ. Luke 7:5
19. ⲟⲩ ⲧⲉ. ⲁⲩⲱ ⲟⲩⲁϣ ⲙ̅–ⲙⲓⲛⲉ ⲧⲉ ⲧⲉïⲥϩⲓⲙⲉ. ⲟⲩⲣⲉϥ–ⲣ̅–$^{\emptyset}$ⲛⲟⲃⲉ ⲧⲉ. Luke 7:39 alt.

[21] ⲕⲁⲫⲁⲣⲛⲁⲟⲩⲙ (place name) Capernaum.
[22] ⲡⲁⲣⲁⲃⲟⲗⲏ parable.
[23] ⲡⲉⲧⲣⲁ rock, rocky outcrop.
[24] ⲃⲁⲣⲁⲃⲃⲁⲥ (personal name) Barabbas.
[25] ⲥⲩⲙⲉⲱⲛ (personal name) Simeon.

20. ⲃⲱⲕ. ⲧⲁϣⲉ-ᵠⲟⲉⲓϣ ⲛ̄-ⲧⲙⲛ̄ⲧ-ⲉⲣⲟ ⲙ̄-ⲡⲛⲟⲩⲧⲉ. Luke 9:60
21. ⲡⲁⲉⲓⲱⲧ ⲁⲓ̈-ⲣ̄-ᵠⲛⲟⲃⲉ ⲉ-ⲧⲡⲉ ⲁⲩⲱ ⲙ̄-ⲡⲉⲕⲙ̄ⲧⲟ ⲉⲃⲟⲗ. Luke 15:18
22. ⲙ̄ⲡⲁⲧⲉ-ⲧⲁⲟⲩⲛⲟⲩ ⲉⲓ. John 2:4
23. . . . sent His son not ϫⲉ-ⲉϥⲉ-ⲕⲣⲓⲛⲉ ⲙ̄-ⲡⲕⲟⲥⲙⲟⲥ ⲁⲗⲗⲁ ϫⲉⲕⲁⲥ ⲉⲣⲉ-ⲡⲕⲟⲥⲙⲟⲥ ⲟⲩϫⲁⲓ̈ ⲉⲃⲟⲗ ϩⲓⲧⲟⲟⲧ-ϥ̄. John 3:17
24. ⲙⲉϥ-ⲉⲓ ϣⲁ-ⲡⲟⲩⲟⲉⲓⲛ. John 3:20
25. ⲙⲛ̄-ᵠⲡⲣⲟⲫⲏⲧⲏⲥ ⲧⲁⲉⲓⲏⲩ ϩⲣⲁⲓ̈ ϩⲙ̄-ⲡⲉϥϯⲙⲉ²⁶. John 4:44
26. ⲡⲉⲓⲱⲧ ⲅⲁⲣ ⲙⲉ ⲙ̄-ⲡϣⲏⲣⲉ ⲁⲩⲱ ϥ-ⲧⲥⲁⲃⲟ²⁷ ⲙ̄ⲙⲟ-ϥ ⲉ-ϩⲱⲃ ⲛⲓⲙ. John 5:20
27. ⲡⲁⲟⲩⲟⲉⲓϣ ⲙ̄ⲡⲁⲧϥ̄-ⲉⲓ. John 7:6 alt.
28. ⲙ̄ⲡϥ̄-ⲟⲩⲱⲙ ⲟⲩⲇⲉ ⲙ̄ⲡϥ̄-ⲥⲱ. Acts 9:9
29. ⲧⲉⲧⲛ̄-ⲙ̄ⲡϣⲁ ⲙ̄-ⲡⲱⲛϩ̄. Acts 13:46
30. ⲧⲉⲛⲟⲩ ϭⲉ ⲉⲓⲥϩⲏⲏⲧⲉ ϯ-ⲙⲏⲣ ϩⲙ̄-ⲡⲉⲡ̄ⲛ̄ⲁ. Acts 20:22 alt.
31. ⲁⲛ-ⲃⲱⲕ ⲉϩⲟⲩⲛ ⲉ-ⲡⲏⲓ̈ ⲙ̄-ⲫⲓⲗⲓⲡⲡⲟⲥ²⁸ ⲡⲣⲉϥ-ⲧⲁϣⲉ-ᵠⲟⲉⲓϣ. Acts 21:8
32. ⲛ̄ⲛⲉⲛ-ⲟⲩⲱⲙ ⲟⲩⲇⲉ ⲛ̄ⲛⲉⲛ-ⲥⲱ. Acts 23:12
33. ⲁⲩ-ⲣ̄-ᵠⲛⲟⲃⲉ ⲁⲩⲱ ⲥⲉ-ϣⲁⲁⲧ ⲙ̄-ⲡⲉⲟⲟⲩ ⲙ̄-ⲡⲛⲟⲩⲧⲉ. Romans 3:23 alt.
34. ⲙⲛ̄-ᵠⲁⲅⲁⲑⲟⲛ²⁹ ⲟⲩⲏϩ ⲛ̄ϩⲏⲧ-ᵠ. Romans 7:18
35. ⲛ̄-ⲧⲙⲛ̄ⲧ-ⲉⲣⲟ ⲅⲁⲣ ⲁⲛ ⲙ̄-ⲡⲛⲟⲩⲧⲉ ⲡⲉ ᵠⲟⲩⲱⲙ ϩⲓ-ᵠⲥⲱ. Romans 14:17
36. ⲧⲉⲧⲛ̄-ⲣ̄-ᵠⲛⲟⲃⲉ ⲉ-ⲡⲉⲭ̄ⲥ̄. 1 Corinthians 8:12
37. ⲙⲁⲣⲉϥ-ϣⲗⲏⲗ ϫⲉⲕⲁⲁⲥ ⲉϥⲉ-ⲃⲱⲗ. 1 Corinthians 14:13
38. ⲁⲛ-ϩⲉⲛⲧⲉⲓ̈ⲙⲓⲛⲉ ⲟⲛ (**44**). 2 Corinthians 10:11
39. ⲙ̄ⲡⲓ-ϣⲱⲱⲧ ⲛ̄-ⲗⲁⲁⲩ ⲡⲁⲣⲁ³⁰-ⲛ̄ⲛⲟϭ ⲛ̄-ⲁⲡⲟⲥⲧⲟⲗⲟⲥ. 2 Corinthians 11:5
40. ϣⲁⲩ-ⲧⲃ̄ⲃⲟ ⲅⲁⲣ ϩⲓⲧⲙ̄-ⲡϣⲁϫⲉ ⲙ̄-ⲡⲛⲟⲩⲧⲉ ⲙⲛ̄-ⲡⲉϣⲗⲏⲗ. 1 Timothy 4:5 alt.
41. ⲙ̄-ⲡϣⲁϫⲉ ⲙ̄-ⲡⲛⲟⲩⲧⲉ ⲙⲏⲣ ⲁⲛ. 2 Timothy 2:9
42. ⲙⲁⲣⲟⲩ-ⲟⲩⲱϣⲧ ⲛⲁ-ϥ. Hebrews 1:6
43. ⲟⲩⲡⲓⲥⲧⲟⲥ ⲡⲉ ⲁⲩⲱ ⲟⲩⲙⲉ ⲡⲉ ϫⲉⲕⲁⲥ ⲉϥⲉ-ⲕⲱ ⲉⲃⲟⲗ ⲛ̄-ⲛⲉⲛⲛⲟⲃⲉ. 1 John 1:9

---

²⁶ ϯⲙⲉ village.
²⁷ ⲧⲥⲁⲃⲟ teach, inform.
²⁸ ⲫⲓⲗⲓⲡⲡⲟⲥ (personal name) Philipp.
²⁹ ⲁⲅⲁⲑⲟⲥ, -ⲟⲛ good person, thing.
³⁰ Lesson 7, box "The Simple Prepositions."

LESSON 12

NON-DURATIVE CONJUGATION:
SUBORDINATE CLAUSE CONJUGATION BASES.
INFLECTED MODIFIER.
SOME STYLISTIC DEVICES.

90. In this lesson you will complete the survey of non-durative conjugation, which was begun in lesson 10. Now you will learn the five subordinate clause conjugation bases—they occur very frequently, and you will see them everywhere. [CG 342–43] They appear in the same three part pattern as the main-clause bases (**75**), namely

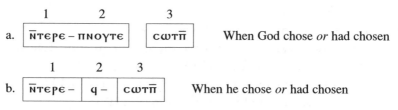

a. | 1 ̄ⲚⲦⲈⲢⲈ – ⲠⲚⲞⲨⲦⲈ 2 | 3 ⲤⲰⲦ̄Ⲡ | When God chose *or* had chosen

b. | ̄ⲚⲦⲈⲢⲈ – ϥ – ⲤⲰⲦ̄Ⲡ | When he chose *or* had chosen

(1) A conjugation base, which has two states, such as ⲚⲦⲈⲢⲈ–, ⲚⲦⲈⲢ(Ⲉ)⸗.
(2) A subject suffixed to the base.
(3) An infinitive (separated in pattern a, attached in pattern b).

Negation. The five subordinate bases are negatived by adding ⲦⲘ̄– (= *not*), which comes before a nominal subject and after a personal one: ⲚⲦⲈⲢⲈ–ⲦⲘ̄–ⲠⲚⲞⲨⲦⲈ ⲤⲰⲦ̄Ⲡ = When God did not choose; ⲚⲦⲈⲢⲈ–ϥ–ⲦⲘ̄–ⲤⲰⲦ̄Ⲡ = After he did not choose.

The five subordinate-clause bases are

Precursive: ⲚⲦⲈⲢⲈ–, ⲚⲦⲈⲢ(Ⲉ)⸗	When *or* After he chose *or* had chosen
Conditional: ⲈⲢϢⲀⲚ–, Ⲉ⸗ϢⲀⲚ– and ⲈⲢⲈ–, Ⲉ⸗	If *or* When *or* Since *or* Whenever he chooses *or* chose
Limitative: ϢⲀⲚⲦⲈ–, ϢⲀⲚⲦ⸗	Until he chose *or* chooses *or* has chosen *or* had chosen

Conjunctive: ⲛ̄ⲧⲉ-, ⲛ̄⸗   (tenseless)

Future conjunctive: ⲧⲁⲣⲉ-, ⲧⲁⲣ⸗   . . . and he shall choose

91. The Precursive, ⲛ̄ⲧⲉⲣⲉ-, ⲛ̄ⲧⲉⲣ(ⲉ)⸗ "When, After" (past time)

ⲛ̄ⲧⲉⲣⲓ-	ⲛ̄ⲧⲉⲣⲛ̄- or ⲛ̄ⲧⲉⲣⲉⲛ-
ⲛ̄ⲧⲉⲣⲉⲕ-	ⲛ̄ⲧⲉⲣⲉⲧⲛ̄-
ⲛ̄ⲧⲉⲣⲉ- or ⲛ̄ⲧⲉⲣⲉⲣ-	
ⲛ̄ⲧⲉⲣⲉϥ-	ⲛ̄ⲧⲉⲣⲟⲩ-
ⲛ̄ⲧⲉⲣⲉⲥ-	

ⲛ̄ⲧⲉⲣⲉ-ⲡⲛⲟⲩⲧⲉ

Speaks of an immediately preceding event, as completed and past: *when* he *had* chosen, *after* he chose. Belongs to narration, where it supplies background information; typically combined with the past tense ⲁ-/ⲁ⸗; occurs before or after the main clause. ⲛ̄ⲧⲉⲣⲉϥ-ⲛⲁⲩ ⲁϥ-ⲡⲓⲥⲧⲉⲩⲉ = When he had seen, he believed. ⲁϥ-ⲡⲓⲥⲧⲉⲩⲉ ⲛ̄ⲧⲉⲣⲉϥ-ⲛⲁⲩ = He believed, once he had seen. ⲛ̄ⲧⲉⲣⲉϥ-ⲧⲙ̄-ⲛⲁⲩ ⲉⲣⲟ-ⲥ ⲁϥ-ⲃⲱⲕ = When he did not see her, he left. [CG 344–45, 348]

92. The Conditional ⲉⲣϣⲁⲛ-, ⲉ⸗ϣⲁⲛ- and ⲉⲣⲉ-, ⲉ⸗ 'If, When, Since, Whenever'

The prepersonal is a split base, ⲉ⸗ϣⲁⲛ. The personal suffixes are inserted into the middle of the base. A short form (without ϣⲁⲛ) also occurs, but rarely.

ⲉⲓ̈ϣⲁⲛ- or ⲉⲓ̈-	ⲉⲛϣⲁⲛ- or ⲉⲛ-
ⲉⲕϣⲁⲛ- or ⲉⲕ-	ⲉⲧⲉⲧⲛ̄ϣⲁⲛ- or ⲉⲧⲉⲧⲛ̄-
ⲉⲣϣⲁⲛ-, ⲉⲣⲉϣⲁⲛ- or ⲉⲣⲉ-	
ⲉϥϣⲁⲛ- or ⲉϥ-	ⲉⲩϣⲁⲛ- or ⲉⲩ-
ⲉⲥϣⲁⲛ- or ⲉⲥ-	

ⲉⲣϣⲁⲛ-ⲡⲛⲟⲩⲧⲉ or ⲉⲣⲉ-ⲡⲛⲟⲩⲧⲉ

Forms a logically ambiguous *'If'* clause, including both *'Since'* (factual cause) and *'If ever, Whenever'*. More or less simultaneous to the main clause. ⲉϥϣⲁⲛ-ⲛⲁⲩ ϥ-ⲛⲁ-ⲡⲓⲥⲧⲉⲩⲉ = If *or* Whenever he sees, he will believe. ⲉϥϣⲁⲛ-ⲧⲙ̄-ⲛⲁⲩ ⲛ̄-ϥ-ⲛⲁ-ⲡⲓⲥⲧⲉⲩⲉ ⲁⲛ = If *or* Whenever he does not see, he will not believe. ⲉϥϣⲁⲛ-ⲛⲁⲩ ϥ-ⲡⲓⲥⲧⲉⲩⲉ = If *or* Whenever *or* Since he sees, he believes. When combined with the Past, ⲉⲣϣⲁⲛ- expresses a generalization (*whenever*)—unlike ⲛ̄ⲧⲉⲣⲉ-, which expresses a single event: ⲉϥϣⲁⲛ-ⲛⲁⲩ ⲁϥ-ⲡⲓⲥⲧⲉⲩⲉ = Whenever he saw, he believed. Occurs before or after the main clause. [CG 346–48]

The ambiguity of ⲉⲣϣⲁⲛ- can be resolved by inserting a conjunction before it: ⲉϣⲱⲡⲉ = if, if ever; ⲉⲓⲙⲏⲧⲓ = unless, except, ⲕⲁⲛ = even though, even if, ϩⲟⲧⲁⲛ = as soon as, whenever, such that.

93. The Limitative, ϣⲁⲛⲧⲉ-, ϣⲁⲛⲧ⸗ "Until such time as"

ϣⲁⲛϯ-	ϣⲁⲛⲧⲛ̄-
ϣⲁⲛⲧⲕ̄-	ϣⲁⲛⲧⲉⲧⲛ̄-
ϣⲁⲛⲧⲉ-	
ϣⲁⲛⲧⲩ̄-	ϣⲁⲛⲧⲟⲩ-
ϣⲁⲛⲧⲥ̄-	

ϣⲁⲛⲧⲉ-ⲡⲛⲟⲩⲧⲉ

Expresses the limit beyond which the main event no longer continues, continued, or will continue: *until, until such time as, until the point where.* ⲁⲩ-ϣⲗⲏⲗ ϣⲁⲛⲧⲩ̄-ⲕⲁⲁ-ⲩ ⲉⲃⲟⲗ = They prayed until he forgave them. [CG 349]

94. The Conjunctive, ⲛ̄ⲧⲉ-, ⲛ̄⸗

ⲛ̄ⲧⲁ- or ⲧⲁ-	ⲛ̄ⲧⲛ̄-
ⲛ̄ⲅ- or ⲛ̄ⲕ-	ⲛ̄ⲧⲉⲧⲛ̄-
ⲛ̄ⲧⲉ-	
ⲛ̄ⲩ-	ⲛ̄ⲥⲉ-
ⲛ̄ⲥ-	

ⲛ̄ⲧⲉ-ⲡⲛⲟⲩⲧⲉ

Forms a subordinate (dependent) clause consisting of subject + verb; signals that the clause is closely connected to what precedes it; does not express any tense or other content. It expresses only a connected, subordinated, "next" event or process. Like the aorist (**79**), the conjunctive is a distinctly Coptic device; there is nothing quite like it in English. To the English speaker, the conjunctive seems to mirror the tense of the immediate context in which it occurs. [CG 351–56] Main uses:

i. The conjunctive continues verbs that do *not* occur in the main line of past narration and are not durative statements about the present. E.g. ⲡⲛⲟⲩⲧⲉ ⲉϥⲉ-ⲥⲙⲟⲩ ⲉⲣⲱ-ⲧⲛ̄ ⲛ̄ⲧⲛ̄-ⲕⲱ ⲛⲏ-ⲧⲛ̄ ⲉⲃⲟⲗ = God shall bless you *and* we shall forgive you. ⲙ̄ⲡⲣ̄ⲧⲣⲉⲩ-ⲟⲩⲱⲙ ϣⲁⲛⲧⲟⲩ-ⲃⲱⲕ ⲉϩⲟⲩⲛ ⲉ-ⲧⲡⲟⲗⲓⲥ ⲛ̄ⲥⲉ-ⲛⲁⲩ ⲉ-ⲡⲣ̄ⲣⲟ = Let them not eat until they have entered the city *and* seen the emperor. ⲕⲁⲁ-ⲩ ⲙ̄ⲡⲉⲓⲙⲁ ⲛ̄ⲧⲁ-ⲭⲓⲧ-ⲟⲩ = Leave them here *and* I will take them. ⲕ-ⲛⲁ-ⲟⲩⲱⲙ ⲛ̄ⲅ-ⲥⲱ = You will eat *and* drink. ϯ-ⲛⲁ-ⲟⲩⲱⲙ ⲛ̄ⲧⲁ-ⲧⲙ̄-ⲥⲱ = I shall eat and not drink.

ii. It also forms subordinate clauses headed by expressions such as ⲉⲓⲙⲏⲧⲓ (unless), ⲙⲛ̄ⲛ̄ⲥⲁ- (after), ⲙⲏⲡⲱⲥ (lest), ϩⲱⲥⲧⲉ (so that), ⲁⲣⲏⲩ (perhaps), ⲕⲉ-ⲕⲟⲩⲓ̈ ⲡⲉ (Just a little while longer and), ⲙⲏⲅⲉⲛⲟⲓⲧⲟ (God forbid that), etc. [CG 354] ⲙ̄ⲡⲣ̄-ⲟⲩⲱⲙ ⲙⲏⲡⲟⲧⲉ ⲛ̄ⲕ-ⲙⲟⲩ = Do not eat *lest* you die. ⲙⲛ̄ⲛ̄ⲥⲁ-ⲛ̄ⲥⲉ-ⲡⲁⲣⲁⲇⲓⲇⲟⲩ ⲛ̄-ⲓⲱϩⲁⲛⲛⲏⲥ = *After* they betrayed John.

Some additional uses are described in CG 353, 355–56.

95. The Future Conjunctive, ⲧⲁⲣⲉ-, ⲧⲁⲣ⸗

ⲧⲁⲣⲓ-	ⲧⲁⲣⲡ̄-
ⲧⲁⲣⲉⲕ-	ⲧⲁⲣⲉⲧⲛ̄-
ⲧⲁⲣⲉ-	
ⲧⲁⲣⲉϥ-	ⲧⲁⲣⲟⲩ-
ⲧⲁⲣⲉⲥ-	

ⲧⲁⲣⲉ-ⲡⲛⲟⲩⲧⲉ

Occurs after an affirmative command, in dialogue. It promises that an event will happen in the future if the command is fulfilled. ϣⲗⲏⲗ ⲧⲁⲣⲉϥ-ⲕⲱ ⲛⲁ-ⲕ ⲉⲃⲟⲗ = Pray *and he will* forgive you. ⲙⲁⲣⲡ̄-ⲉⲓ ⲉϩⲟⲩⲛ ⲧⲁⲣⲡ̄-ⲛⲁⲩ ⲉⲣⲟ-ϥ = Let us go in *and we shall* see him. It can be used independently to form a deliberative question: ⲧⲁⲣⲡ̄-ⲉⲓ ⲉϩⲟⲩⲛ = Shall we enter? [CG 357–58]

THE INFLECTED MODIFIERS

96. You have already learned the eight independent personal pronouns ⲁⲛⲟⲕ, ⲛ̄ⲧⲟⲕ, ⲛ̄ⲧⲟ etc. 40. The ⲁⲛⲟⲕ pronoun also has the ability to float around in the sentence, bobbing up between one bound group and another, provided that it agrees in person and number/gender with some other pronoun in the same sentence.

ⲧⲉ-ⲥⲙⲁⲙⲁⲁⲧ ⲛ̄ⲧⲟ ϩⲛ̄-ⲛⲉϩⲓⲟⲙⲉ
= You are blessed, ⲛ̄ⲧⲟ, among women

ⲡⲁⲟⲩⲟⲉⲓϣ ⲁⲛⲟⲕ ⲙ̄ⲡⲁⲧϥ̄-ⲉⲓ
= My time, ⲁⲛⲟⲕ, has not yet come

This device is typically Coptic, and it is sometimes hard to capture in normal English without seeming clumsy ("You, *in a personal way,* are blessed among women. — My *own particular* time has not yet come.")

There are five other words—called the inflected modifiers—that have the same ability to float around in the sentence, adding stylistic nuance and interest to sentence structure as well as conveying valuable information. All of these occur in the usual pattern of eight persons; indeed, they are so regular that we can represent them simply as prepersonal states that are completed by the personal suffixes. [CG 152–58]

(*a*) ⲧⲏⲣ⸗ = . . . all, entirely, all . . . ; utterly
ϩⲱⲱ⸗ = . . . too; for (my *etc.*) part

(*b*) ⲙ̄ⲙⲓⲛⲙ̄ⲙⲟ⸗ = . . . (my- *etc.*) self [often reflexive]; own
ⲙⲁⲩⲁⲁ⸗ and ⲙⲁⲩⲁⲁⲧ⸗ = alone, only, mere; (my- *etc.*) self; own
ⲟⲩⲁⲁ⸗ and ⲟⲩⲁⲁⲧ⸗ = only, alone

ⲧⲏⲡ̄ⲧ, ⲧⲏⲡ̄ⲕ, ⲧⲏⲡⲉ, ⲧⲏⲡ̄ϥ, ⲧⲏⲡ̄ⲥ, ⲧⲏⲡ̄ⲛ, ⲧⲏⲡⲧ̄ⲛ, ⲧⲏⲣⲟⲩ

ϩⲱⲱⲧ (or ϩⲱ), ϩⲱⲱⲕ, ϩⲱⲱⲧⲉ, ϩⲱⲱϥ, ϩⲱⲱⲥ, ϩⲱⲱⲛ, ϩⲱⲧⲧⲏⲩⲧ̄ⲛ, ϩⲱⲟⲩ

ⲙ̄ⲙⲓⲛⲙ̄ⲙⲟ⸗ just like the preposition ⲙ̄ⲙⲟ⸗

ⲙⲁⲩⲁⲁⲧ, ⲙⲁⲩⲁⲁⲕ, ⲙⲁⲩⲁⲁⲧⲉ, ⲙⲁⲩⲁⲁϥ, ⲙⲁⲩⲁⲁⲥ, ⲙⲁⲩⲁⲁⲛ, ⲙⲁⲩⲁⲧⲧⲏⲩⲧ̄ⲛ, ⲙⲁⲩⲁⲁⲩ *or*

ⲙⲁⲩⲁⲁⲧ, ⲙⲁⲩⲁⲁⲧ̄ⲕ, ⲙⲁⲩⲁⲁⲧⲉ, ⲙⲁⲩⲁⲁⲧ̄ϥ, ⲙⲁⲩⲁⲁⲧ̄ⲥ, ⲙⲁⲩⲁⲁⲧ̄ⲛ, ⲙⲁⲩⲁⲁⲧ-ⲧⲏⲩⲧ̄ⲛ, ⲙⲁⲩⲁⲁⲧⲟⲩ

ⲟⲩⲁⲁⲧ, ⲟⲩⲁⲁⲕ, ⲟⲩⲁⲁⲧⲉ, ⲟⲩⲁⲁϥ (or ⲟⲩⲁⲁⲧ̄ϥ), ⲟⲩⲁⲁⲥ (or ⲟⲩⲁⲁⲧ̄ⲥ), ⲟⲩⲁⲁⲛ, ⲟⲩⲁ(ⲁ)ⲧⲧⲏⲩⲧ̄ⲛ, ⲟⲩⲁⲁⲧⲟⲩ

Position in the sentence. None of these five can be the first word of a clause. Those in group (*a*) can either preceed or follow the pronoun with which they agree.

ⲧⲉⲧ̄ⲛ-ⲥⲟⲟⲩⲛ̄ ⲧⲏⲡ-ⲧⲛ̄ = You all know.

ⲉⲓⲥϩⲏⲏⲧⲉ ⲧⲏⲡ-ⲧⲛ̄ ⲧⲉⲧ̄ⲛ-ⲥⲟⲟⲩⲛ̄ = You all know.

Those in group (*b*) always follow the person with which they agree.

ⲛⲉϥⲙⲁⲑⲏⲧⲏⲥ ⲙⲁⲩⲁⲁ-ⲩ ⲁⲩ-ⲃⲱⲕ = Only his disciples went away

ⲥⲟⲟⲩⲛ̄ ⲙ̄ⲙⲟ-ⲕ ⲙ̄ⲙⲓⲛⲙ̄ⲙⲟ-ⲕ = Know thyself (Know your own self)

SOME STYLISTIC DEVICES

97. *Postponed subjects* (ⲛ̄ϭⲓ-). In all sentence types except the nominal sentence, a 3d person subject of the type ϥ, ⲥ, ⲥⲉ, ⲩ, and ⲟⲩ can be made explicit later in the sentence by an article phrase, pronoun, or specifier phrase, of the same number (and gender) introduced by the preposition ⲛ̄ϭⲓ-. (Caution: ⲛ̄ϭⲓ- is not translated.) [CG 87(b)]

ϥ-ⲥⲱⲧⲡ̄ ⲛ̄ϭⲓ-ⲡⲣⲱⲙⲉ = ⲡⲣⲱⲙⲉ ⲥⲱⲧⲡ̄
The man is choosing *or* chooses (he-choosing ⲛ̄ϭⲓ- the-man)

ⲁⲩ-ⲥⲱⲧⲡ̄ ⲛ̄ϭⲓ-ⲛ̄ϣⲏⲣⲉ = ⲁ-ⲛ̄ϣⲏⲣⲉ ⲥⲱⲧⲡ̄
The children chose *or* have chosen

ⲟⲩⲛⲧⲁ-ϥ ⲛ̄ϭⲓ-ⲡⲣⲱⲙⲉ = ⲟⲩⲛ̄ⲧⲉ-ⲡⲣⲱⲙⲉ
The man has (cf. below, **103**)

ⲡⲉϫⲁ-ϥ ⲛ̄ϭⲓ-ⲓ̄ⲥ̄ = ⲡⲉϫⲉ-ⲓ̄ⲥ̄
Jesus said (cf. below, **105**)

98. *Extraposited subject or object.* In studying the nominal sentence, you have already seen how a component of the sentence can be *extraposited*—literally, "put outside"—before a simple form of sentence pattern **39**. This is a typical way of speaking in Coptic, and all kinds of sentences can be equipped with an extraposition before the sentence pattern begins, or even several. [CG 253, 313, 322, 330, 374, 387] Thus

ⲡⲣⲱⲙⲉ, ϥ-ⲥⲱⲧⲡ̄ = ⲡⲣⲱⲙⲉ ⲥⲱⲧⲡ̄
The man is choosing *or* chooses (as-for-the-man, he-is-choosing)

ⲛ̄ϣⲏⲣⲉ, ⲁⲩ-ⲥⲱⲧⲡ̄ = ⲁ-ⲛ̄ϣⲏⲣⲉ ⲥⲱⲧⲡ̄
The children chose *or* have chosen (the-children, they-chose)

ⲛ̄ϣⲏⲣⲉ, ⲛ̄ⲧⲉⲣⲟⲩ-ⲥⲱⲧⲡ̄ = ⲛ̄ⲧⲉⲣⲉ-ⲛ̄ϣⲏⲣⲉ ⲥⲱⲧⲡ̄
After the children chose *or* had chosen (the-children, after-they-chose) . . .

ⲡⲣⲱⲙⲉ, ⲟⲩⲛ̄ⲧⲁ-ϥ = ⲟⲩⲛ̄ⲧⲉ-ⲡⲣⲱⲙⲉ
The man has (cf. below, **103**) (the-man, he-has)

ⲓ̄ⲥ, ⲡⲉϫⲁ-ϥ = ⲡⲉϫⲉ-ⲓ̄ⲥ
Jesus said (cf. below, **105**) (Jesus, he-said)

As you see from these examples, the extraposited element must also be represented by a personal pronoun of the same number (and gender) within the sentence pattern itself: ⲡⲣⲱⲙⲉ ϥ-, ⲛ̄ϣⲏⲣⲉ ⲁⲩ-, ⲛ̄ϣⲏⲣⲉ ⲛ̄ⲧⲉⲣⲟⲩ-, ⲡⲣⲱⲙⲉ ⲟⲩⲛ̄ⲧⲁ-ϥ, ⲓ̄ⲥ ⲡⲉϫⲁ-ϥ.

Also objects can be extraposited at the head of the sentence, and they too must be represented within the pattern by a personal pronoun.

ⲛⲉⲓ̈ϩⲃⲏⲩⲉ ⲁⲓ̈-ⲛⲁⲩ ⲉⲣⲟ-ⲟⲩ = ⲁⲓ̈-ⲛⲁⲩ ⲉ-ⲛⲉⲓ̈ϩⲃⲏⲩⲉ
I saw these things (these-things, I-saw them)

Indeed, both a subject and an object can be extraposited in the same sentence.

ⲡⲉⲡⲣⲟⲫⲏⲧⲏⲥ ⲛⲉⲓ̈ϩⲃⲏⲩⲉ ⲁϥ-ⲛⲁⲩ ⲉⲣⲟ-ⲟⲩ = ⲁ-ⲡⲉⲡⲣⲟⲫⲏⲧⲏⲥ ⲛⲁⲩ ⲉ-ⲛⲉⲓ̈-
ϩⲃⲏⲩⲉ
The prophet saw these things (the-prophet, these-things, he-saw them)

Postponed subjects and extraposited subjects and objects add stylistic flexibility. They are typical devices in Coptic literary style, but less so in English.

99. *The position of prepositional phrases and adverbs* is fairly free. They can occur at the head of a sentence, sometimes accompanied by an extraposited subject or object (**98**).

ϩⲛ̄-ⲧⲉϩⲟⲩⲉⲓⲧⲉ, ⲛⲉϥ-ϣⲟⲟⲡ ⲛ̄ϭⲓ-ⲡϣⲁϫⲉ
In the beginning, there was the Word

ⲛ̄ⲧⲉⲩⲛⲟⲩ ⲇⲉ, ⲁⲩ-ⲕⲁ-ⲛⲉⲩϣⲛⲏⲩ
And immediately, they left their nets

ⲁϫⲛ̄ⲧ-ϥ, ⲙ̄ⲡⲉ-ⲗⲁⲁⲩ ϣⲱⲡⲉ
Without Him, nothing came into existence

ⲁⲩⲱ ⲛ̄ⲧⲉⲩⲛⲟⲩ ϩⲛ̄-ⲛ̄ⲥⲁⲃⲃⲁⲧⲟⲛ, ⲁϥ-ϯ-ᵉⲥⲃⲱ ϩⲛ̄-ⲧⲥⲩⲛⲁⲅⲱⲅⲏ
And right away, on the Sabbath, He taught in the synagogue

ⲁⲩⲱ ⲛ̄ⲧⲉⲩⲛⲟⲩ ⲡⲉⲡⲛ̄ⲁ̄, ⲁϥ-ϫⲓⲧ-ϥ̄
And right away, as for the spirit, it seized Him

ⲡⲁⲓ̈ ϩⲛ̄-ⲧⲉϩⲟⲩⲉⲓⲧⲉ, ⲛⲉϥ-ϣⲟⲟⲡ ϩⲁⲧⲙ̄-ⲡⲛⲟⲩⲧⲉ
As for Him, in the beginning, He existed with God

And they very often occur late in the sentence.

ⲁⲓ̈-ϯ-ᵉⲃⲁⲡⲧⲓⲥⲙⲁ ⲛⲏ-ⲧⲛ̄ ϩⲛ̄-ⲟⲩⲙⲟⲟⲩ
I have given baptism *to you by means of water*

ⲁⲩ-ⲕⲁ-ⲡⲉⲩⲉⲓⲱⲧ ⲍⲉⲃⲉⲇⲁⲓⲟⲥ ϩⲙ̄-ⲡϫⲟⲓ̈ ⲙⲛ̄-ⲛ̄ϫⲁⲓ̈-ᵉⲃⲉⲕⲉ
They left their father Zebedee *in the boat with the employees*

ⲁⲩ-ⲭⲁⲗⲁ ⲙ̄-ⲡⲉⲃⲗⲟϭ ⲉⲡⲉⲥⲏⲧ
They lowered the cot *downwards*

ⲁⲩ-ⲥⲡ̄ⲥⲱⲡ-ϥ̄ ⲉⲙⲁⲧⲉ
They implored him *greatly*

VOCABULARY 12

More verbs: Change of condition (ingr. = ingressive meaning **74**)

M̄TON, MOTN̄†	make to rest; ingr. become rested	ἐπαναπαύειν
M̄TON M̄MO= reflexive	rest	ἀναπαύεσθαι
ϢTOPTP̄ (ϢTP̄TP̄-, ϢTP̄TⲰP=) ϢTP̄TⲰP†	disturb; ingr. become disturbed	ταράσσεσθαι
MOY2 (ME2-, MA2=) ME2†	fill, complete, amount to; finish; ingr. become full, complete	πιμπλάναι, πληροῦν
ⲬⲰK EBOⲖ (ⲬEK-, ⲬOK=) ⲬHK† EBOⲖ	complete, amount to; ingr. become perfect, complete; reach (one's) limit	πληροῦν
OYⲰN, OYHN†	open; ingr. become open	ἀνοίγειν
ΠⲰϢ (ΠEϢ-, ΠOϢ=) ΠHϢ†	divide; ingr. become divided	κλᾶν
TAⲬPO (TAⲬPE-, TAⲬPO=) TAⲬPHY†	make firm; ingr. become firm	στηρίζειν
TAKO (TAKE-, TAKO=) TAKHY(T)†	destroy, ruin; ingr. become ruined	ἀπολλύναι
2OOY† (stative only)	bad, evil	πονηρός, κακός
BⲰⲖ EBOⲖ (BⲀ-, BOⲖ=) BHⲖ† EBOⲖ	loosen, destroy; ingr. become loose, destroyed	λύειν
2E EBOⲖ, 2HY† EBOⲖ **89**	perish	ἀπόλλυσθαι
MOYOYT (MOYT- or MEYT-, MOYOYT=)	kill	θανατοῦν
TOYNOC (TOYNEC-, TOYNOC=)	awaken, raise	ἐγείρειν
COBTE (CB̄TE-, CB̄TⲰT=) CB̄TⲰT†	prepare; ingr. become prepared	ἀνοίγειν
EINE N̄-/M̄MO= [not same as EINE "bring"]	resemble	ὅμοιος εἶναι
2ICE, 2OCE†	become tired, exert oneself, labor	κοπιᾶν

105

LESSON TWELVE

ϩⲓⲥⲉ ⲙ̄ⲙⲟⲥ reflexive	labor, exert oneself	κοπιᾶν
ϣⲓⲡⲉ ϩⲏⲧⲥ	feel great respect (shame) before	ἐντρέπεσθαι
†-ᵠϣⲓⲡⲉ	shame (= cause . . . to feel ashamed)	ἐπαισχύνεσθαι
ϫⲓ-ᵠϣⲓⲡⲉ	be put to shame, be ashamed	καταισχύνεσθαι
ⲙⲟⲥⲧⲉ (ⲙⲉⲥⲧⲉ-, ⲙⲉⲥⲧⲱⲥ)	hate	μισεῖν

Conjunctions

| *ⲉⲓⲙⲏⲧⲓ | unless indeed, unless perhaps |
| *ϩⲱⲥⲧⲉ | so that . . . |

EXERCISES 12

A. *Translate rapidly into Coptic, giving all eight persons and the noun (ⲡⲣⲱⲙⲉ) as subject (I, you, . . . , etc.).*

a. After I divided (After you divided, . . . , etc.)
b. Whenever I strengthen . . .
c. Until I perish . . .
d. After I had not loosened . . .
e. When I do not open . . .
f. Until I do not become tired . . .

B. *Translate (most of these are incomplete sentences).* a. ⲛ̄ⲧⲉⲣⲉⲕ-ⲙ̄ⲧⲟⲛ ⲙ̄ⲙⲟ-ⲕ. b. ⲉϥϣⲁⲛ-ϣⲧⲟⲣⲧⲣ̄. c. ϣⲁⲛ†-ⲙⲟⲩϩ. d. ⲛ̄ⲧⲉⲣⲟⲩ-ⲧⲙ̄-ϫⲱⲕ ⲉⲃⲟⲗ. e. ⲉⲓ̈ϣⲁⲛ-ⲧⲙ̄-ⲡⲱϣ. f. ϣⲁⲛⲧⲉ-ⲧⲙ̄-ⲧⲁϫⲣⲟ. g. ⲛ̄ⲧⲉⲣⲉⲥ-ⲧⲁⲕⲟ. h. ⲉⲧⲉⲧⲛ̄ϣⲁⲛ-ⲃⲱⲗ ⲉⲃⲟⲗ. i. ϣⲁⲛⲧⲕ̄-ⲙⲟⲩⲟⲩⲧ. j. ⲥⲉ-ϩⲟⲟⲩ. k. ⲛ̄-ϥ-ϩⲟⲟⲩ ⲁⲛ. l. ϣⲁⲛⲧⲟⲩ-ⲧⲟⲩⲛⲟⲥ. m. ⲛ̄ⲧⲉⲣⲓ-ⲥⲟⲃⲧⲉ. n. ⲉⲣϣⲁⲛ-ⲟⲩⲱⲛ. o. ϣⲁⲛⲧϥ̄-ⲉⲓⲛⲉ. p. ⲛ̄ⲧⲉⲣⲉⲧⲛ̄-ϩⲓⲥⲉ. q. ⲉⲕϣⲁⲛ-ⲣⲁϣⲉ. r. ϣⲁⲛⲧϥ̄-ⲙ̄ⲧⲟⲛ. s. ⲛ̄ⲧⲉⲣⲓ-†-ᵠϣⲓⲡⲉ. t. ⲉⲩϣⲁⲛ-ϫⲓ-ᵠϣⲓⲡⲉ. u. ϣⲁⲛ†-ⲙⲟⲥⲧⲉ.

C. *Translate into Coptic, using the conjunctive (ⲛ̄ⲧⲉ-, ⲛ̄ⲥ) for (a)–(f) and the future conjunctive (ⲧⲁⲣⲉ- ⲧⲁⲣⲥ) for (g)–(h).* a. Rest and do not become disturbed. b. He is going to build you up and you will become perfect. c. If you do not go and see, you will be put to shame. *d.* You shall rejoice and live. *e.* You shall die and not live. *f.* If you come and God hates you, you will perish. *g.* Come and you will become full. *h.* Exert yourselves and you will become perfect.

D. Reading selections from the New Testament.

1. ⲁϥ-ⲉⲓ ⲛ̄ϭⲓ-ⲓⲥ̄ ⲉⲃⲟⲗ ϩⲛ̄-ⲛⲁⲍⲁⲣⲉⲧ ⲛ̄ⲧⲉ-ⲧⲅⲁⲗⲓⲗⲁⲓⲁ. Mark 1:9
2. ϩⲛ̄-ⲧⲉⲩⲛⲟⲩ ⲡⲉⲡⲛ̄ⲁ̄ ⲁϥ-ϫⲓⲧ-ϥ̄. Mark 1:12
3. ⲛⲉⲧⲙ̄ⲙⲁⲩ ϩⲱ-ⲟⲩ ⲟⲛ ⲁⲩ-ⲃⲱⲕ. Mark 16:13
4. ⲁⲩ-ⲃⲱⲕ ⲙⲁⲩⲁⲁ-ⲩ ⲉ-ⲩⲙⲁ ⲛ̄-ϫⲁⲉⲓⲉ[31]. Mark 6:32
5. ⲁ-ϩⲁϩ ⲇⲉ ⲛⲁⲩ ⲉⲣⲟ-ⲟⲩ . . . ⲁⲩ-ⲥⲟⲩⲱⲛ-ⲟⲩ ⲁⲩⲱ ⲁⲩ-ⲉⲓ ⲉⲃⲟⲗ ϩⲛ̄-ⲙ̄ⲡⲟⲗⲓⲥ. Mark 6:33
6. ⲁⲩⲱ ⲛ̄ⲧⲉⲣⲉϥ-ⲉⲓ ⲉⲃⲟⲗ ⲁϥ-ⲛⲁⲩ ⲉ-ⲩⲛⲟϭ ⲙ̄-ⲙⲏⲏϣⲉ. Mark 6:34
7. ⲡϣⲏⲣⲉ ϩⲱⲱ-ϥ ⲙ̄-ⲡⲣⲱⲙⲉ ⲛⲁ-ϯ-⁰ϣⲓⲡⲉ ⲛⲁ-ϥ ⲉϥϣⲁⲛ-ⲉⲓ ϩⲙ̄-ⲡⲉⲟⲟⲩ ⲙ̄-ⲡⲉϥⲉⲓⲱⲧ. Mark 8:38
8. ⲛ̄ⲧⲉⲩⲛⲟⲩ ⲇⲉ ⲛ̄ⲧⲉⲣⲉ-ⲡⲙⲏⲏϣⲉ ⲧⲏⲣ-ϥ̄ ⲛⲁⲩ ⲉⲣⲟ-ϥ ⲁⲩ-ϣⲧⲟⲣⲧⲣ̄ ⲁⲩⲱ ⲁⲩ-ⲡⲱⲧ ⲉⲣⲁⲧ-ϥ̄. Mark 9:15
9. ⲓⲥ̄ ⲇⲉ ⲙ̄ⲡϥ̄-ϣⲁϫⲉ ⲗⲁⲁⲩ ϩⲱⲥⲧⲉ ⲛ̄ⲧⲉ-ⲡⲓⲗⲁⲧⲟⲥ ⲣ̄-⁰ϣⲡⲏⲣⲉ. Mark 15:5
10. ⲙⲛ̄ⲛⲥⲁ-ⲛⲁⲓ̈ ⲁϥ-ⲉⲓ ⲛ̄ϭⲓ-ⲓⲥ̄ ⲙⲛ̄-ⲛⲉϥⲙⲁⲑⲏⲧⲏⲥ ⲉ-ⲡⲕⲁϩ ⲛ̄-ϯⲟⲩⲇⲁⲓⲁ. John 3:22

---

[31] ϫⲁⲉⲓⲉ Wilderness, desert.

LESSON 13

CAUSATIVE INFINITIVE. VERBOIDS. *'TO HAVE'.* DYNAMIC PASSIVE.

---

100. The Causative Infinitive ⲧⲣⲉ-, ⲧⲣⲉ⸗ "(Cause) ... to"

ⲧⲣⲁ-	ⲧⲣⲉⲛ-
ⲧⲣⲉⲕ-	ⲧⲣⲉⲧⲛ̄- or ⲧⲣⲉⲧⲉⲧⲛ̄-
ⲧⲣⲉ-	
ⲧⲣⲉϥ-	ⲧⲣⲉⲩ-
ⲧⲣⲉⲥ-	

ⲧⲣⲉ-ⲡⲛⲟⲩⲧⲉ

The causative infinitive ends with a hyphen (as shown above), and it must be completed by another infinitive: ⲧⲣⲉϥ-ⲥⲱⲧⲛ̄ = (cause) him to choose, ⲧⲣⲉ-ⲡⲛⲟⲩⲧⲉ ⲥⲱⲧⲛ̄ = (cause) God to choose. It can be conjugated like any other infinitive: ⲁⲓ̈-ⲧⲣⲉ- = I caused, ⲁⲕ-ⲧⲣⲉ- = you caused, ⲁⲣⲉ-ⲧⲣⲉ- = you caused, ⲁϥ-ⲧⲣⲉ- = he caused, etc. (below, a). The causative infinitive is also used as a masculine noun (below, b).

It has two meanings. [CG 359–63]

    i. When conjugated or when completing ⲛⲁ- (future) or another verb, ⲧⲣⲉ- means *"cause him (etc.) to ... "*

        ⲁⲓ̈-ⲧⲣⲉϥ-ⲥⲱⲧⲛ̄   = I caused him (or have caused him) to choose
        ϯ-ⲧⲣⲉϥ-ⲥⲱⲧⲛ̄   = I am causing him (or cause him) to choose
        ϯ-ⲛⲁ-ⲧⲣⲉϥ-ⲥⲱⲧⲛ̄ = I shall cause him to choose

    ii. As a masc. noun in fixed prepositional phrases, ⲧⲣⲉ- does not have causal meaning: *"him (etc.) choosing; him to choose."* For a list of these phrases, see box below.

        ⲁⲛⲧⲓ-⁰ⲧⲣⲉϥ-ⲥⲱⲧⲛ̄   = instead of him choosing
        ⲉ-⁰ⲧⲣⲉϥ-ⲥⲱⲧⲛ̄   = in order for him to choose
        ϩⲙ̄-ⲡⲧⲣⲉϥ-ⲥⲱⲧⲡ   = while he was/is choosing

Negations: (*a*) The preceding conjugation base is negatived: ⲙ̄ⲡⲓ-ⲧⲣⲉϥ-ⲥⲱⲧⲛ̄ = I did not cause him to choose. (*b*) ⲉ-⁰ⲧⲙ̄-ⲧⲣⲉ- but ϩⲙ̄-ⲡ-ⲧⲣⲉϥ-ⲧⲙ̄-.

Fixed prepositional expressions containing ⲧⲣⲉ-, ⲧⲣⲉ⸗ [CG 363(4)]

ⲁⲛⲧⲓ-⁰ⲧⲣⲉ- Instead of . . . -ing
ⲁⲭⲛ̄-⁰ⲧⲣⲉ- Without . . . -ing
ⲉ-ⲡⲙⲁ ⲉ-⁰ⲧⲣⲉ- Instead of . . . -ing
ⲉ-ⲡⲧⲣⲉ- and ⲉ-⁰ⲧⲣⲉ- In order for . . . to
ⲉⲓⲙⲏⲧⲓ ⲉ-⁰ⲧⲣⲉ- Unless
ⲙⲛ̄ⲛ̄ⲥⲁ-⁰ⲧⲣⲉ- and ⲙⲛ̄ⲛ̄ⲥⲁ-ⲉ-⁰ⲧⲣⲉ- After . . . -ing
ⲭⲱⲣⲓⲥ-⁰ⲧⲣⲉ- Except when/Unless
ϩⲁⲑⲏ ⲉ-⁰ⲧⲣⲉ- Before . . . -ing
ϩⲙ̄-ⲡⲧⲣⲉ- While . . . -ing
ϩⲱⲥⲧⲉ ⲉ-⁰ⲧⲣⲉ- So that
ϩⲓⲧⲙ̄-ⲡⲧⲣⲉ- Because of . . . -ing

After ϩⲛ̄- and ϩⲓⲧⲛ̄- the definite article must be used.

Negations: note ⲉ-⁰ⲧⲙ̄-ⲧⲣⲉ- but ϩⲙ̄-ⲡⲧⲣⲉ- . . . ⲧⲙ̄-.

---

101. The verboids ["Suffixally conjugated verboids" in CG 373–82] are a miscellaneous group of verb-like words that exist only in bound states and which are conjugated by sticking the subject onto the end. Especially important are the ⲛⲁ group, ⲟⲩⲛⲧⲉ- *'have'*, and ⲡⲉϫⲉ- *'said'*.

102. *The* ⲛⲁ *Group* are seven verboids that begin with the letters ⲛⲁ or ⲛⲉ and express adjectival meaning; cf. **70.** ⲛⲁⲛⲟⲩ-ⲕ = You are good. ⲛⲁⲛⲟⲩ-ϥ = He *or* it is good. ⲛⲁⲛⲟⲩ-ⲡⲉⲕⲉⲓⲱⲧ = Your father is good. The attachment of the personal suffixes follows the usual pattern (**52** table). [CG 376–78]

ⲛⲁⲁ-, ⲛⲁⲁⲁ⸗ = is great
ⲛⲁⲛⲟⲩ-, ⲛⲁⲛⲟⲩ⸗ = is good
ⲛⲉⲥⲉ-, ⲛⲉⲥⲱ⸗ = is beautiful
——, ⲛⲉⲥⲃⲱⲱ⸗ = is intelligent
ⲛⲁϣⲉ-, ⲛⲁϣⲱ⸗ = is many, much, plentiful
——, ⲛⲁϩⲗⲱϭ⸗ = is pleasant
——, ⲛⲉϭⲱ⸗ = is ugly

Negation: (ⲛ-) . . . ⲁⲛ

For example: ⲛⲁⲁ-ⲡⲛⲟⲩⲧⲉ God is great, ⲛⲁⲁⲁ-ϥ He is great, ⲛⲁⲁⲁ-ï I am great, ⲛ̄-ⲛⲁⲛⲟⲩ-ⲡⲁï ⲁⲛ this is not good, ⲛⲉϭⲱ-ⲟⲩ ⲁⲛ they are not ugly, etc.

For the comparative (is *greater* etc.) cf. **71.**

103. **To Have,** affirm. ⲟⲩⲛ̄ⲧⲉ-, ⲟⲩⲛ̄ⲧⲁ⸗ / neg. ⲙⲛ̄ⲧⲉ-, ⲙⲛ̄ⲧⲁ⸗ or ⲙ̄ⲙⲛ̄ⲧⲉ-, ⲙ̄ⲙⲛ̄ⲧⲁ⸗ [CG 383-92]

ⲟⲩⲛ̄ⲧⲁ-ï	ⲙⲛ̄ⲧⲁ-ï
ⲟⲩⲛ̄ⲧⲁ-ⲕ	ⲙⲛ̄ⲧⲁ-ⲕ
ⲟⲩⲛ̄ⲧⲉ-⁰	ⲙⲛ̄ⲧⲉ-⁰
ⲟⲩⲛ̄ⲧⲁ-ϥ	ⲙⲛ̄ⲧⲁ-ϥ
ⲟⲩⲛ̄ⲧⲁ-ⲥ	ⲙⲛ̄ⲧⲁ-ⲥ
ⲟⲩⲛ̄ⲧⲁ-ⲛ	ⲙⲛ̄ⲧⲁ-ⲛ
ⲟⲩⲛ̄ⲧⲏ-ⲧⲛ̄	ⲙⲛ̄ⲧⲏ-ⲧⲛ̄
ⲟⲩⲛ̄ⲧⲁ-ⲩ	ⲙⲛ̄ⲧⲁ-ⲩ
ⲟⲩⲛ̄ⲧⲉ-ⲡⲛⲟⲩⲧⲉ	ⲙⲛ̄ⲧⲉ-ⲡⲛⲟⲩⲧⲉ

Constructions of *have* are often followed by the untranslatable adverb ⲙ̄ⲙⲁⲩ. (The linguistic function of this seemingly meaningless part of the construction is not yet understood.)

Because *have* can take a direct object, the complicated problem arises of how the direct object can be combined with the suffixed subject. There are four possibilities:

    i. The man has the boats. ⲟⲩⲛ̄ⲧⲉ-ⲡⲣⲱⲙⲉ ⲛ̄ⲉϫⲏⲩ

    ii. He has the boats. ⲟⲩⲛ̄ⲧⲁ-ϥ ⲛ̄-ⲛ̄ⲉϫⲏⲩ or ⲟⲩⲛ̄ⲧϥ̄-ⲛ̄ⲉϫⲏⲩ or ⲟⲩⲛ̄ⲧⲁϥ-
       ⲛ̄ⲉϫⲏⲩ

    iii. He has them. ⲟⲩⲛ̄ⲧⲁ-ϥ-ⲥⲟⲩ

    iv. The man has them.

A few comments:

    i. In *the man has the boats,* the direct object (ⲛ̄ⲉϫⲏⲩ) floats alone and independent, without any direct object preposition. ⲟⲩⲛ̄ⲧⲉ-ⲡⲣⲱⲙⲉ ⲛ̄ⲉϫⲏⲩ.

    ii. In *he has the boats,* the direct object (ⲛ̄ⲉϫⲏⲩ) can be either marked by the preposition ⲛ̄- (ⲟⲩⲛ̄ⲧⲁ-ϥ ⲛ̄-ⲛ̄ⲉϫⲏⲩ) or suffixed directly (ⲟⲩⲛ̄ⲧⲁ-ϥ-ⲛ̄ⲉϫⲏⲩ), in which case the verboid may or may not be spelled in a bound state (ⲟⲩⲛ̄ⲧ⸗), as follows:

ⲟⲩⲛ̄ϯ- ⲛ̄ⲉϫⲏⲩ etc.	ⲙⲛ̄ϯ-
ⲟⲩⲛ̄ⲧⲕ̄-	ⲙⲛ̄ⲧⲕ̄-
ⲟⲩⲛ̄ⲧⲉ-	ⲙⲛ̄ⲧⲉ-
ⲟⲩⲛ̄ⲧϥ̄-	ⲙⲛ̄ⲧϥ̄-
ⲟⲩⲛ̄ⲧⲥ̄-	ⲙⲛ̄ⲧⲥ̄-
ⲟⲩⲛ̄ⲧⲛ̄-	ⲙⲛ̄ⲧⲛ̄-
ⲟⲩⲛ̄ⲧⲉⲧⲛ̄-	ⲙⲛ̄ⲧⲉⲧⲛ̄-
ⲟⲩⲛ̄ⲧⲟⲩ-	ⲙⲛ̄ⲧⲟⲩ-

E.g. ⲟⲩⲛ̄ⲧⲉⲧⲛ̄-⁰ⲡⲓⲥⲧⲓⲥ ⲙ̄ⲙⲁⲩ = You have faith. ⲟⲩⲛ̄ϯ-ⲧⲉϫⲟⲩⲥⲓⲁ = I have the power. (Also ⲟⲩⲛ̄ⲧⲏⲧⲛ̄-⁰ⲡⲓⲥⲧⲓⲥ, ⲟⲩⲛ̄ⲧⲁï-ⲧⲉϫⲟⲩⲥⲓⲁ.)

iii. In *he has them* the direct object (*them*) must be taken from a special set of "personal second suffixes" used for this purpose.

−т	−cн̄
−к, −cк̄, or −тк̄	−тнγтн̄
[? form unknown]	
−q or −cq̄	−ce or −coγ
−c	

Thus oγн̄та−q−ce or oγн̄та−q−coγ = He has them.

iv. The fourth possibility, *the man has them,* is not well attested. An esoteric solution to this problem is described in CG 390(b).

The personal second suffixes [CG 88] also must be used as direct object of

тн̄нооγ⸗	send hither
хооγ⸗	send thither
тооγ⸗	buy
бооγ⸗	make narrow
cϩaï⸗	write

special affirmative imperatives ending in ı⸗ (e.g. anı⸗ = bring **87** [box])

Negations are formed identically, but based on мн̄те−, мн̄та⸗ (or м̄мн̄те−, м̄мн̄та⸗) instead of oγн̄те−.

For now, you should treat all this information as reference material, coming back to it whenever you need to translate a oγн̄те− sentence. Remember that м̄маγ (untranslatable) sometimes appears near the end of such sentences.

104. *Other expressions of 'having'.* To express integral membership in an organism (a tree 'has' leaves, a man 'has' hands), custody (I 'have' some money), infection (she 'has' an illness or a demon), etc. Coptic often uses a prepositional predicate such as м̄мо⸗ in a durative sentence, as illustrated below. [CG 393–94]

oγn−⁰ваλ м̄мо−oγ
They *have* eyes (There are eyes in them)

oγn̄−ωтнn cн̄те ϩιωт−тнγтн̄
You *have on* two tunics (There are two tunics upon you)

oγn̄−oγπ̄na n̄−акаθартоn n̄ϩнт−q̄
He *has* an unclean spirit (There is an unclean spirit in him)

105. The other verboids [CG 379–82] are

пехе−, пеха⸗ = *said.* Marks direct discourse, only in past narration **145**. Very common. No negation. пехе−ı̄c = Jesus said. пеха−q = He said. The content of what was said is introduced by the conjunction ϫⲉ– (Greek ὅτι): ⲡⲉϫⲉ-ⲓ̅ⲥ̅ ϫⲉ-ⲙⲉⲣⲉ-ⲡⲛⲟⲩⲧⲉ = Jesus said, Love God.

ϩⲛⲉ–, ϩⲛⲁ⸗ = *is willing, is content, agrees to.* Negation, (ⲛ̅–) . . . ⲁⲛ. E.g. ϩⲛⲁ-ⲛ ⲉ-$^{\emptyset}$ⲉⲓ ⲉⲃⲟⲗ ϩⲙ̅-ⲡⲥⲱⲙⲁ = We are willing to come out of the body.

ⲙⲉϣⲁ⸗ = *not know.* ⲙⲉϣⲁ-ϥ = He does not know.

ⲛⲉϥⲣ̅– = *is pleasant.*

ⲟⲩⲉⲧ– = *is distinct, is different.* E.g. ⲟⲩⲉⲧ-ⲡϫⲟⲉⲓⲥ ⲁⲩⲱ ⲟⲩⲉⲧ-ⲡϩⲙ̅ϩⲁⲗ = The master is one thing, but the servant is quite another.

THE DYNAMIC PASSIVE

106. The *dynamic passive* (something being done to someone). [CG 175] The term "passive" has two meanings in Coptic. First, you have already learned the static passive or *stative,* which describes the enduring state of a subject after an action or process or quality has been achieved: thus statives ⲃⲏⲗ† = free, ⲙⲟⲟⲩⲧ† = dead, ⲟⲩⲟⲃϣ† = white (see above, **66**).

The other kind of passive is the *dynamic passive,* which describes something that is happening to someone or something (dynamic, not static). Coptic has no special verb form to express the dynamic passive. Rather, the dynamic passive is expressed by a pro forma 3d person plural actor "they."

ⲥⲉ-ⲛⲁ-ϫⲡⲟ-ϥ = He will be born ("they-will-bear-him")
ⲁⲩ-ϫⲡⲉ-ⲓ̅ⲥ̅ ϩⲛ̅-ⲃⲏⲑⲗⲉⲉⲙ = Jesus was born in Bethlehem ("they-bore-Jesus in-Bethlehem")

Sentences such as these are ambiguous, since the 3d person might also be understood to mean a group of actors who did something. Fortunately, the matter can be cleared up where necessary: the real actor (the cause of the process) can be specified by an agential preposition ⲉⲃⲟⲗ ϩⲓⲧⲛ̅– or ϩⲓⲧⲛ̅– or ⲉⲃⲟⲗ ϩⲛ̅–.

ⲁⲩ-ϫⲡⲉ-ⲓ̅ⲥ̅ ϩⲛ̅-ⲃⲏⲑⲗⲉⲉⲙ ⲉⲃⲟⲗ ϩⲙ̅-ⲙⲁⲣⲓⲁ = Jesus was born of Mary in Bethlehem (they-bore-Jesus in-Bethlehem out-of-Mary)
ⲁⲩ-ϫⲟⲟ-ⲥ ϩⲓⲧⲙ̅-ⲡⲉⲡⲣⲟⲫⲏⲧⲏⲥ = It was said by the prophet (they-said-it by-the-prophet)

Such sentences, because they contain an agential preposition, are unambiguous.

VOCABULARY 13

More verbs: Communication and mental activity

ϫⲛⲟⲩ (ϫⲛⲉ-, ϫⲛⲟⲩ⸗)	ask; question; tell	ἐρωτᾶν
ⲟⲩⲱϣⲃ	answer	ἀποκρίνεσθαι
ϫⲱ (ϫⲉ-, ϫⲟⲟ⸗) (not same as as ϫⲟ, ϫⲉ-, ϫⲟⲟ⸗ sow)	say, utter; talk about; sing	λέγειν
ϫⲱ ⲙ̄ⲙⲟ-ⲥ ϫⲉ-, ϫⲟⲟ-ⲥ ϫⲉ-	say . . . (ϫⲉ- = Greek ὅτι)	λέγειν
ⲡⲉϫⲉ-, ⲡⲉϫⲁ⸗ (105)	said (always narrative past tense)	λαλεῖν
ⲟⲩⲉϩ-⁰ⲥⲁϩⲛⲉ ⲛ̄-/ ⲙ̄ⲙⲟ⸗ + ⲛ̄-/ⲛⲁ⸗	command; give (a command) + to (a person)	κελεύειν
ⲥⲱⲧⲙ̄ ⲉ-	listen to (words *or* person)	ἀκούειν
ⲥⲱⲧⲙ̄ ⲛ̄-/ⲛⲁ⸗ or ⲛ̄ⲥⲁ-	obey	ἀκούειν
ⲣ̄-ⲡⲙⲉⲉⲩⲉ ⲛ̄-, ⲣ̄-ⲡⲉϥ- ⲙⲉⲉⲩⲉ (etc.)	remember	μιμνήσκειν
ⲱⲡ (ⲉⲡ-, ⲟⲡ⸗) ⲏⲡ†	count; consider to be	λογίζεσθαι
ⲧⲁⲙⲟ (ⲧⲁⲙⲉ-, ⲧⲁⲙⲟ⸗)	inform (someone + ⲉ- about something)	ἀπαγγέλλειν
ϩⲱⲡ (ϩⲉⲡ-, ϩⲟⲡ⸗) ϩⲏⲡ†	conceal, hide; ingr. become hidden	κρύπτειν
ⲟⲩⲱⲛϩ̄ (ⲟⲩⲉⲛϩ̄-, ⲟⲩⲟⲛϩ⸗) ⲟⲩⲟⲛϩ̄†	reveal; ingr. become manifest	φανεροῦν
ⲉⲓⲙⲉ	know (ⲉ- about a thing; ϫⲉ- that . . .); understand, become acquainted with	γιγνώσκειν, εἰδέ- ναι
ⲥⲟⲟⲩⲛ (ⲥⲟⲩⲛ̄-, ⲥⲟⲩⲱⲛ⸗)	become acquainted with; know (ϫⲉ- that . . .)	γιγνώσκειν, εἰδέ- ναι
ϣⲓⲛⲉ ⲛ̄ⲥⲁ-	seek	ζητεῖν
ϣⲓⲛⲉ ⲉ-	greet	ἀσπάζεσθαι
*ⲁⲓⲧⲉⲓ ⲛ̄-/ⲙ̄ⲙⲟ⸗	ask (a person); request (a thing)	εὑρίσκειν
ϩⲉ ⲉ-, ϩⲏⲩ† ⲉ-	find	

cⲻ2ⲁï (cⲉ2-, cⲁ2= or cⲻ2ⲁï-, cⲻ2ⲁï=ᵃ), cH2†	write	γράφειν
ⲱⲱ (ⲉⲱ-, oⲱ=)	read	ἀναγιγνώσκειν
ⲱⲱ ⲉⲃoⲗ (ⲉⲱ-, oⲱ=)	cry out	κράζειν
ⲣⲓⲙⲉ	weep	κλαίειν
ⲛⲁⲅ ⲉ-	look (at)	ἰδεῖν, ὁρᾶν
6ⲱⲱⲧ̄ ⲉ-	look (at), stare (at)	βλέπειν
ⲉⲣHⲧ	promise	ἐπαγγέλλειν
ⲙoⲩⲧⲉ ⲉ-	call out to, summon, invoke	καλεῖν
ⲙoⲩⲧⲉ ⲉ- (person) ⲭⲉ- (name)	call (*person* by *the name of*)	λέγειν

Conjunctions

n̄ⲑⲉ n̄-oⲩ- . . .	like a . . .	ὡς
n̄ⲑⲉ m̄-ⲡ-/ⲧ-/n̄- . . .	like the . . .	ὡς ὁ . . .
n̄ⲑⲉ n̄-ni- . . .	like a (sicᵇ) . . . , like . . .	ὡς

Other expressions

oⲩ- . . . n̄-oⲩⲱⲧ	a single . . . , an only . . .	εἷς, μονο-
ⲡi- . . . n̄-oⲩⲱⲧ	the very same . . .	ὁ αὐτός
ⲡ- . . . n̄-oⲩⲱⲧ	the only	ὁ μονο-
ⲁ2ⲣo=	What's the matter with . . . ?; Why . . . ?ᶜ	τί

ᵃcⲻ2ⲁï= takes the personal second suffixes. Cf. **103** (box).

ᵇE.g. n̄ⲑⲉ n̄-niⲱHⲣⲉ = like a child *or* like children.

ᶜⲁ2ⲣo= is completed by a personal suffix, which agrees with the subject of a following independent clause. E.g. ⲁ2ⲣⲱ-ⲧn̄ ⲧⲉⲧn̄-ⲣ̄-⁰2oⲧⲉ "Why are you afraid?"; ⲁ2ⲣo-ⲕ ⲕ-ⲙoⲩⲧⲉ ⲉⲣo-ï "Why are you calling me?"; ⲁ2ⲣo-⁰ ⲧⲉ-ⲣⲓⲙⲉ "Why are you weeping?"

EXERCISES 13

A. *Translate.* a. ϥ-ⲧⲣⲉ-ⲡⲉϥⲗⲁⲟⲥ ⲙⲟⲩⲧⲉ ⲉⲣⲟ-ϥ. b. ⲁϥ-ⲧⲣⲁ-ⲥϩⲁⲓ̈
ⲛ̄-ⲛⲉⲓ̈ϣⲁϫⲉ. c. ⲁⲥ-ⲉⲓ ϫⲉⲕⲁⲁⲥ ⲉⲥⲉ-ⲧⲣⲉⲧⲛ̄-ⲥⲱⲧⲙ̄. d. ϩⲙ̄-ⲡⲧⲣⲉⲕ-
ⲃⲱϣⲧ ⲉⲣⲟ-ⲟⲩ ⲁϥ-ⲟⲩⲱϣⲃ̄. e. ϩⲙ̄-ⲡⲧⲣⲉⲕ-ⲃⲱϣⲧ ⲉⲣⲟ-ⲟⲩ ϥ-ⲛⲁ-
ⲟⲩⲱϣⲃ̄. f. ⲛ̄-ϯ-ⲟⲩⲱϣ ⲁⲛ ⲉ-⁰ⲧⲣⲉ-ⲧⲉⲓ̈ϣⲉⲉⲣⲉ ⲙⲟⲩ. g. ϯ-ⲟⲩⲱϣ
ⲉ-⁰ⲧⲙ̄-ⲧⲉⲓ̈ϣⲉⲉⲣⲉ ⲙⲟⲩ.

B. *Translate into Coptic.* a. I made him look at me. b. You (sing. fem.) made
me promise. c. He made them listen to her. d. He made them obey her. e. We
have not yet made them conceal it. f. They did not cause her to write it.

C. *Recite the paradigm (with all eight persons and the noun subject),*
forwards and backwards. a. ⲛⲁⲛⲟⲩ⸗ (I am good, you are good, etc.).
b. (ⲛ̄-)ⲛⲁⲛⲟⲩ⸗ ⲁⲛ I am not good . . . c. ⲛⲁϣⲱ⸗ (I am plentiful . . .).
d. ⲡⲉϫⲁ⸗ (I said . . .). e. ⲟⲩⲛ̄ⲧⲁ⸗ (I have . . .). f. ⲙ̄ⲙⲛ̄ⲧⲁ⸗ (I do not
have . . .).

D. *Translate.*

a. ⲟⲩⲛ̄ⲧⲉ-ⲡⲛⲟⲩⲧⲉ ⲟⲩⲣⲡⲉ ϩⲛ̄-ⲙ̄ⲡⲏⲩⲉ.
b. ⲙⲛ̄ⲧⲉ-ⲡⲉⲡⲣⲟⲫⲏⲧⲏⲥ ⲕⲉⲛⲓ̈ ⲙ̄ⲙⲁⲩ.
c. ⲟⲩⲛ̄ⲧⲉ-ⲡⲣ̄ⲣⲟ ⲧⲉϩⲟⲩⲥⲓⲁ ⲙ̄-ⲡⲱⲛϩ ⲙⲛ̄-ⲡⲙⲟⲩ.
d. ⲟⲩⲛ̄ⲧⲁ-ϥ ⲙ̄ⲙⲁⲩ ⲛ̄-ⲟⲩⲣⲡⲉ.
e. ⲟⲩⲛ̄ⲧⲁ-ϥ ⲛ̄-ⲟⲩⲣ̄ⲡⲉ.
f. ⲟⲩⲛ̄ⲧ-ϥ̄-ⲟⲩⲣ̄ⲡⲉ.
g. ⲙⲛ̄ⲧⲁ-ϥ ⲛ̄-ⲕⲉⲛⲓ̈.
h. ⲙ̄ⲙⲛ̄ⲧ-ϥ̄-ⲕⲉⲛⲓ̈ ⲙ̄ⲙⲁⲩ.
i. ⲟⲩⲛ̄ⲧⲁ-ϥ ⲛ̄-ⲧⲉϩⲟⲩⲥⲓⲁ.
j. ⲟⲩⲛ̄ⲧⲁ-ϥ-ⲥⲉ.
k. ⲟⲩⲛ̄ⲧ-ϥ̄-ⲧⲉϩⲟⲩⲥⲓⲁ.
l. ⲟⲩⲛ̄ⲧⲁ-ϥ-ⲥⲟⲩ.
m. ⲟⲩⲛ̄ⲧⲁ-ϥ-ⲥϥ̄.
n. ⲟⲩⲛ̄ⲧⲁ-ϥ-ⲥ̄.
o. ⲟⲩⲛ̄ⲧⲁ-ϥ-ⲥⲛ̄.
p. ⲟⲩⲛ̄ⲧⲁ-ϥ-ⲥⲕ̄.
q. ⲟⲩⲛ̄ⲧⲁ-ϥ-ⲧⲏⲩⲧⲛ̄.

E. Translate into Coptic, giving alternate translations where possible. a. My father has three large houses. *b.* You do not all have them. *c.* We have another wise prophet. *d.* These emperors have four kingdoms. *e.* They do not have five kingdoms. *f.* They have us. *g.* I am better than you are. *h.* God is greater than the emperors. *i.* She is more intelligent than he is.

F. Reading selections from the New Testament.

1. ⲙⲛ̄ⲧⲁ-ⲛ-ⲗⲁⲁⲩ ⲙ̄ⲡⲉⲓ̈ⲙⲁ. (textual variants have ⲙ̄ⲙⲛ̄ⲧⲛ̄- and ⲙⲛ̄ⲧⲛ̄-) Matthew 14:17

2. ⲟⲩⲛ̄ⲧⲁ-ϥ ⲅⲁⲣ ⲙ̄ⲙⲁⲩ ⲛ̄-ϩⲁϩ ⲛ̄-ⲛ̄ⲕⲁ. Matthew 19:22 alt.

3. ⲟⲩⲛ̄ⲧⲏ-ⲧⲛ̄-ⲟⲩⲏⲣ ⲛ̄-ⲟⲉⲓⲕ. Mark 6:38

4. ⲙⲛ̄ⲧⲟⲩ-⁰ϣⲏⲣⲉ ⲙ̄ⲙⲁⲩ. Luke 1:7 alt.

5. ⲟⲩⲛ̄ⲧ-ⲥ̄-ⲟⲩⲥⲱⲛⲉ ⲇⲉ. Luke 10:39 alt.

6. ⲙⲛ̄ⲧⲛ̄-ⲕⲉⲣ̄ⲣⲟ ⲙ̄ⲙⲁⲩ ⲉⲓⲙⲏⲧⲓ ⲡⲣ̄ⲣⲟ ⲕⲁⲓⲥⲁⲣ[32]. John 19:15

7. ⲟⲩⲛ̄ⲧⲁ-ⲓ̈ ⲙ̄ⲙⲁⲩ ⲙ̄-ⲡⲉⲡ̄ⲛ̄ⲁ̄ ⲙ̄-ⲡⲛⲟⲩⲧⲉ. 1 Corinthians 7:40

8. ⲟⲩⲛ̄ⲧⲁ-ⲛ ⲙ̄ⲙⲁⲩ ⲛ̄-ⲟⲩⲕⲱⲧ ⲉⲃⲟⲗ ϩⲓⲧⲙ̄-ⲡⲛⲟⲩⲧⲉ. 2 Corinthians 5:1

9. ⲙⲛ̄ⲧⲁ-ⲛ-⁰ⲡⲟⲗⲓⲥ ⲅⲁⲣ ⲙ̄ⲡⲉⲓ̈ⲙⲁ. Hebrews 13:14

10. ⲟⲩⲛ̄ⲧⲁⲛ ⲙ̄ⲙⲁⲩ ⲛ̄-ⲟⲩⲡⲁⲣⲣⲏⲥⲓⲁ[33] ⲛ̄ⲛⲁϩⲣⲙ̄-ⲡⲛⲟⲩⲧⲉ. 1 John 3:21

11. ⲉⲃⲟⲗ ϩⲓⲧⲙ̄-ⲡⲉⲓ̈ⲓ̄ⲥ̄ ⲥⲉ-ⲧⲁϣⲉ-⁰ⲟⲉⲓϣ ⲛⲏ-ⲧⲛ̄ ⲙ̄-ⲡⲕⲱ ⲉⲃⲟⲗ ⲛ̄-ⲛⲉ-ⲧⲛ̄ⲛⲟⲃⲉ. Acts 13:38

12. ⲁⲩ-ⲧⲁϣⲉ-⁰ⲟⲉⲓϣ ⲙ̄-ⲡϣⲁϫⲉ ⲙ̄-ⲡⲛⲟⲩⲧⲉ ⲉⲃⲟⲗ ϩⲓⲧⲙ̄-ⲡⲁⲩⲗⲟⲥ. Acts 17:13 alt.

13. ⲟⲩⲥⲙⲏ ⲁⲩ-ⲥⲱⲧⲙ̄ ⲉⲣⲟ-ⲥ ϩⲛ̄-ⲣⲁⲙⲁ[34]. Matthew 2:18

G. Translate.

a. ⲁⲩ-ϫⲛⲟⲩ-ⲓ̈ ⲁⲩⲱ ⲁⲓ̈-ⲟⲩⲱϣⲃ̄. b. ⲁϥ-ϫⲱ ⲙ̄ⲙⲟ-ⲥ ϫⲉ-ⲧⲁⲙⲟ-ⲓ̈ ⲉ-ⲡⲉⲓ̈ϩⲱⲃ. c. †-ⲟⲩⲉϩ-ⲥⲁϩⲛⲉ ⲛⲏ-ⲧⲛ̄ ⲉ-⁰ⲧⲙ̄-ⲣⲓⲙⲉ. d. ⲁⲥ-ϩⲉ ⲉⲣⲟ-ϥ ϩⲙ̄-ⲡⲉϥⲏⲓ̄. e. ⲁⲩ-ⲣ̄-ⲡⲙⲉⲉⲩⲉ ⲛ̄-ⲛⲉϥϣⲁϫⲉ. f. ⲛ̄-†-ⲥⲟⲟⲩⲛ ⲁⲛ ⲙ̄-ⲡⲣⲱⲙⲉ. g. ⲙ̄ⲡϥ̄-ⲉⲓⲙⲉ ⲙ̄-ⲡϩⲱⲃ. h. ⲙ̄ⲡⲣ̄-ⲱϣ ⲛ̄-ⲧⲉⲓ̈ⲅⲣⲁⲫⲏ ⲛ̄-ⲗⲁⲁⲩ ⲛ̄-ⲣⲱⲙⲉ. i. ⲡⲉϫⲁ-ⲩ ⲛⲁ-ϥ ϫⲉ-ⲧⲛ̄-ϣⲓⲛⲉ ⲛ̄ⲥⲁ-ⲓ̄ⲥ̄.

H. Translate into Coptic. a. This was said by Moses. *b.* His kingdom will be hidden until the last day. *c.* Truth was revealed by Jesus. *d.* She will be sought in the city. *e.* She will be sought in the city by everyone. *f.* You will be called "John."

---

[32] ⲕⲁⲓⲥⲁⲣ Caesar.
[33] ⲡⲁⲣⲣⲏⲥⲓⲁ freedom to speak.
[34] ⲣⲁⲙⲁ (place name) Rama.

LESSON 14

IMPERSONAL PREDICATES.
THE FOUR CONVERSIONS.
PRETERIT CONVERSION.
HOW CONVERSION WORKS.

107. The eight impersonal predicates are single words that express a short impersonal statement. [CG 487]

(a) ⲁⲛⲁⲅⲕⲏ It is necessary. Negation (ⲛ̄–) ⲁⲛⲁⲅⲕⲏ ⲁⲛ.
　　ⲣⲱ It is sufficient, It is enough. Neg. (ⲛ̄–) ⲣⲱ ⲁⲛ.
　　ⲣⲁⲡⲥ̄ It is necessary. Neg. (ⲛ̄–) ⲣⲁⲡⲥ̄ ⲁⲛ.
　　ⲣⲛⲉ–, ⲣⲛⲁ⸗ It is pleasing unto . . . Neg. (ⲛ̄–) ⲣⲛⲉ– (or ⲣⲛⲁ⸗) ⲁⲛ. **105**

(b) ⲅⲉⲛⲟⲓⲧⲟ May it come to pass. Neg. ⲙⲏⲅⲉⲛⲟⲓⲧⲟ.
　　ⲉⲝⲉⲥⲧⲓ It is permitted, possible, proper. Neg. ⲟⲩⲕⲉⲝⲉⲥⲧⲓ.

(c) ϣϣⲉ (or ⲉϣϣⲉ) It is right, fitting, necessary. Neg. (ⲛ̄–)ϣϣⲉ ⲁⲛ and ⲙⲉϣϣⲉ[35].

(d) ⲣⲁⲙⲟⲓ̈ How good it would be if . . . ! If only . . . No negation.

The impersonal predicates are most often completed by a verbal clause or phrase. [CG 486] E.g.

ⲁⲛⲁⲅⲕⲏ ⲅⲁⲣ ⲉ–ᵒⲧⲣⲉ–ⲛⲉⲥⲕⲁⲛⲇⲁⲗⲟⲛ ⲉⲓ
For, it is necessary *that temptations come*

ⲉⲝⲉⲥⲧⲓ ⲣⲛ̄–ⲛ̄ⲥⲁⲃⲃⲁⲧⲟⲛ ⲉ–ᵒⲣ̄–ᵒⲡⲉⲧⲛⲁⲛⲟⲩϥ ⲭⲛ̄–ᵒⲣ̄–ᵒⲡⲉⲑⲟⲟⲩ
Is it lawful on the sabbath *to do good or to do harm?*

Similar in content are other impersonal expressions meaning *It is evident, obligatory, necessary, sufficient, a good thing, hard, shameful*, etc. E.g. ϥ–ⲟⲩⲟⲛⲍ̄ ⲉⲃⲟⲗ ⲭⲉ– = It is obvious that . . . , ⲟⲩⲙⲟⲉⲓⲣⲉ ⲧⲉ ⲛ̄ⲧⲉ– (conjunctive) = It is amazing that . . . , ϥ–ⲙⲟⲕⲍ̄ ⲉ–ᵒⲧⲣⲉ⸗ = It is hard for . . . .

---

[35] ⲛ̄–ϣϣⲉ ⲁⲛ in unconverted clauses and some relative conversions (ⲉⲧⲉ–ⲛ̄–ϣϣⲉ ⲁⲛ); ⲙⲉϣϣⲉ in circumstantials and some relative conversions (ⲉ–ⲙⲉϣϣⲉ, ⲉⲧⲉ–ⲙⲉϣϣⲉ) [CG 488].

THE FOUR CONVERSIONS—A GENERAL SURVEY

108. Up to this point, you have been learning the basic sentence types:

nominal sentence
durative sentence
non-durative conjugation
verboids
impersonal predicates

These are used as the basis of important grammatical patterns called *conversions,* which we shall now study, one at a time. There are four conversions:

Preterit Conversion
Circumstantial Conversion
Relative Conversion
Focalizing Conversion

With a few exceptions, each of the five basic sentence patterns can occur in these four conversions, as well as in unconverted form: roughly twenty-five possibilities. [CG 395–398]

109. Converted clauses are marked as having a special relationship to the surrounding text, in syntax and/or in the way that they present information.

The *preterit* (lesson 14) often moves things one step back in time or into non-factuality: q–κⲱⲧ he builds; preterit ⲛⲉq–κⲱⲧ he was building, ⲛⲉq–ⲛⲁ–κⲱⲧ he would build

The *circumstantial* (lesson 15) expresses something like a participle or a Greek genitive absolute (Latin ablative absolute): ⲥ–ⲣⲓⲙⲉ she is weeping; circumstantial ⲉⲥ–ⲣⲓⲙⲉ weeping, while she weeps/wept, as she weeps/wept

The *relative* (lessons 16–17) forms a modifying clause (attributive clause): q–κⲱⲧ he is building; relative ⲡⲏⲓ̈ ⲉⲧⲁ̄q–κⲱⲧ ⲙ̄ⲙⲟ–q the house that he is building

The *focalizing* (lesson 18) signals that some element in the sentence should be read with special focus or intensity: q–ⲛⲁ–ⲃⲁⲡⲧⲓⲍⲉ ⲙ̄ⲙⲱ–ⲧⲛ̄ ϩⲛ̄–ⲟⲩⲡ̄ⲛⲁ he will baptize you with spirit; focalizing ⲉq–ⲛⲁ–ⲃⲁⲡⲧⲓⲍⲉ ⲙ̄ⲙⲱ–ⲧⲛ̄ ϩⲛ̄–ⲟⲩⲡ̄ⲛⲁ he will *baptize* you with spirit, or he will baptize *you* with spirit, or he will baptize you *with spirit,* or what he will do is *baptize you with spirit*

Conversions occur frequently. You must learn to recognize the four conversion wherever they are present.

110. You can recognize a conversion by the presence of a *converter* at (or near) the beginning of the converted clause:

Preterit Converter	ⲛⲉⲣⲉ-, ⲛⲉ⸗; ⲛⲉ-
Circumstantial Converter	ⲉⲣⲉ-, ⲉ⸗; ⲉ-
Relative Converter	ⲉⲧⲉⲣⲉ-, ⲉⲧ⸗; ⲉⲛⲧ- or ⲛⲧ̄, ⲉⲧ-, ⲉⲧⲉ-, and ⲉ-
Focalizing Converter	ⲉⲣⲉ-, ⲉ⸗; ⲉ-, ⲛ̄ⲧ-, and ⲉⲧⲉ-

The converter is substituted or prefixed at the beginning of the clause as a signal of conversion. As you can see from the list above, there is ambiguity in identifying the converters spelled ⲉⲣⲉ-, ⲉ⸗, ⲉ- and ⲛ̄ⲧ-.

For example,

ⲛⲉ-ϣⲁϥ-ⲥⲱⲧⲛ̄ = Preterit (marked by ⲛⲉ-)
ⲉⲧⲉ-ϣⲁϥ-ⲥⲱⲧⲛ̄ = Relative (marked by ⲉⲧⲉ-)

But ⲉ-ϣⲁϥ-ⲥⲱⲧⲛ̄ is ambiguous = Circumstantial or Relative or Focalizing (ⲉ-). The ambiguity of ⲉ- in such a case is resolved either when the larger context rules out some interpretations or by a particular interpretive decision made by the reader.

In this lesson we shall study the preterit conversion.

THE PRETERIT CONVERSION

111. The preterit conversion [CG 434–43] often moves things back one step in time

Basic	Preterit
ϥ-ⲕⲱⲧ He builds, He is building	ⲛⲉϥ-ⲕⲱⲧ He used to build, He was building
ⲁϥ-ⲕⲱⲧ He built	ⲛⲉ-ⲁϥ-ⲕⲱⲧ He had built

or expresses a remote hypothetical possibility or wish[36]

Basic	Preterit
ϥ-ⲛⲁ-ⲕⲱⲧ He will build, He is going to build	ⲛⲉϥ-ⲛⲁ-ⲕⲱⲧ He would build (if he could)

The ordinary way to tell a story is the past tense ⲁϥ- (and ⲡⲉϫⲁ⸗ "said"), e.g. ⲁⲩ-ⲡⲱⲧ "They fled." In contrast, preterit ⲛⲉϥ- is a literary device that expresses information in a descriptive, static (durative) way, which provides a background for the ordinary story line

ⲁⲩ-ⲡⲱⲧ. ⲛⲉⲣⲉ-ⲟⲩϩⲟⲧⲉ ⲅⲁⲣ ⲛⲙ̄ⲙⲁ-ⲩ.
They fled (narration). For, fear *was with them* (explanatory background information)

---

[36] See below **152**, where contrary-to-fact conditional sentences are discussed.

and changes the tempo. The background scenery is painted in Ⲛⲉϥ–, the main actions are clothed in ⲁϥ–.

ⲂⲎⲐⲀⲚⲓⲀ Ⲇⲉ Ⲛⲉⲥ–ϨⲎⲚ ⲉϨⲞⲨⲚ ⲉ–ⲐⲒⲉⲢⲞⲨⲤⲀⲖⲎⲘ. ⲞⲨⲘⲎⲎ⳩ⲉ Ⲇⲉ ⲉⲂⲞⲖ
ϨⲚ–ⲚⲒⲞⲨⲆⲀⲒ Ⲛⲉ–ⲀⲨ–ⲉⲒ ⳙⲀ–ⲘⲀⲢⲐⲀ ⲘⲚ–ⲘⲀⲢⲒⲀ. ⲘⲀⲢⲐⲀ ⳝⲉ ⲚⲦⲉⲢⲉⲤ–
ⲤⲰⲦⲘ̄ . . . ⲀⲤ–ⲉⲒ ⲉⲂⲞⲖ

Bethany *was near* [background] Jerusalem. And a crowd of the Jews *had come* [background] to Martha and Mary. So when Martha heard, she *came out* [main story line]

The literary value of the preterit, indeed its meaning, is to switch out of the main line of discourse (ⲁϥ–, ⲚⲦⲉⲢⲉϥ–, ⲡⲉϪⲀ–ϥ) into a descriptive or slow-motion mode (Ⲛⲉϥ–), and then back again (ⲁϥ–). [CG 439] The translation exercises with this lesson will include large amounts of context, so you can study this process of switching back and forth. Other "switching signals" may also be present, such as ⳝⲉ to mark a switch or ⲚⲦⲉⲨⲚⲞⲨ to signal a return to the main action line (especially in Mark).

HOW THE CONVERSION PROCESS WORKS FORMALLY

112. Each converter appears in two types:

i. As a *conversion base* in the two states[37] [CG 396]; occurs only in durative sentences

Preterit	ⲚⲉⲢⲉ–, Ⲛⲉ⸗
Circumstantial	ⲉⲢⲉ–, ⲉ⸗
Relative	ⲉⲦⲉⲢⲉ–, ⲉⲦ⸗
Focalizing	ⲉⲢⲉ–, ⲉ⸗

ii. As a *sentence converter*

Preterit	Ⲛⲉ–
Circumstantial	ⲉ–
Relative	ⲉⲚⲦ– or ⲚⲦ–, ⲉⲦ–, ⲉⲦⲉ–, or ⲉ– (depending on sentence type)
Focalizing	ⲉ– or ⲚⲦ– (depending on sentence type); ⲉⲦⲉ–

The following three paragraphs give details about the exact formation of conversions. But you should concentrate first on learning how to recognize and translate them. You will gain a more detailed knowledge from practice and reading experience. The preterit will be used here as an example.

113. (*a*) *To convert a basic durative sentence,* remove the personal subject prefix (ϯ–, ⲕ–, etc.) and substitute the conversion base (Ⲛⲉ⸗) conjugated with a personal suffix. [CG 320]

---

[37] Just like the non-durative conjugation bases. Cf. lesson 10 and the chart with **52**.

Basic	Converted (Preterit)
ϯ–ⲃⲱⲗ	ⲛⲉⲓ̈–ⲃⲱⲗ
ϯ–ⲃⲏⲗ†	ⲛⲉⲓ̈–ⲃⲏⲗ†
ϯ–ϩⲙ̄–ⲡⲉϥⲏⲓ̈	ⲛⲉⲓ̈–ϩⲙ̄–ⲡⲉϥⲏⲓ̈
ϯ–ⲛⲁ–ⲃⲱⲗ	ⲛⲉⲓ̈–ⲛⲁ–ⲃⲱⲗ
ϯ–	ⲛⲉⲓ̈–
ⲕ–	ⲛⲉⲕ–
ⲧⲉ–	ⲛⲉⲣⲉ–
ϥ–	ⲛⲉϥ–
ⲥ–	ⲛⲉⲥ–
ⲧⲛ̄–	ⲛⲉⲛ–
ⲧⲉⲧⲛ̄–	ⲛⲉⲧⲉⲧⲛ̄–
ⲥⲉ–	ⲛⲉⲩ–

If the subject is an article phrase, pronoun, etc., prefix the prenominal conversion base (ⲛⲉⲣⲉ–) to it.

ⲡⲣⲱⲙⲉ ⲥⲱⲧⲡ̄   ⲛⲉⲣⲉ–ⲡⲣⲱⲙⲉ ⲥⲱⲧⲡ̄

Negations are formed by adding ⲁⲛ after the predicate. E.g. ⲛⲉⲓ̈–ⲥⲱⲧⲡ̄ ⲁⲛ, ⲛⲉⲣⲉ–ⲡⲣⲱⲙⲉ ⲥⲱⲧⲡ̄ ⲁⲛ.

114. (b) *To convert a durative sentence formed with affirmative* ⲟⲩⲛ̄– *"there is,"* it is possible to simply substitute a prenominal conversion base (ⲛⲉⲣⲉ–, ⲉⲣⲉ–, ⲉⲧⲉⲣⲉ–, ⲉⲣⲉ–) in place of ⲟⲩⲛ̄–[38]. [CG 324]

ⲟⲩⲛ̄–ᵠⲣⲱⲙⲉ ⲥⲱⲧⲡ̄   ⲛⲉⲣⲉ–ᵠⲣⲱⲙⲉ–ⲥⲱⲧⲡ̄
Etc.

115. (c) *To convert all other sentence types*[39], simply prefix the sentence converter to the basic sentence, whether affirmative or negative. [CG 396–98] For example,

ⲛⲉ–ⲁⲛⲅ̄–ⲟⲩⲡⲣⲟⲫⲏⲧⲏⲥ[40]
ⲛⲉ–ⲟⲩⲡⲣⲟⲫⲏⲧⲏⲥ ⲡⲉ
ⲛⲉ–ⲟⲩⲡⲣⲟⲫⲏⲧⲏⲥ ⲁⲛ ⲡⲉ
ⲛⲉ–ⲁϥ–ⲥⲱⲧⲡ̄, ⲛⲉ–ⲙ̄ⲡϥ̄–, ⲛⲉ–ⲙ̄ⲡⲁⲧϥ̄–, ⲛⲉ–ϣⲁϥ–, ⲛⲉ–ⲙⲉϥ–
ⲛⲉ–ⲛⲁⲛⲟⲩ–ϥ
ⲛⲉ–ⲛⲁⲛⲟⲩ–ϥ ⲁⲛ
ⲛⲉ–ⲁⲛⲁⲅⲕⲏ . . .
ⲛⲉ–ⲁⲛⲁⲅⲕⲏ ⲁⲛ . . .

---

[38] Or, optionally, prefix the sentence converter to ⲟⲩⲛ̄–, thus ⲛⲉ–ⲟⲩⲛ̄–ᵠⲣⲱⲙⲉ ⲃⲱⲗ (all four conversions).

[39] There is no preterit conversion of the optative affirmative ⲉ≠ⲉ–.

[40] The negation of ⲛⲉ–ⲁⲛⲅ̄–ⲟⲩⲡⲣⲟⲫⲏⲧⲏⲥ apparently does not occur.

ⲛⲉ-ⲟⲩⲛ̄-⁰ⲣⲱⲙⲉ ⲥⲱⲧⲡ̄[41]
ⲛⲉ-ⲙⲛ̄-⁰ⲣⲱⲙⲉ ⲥⲱⲧⲡ̄
ⲛⲉ-ⲡⲁⲓ̈ ⲡⲉ-ⲉⲧϥ̄-ⲥⲱⲧⲡ̄ ⲙ̄ⲙⲟ-ϥ[42]
Etc.

The non-durative subordinate clauses (ⲛ̄ⲧⲉⲣⲉ- etc.) cannot be converted.

116. *The preterit particle* ⲡⲉ. [CG 438] The word ⲡⲉ sometimes occurs in preterit sentences, towards the end of the sentence. Its function and meaning are unknown[43]. E.g. ⲛⲉϥ-ⲥⲱⲧⲡ̄ ⲡⲉ.

117. To summarize: It will be easy to recognize a preterit conversion when you read, because the converted clause begins with the signal ⲛⲉⲣⲉ-, ⲛⲉ⸗, or ⲛⲉ-. Also, ⲡⲉ may occur towards the end of a preterit clause.

---

[41] Also ⲛⲉⲣⲉ-⁰ⲣⲱⲙⲉ ⲥⲱⲧⲡ̄.

[42] Preterit of a cleft sentence (see lesson 19).

[43] This ⲡⲉ does not occur in the preterit of nominal sentences formed with ⲡⲉ. In other words, ⲡⲉ ⲡⲉ is not written.

VOCABULARY 14

More verbs: Miscellaneous basic actions

ογωϣ (ογεϣ–, ογαϣ⸗)	want to; love; like	θέλειν
ειρε (ⲣ̄–, ⲁⲁ⸗) ⲟ†	make; cause . . . to be; function as . . . ; amount to; perform, accomplish; be (ⲟ† ⲛ̄–)	ποιεῖν, εἶναι
*ⲁⲣⲭⲉⲓ ⲛ̄– or ⲉ– (+ infin.)	begin	
ϭⲱ, ϭⲉⲉⲧ†	stay, tarry, remain (w. circumstantial 120)	μένειν
ⲗⲟ	cease (w. circumstantial 120); get well	παύεσθαι, ἰᾶσθαι
ϣⲱⲡⲉ, ϣⲟⲟⲡ†	become, come into existence; happen, come to pass; be	γίνεσθαι; εἶναι
ⲭⲡⲟ (ⲭⲡⲉ–, ⲭⲡⲟ⸗) (=ⲧϣⲡⲟ)	bring into existence; give birth to; produce; get (literally "cause to exist")	γεννᾶν
ⲁⲙⲁϩⲧⲉ	seize, grasp	κρατεῖν
ⲕⲱ (ⲕⲁ–, ⲕⲁⲁ⸗) ⲕⲏ†	place, appoint, put down; permit; leave, abandon; lie, be (ⲕⲏ†)	τιθέναι, ἀφιέναι; κεῖσθαι
ϩⲓⲟⲩⲉ (ϩⲓ–, ϩⲓⲧ⸗)	strike, cast	δέρειν, τύπτειν
ϩⲁⲣⲉϩ ⲉ–	keep, guard	τηρεῖν, φυλάσσειν

Verbs of position: (a) Motion

ⲙⲟⲟϣⲉ	go, travel, walk	πορεύεσθαι, περιπατεῖν
ⲡⲱⲧ, ⲡⲏⲧ†	run, flee	τρέχειν
ϩⲱⲛ ⲉϩⲟⲩⲛ, ϩⲏⲛ† ⲉϩⲟⲩⲛ	draw near, approach	ἐγγίζειν, ἐγγὺς εἶναι
ϥⲓ (ϥⲓ–, ϥⲓⲧ⸗)	take up; take away; ϩⲁ– carry	αἴρειν

(b) Stasis

ϨⲘⲞⲞⲤ	sit, dwell; ⲘⲚ̄– be married to	καθῆσθαι
ⲀϨⲈⲢⲀⲦ⸗ or ⲀϨⲈ ⲈⲢⲀⲦ⸗ (filed under ⲱϨⲈ)	stand (stand-on-feet-of self [reflexive])	ἱστάναι

(c) Rotation

ⲔⲰⲦⲈ (ⲔⲈⲦ–, ⲔⲞⲦ⸗)	Ⲛ̄– turn (transitive, often reflexive); ⲉ– surround, repeat	ἐπιστρέφειν, κυ-κλοῦν
ⲔⲦⲞ (ⲔⲦⲈ–, ⲔⲦⲞ⸗)	turn (transitive, often reflex-ive; properly, "cause to turn" = ⲦⲔⲦⲞ), go round, surround	ὑποστρέφειν, στρέφειν

Conjunctions

ⲈⲂⲞⲖ ϪⲈ–	because (less ambiguous than ϪⲈ–)	ὅτι, ἐπεί
ⲈⲦⲂⲈ–ϪⲈ–	because (less ambiguous than ϪⲈ–)	διὰ τὸ + infini-tive, ἐπεί

Logical particles

ⲈⲚⲈ–	(1) before indirect question: whether (2) before direct question: not translated	εἰ
ⲈⲒⲈ–	then (in If-Then sentence); *ergo, igitur, profecto*	ἄρα

Reciprocal pronoun

ⲈⲢⲎⲨ (always w. posses-sive article agreeing with subject)	one another (literally compan-ion, fellow)[a]	ἀλλήλων

The noun ⲤⲞⲠ forming adverbs

Ⲡ–ⲤⲞⲠ (noun)	time, turn, occasion	
ϨⲀϨ Ⲛ̄–ⲤⲞⲠ, Ⲛ̄ϨⲀϨ Ⲛ̄–ⲤⲞⲠ	often, many times	πολλάκις
ϮⲞⲨ Ⲛ̄–ⲤⲞⲠ, Ⲛ̄ϮⲞⲨ Ⲛ̄–ⲤⲞⲠ, etc. (any num-ber from ϢⲞⲘⲚ̄Ⲧ on up is constructed thus)	five times, etc.	πεντάκις

оүнр ⲛ̄-cоⲡ, ⲛ̄оүнр ⲛ̄-cоⲡ	how many times?, how often?	ποσάκις
кecоⲡ, ⲛ̄кecоⲡ	again, anew	ἄνωθεν, πάλιν
оүcоⲡ, ⲛ̄оүcоⲡ, ⲛ̄оү-cоⲡ ⲛ̄-оүⲱⲧ	one time, once	ἅπαξ
ϩι-оүcоⲡ	together, with one accord	ὁμοθυμαδόν

Special forms of cоⲡ:

ⲛ̄cⲉⲡ cⲛⲁү, ⲛ̄cⲡ̄-cⲛⲁү	twice	δίς
ⲛ̄ϣⲙ̄ⲛ̄ⲧ-cⲱⲱⲡ	three times	τρίς
ⲙ̄ⲡⲙⲉϩ-cⲉⲡ cⲛⲁү (yet ⲙ̄ⲡⲙⲉϩ-ϣⲟⲙⲛ̄ⲧ ⲛ̄-cоⲡ etc. from *Three* up)	for a second time	δεύτερον

ᵃE.g. ⲁү-ϣⲁϫⲉ ⲙⲛ̄-ⲛⲉүⲉⲣнү = They spoke with one another, ⲁⲛ-ⲛ̄ϩⲙ̄ϩⲁⲗ ⲛ̄-ⲛⲉⲛⲉⲣнү = We are one another's servants.

EXERCISES 14

A. *Study these preterit conversions and their context, noting carefully where there are switches between main-line past narrative (ⲁq-, ⲛ̄ⲧⲉⲣⲉq-, ⲡⲉϫⲁ-q) and the descriptive or slow-motion preterit (ⲛⲉq-). Notice other signals of switching in the text, such as ⲇⲉ, ⲅⲁⲣ, or ⲛ̄ⲧⲉүⲛоү. In each passage, what is the cause, or the effect, of the switching?*

1. The whole region came (ⲁc-ⲃⲱк) and were baptized (ⲁү-ϫι-ᵉⲃⲁⲡ-ⲧιcⲙⲁ) by him (John). ⲁүⲱ ιⲱϩⲁⲛⲛнⲥ ⲛⲉⲣⲉ-ϩⲉⲛqⲱ⁴⁴ ⲛ̄-бⲁⲙоүⲗ ⲧⲟ ϩιⲱⲱ-q⁴⁵ . . . ⲁүⲱ ⲛⲉq-ⲧⲁϣⲉ-ᵉоⲉιϣ . . . Now it happened (ⲁүⲱ ⲁc-ϣⲱⲡⲉ) that Jesus came (ⲁq-ⲉι) from Nazareth of Galilee and was baptized (ⲁq-ϫι-ᵉⲃⲁⲡⲧιcⲙⲁ). Mark 1:5–9

2. While He (Jesus) was walking by the Sea of Galilee, He saw (ⲁq-ⲛⲁү) Simon and Simon's brother Andrew casting nets into the lake. ⲛⲉ-ϩⲉⲛоүⲱϩⲉ⁴⁶ ⲅⲁⲣ ⲛⲉ. He said (ⲡⲉϫⲁ-q) to them, Come . . . Mark 1:16–17

---

⁴⁴ qⲱ skin; бⲁⲙоүⲗ camel.

⁴⁵ ⲧⲟ ϩιⲱⲱ-q Stative of ϯ ϩιⲱⲱ= to dress (someone), lit. put upon.

⁴⁶ оүⲱϩⲉ fisherman.

3. As soon as they had left (ⲛ̄ⲧⲉⲩⲛⲟⲩ ⲇⲉ ⲛ̄ⲧⲉⲣⲟⲩ-ⲉⲓ ⲉⲃⲟⲗ ϩⲛ̄-) the synagogue He (Jesus) went (ⲁϥ-ⲃⲱⲕ) into the house of Simon and Andrew, with James and John. Now (ⲇⲉ) Simon's mother-in-law ⲛⲉⲥ-ⲛⲏⲭ[47] with a fever. And immediately they spoke (ⲛ̄ⲧⲉⲩⲛⲟⲩ ⲁⲩ-ϣⲁϫⲉ) with Him about her. And He went to her (ⲁϥ-) and lifted her up (ⲁϥ-ⲧⲟⲩⲛⲟⲥ-ⲥ̄) . . . and the fever ceased (ⲁϥ-ⲗⲟ). Mark 1:29–31

4. And He went back (ⲁϥ-ⲃⲱⲕ ⲟⲛ) into the synagogue. ⲛⲉ-ⲩⲛ̄-ⲟⲩⲣⲱⲙⲉ ⲇⲉ ⲙ̄ⲙⲁⲩ whose hand was withered. ⲁⲩⲱ ⲛⲉⲩ-ⲡⲁⲣⲁⲧⲏⲣⲉⲓ[48] ⲉⲣⲟ-ϥ to heal him on the Sabbath so that they might press charges against Him. And He said (ⲁⲩⲱ ⲡⲉϫⲁ-ϥ) to the man whose hand was withered, Arise, come forth . . . He said (ⲡⲉϫⲁ-ϥ) to the man, Stretch out your hand. He stretched it out (ⲁϥ-ⲥⲟⲩⲧⲱⲛ-ⲥ̄) and his hand was cured (ⲁⲥ-ⲗⲟ ⲛ̄ϭⲓ-ⲧⲉϥϭⲓϫ). Mark 3:1–5

5. And His mother and brothers came (ⲁⲩ-ⲉⲓ) and positioned themselves (ⲁⲩ-ⲁϩⲉⲣⲁⲧ-ⲟⲩ) outside, and they sent (ⲁⲩ-ϫⲟⲟⲩ) in to Him summoning Him. ⲁⲩⲱ ⲛⲉϥ-ϩⲙⲟⲟⲥ ϩⲙ̄-ⲡⲉϥⲕⲱⲧⲉ[49] ⲛ̄ϭⲓ-ⲟⲩⲙⲏⲏϣⲉ ⲡⲉ. They said (ⲡⲉϫⲁ-ⲩ), Excuse me, Your mother and brothers are outside looking for You. He replied (ⲁϥ-ⲟⲩⲱϣⲃ̄ ⲇⲉ), Who are my "mother" and my "brothers!" Mark 3:31–33

6. And a large crowd gathered (ⲁⲩⲱ ⲁ-ⲩⲛⲟϭ ⲙ̄-ⲙⲏⲏϣⲉ ⲥⲱⲟⲩϩ) to Him, so that He got into a boat and sat there in the lake. ⲁⲩⲱ ⲡⲙⲏⲏϣⲉ ⲧⲏⲣ-ϥ̄ ⲛⲉϥ-ⲁϩⲉⲣⲁⲧ-ϥ̄ ϩⲓ-ⲡⲉⲕⲣⲟ ⲛ̄-ⲧⲉⲑⲁⲗⲁⲥⲥⲁ. ⲁϥ-ϯ-ᵠⲥⲃⲱ ⲇⲉ ⲛⲁ-ⲩ ⲉⲙⲁⲧⲉ[50] ϩⲛ̄-ϩⲉⲛⲡⲁⲣⲁⲃⲟⲗⲏ[51]. ⲁⲩⲱ ⲛⲉϥ-ϫⲱ ⲙ̄ⲙⲟ-ⲥ[52] ⲛⲁ-ⲩ ϫⲉ- Listen here, a sower came forth to sow. And when he sowed, some fell on the road (etc . . . . [*the Parable of the Sower is now told at length, using only* ⲁϥ-, ⲛ̄ⲧⲉⲣⲉϥ-, *and* ⲙ̄ⲡϥ̄-; *the parable ends, and Mark continues as follows*). ⲛⲉϥ-ϫⲱ ⲇⲉ ⲙ̄ⲙⲟ-ⲥ ⲛⲁ-ⲩ ϫⲉ- He who has ears to hear, let him hear! ⲛ̄ⲧⲉⲣⲉϥ-ⲕⲁ-ⲡⲙⲏⲏϣⲉ ⲇⲉ ⲁⲩ-ϫⲛⲟⲩ-ϥ . . . ⲉ-ⲙ̄ⲡⲁⲣⲁⲃⲟⲗⲏ. ⲡⲉϫⲁ-ϥ ⲛⲁ-ⲩ . . . Mark 4:1–11

7. Now, they left the crowd (ⲁⲩ-ⲕⲁ-ⲡⲙⲏⲏϣⲉ ϭⲉ) and got Him into the boat (ⲁⲩ-ⲧⲁⲗⲟ-ϥ ⲉ-ⲡϫⲟⲉⲓ) . . . And a great tempest occurred (ⲁⲩⲱ ⲁ-ⲩⲛⲟϭ ⲛ̄-ϩⲁⲧⲏⲩ ϣⲱⲡⲉ), and the waves pounded the boat to the point of capsizing it. ⲛ̄ⲧⲟϥ ⲇⲉ ⲛⲉϥ-ϩⲓⲡⲁϩⲟⲩ ⲙ̄-ⲡϫⲟⲓ̈[53] sleeping on a pillow. And

---

[47] ⲛⲏⲭ was in bed (ⲛⲟⲩϫⲉ = throw, ⲛⲏⲭ† = lie).

[48] ⲡⲁⲣⲁⲧⲏⲣⲉⲓ entreat.

[49] ϩⲙ̄-ⲡⲉϥⲕⲱⲧⲉ around Him, in His vicinity.

[50] ⲉⲙⲁⲧⲉ very much.

[51] ⲡⲁⲣⲁⲃⲟⲗⲏ parables, short symbolic stories.

[52] ϫⲱ ⲙ̄ⲙⲟ-ⲥ ϫⲉ- to say.

[53] ϩⲓⲡⲁϩⲟⲩ ⲙ̄-ⲡϫⲟⲓ̈ in the stern of the boat.

they woke Him (ⲁⲩⲱ ⲁⲩ-ⲛⲉ2ⲥⲉ ⲙⲙⲟ-ϥ) saying to Him, Teacher, don't you care about the fact that we're going to die! Mark 4:36–38

8. 2ⲛ-ⲧⲉ2ⲟⲩⲉⲓⲧⲉ⁵⁴ ⲛⲉϥ-ϣⲟⲟⲡ ⲛ6ⲓ-ⲡϣⲁⲭⲉ. ⲁⲩⲱ ⲡϣⲁⲭⲉ ⲛⲉϥ-ϣⲟⲟⲡ ⲛⲛⲁ2ⲣⲛ-ⲡⲛⲟⲩⲧⲉ. ⲁⲩⲱ ⲛⲉ-ⲩⲛⲟⲩⲧⲉ ⲡⲉ ⲡϣⲁⲭⲉ. ⲡⲁⲓ 2ⲛ-ⲧⲉ2ⲟⲩⲉⲓⲧⲉ ⲛⲉϥ-ϣⲟⲟⲡ 2ⲁⲧⲙ-ⲡⲛⲟⲩⲧⲉ . . . Once upon a time there was (ⲁϥ-ϣⲱⲡⲉ) a man sent by God, named John. ⲡⲁⲓ ⲁϥ-ⲉⲓ ⲉ-ⲩⲙⲛⲧ-ⲙⲛⲧⲣⲉ ⲭⲉ-ⲉϥⲉ-ⲣ̄-⁰ⲙⲛⲧⲣⲉ ⲉⲧⲃⲉ-ⲡⲟⲩⲟⲉⲓⲛ . . . ⲛⲉ-ⲡⲉⲧⲙⲙⲁⲩ ⲁⲛ ⲡⲉ ⲡⲟⲩⲟⲉⲓⲛ, ⲁⲗⲗⲁ ⲭⲉⲕⲁⲥ ⲛⲧⲟϥ ⲉϥⲉ-ⲣ̄-⁰ⲙⲛⲧⲣⲉ ⲉⲧⲃⲉ-ⲡⲟⲩⲟⲉⲓⲛ. John 1:1–8

9. And on the third day, a wedding occurred (ⲁ-ⲩϣⲉⲗⲉⲉⲧ ϣⲱⲡⲉ) in Cana of Galilee. ⲁⲩⲱ ⲛⲉⲣⲉ-ⲧⲙⲁⲁⲩ ⲛ-ⲓⲥ ⲙⲙⲁⲩ. ⲁⲩ-ⲧⲱ2ⲙ ⲇⲉ 2ⲱⲱ-ϥ ⲛ-ⲓⲥ ⲙⲛ-ⲛⲉϥⲙⲁⲑⲏⲧⲏⲥ ⲉ-ⲧϣⲉⲗⲉⲉⲧ. John 2:1–2

10. They arrested (ⲁⲩ-6ⲱⲡⲉ) Jesus, tied Him up (ⲁⲩ-ⲙⲟⲣ-ϥ) and brought Him (ⲁⲩ-ⲛⲧ-ϥ) first to Annas. ⲛⲉ-ⲡϣⲟⲙ⁵⁵ ⲇⲉ ⲡⲉ ⲛ-ⲕⲁⲓⲫⲁⲥ⁵⁶, who was high priest that year. Kaiphas is the one who consulted with the Jews as to whether it was useful for one man to die for the sake of the people. ⲛⲉϥ-ⲟⲩⲏ2⁵⁷ ⲇⲉ ⲛⲥⲁ-ⲓⲥ ⲛ6ⲓ-ⲥⲓⲙⲱⲛ ⲡⲉⲧⲣⲟⲥ ⲙⲛ-ⲕⲉⲙⲁⲑⲏⲧⲏⲥ. ⲡⲙⲁⲑⲏⲧⲏⲥ ⲇⲉ ⲉⲧⲙⲙⲁⲩ ⲛⲉⲣⲉ-ⲡⲁⲣⲭⲓⲉⲣⲉⲩⲥ ⲥⲟⲟⲩⲛ ⲙⲙⲟ-ϥ. And he went (ⲁϥ-ⲃⲱⲕ) into the praetorium with Jesus. ⲡⲉⲧⲣⲟⲥ ⲇⲉ ⲛⲉϥ-ⲁ2ⲉⲣⲁⲧ-ϥ ⲡⲉ ⲙⲃⲟⲗ⁵⁸ 2ⲓⲣⲙ-ⲡⲣⲟ⁵⁹. Then the disciple whom the high priest knew came (ⲁϥ-ⲉⲓ ⲇⲉ), spoke (ⲁϥ-ⲭⲟⲟ-ⲥ) to the doorkeeper, and brought Peter in (ⲁϥ-ⲭⲓ ⲙ-ⲡⲉⲧⲣⲟⲥ ⲉ2ⲟⲩⲛ). And the servant of the doorkeeper said (ⲡⲉⲭⲁ-ⲥ) to Peter, Aren't you also one of the disciples of this man? He said (ⲡⲉⲭⲁ-ϥ), No. ⲛⲉⲩ-ⲁ2ⲉⲣⲁⲧ-ⲟⲩ ⲇⲉ ⲛ6ⲓ-ⲛ2ⲙ2ⲁⲗ ⲙⲛ-ⲛ2ⲩⲡⲏⲣⲉⲧⲏⲥ⁶⁰. And they lit (ⲁⲩ-) a fire, warming themselves. ⲭⲉ-ⲛⲉⲣⲉ-ⲡⲭⲁϥ ⲛⲃⲟⲗ⁶¹. ⲡⲉⲧⲣⲟⲥ 2ⲱⲱ-ϥ ⲟⲛ ⲛⲉϥ-ⲁ2ⲉⲣⲁⲧ-ϥ warming himself. ⲡⲁⲣⲭⲓⲉⲣⲉⲩⲥ ⲇⲉ ⲁϥ-ⲭⲛⲉ-ⲓⲥ ⲉⲧⲃⲉ-ⲛⲉϥⲙⲁⲑⲏⲧⲏⲥ ⲁⲩⲱ ⲉⲧⲃⲉ-ⲧⲉϥⲥⲃⲱ. ⲁϥ-ⲟⲩⲱϣⲃ ⲛⲁ-ϥ ⲛ6ⲓ-ⲓⲥ . . . John 18:12–20

11. So Jesus stood (ⲁϥ-ⲁ2ⲉⲣⲁⲧ-ϥ) before the governor. And the governor questioned Him (ⲁϥ-ⲭⲛⲟⲩ-ϥ ⲇⲉ), saying, Is it You who are the king of the Jews? Jesus said (ⲡⲉⲭⲁ-ϥ), It is you who say this . . . Next Pilate said (ⲧⲟⲧⲉ ⲡⲉⲭⲁ-ϥ) to Him, Don't You hear how much they are testifying against You? But He did not answer (ⲙⲡⲉϥ-ⲟⲩⲟϣⲃ-ⲉϥ) a single word, so

---

⁵⁴ 2ⲟⲩⲉⲓⲧⲉ beginning.
⁵⁵ ϣⲟⲙ father-in-law.
⁵⁶ ⲕⲁⲓⲫⲁⲥ (personal name) Kaiphas.
⁵⁷ ⲟⲩⲏ2 (stative) ⲛⲥⲁ- follow, be behind.
⁵⁸ ⲙⲃⲟⲗ outside.
⁵⁹ 2ⲓⲣⲙ-ⲡⲣⲟ at the door.
⁶⁰ 2ⲩⲡⲏⲣⲉⲧⲏⲥ official, officer.
⁶¹ ⲡⲭⲁϥ ⲛⲃⲟⲗ, literally "the cold was outside" i.e. it was cold.

that the governor was really surprised. Now on every feastday (ⲕⲁⲧⲁ-⁰ⲱϣⲁ
ⲗⲉ), ⲛⲉ-ϣⲁⲣⲉ-ⲡϨⲏⲅⲉⲙⲱⲛ ⲕⲁ-ⲟⲩⲁ ⲉⲃⲟⲗ ⲙ̄-ⲡⲙⲏⲏϣⲉ—someone
under arrest, whoever they wanted. ⲛⲉ-ⲩⲛ̄ⲧⲁ-ⲩ ⲗⲉ ⲙ̄ⲙⲁⲩ ⲙ̄-ⲡⲉⲟⲩⲟⲉⲓϣ
ⲉⲧⲙ̄ⲙⲁⲩ ⲛ̄-ⲟⲩⲁ . . . ϫⲉ-ⲃⲁⲣⲁⲃⲃⲁⲥ. And (ⲗⲉ) as they gathered together,
Pilate said (ⲡⲉϫⲁ-ϥ) to them, Do you want me to release Barabbas to you,
or Jesus, who is called "Messiah?" Matthew 27:11–17

12. After this, Jesus came (ⲙⲛ̄ⲛ̄ⲥⲁ-ⲛⲁⲓ̈ ⲁϥ-ⲉⲓ) with His disciples to the
region of Judaea. ⲁⲩⲱ ⲛⲉϥ-ⲙ̄ⲙⲁⲩ ⲡⲉ ⲛⲙ̄ⲙⲁ-ⲩ, baptizing. ⲛⲉⲣⲉ-
ⲡⲕⲉⲓⲱϨⲁⲛⲛⲏⲥ ⲗⲉ ⲃⲁⲡⲧⲓⲍⲉ Ϩⲛ̄-ⲁⲓⲛⲱⲛ Ϩⲁⲧⲛ̄-ⲥⲁⲗⲉⲓⲙ[62]. ϫⲉ ⲛⲉ-ⲩⲛ̄-
ϨⲁϨ ⲙ̄-ⲙⲟⲟⲩ Ϩⲙ̄-ⲡⲙⲁ ⲉⲧⲙ̄ⲙⲁⲩ. ⲁⲩⲱ ⲛⲉⲩ-ⲛⲏⲩ ⲡⲉ to be baptized. ⲛⲉ-
ⲙ̄ⲡⲁⲧⲟⲩ-ⲛⲉϫ-ⲓⲱϨⲁⲛⲛⲉⲥ ⲅⲁⲣ ⲡⲉ ⲉ-ⲡⲉϣⲧⲉⲕⲟ[63]. So, a dispute occurred
(ⲁ-ⲩⲍⲏⲧⲏⲥⲓⲥ ϭⲉ ϣⲱⲡⲉ), consisting of the disciples of John and a certain
Jew, on the subject of purification. They came (ⲁⲩ-ⲉⲓ) to John and said
(ⲡⲉϫⲁ-ⲩ) to him . . . John 3:22–26

13. And He came back (ⲁϥ-ⲉⲓ ⲗⲉ ⲟⲛ) to Cana of Galilee, where He had
made the water turn into wine. ⲁⲩⲱ ⲛⲉ-ⲩⲛ̄-ⲟⲩⲃⲁⲥⲓⲗⲓⲕⲟⲥ[64] whose son
was sick in Capharnaum. When this man heard (ⲛ̄ⲧⲉⲣⲉϥ-ⲥⲱⲧⲙ̄) that Jesus
had come from Judaea to Galilee, he went (ⲁϥ-ⲃⲱⲕ) to Him and begged
Him (ⲁϥ-ⲥⲉⲡⲥⲱⲡ-ϥ̄) to come down and heal his son. ⲛⲉϥ-ⲛⲁ-ⲙⲟⲩ ⲅⲁⲣ
ⲡⲉ. So Jesus said (ⲡⲉϫⲉ-ⲓⲥ̄ ϭⲉ) to him, Unless you see signs and wonders
you will not believe! John 4:46–48

14. The tribune commanded (ⲁ-ⲡϫⲓⲗⲓⲁⲣⲭⲟⲥ ⲗⲉ ⲟⲩⲉϨ-⁰ⲥⲁϨⲛⲉ) for him
(Paul) to be brought into the barracks, and he said he should be scourged
with whips . . . But when (ⲛ̄ⲧⲉⲣⲟⲩ-) he had been tied up with thongs, Paul
said (ⲡⲉϫⲁ-ϥ) to the tribune who was standing there, Is it within your
capacity to beat a man who is a Roman and has done no wrong? . . . I was
born with this citizenship. And immediately those who were about to inter-
rogate him withdrew (ⲁⲩ-ⲥⲁϨⲱ-ⲟⲩ ⲉⲃⲟⲗ). And the tribune became afraid
(ⲁϥ-ⲣ̄-⁰Ϩⲟⲧⲉ) when he learned that he was a Roman citizen, ⲉⲃⲟⲗ
ϫⲉ-ⲛⲉ-ⲁϥ-ⲙⲟⲣ-ϥ̄ ⲡⲉ. And immediately he released him (ⲁⲩⲱ
ⲛ̄ⲧⲉⲩⲛⲟⲩ ⲁϥ-ⲃⲟⲗ-ϥ̄ ⲉⲃⲟⲗ). Acts 22:24–29

B. *Translate rapidly into Coptic, using the preterit conversion of the durative sentence.*

a. I wanted, you (sing. masc.) wanted, you (sing. fem.) wanted, he... etc. etc.

b. The man wanted, the woman wanted, the brothers wanted, someone
(⁰ⲣⲱⲙⲉ) wanted.

---

[62] ⲁⲓⲛⲱⲛ Ϩⲁⲧⲛ̄-ⲥⲁⲗⲉⲓⲙ (place name) Ainon by Salim.

[63] ϣⲧⲉⲕⲟ prison.

[64] ⲃⲁⲥⲓⲗⲓⲕⲟⲥ official.

c. I did not want, you (sing. masc.) did not want, etc. etc.

d. The man did not want, the woman did not want, the brothers did not want, no one wanted.

e. My mother was sitting in the house. The Lord was in His temple. I was with them. They were with me. You (pl.) were with us.

C. Translate. a. ετβε-ογ ακ-ρ̄-πειϩωβ. b. εϣϣε ϫν ε-⁰ειρε ⲙ̄-πειϩωβ. c. ⲛⲉⲩ-ⲁⲣⲭⲉⲓ ⲛ̄-⁰ⲕⲱⲧⲉ ⲉ-ⲧⲉⲥϩⲓⲙⲉ. d. ⲁⲛ-ⲁⲙⲁϩⲧⲉ ⲙ̄-ⲡⲉϥϭⲓϫ ⲛ̄ⲕⲉⲥⲟⲡ. e. ⲁⲥ-ϫⲡⲉ-ⲟⲩϣⲏⲣⲉ ϫⲉ-ⲓⲱϩⲁⲛⲛⲏⲥ⁶⁵. f. ⲛⲉⲩ-ϭⲱ ϩⲛ̄-ⲧⲡⲟⲗⲓⲥ ϩⲓ-ⲟⲩⲥⲟⲡ. g. ⲡⲉϫⲉ-ⲡϩⲗ̄ⲗⲟ ϫⲉ-ϩⲁⲣⲉϩ ⲉ-ⲧⲉⲕⲧⲁⲡⲣⲟ ⲛⲅ̄-ϥⲓ ⲙ̄-ⲡⲉⲕⲥⲧⲁⲩⲣⲟⲥ. h. ⲛⲉⲣⲉ-ⲛ̄ⲇⲁⲓⲙⲟⲛⲓⲟⲛ ⲡⲏⲧ ⲉⲃⲟⲗ. i. ⲁⲥ-ⲕⲧⲟ-ⲥ ⲁⲥ-ϩⲱⲛ ⲉϩⲟⲩⲛ.

---

⁶⁵ Cf. **23** (box "The Special Grammar of Proper Nouns").

LESSON 15

ASYNDETIC CONNECTION OF CLAUSES. ADVERB. CIRCUMSTANTIAL CONVERSION.

118. *Asyndetic Connection of Clauses.* [CG 237]

When two or more past tense clauses (ⲁϥ–) are strung together without a word for *'And'*, this indicates very close connection. ⲡⲉϫⲁⲥ is also connected in this way.

ⲁϥ–ⲥⲱⲧⲙ̄ ⲇⲉ ⲛ̄ϭⲓ–ϩⲏⲣⲱⲁⲛⲥ ⲡⲣ̄ⲣⲟ ⲁϥ–ϣⲧⲟⲣⲧⲣ̄
Then King Herod heard the news and was alarmed

ⲁϥ–ⲟⲩⲱϣⲃ̄ ⲡⲉϫⲁ–ϥ
He answered, saying . . .

ⲁⲥ–ⲧⲱⲟⲩⲛ–ⲥ̄ ⲛ̄ϭⲓ–ⲧϣⲉⲉⲣⲉ ϣⲏⲙ ⲁⲥ–ⲙⲟⲟϣⲉ
The girl got up and walked

ⲁⲩ–ⲛⲁⲩ ⲉ–ⲡϣⲏⲣⲉ ϣⲏⲙ ⲙⲛ̄–ⲙⲁⲣⲓⲁ ⲧⲉϥⲙⲁⲁⲩ ⲁⲩ–ⲡⲁϩⲧ–ⲟⲩ ⲁⲩ–ⲟⲩⲱϣⲧ̄
ⲛⲁ–ϥ ⲁⲩ–ⲟⲩⲱⲛ ⲛ̄–ⲛⲉⲩⲁϩⲱⲱⲣ ⲁⲩ–ⲉⲓⲛⲉ ⲛⲁ–ϥ ⲛ̄–ϩⲉⲛⲁⲱⲣⲟⲛ
Seeing the child and Mary His mother they bowed themselves down, worshipped
    Him, opened their treasures, and brought Him gifts

119. *Adverbs* [CG 194–99, 215–29] are words such as

ⲉⲙⲁⲧⲉ greatly
ⲉⲙⲁⲩ thither
ⲉⲛⲉϩ ever (as in "not *ever*")
*ⲕⲁⲗⲱⲥ well
*ⲕⲁⲕⲱⲥ badly
ⲗⲁⲁⲩ at all
ⲙ̄ⲙⲏⲛⲉ daily
ⲙ̄ⲙⲁⲧⲉ only, exclusively
ⲙ̄ⲙⲁⲩ there
ⲟⲛ again
*ⲡⲱⲥ how?
ⲧⲱⲛ where? when? how?
ⲉⲃⲟⲗ ⲧⲱⲛ whence?
ⲧⲛⲁⲩ when?

ⲧⲉⲛⲟⲩ now
ⲅⲉ any more

Some adverbs are prepositional phrases used as fixed expressions; many are formed with initial ⲛ̄.

ⲛ̄ⲁϣ ⲛ̄-ϩⲉ how?
ⲛ̄ⲥⲁϣϥ̄ ⲛ̄-ⲥⲟⲡ for seven times
ⲛ̄ⲧⲉⲩϣⲏ by night
ⲛ̄ⲟⲩⲕⲟⲩⲓ̈ to a small degree
ⲛ̄ⲟⲩⲙⲁ somewhere
ⲛ̄ⲟⲩⲏⲣ ⲛ̄-ⲥⲟⲡ how many times?
ⲛ̄ϩⲁⲉ finally
ⲉ-ⲡⲧⲏⲣ-ϥ wholly
ⲉ-ⲡⲉϩⲟⲩⲟ too much
ⲉ-ⲧⲱⲛ whither?
ⲉⲧⲃⲉ-ⲟⲩ why?
ϣⲁ-ⲡⲉⲓ̈ⲙⲁ thus far, up to now
ⲭⲉ-ⲟⲩ why?

Negation of these is by a following ⲁⲛ: ⲉⲙⲁⲧⲉ ⲁⲛ = not greatly, ⲉⲙⲁⲩ ⲁⲛ = not thither, ⲛ̄ⲥⲁϣϥ̄ ⲛ̄-ⲥⲟⲡ ⲁⲛ = not seven times, etc.

Adverbs of manner are formed freely in the pattern ϩⲛ̄-ⲟⲩ . . . (and negative ⲁⲭⲛ̄-⁰ . . .).

ϩⲛ̄-ⲟⲩⲙⲉ truly, ϩⲛ̄-ⲟⲩⲇⲓⲕⲁⲓⲟⲥⲩⲛⲏ justly, etc. etc.
ⲁⲭⲛ̄-⁰ⲛⲟⲙⲟⲥ lawlessly, ⲁⲭⲛ̄-⁰ϩⲟⲧⲉ fearlessly, etc. etc.

The placement of adverbs within the sentence is fairly free.

THE CIRCUMSTANTIAL CONVERSION

120. The circumstantial conversion [CG 413–33] is marked by the converter

ⲉⲣⲉ-, ⲉⲑ   conversion base
ⲉ-   sentence converter

As you already know (**110**), there is some ambiguity in identifying circumstantials.

The circumstantial, both affirmative and negative, is formed in the same way as the preterit (cf. **112**). Note that there is a circumstantial of the preterit.

ⲉ-ⲁⲛⲅ̄-ⲟⲩⲡⲣⲟⲫⲏⲧⲏⲥ
ⲉ-ⲁⲛⲅ̄-ⲟⲩⲡⲣⲟⲫⲏⲧⲏⲥ ⲁⲛ
ⲉ-ⲟⲩⲡⲣⲟⲫⲏⲧⲏⲥ ⲡⲉ
ⲉ-ⲟⲩⲡⲣⲟⲫⲏⲧⲏⲥ ⲁⲛ ⲡⲉ
ⲉ-ⲛ̄-ⲟⲩⲡⲣⲟⲫⲏⲧⲏⲥ ⲁⲛ ⲡⲉ

ⲉⲣⲉ-ⲡⲣⲱⲙⲉ ⲥⲱⲧⲡ̄
ⲉⲣⲉ-ⲡⲣⲱⲙⲉ ⲥⲱⲧⲡ̄ ⲁⲛ
ⲉ-ⲙ̄-ⲡⲣⲱⲙⲉ ⲥⲱⲧⲡ ⲁⲛ
ⲉϥ-ⲥⲱⲧⲡ̄
ⲉϥ-ⲥⲱⲧⲡ̄ ⲁⲛ
ⲉ-ⲛ̄-ϥ-ⲥⲱⲧⲡ̄ ⲁⲛ
ⲉ-ⲁϥ-ⲥⲱⲧⲡ̄, ⲉ-ⲙ̄ⲡϥ̄-, etc.
ⲉ-ⲛⲁⲛⲟⲩ-ϥ
ⲉ-ⲛⲁⲛⲟⲩ-ϥ ⲁⲛ
ⲉ-ⲟⲩⲛ̄-⁰ⲣⲱⲙⲉ ⲥⲱⲧⲡ̄
ⲉⲣⲉ-⁰ⲣⲱⲙⲉ ⲥⲱⲧⲡ̄
ⲉ-ⲙⲛ̄-⁰ⲣⲱⲙⲉ ⲥⲱⲧⲡ̄
ⲉ-ⲛⲉϥ-ⲥⲱⲧⲡ̄
ⲉ-ⲛⲉϥ-ⲥⲱⲧⲡ̄ ⲁⲛ
ⲉ-ⲡⲁⲓ̈ ⲡⲉ-ⲉⲧϥ-ⲥⲱⲧⲡ̄ ⲙ̄ⲙⲟ-ϥ[66]
Etc.

To convert a sentence formed with ⲟⲩⲛ̄-, it is possible to substitute the prenominal base ⲉⲣⲉ- in place of ⲟⲩⲛ̄-:

ⲟⲩⲛ̄-⁰ⲣⲱⲙⲉ ⲥⲱⲧⲡ̄   ⲉⲣⲉ-⁰ⲣⲱⲙⲉ-ⲥⲱⲧⲡ̄

Conjugation of the conversion base ⲉⲣⲉ-, ⲉ⸗.

ⲉⲓ̈-	ⲉⲛ-
ⲉⲕ-	ⲉⲧⲉⲧⲛ̄-
ⲉⲣⲉ-	
ⲉϥ-	ⲉⲩ-
ⲉⲥ-	
ⲉⲣⲉ-ⲡⲛⲟⲩⲧⲉ	

THE MEANING OF THE CIRCUMSTANTIAL CONVERSION

121. The circumstantial is a subordinate (dependent) clause. It has several functions. Three will be described in this lesson. The fourth is shared between circumstantial and relative, and will be discussed in lesson 17. Generally, the circumstantial is something like a combination of the English *-ing* participle (*going, seeing*) and the Greek genitive absolute or Latin ablative absolute. "*Coming* up from the water, He saw the heavens opened"; "He was in the wilderness, *with-Satan-testing-Him*" (i.e. While Satan was testing Him).

---

[66] Circumstantial of a cleft sentence (see lesson 19).

THE CIRCUMSTANTIAL CONVERSION

122. (*a*) *Adverbial Function.* [CG 421–25]

In this function, the circumstantial plays the role of an adverb, stating the circumstances under which a main clause is envisaged or said to be valid.

   i. ϥϥ-ⲛⲏⲩ ⲉϩⲣⲁⲓ ϩⲙ̄-ⲡⲙⲟⲟⲩ ⲁϥ-ⲛⲁⲩ ⲉ-ⲙⲡⲏⲩⲉ
      As He was coming up from the waters, He saw the heavens

   ii. ⲁⲩ-ϫⲓ-⁰ⲃⲁⲡⲧⲓⲥⲙⲁ ⲉⲩ-ⲉϧⲟⲙⲟⲗⲟⲅⲉⲓ ⲛ̄-ⲛⲉⲩⲛⲟⲃⲉ
      They got baptized, *confessing their sins*

   iii. ⲉϥ-ⲛⲁ-ⲥⲃ̄ⲧⲉ-ⲧⲡⲉ ⲛⲉⲓ̄-ⲛⲙ̄ⲙⲁ-ϥ
      When He was going to prepare the heaven, I was with Him
      (He-going-to-prepare the heaven I was with him)

   iv. ⲛⲉϥ-ϩⲛ̄-ⲧⲉⲣⲏⲙⲟⲥ ⲛ̄-ϩⲙⲉ ⲛ̄-ϩⲟⲟⲩ ⲉⲣⲉ-ⲡⲥⲁⲧⲁⲛⲁⲥ ⲡⲓⲣⲁϧⲉ ⲙ̄ⲙⲟ-ϥ
      He was in the wilderness forty days, *with Satan testing Him*

As these examples show, a circumstantial can either precede or follow the main clause that it relates to. Note that the subject of the circumstantial and the main clause may be the same (examples i and ii) or different (iii and iv). All kinds of main clause can be modified by an adverbial circumstantial.

The logical relationship between the adverbial circumstantial and the main clause is not specified, and English style usually leads translators to add *when, if, although, because,* etc. (Compare translation of the Greek genitive absolute or Latin ablative absolute.) It is important to be very flexible when translating the circumstantial into English. Optionally, Coptic can resolve this logical ambiguity by putting a conjunction before the circumstantial (for a list of these, see box p. 134.)

(*b*) *Completive Function.* [CG 426–27]

The circumstantial can complete a subject or object of certain verbs whose meaning makes this appropriate. The pronoun subject of the circumstantial clause must agree with the subject or object of the main clause that it completes.

   i. Completing the subject of verbs meaning *appear to, cease to, continue to, happen to,* etc.

     ϫⲉⲕⲁⲁⲥ ⲛ̄ⲛⲉⲕ-ⲟⲩⲱⲛϩ̄ ⲉⲃⲟⲗ ⲉⲕ-ⲛⲏⲥⲧⲉⲩⲉ
     So that you [subject] may not appear to be fasting
     (That you may not appear you-fasting)

     ⲁⲩ-ⲗⲟ ⲉⲩ-ⲙⲟⲟϣⲉ ⲛⲙ̄ⲙⲁ-ϥ
     They [subject] ceased going about with Him
     (They stopped they-travelling with Him)

Conjunctions that can precede the adverbial circumstantial [CG 422]

ⲁⲗⲗⲁ ⲉ= though, but, rather

ⲁⲩⲱ ⲉ= and, and indeed, too, furthermore

ⲉⲓⲙⲏⲧⲓ ⲉ= unless, except for . . . -ing

ⲉⲛϩⲟⲥⲟⲛ ⲉ= as long as

ⲉⲫⲟⲥⲟⲛ (ⲉⲡϩⲟⲥⲟⲛ) ⲉ= as long as, inasmuch as

ⲉⲧⲓ ⲉ= while . . . still . . .

ⲉϣⲱⲡⲉ ⲉ= if (ever)

ⲉϣϫⲉ-ⲉ= supposing that

ⲕⲁⲛ ⲉ= even if, even though

ⲕⲁⲓⲡⲉⲣ ⲉ= although

ⲕⲁⲧⲁ-ⲑⲉ ⲉ= just as

ⲕⲁⲓⲧⲟⲓ ⲉ= although

ⲙⲁⲗⲓⲥⲧⲁ ⲉ= especially if/since

ⲛ̄ⲑⲉ ⲉ= just as

ⲡⲁⲗⲓⲛ ⲟⲛ ⲉ= moreover, and yet

⁰ⲥⲟⲡ ⲉ= . . . ⁰ⲥⲟⲡ ⲉ= . . . at one time . . . at another time . . .

ⲭⲱⲣⲓⲥ ⲉ= except when, unless

ϩⲁⲑⲏ ⲉ-ⲙ̄ⲡⲁⲧ= before

ϩⲁⲙⲁ ⲉ= at the same time

ϩⲱⲥ ⲉ= as, as if, on the grounds that

ϩⲱⲥ ⲉϣϫⲉ-ⲉ= as if

ϩⲟⲥⲟⲛ ⲉ= as long as

ϩⲟⲧⲁⲛ ⲉ= whenever, as soon as, such that

---

ii. Completing the direct object of verbs meaning *find, forget, keep, know, leave, ordain, see,* etc.

ⲁϥ-ⲕⲁⲁ-ϥ ⲉϥ-ⲟⲛϩ
He left him [object] alive
(He left him he-living)

ⲁⲛ-ⲛⲁⲩ ⲉ-ⲟⲩⲁ ⲉϥ-ⲛⲉⲝ-⁰ⲇⲁⲓⲙⲟⲛⲓⲟⲛ ⲉⲃⲟⲗ
We saw someone [object] casting out demons
(We saw one he-casting-demons out)

(*c*) *Sequential Function.* [CG 428–29]

This typically occurs in narrative, especially after the past tense ⲁϥ-. The circumstantial expresses the next event, or reexpresses the main clause somewhat differently (*not* relative tense).

ⲁϥ-ϫⲛⲟⲩ-ï ⲉ-ⲁï-ϫⲉ-ⲡⲁï
He asked me, and (next) I said this

ⲁ-ⲫⲓⲗⲓⲡⲡⲟⲥ ⲟⲩⲱⲛ ⲛ̄-ⲣⲱ-ϥ ⲉ-ⲁϥ-ⲁⲣⲭⲉⲓ
Philip opened his mouth and began

In this function, the circumstantial past tense (ⲉ-ⲁ⸗) is not prior to the main clause but happens after it.

However, this function is more often expressed by the adverbial circumstantial, with relative tense: ⲁ-ⲓ̄ⲥ̄ ⲟⲩⲱϣⲃ̄ ⲉϥ-ϫⲱ ⲙ̄ⲙⲟ-ⲥ = Jesus answered, saying (Jesus answered he-saying) or by two past tenses: ⲁϥ-ⲛⲁⲩ ⲁϥ-ⲟⲩⲱϣⲃ̄ = He looked and replied.

(*d*) *Attributive Function.*

This function is shared with the relative conversion and will be described in lesson sixteen (**127**).

123. *Relative Tense.* [CG 529–30]

The circumstantial *present* expresses action *simultaneous* with the main verb

ⲉⲩ-ⲣⲓⲙⲉ ⲁⲥ-ⲃⲱⲕ While they were weeping, she left
ⲉⲩ-ⲣⲓⲙⲉ ⲥ-ⲃⲏⲕ As they weep, she leaves
ⲉⲩ-ⲣⲓⲙⲉ ⲥ-ⲛⲁ-ⲃⲱⲕ When they weep she will leave

the circumstantial *past* expresses action *before* the main verb

ⲉ-ⲁⲩ-ⲣⲓⲙⲉ ⲁⲥ-ⲃⲱⲕ Since/When/Because *etc.* they had wept, she left
ⲉ-ⲁⲩ-ⲣⲓⲙⲉ ⲥ-ⲃⲏⲕ Because they wept she is leaving

and the circumstantial *future* looks forward to action *after* the main verb

ⲉⲩ-ⲛⲁ-ⲣⲓⲙⲉ ⲁⲥ-ⲃⲱⲕ As they were about to weep, she left

VOCABULARY 15

Verbs of position: (d) Motion upwards

ⲧⲁⲗⲟ (ⲧⲁⲗⲉ-, ⲧⲁⲗⲟ=) ⲧⲁⲗⲏⲩ†	lift up, take up, make to go up (onto)	ἀναλαμβάνειν (κεῖσθαι)
ⲧⲱⲟⲩⲛ (intransitive)	arise	ἐγείρειν
ⲧⲱⲟⲩⲛ ⲙ̄ⲙⲟ= (ⲧⲟⲩⲛ̄-, ⲧⲱⲟⲩⲛ=)	(reflexive) arise; (transitive) raise	ἐγείρειν
ⲧⲁϩⲟ (ⲧⲁϩⲉ-, ⲧⲁϩⲟ=)	seize, attain, get to; reach, befall; set up	καταλαμβάνειν
ⲧⲁϩⲟ ⲙ̄ⲙⲟ= (ⲧⲁϩⲉ-, ⲧⲁϩⲟ=) ⲉⲣⲁⲧ=	establish, make to stand	ἱστάναι
ϫⲓⲥⲉ (ϫⲉⲥⲧ-, ϫⲁⲥⲧ=) ϫⲟⲥⲉ†	elevate, lift up; (ingressive) become lifted up, rise	ὑψοῦν

(e) Motion downwards

ϩⲉ, ϩⲏⲩ†	fall	πίπτειν

(f) Motion towards/away from the speaker

ⲉⲓⲛⲉ (ⲛ̄-, ⲛ̄ⲧ=)	bring; (ⲉⲃⲟⲗ) bring, publish; (ⲉⲡⲉⲥⲏⲧ) bring down; (ⲉϩⲟⲩⲛ) bring in	φέρειν
ϥⲓ (ϥⲓ-, ϥⲓⲧ=) ⲉⲃⲟⲗ or ⲙ̄ⲙⲁⲩ	take away	αἴρειν
ⲧⲛ̄ⲛⲟⲟⲩ (ⲧⲛ̄ⲛⲉⲩ-, ⲧⲛ̄ⲛⲟⲟⲩ=)[a]	send (towards speaker), fetch, send word	ἀποστέλλειν
ϫⲟⲟⲩ (ϫⲉⲩ-, ϫⲟⲟⲩ-)[a]	send (away from speaker), dispatch	ἀποστέλλειν
ⲉⲓ, ⲛⲏⲩ†	come; (ⲉⲃⲟⲗ) come forth; (ⲉⲡⲉⲥⲏⲧ) come down; (ⲉϩⲟⲩⲛ ⲉ-) come into; (ⲉϩⲣⲁⲓ̈) come up	ἔρχεσθαι
ⲃⲱⲕ, ⲃⲏⲕ†	go; (ⲉⲃⲟⲗ) leave; (ⲉϩⲟⲩⲛ ⲉ-) enter; (ⲉϩⲣⲁⲓ̈ ⲉ-) go up; (ⲉⲡⲉⲥⲏⲧ) go down	πορεύεσθαι

ϫⲓ (ϫⲓ-, ϫⲓⲧ⸗)	take, receive, get	λαμβάνειν
ϯ (ϯ-, ⲧⲁⲁ-) ⲧⲟ†	give, give back, give away, repay; ⲥ-ⲧⲟ† It is fated	(ἀπο)διδόναι
ϯ (ϯ-, ⲧⲁⲁ⸗) ⲉⲃⲟⲗ, ⲧⲟ† ⲉⲃⲟⲗ	sell	πωλεῖν
ϣⲱⲡ (ϣⲉⲡ-, ϣⲟⲡ⸗) ϣⲏⲡ†	receive, take, buy; (stative) acceptable	δέχεσθαι, ἀγορά-ζειν
ⲥⲱⲟⲩϩ (ⲥⲉⲩϩ-, ⲥⲟⲟⲩϩ-) ⲥⲟⲟⲩϩ†	gather	συνάγειν
ⲧⲁⲟⲩⲟ (ⲧⲁⲟⲩⲉ-, ⲧⲁⲟⲩⲟ⸗)	send forth; utter, proclaim	πέμπειν
ⲛⲟⲩϫⲉ (ⲛⲉϫ-, ⲛⲟϫ-) ⲛⲏϫ†	throw; (ⲉⲃⲟⲗ) cast forth	βάλλειν

Other verbs

(a) Formed with ⲛ̄ϭⲟⲛⲥ̄

ϫⲓ (ϫⲓ-, ϫⲓⲧ-) ⲛ̄ϭⲟⲛⲥ̄	treat violently, violate, treat unjustly	ἀδικεῖν κτλ.
Inf. as nn ⲡϫⲓ ⲛ̄ϭⲟⲛⲥ̄	injustice, unjust action, violence	
ⲣⲉϥ-ϫⲓ ⲛ̄ϭⲟⲛⲥ̄	unjust or violent person	ἄδικος

(b) Based on ⲡ-ⲟⲩⲟⲉⲓ "quick advance, approach"

ϯ-ⲡⲉ(ϥ)ⲟⲩⲟⲉⲓ ⲉ-	approach, meet (ⲁⲥ-ϯ-ⲡⲉⲥ-ⲟⲩⲟⲉⲓ ⲉⲣⲟ-ϥ "She met or approached him")	προσέρχεσθαι

(c) "Be able to, Can"

ϣ-, also spelled ⲉϣ- must be completed by an infinitive [CG 184(c)]	is able to, can	δύνασθαι
ⲛⲁ-ϣ- (future ⲛⲁ-63 + ϣ-), completed by an infinitive, is formally a future tense but often has present meaning	is *or* will be able to, can	δύνασθαι
ⲟⲩⲛ̄-⁰ϭⲟⲙ (or ⲟⲩⲛ̄-⁰ϣϭⲟⲙ) ⲛ̄-/ⲙ̄ⲙⲟ⸗ ⲉ-;[b] negation ⲙⲛ̄-⁰ϭⲟⲙ	is able to, can ("there is power in... to...")[b]	δύνασθαι

ϭⲙ̅–⁰ϭⲟⲙ ⲉ–, ϣϭⲙ̅–   is able to, can   δύνασθαι
⁰ϭⲟⲙ ⲉ– (+ infinitive)

Adverbs in paragraph **119**

---

[a]ⲧⲛ̅ⲛⲟⲟⲩ⸗ and ⲭⲟⲟⲩ⸗ take the personal second suffixes. Cf. **103** (box).
[b]E.g. ⲟⲩⲛ̅–⁰ϭⲟⲙ ⲙ̅ⲙⲟ–ⲕ ⲉ–⁰ⲧⲃ̅ⲃⲟ–ⲓ̈ "You can purify me."

EXERCISES 15

A. *Reading selections from the New Testament.*

1. ϩⲛ̅–ⲧⲉⲩⲛⲟⲩ ⲡⲉⲡ̅ⲛ̅ⲁ ⲁϥ–ϫⲓⲧ–ϥ̅. Mark 1:12

2. ⲁϥ–ⲉⲓ ⲛ̅ϭⲓ–ⲓⲥ̅ ⲉϩⲣⲁⲓ̈ ⲉ–ⲧⲅⲁⲗⲓⲗⲁⲓⲁ ⲉϥ–ⲕⲏⲣⲩⲥⲥⲉ[67] ⲙ̅–ⲡⲉⲩⲁⲅⲅⲉ-ⲗⲓⲟⲛ ⲙ̅–ⲡⲛⲟⲩⲧⲉ. Mark 1:14

3. ⲁⲩⲱ ⲉϥ–ⲙⲟⲟϣⲉ ϩⲁⲧⲛ̅–ⲧⲉⲑⲁⲗⲁⲥⲥⲁ ⲛ̅–ⲧⲅⲁⲗⲓⲗⲁⲓⲁ ⲁϥ–ⲛⲁⲩ ⲉ–ⲥⲓ-ⲙⲱⲛ ⲙⲛ̅–ⲁⲛⲇⲣⲉⲁⲥ ⲡⲥⲟⲛ ⲛ̅–ⲥⲓⲙⲱⲛ ⲉⲩ–ⲛⲉϫ–⁰ϣⲛⲉ[68] ⲉ–ⲧⲉ-ⲑⲁⲗⲁⲥⲥⲁ. Mark 1:16

4. ⲁϥ–ⲛⲁⲩ ⲉ–ⲓⲁⲕⲱⲃⲟⲥ ⲡϣⲏⲣⲉ ⲛ̅–ⲍⲉⲃⲉⲇⲁⲓⲟⲥ ⲙⲛ̅–ⲓⲱϩⲁⲛⲛⲏⲥ ⲡⲉϥ-ⲥⲟⲛ ⲛ̅ⲧⲟⲟⲩ ϩⲱ–ⲟⲩ ⲉⲩ–ϩⲙ̅–ⲡϫⲟⲓ̈. Mark 1:19

5. ⲁⲩⲱ ⲟⲩⲙⲏⲏϣⲉ ⲛ̅–⁰ⲇⲁⲓⲙⲟⲛⲓⲟⲛ ⲁϥ–ⲛⲟϫ–ⲟⲩ ⲉⲃⲟⲗ ⲉ–ⲙⲉϥ–ⲕⲁ-ⲛ̅ⲇⲁⲓⲙⲟⲛⲓⲟⲛ ⲉ–⁰ϣⲁϫⲉ. Mark 1:34

6. ⲁⲩⲱ ⲁϥ–ⲃⲱⲕ ⲉϥ–ⲕⲏⲣⲩⲥⲥⲉ ϩⲛ̅–ⲛⲉⲩⲥⲩⲛⲁⲅⲱⲅⲏ ϩⲛ̅–ⲧⲅⲁⲗⲓⲗⲁⲓⲁ ⲧⲏⲣ–ⲥ̅ ⲁⲩⲱ ⲛ̅ⲕⲉⲇⲁⲓⲙⲟⲛⲓⲟⲛ ⲉϥ–ⲛⲟⲩϫⲉ ⲙ̅ⲙⲟ–ⲟⲩ ⲉⲃⲟⲗ. Mark 1:39

7. ⲁⲩⲱ ⲉϥ–ⲡⲁⲣⲁⲅⲉ[69] ⲁϥ–ⲛⲁⲩ ⲉ–ⲗⲉⲟⲩⲉⲓ[70] ⲡϣⲏⲣⲉ ⲛ̅–ⲁⲗⲫⲁⲓⲟⲥ ⲉϥ-ϩⲙⲟⲟⲥ ϩⲓ–ⲡⲉϥⲧⲉⲗⲱⲛⲓⲟⲛ[71]. Mark 2:14

8. ⲉ–ϣⲁⲩ–ⲥⲱⲧⲙ̅ ⲉ–ⲡϣⲁϫⲉ ⲛ̅ⲧⲉⲩⲛⲟⲩ ϣⲁⲩ–ϫⲓⲧ–ϥ̅ ϩⲛ̅–ⲟⲩⲣⲁϣⲉ. Mark 4:16

---

[67] ⲕⲏⲣⲩⲥⲥⲉ proclaim.
[68] ϣⲛⲉ fishnet.
[69] ⲡⲁⲣⲁⲅⲉ pass by.
[70] ⲗⲉⲟⲩⲉⲓ . . . ⲁⲗⲫⲁⲓⲟⲥ (personal names) Levi, Alphaios.
[71] ⲧⲉⲗⲱⲛⲓⲟⲛ money changer's booth.

9. ⲉⲧⲓ[72] ⲛ̄ⲧⲟϥ ⲉϥ-ϣⲁϫⲉ ⲁⲩ-ⲉⲓ ⲛ̄ϭⲓ-ⲛ̄ⲣⲱⲙⲉ ⲙ̄-ⲡⲁⲣⲭⲓⲥⲩⲛⲁⲅⲱⲅⲟⲥ[73]. Mark 5:35

10. ⲁϥ-ⲛⲁⲩ ⲉⲣⲟ-ⲟⲩ ⲉⲩ-ϣⲧⲣ̄ⲧⲱⲣ ⲁⲩⲱ ⲉⲩ-ⲣⲓⲙⲉ. Mark 5:38

11. ⲁⲩⲱ ⲡⲙⲏⲛϣⲉ ⲉⲩ-ⲥⲱⲧⲙ̄ (20 [box]) ⲁⲩ-ⲣ̄-⁰ϣⲡⲏⲣⲉ[74]. Mark 6:2

12. ⲁ-ϩⲁϩ ⲇⲉ ⲛⲁⲩ ⲉⲣⲟ-ⲟⲩ ⲉⲩ-ⲃⲏⲕ. Mark 6:33

13. ⲁϥ-ⲉⲓ ϣⲁⲣⲟ-ⲟⲩ ⲉϥ-ⲙⲟⲟϣⲉ ϩⲓϫⲛ̄-ⲧⲉⲑⲁⲗⲁⲥⲥⲁ. ⲁⲩⲱ ⲛⲉϥ-
ⲟⲩⲱϣ ⲉ-⁰ⲡⲁⲣⲁⲅⲉ ⲙ̄ⲙⲟ-ⲟⲩ. Mark 6:48

14. ⲡⲥⲁϩ ⲁⲛ-ⲛⲁⲩ ⲉ-ⲟⲩⲁ ⲉϥ-ⲛⲉϫ-⁰ⲇⲁⲓⲙⲟⲛⲓⲟⲛ ⲉⲃⲟⲗ ϩⲙ̄-ⲡⲉⲕⲣⲁⲛ.
Mark 9:38

15. ⲁϥ-ⲥⲙⲟⲩ ⲉⲣⲟ-ⲟⲩ ⲉ-ⲁϥ-ⲕⲁ-ⲧⲟⲟⲧ-ϥ̄ ϩⲓⲭⲱ-ⲟⲩ. Mark 10:16

16. ⲁⲩⲱ ⲉϥ-ⲛⲏⲩ ⲉⲃⲟⲗ ϩⲛ̄-ϩⲓⲉⲣⲓⲭⲱ[75] ⲙⲛ̄-ⲛⲉϥⲙⲁⲑⲏⲧⲏⲥ ⲁⲩⲱ ⲟⲩⲛⲟϭ
ⲙ̄-ⲙⲏⲛϣⲉ ⲃⲁⲣⲧⲓⲙⲁⲓⲟⲥ[76] ⲉ-ⲩⲃⲗ̄ⲗⲉ[77] ⲡⲉ ⲡϣⲏⲣⲉ ⲛ̄-ⲧⲓⲙⲁⲓⲟⲥ[78]
ⲛⲉϥ-ϩⲙⲟⲟⲥ ⲉϩⲣⲁⲓ̈ ϩⲁ-ⲧⲉϩⲓⲏ ⲉϥ-ⲭⲓ-⁰ⲙⲛ̄ⲧ-ⲛⲁ[79]. Mark 10:46

B. Translate into Coptic, using the circumstantial conversion. a. As I was
bringing them, I fell down. *b.* As I was bringing them, he fell down. *c.* He
arose, lifting them up with him. *d.* They arose as he was lifting them up with
him. *e.* She saw them bringing it. *f.* They saw her bringing it. *g.* We did not
see her coming (**89**).

C. Translate. a. ϯ-ⲛⲁ-ⲧⲁϩⲟ-ⲟⲩ ⲛ̄ⲧⲁ-ϥⲓⲧ-ⲟⲩ. b. ⲁⲩ-ⲧⲛ̄ⲛⲟⲟⲩ-ⲥⲟⲩ
ϣⲁⲣⲟ-ϥ ⲙ̄ⲙⲏⲛⲉ ⲁⲩⲱ ⲁϥ-ⲭⲓⲧ-ⲟⲩ. c. ϣⲁⲣⲉ-ⲡⲣⲉϥ-ⲣ̄-⁰ⲛⲟⲃⲉ ϣⲱⲡ
ⲛ̄ϥ-ⲧⲙ̄-ϯ ⲉⲃⲟⲗ ⲉⲛⲉϩ, ϣⲁϥ-ⲥⲱⲟⲩϩ ⲛ̄ϥ-ⲧⲙ̄-ⲧⲁⲟⲩⲟ ⲉⲛⲉϩ. d. ⲁϥ-ⲭⲓⲥⲉ
ⲙ̄ⲙⲟ-ⲟⲩ ⲁϥ-ϫⲟⲟⲩ-ⲥⲟⲩ ⲉ-ⲡⲕⲟⲥⲙⲟⲥ.

---

[72] ⲉⲧⲓ still (Greek adverb ἔτι).
[73] ⲁⲣⲭⲓⲥⲩⲛⲁⲅⲱⲅⲟⲥ leader of the synagogue.
[74] ϣⲡⲏⲣⲉ omen, wonder, miracle; ⲣ̄-⁰ϣⲡⲏⲣⲉ to marvel, to wonder, to be amazed.
[75] ϩⲓⲉⲣⲓⲭⲱ (place name) Jericho.
[76] ⲃⲁⲣⲧⲓⲙⲁⲓⲟⲥ (personal name) Bartimaios.
[77] ⲃⲗ̄ⲗⲉ blind.
[78] ⲧⲓⲙⲁⲓⲟⲥ (personal name) Timaios.
[79] ⲙⲛ̄ⲧ-ⲛⲁ alms (cf. infinitive ⲛⲁ = to show mercy).

139

LESSON 16

RELATIVE CONVERSION.

124. Relative clauses [CG 399–402, 404] modify a preceding noun, pronoun, or the like.

Thus the italicized relative clauses

the man *who built her house*
the house *that the man built for her*
the one *whose house the man built*
the one *for whom the man built a house*
the town *in which the man built her house*

modify the man, the house, the one, and the town. The modified item (the man, the house, the one, the town) is called the *antecedent* of the relative clause.

In English, relative clauses are connected to their antecedent by a variable relative pronoun *(who, that, which, whose, for whom, in which, etc.)*, whose form helps to express the relationship of the clause to its antecedent.[80]

The Coptic form is very different. Coptic relative clauses do not contain a variable relative pronoun—just a relative converter (such as єNT– in the examples below). The converter only signals the beginning of a relative clause and roughly means "modified by the following complete statement . . . " Study the following equivalents and note all the ways that Coptic and English differ.

English:	the man	who built her house
Coptic form:	the man + *converter* +	he built her house
	ⲡⲣⲱⲙⲉ + єNT– +	ⲁϥ–ⲕⲱⲧ ⲙ̄–ⲡⲉⲥϩⲓ̈
English:	the house	that the man built for her
Coptic form:	the house + *converter* +	the man built it for her
	ⲡϩⲓ̈ + єNT– +	ⲁ–ⲡⲣⲱⲙⲉ ⲕⲟⲧ–ϥ̄ ⲛⲁ–ⲥ
English:	the one	whose house the man built
Coptic form:	the one + *converter* +	the man built her house
	ⲧ– + єNT– +	ⲁ–ⲡⲣⲱⲙⲉ ⲕⲱⲧ ⲙ̄–ⲡⲉⲥϩⲓ̈

---

[80] The English relative pronoun also can signal a distinction of personal: impersonal (who: that, whom: which).

English: the one   for whom the man built the house
Coptic form: the one + *converter* + the man built the house for her
               ⲧ−   + ⲉⲛⲧ−   + ⲁ−ⲡⲣⲱⲙⲉ ⲕⲱⲧ ⲙ̄−ⲡⲏⲓ̈ ⲛⲁ−ⲥ

English: the town   in which the man built her house
Coptic form: the town + *converter* + the man built her house in it
               ⲡ†ⲙⲉ   + ⲉⲛⲧ−   + ⲁ−ⲡⲣⲱⲙⲉ ⲕⲱⲧ ⲙ̄−ⲡⲉⲥⲏⲓ̈ ⲛ̄ϩⲏⲧ−ϥ̄

125. *Translation strategy.* When you translate a Coptic relative clause into English, you must do three things:

   i. Substitute the appropriate English variable relative pronoun (*who, that, which, whose, for whom, in which,* etc.) instead of the converter

   ii. Ignore a redundant Coptic personal pronoun when translating

   iii. Rearrange the words if necessary

ⲡⲣⲱⲙⲉ ⲉⲛⲧ−ⲁϥ−ⲕⲱⲧ ⲙ̄−ⲡⲉⲥⲏⲓ̈
the man + *converter* + he built her house
             who
the man + ~~*converter*~~ + ̶h̶e̶ built her house
→ the man who built her house

ⲡⲏⲓ̈ ⲉⲛⲧ−ⲁ−ⲡⲣⲱⲙⲉ ⲕⲟⲧ−ϥ̄ ⲛⲁ−ⲥ
the house + *converter* + the man built it for her
             that
the house + ~~*converter*~~ + the man built ̶i̶t̶ for her
→ the house that the man built for her

ⲧ−ⲉⲛⲧ−ⲁ−ⲡⲣⲱⲙⲉ ⲕⲱⲧ ⲙ̄−ⲡⲉⲥⲏⲓ̈
the one + *converter* + the man built her house
         whose
the one + ~~*converter*~~ + the man built ̶h̶e̶r̶ (house)
→ the one whose house the man built

ⲧ−ⲉⲛⲧ−ⲁ−ⲡⲣⲱⲙⲉ ⲕⲱⲧ ⲙ̄−ⲡⲏⲓ̈ ⲛⲁ−ⲥ
the one + *converter* + the man built the house for her
        whom
the one + ~~*converter*~~ + the man built the house (for) ̶h̶e̶r̶
→ the one for whom the man built the house

ⲡ†ⲙⲉ ⲉⲛⲧ−ⲁ−ⲡⲣⲱⲙⲉ ⲕⲱⲧ ⲙ̄−ⲡⲉⲥⲏⲓ̈ ⲛ̄ϩⲏⲧ−ϥ̄
the town + *converter* + the man built her house in it
      which
the town + ~~*converter*~~ + the man built her house (in) ̶i̶t̶
→ the town in which the man built her house

Thus in the five examples above,

i. The Coptic converter has been replaced by *who, that, whose, whom,* and *which*

ii. The redundant Coptic pronouns meaning *he, it, her, her,* and *it* have been ignored

iii. In the third, fourth, and fifth examples, *house, for,* and *in* have been moved to make normal sounding English[81].

Notice that the Coptic definite article (π‑, τ‑, ν‑) "the one..." is an antecedent in examples three and four. (As an antecedent, ν‑ never has a superlinear stroke.)

When the antecedent expresses time or manner (*the days, the year, a year, the way*), optionally in step (2) there may be no redundant personal pronoun to delete. [CG 407]

the year + *converter* + he built her house

τερομπε + εντ‑ + ⲁϥ‑ⲕⲱⲧ ⲙ‑ⲡⲉⲥϩⲓ

Thus πεϩοοⲩ εντ‑ⲁⲩ‑ⲁⲛⲁⲗⲁⲙⲃⲁⲛⲉ ⲙⲙⲟ‑ϥ = the day (when) He was taken up. ⲕⲁⲧⲁ‑ⲑⲉ εντ‑ⲁⲛ‑ⲥⲱⲧⲙ = in the way (that) we have heard. ⲛ̄ⲑⲉ ⲟⲛ ⲉⲣⲉ‑ⲡⲁⲣⲭⲓⲉⲣⲉⲩⲥ ⲣ̄‑⁰ⲙⲛ̄ⲧⲣⲉ ⲛⲁ‑ⲓ̈ = just as also the high priest vouches for me.

126. Let's do a quick exercise now. Translate these four relative constructions into good, normal English. The converter here is always εντ‑.

Coptic: τεⲥϩⲓⲙⲉ εντ‑ⲁⲥ‑ϩⲉ ⲉ‑ⲡⲉϥϩⲟⲙⲛ̄ⲧ
Coptic form: the woman + εντ‑ + she found his money

English: _____

Coptic: ⲡⲉϥϩⲟⲙⲛ̄ⲧ εντ‑ⲁ‑τεⲥϩⲓⲙⲉ ϩⲉ ⲉⲣⲟ‑ϥ
Coptic form: his money + εντ‑ + the woman found it

English: _____

Coptic: π‑εντ‑ⲁ‑τεⲥϩⲓⲙⲉ ϩⲉ ⲉ‑ⲡⲉϥϩⲟⲙⲛ̄ⲧ
Coptic form: the one + εντ‑ + the woman found his money

English: _____

Coptic: ⲡⲏⲓ̈ εντ‑ⲁ‑τεⲥϩⲓⲙⲉ ϩⲉ ⲉ‑ⲡⲉϥϩⲟⲙⲛ̄ⲧ ⲛ̄ϩⲏⲧ‑ϥ̄
Coptic form: the house + εντ‑ + the woman found his money in it

English: _____

---

[81] In colloquial English, *for* and *in* can be left where they are.

127. *The choice of converter varies according to the antecedent.* [CG 404]

After a *definite* antecedent (one that contains ⲡ . . . , ⲧ . . . , or ⲛ . . . **60**) a *relative* converter is used.

ⲡⲣⲱⲙⲉ (ⲡⲉⲓⲣⲱⲙⲉ, ⲡⲉⲛⲣⲱⲙⲉ) ⲉⲛⲧ-ⲁϥ-ⲕⲱⲧ ⲙ̄-ⲡⲉⲥⲏⲓ̈
the man who built her house

After a *non-definite* antecedent (with indefinite or zero article) a *circumstantial* converter must be used.

ⲟⲩⲣⲱⲙⲉ ⲉ-ⲁϥ-ⲕⲱⲧ ⲙ̄-ⲡⲉⲥⲏⲓ̈ (ⲉ- is circumstantial converter)
a man who built her house

ᵠⲣⲱⲙⲉ ⲉ-ⲁϥ-ⲕⲱⲧ (or ⲉ-ⲁⲩ-ⲕⲱⲧ) ⲙ̄-ⲡⲉⲥⲏⲓ̈
someone/people who built her house

Antecedents constructed with . . . ⲛⲓⲙ *any, every* or with specifiers such as
ϩⲁϩ ⲛ̄- *many* can be followed by either circumstantial or relative, optionally.

When the antecedent expresses time or manner and is definite (*the days, the way*), either circumstantial or relative can be used. ⲡⲉϩⲟⲟⲩ ⲉⲧⲉⲣⲉ-ⲛⲁⲓ̈ ⲛⲁ-ϣⲱⲡⲉ = The day (when) these things will come to pass. ⲛⲉϩⲟⲟⲩ ⲉⲛ-ϩⲛ̄-ⲧⲥⲁⲣⲝ̄ = The days (when) we were in the flesh.

128. The relative conversion is formed in the same way as the preterit and circumstantial. There are several shapes of the relative converter, most of which we will study in the next lesson. For now, you will learn only

the conversion base ⲉⲧⲉⲣⲉ-, ⲉⲧ⸗ (present tense)
the sentence converter of the past tense affirmative ⲉⲛⲧ-, also spelled ⲛ̄ⲧ-

Remember that a conversion base (ⲉⲧⲉⲣⲉ-, ⲉ⸗) is only used to convert durative sentences **112** (i).

129. *Conjugation of the conversion base* ⲉⲧ⸗.

ⲉϯ- (et-i-)	ⲉⲧⲛ̄-
ⲉⲧⲕ̄-	ⲉⲧⲉⲧⲛ̄-
ⲉⲧⲉ- or ⲉⲧⲉⲣⲉ-	
ⲉⲧϥ̄-	ⲉⲧⲟⲩ-
ⲉⲧⲥ̄-	
ⲉⲧⲉⲣⲉ-ⲡⲛⲟⲩⲧⲉ	

Exercises 16

A. *Review vocabularies 2–4.*

B. *Analyze and translate, giving alternate translations where possible.*

a. ⲡϣⲏⲣⲉ ϣⲏⲙ ⲉⲛⲧ–ⲁ–ⲧⲉⲥϩⲓⲙⲉ ⲛⲁⲩ ⲉⲣⲟ–ϥ

b. ⲧϣⲉⲉⲣⲉ ϣⲏⲙ ⲉⲛⲧ–ⲁ–ⲧⲉⲥϩⲓⲙⲉ ⲛⲁⲩ ⲉⲣⲟ–ⲥ

c. ⲛ̄ϣⲏⲣⲉ ϣⲏⲙ ⲉⲛⲧ–ⲁ–ⲧⲉⲥϩⲓⲙⲉ ⲛⲁⲩ ⲉⲣⲟ–ⲟⲩ

d. ⲡⲉⲣⲡⲉ ⲉⲛⲧ–ⲁⲥ–ⲛⲁⲩ ⲉⲣⲟ–ϥ

e. ⲧⲡⲟⲗⲓⲥ ⲉⲛⲧ–ⲁⲥ–ⲛⲁⲩ ⲉⲣⲟ–ⲥ

f. ⲛ̄ⲏⲓ̈ ⲉⲛⲧ–ⲁϥ–ⲛⲁⲩ ⲉⲣⲟ–ⲟⲩ

g. ⲛ̄ⲏⲓ̈ ⲉⲧϥ̄–ⲛⲁⲩ ⲉⲣⲟ–ⲟⲩ

h. ⲛ̄ⲏⲓ̈ ⲉⲧⲉⲧⲛ̄–ⲛⲁⲩ ⲉⲣⲟ–ⲟⲩ

i. ⲛ̄ⲏⲓ̈ ⲉⲧⲉⲣⲉ–ⲧⲉⲥϩⲓⲙⲉ ⲛⲁⲩ ⲉⲣⲟ–ⲟⲩ

j. ⲧⲉⲥϩⲓⲙⲉ ⲉⲛⲧ–ⲁⲥ–ⲛⲁⲩ ⲉ–ⲧⲡⲟⲗⲓⲥ

k. ⲧⲉⲥϩⲓⲙⲉ ⲉⲛⲧ–ⲁⲥ–ⲛⲁⲩ ⲉⲣⲟ–ϥ

l. ⲧⲉⲥϩⲓⲙⲉ ⲉⲛⲧ–ⲁϥ–ⲛⲁⲩ ⲉⲣⲟ–ⲥ

m. ⲧⲉⲥϩⲓⲙⲉ ⲉⲛⲧ–ⲁⲥ–ⲛⲁⲩ ⲉⲣⲟ–ⲥ (this has two interpretations)

n. ⲡⲣⲉϥ–ⲣ̄–⁰ⲛⲟⲃⲉ ⲉⲛⲧ–ⲁϥ–ⲛⲁⲩ ⲉ–ⲛⲉϥⲛⲟⲃⲉ (two interpretations)

o. ⲧⲡⲟⲗⲓⲥ ⲉⲛⲧ–ⲁϥ–ⲛⲁⲩ ⲉⲣⲟ–ⲟⲩ ⲛ̄ϩⲏⲧ–ⲥ̄

p. ⲧⲡⲟⲗⲓⲥ ⲉⲛⲧ–ⲁϥ–ⲛⲁⲩ ⲉⲣⲟ–ⲥ ⲛ̄ϩⲏⲧ–ⲥ̄ (two interpretations)

q. ⲡⲉⲣⲡⲉ ⲉⲛⲧ–ⲁⲥ–ⲛⲁⲩ ⲉⲣⲟ–ⲟⲩ ⲛ̄ϩⲏⲧ–ϥ̄

r. ⲡⲉⲣⲡⲉ ⲉⲛⲧ–ⲁⲥ–ⲛⲁⲩ ⲉⲣⲟ–ϥ ⲛ̄ϩⲏⲧ–ϥ̄ (two interpretations)

s. ⲡⲁⲓ̈ ⲉⲛⲧ–ⲁϥ–ⲛⲁⲩ ⲉⲣⲟ–ϥ ⲛ̄ϩⲏⲧ–ϥ̄ (three interpretations)

t. ⲛⲁⲓ̈ ⲉⲧⲥ̄–ⲛⲁⲩ ⲉⲣⲟ–ⲥ ⲛ̄ϩⲏⲧ–ⲥ̄ (two interpretations)

u. ⲡⲛⲟⲩⲧⲉ ⲉⲛⲧ–ⲁⲛ–ⲛⲁⲩ ⲉ–ⲛⲉϥⲣ̄ⲡⲏⲩⲉ

v. ⲛ̄ⲉⲣⲡⲏⲩⲉ ⲉⲛⲧ–ⲁⲛ–ⲛⲁⲩ ⲉ–ⲡⲉⲩⲛⲟⲩⲧⲉ

B. *Repeat (1) to (22) as a rapid drill:* a. ⲡϣⲏⲣⲉ ϣⲏⲙ ⲉⲛⲧ–ⲁ–ⲧⲉⲥϩⲓⲙⲉ ⲛⲁⲩ ⲉⲣⲟ–ϥ. b. ⲧϣⲉⲉⲣⲉ ϣⲏⲙ ⲉⲛⲧ–ⲁ–ⲧⲉⲥϩⲓⲙⲉ ⲛⲁⲩ ⲉⲣⲟ–ⲥ. c. ⲛ̄ϣⲏⲣⲉ ϣⲏⲙ ⲉⲛⲧ–ⲁ–ⲧⲉⲥϩⲓⲙⲉ ⲛⲁⲩ ⲉⲣⲟ–ⲟⲩ. d. ⲡⲉⲣⲡⲉ ⲉⲛⲧ–ⲁⲥ–ⲛⲁⲩ ⲉⲣⲟ–ϥ. e. ⲧⲡⲟⲗⲓⲥ ⲉⲛⲧ–ⲁⲥ–ⲛⲁⲩ ⲉⲣⲟ–ⲥ. f. ⲛ̄ⲏⲓ̈ ⲉⲛⲧ–ⲁϥ–ⲛⲁⲩ ⲉⲣⲟ–ⲟⲩ. g. ⲛ̄ⲏⲓ̈ ⲉⲧϥ̄–ⲛⲁⲩ ⲉⲣⲟ–ⲟⲩ. h. ⲛ̄ⲏⲓ̈ ⲉⲧⲉⲧⲛ̄–ⲛⲁⲩ ⲉⲣⲟ–ⲟⲩ. i. ⲛ̄ⲏⲓ̈ ⲉⲧⲉⲣⲉ–ⲧⲉⲥϩⲓⲙⲉ

ⲛⲁⲩ ⲉⲣⲟ-ⲟⲩ. j. ⲧⲉⲥϩⲓⲙⲉ ⲉⲛⲧ-ⲁⲥ-ⲛⲁⲩ ⲉ-ⲧⲡⲟⲗⲓⲥ. k. ⲧⲉⲥϩⲓⲙⲉ ⲉⲛⲧ-
ⲁⲥ-ⲛⲁⲩ ⲉⲣⲟ-ϥ. l. ⲧⲉⲥϩⲓⲙⲉ ⲉⲛⲧ-ⲁϥ-ⲛⲁⲩ ⲉⲣⲟ-ⲥ. m. ⲧⲉⲥϩⲓⲙⲉ ⲉⲛⲧ-
ⲁⲥ-ⲛⲁⲩ ⲉⲣⲟ-ⲥ (this has two interpretations). n. ⲡⲣⲉϥ-ⲣ̄-⁰ⲛⲟⲃⲉ
ⲉⲛⲧ-ⲁϥ-ⲛⲁⲩ ⲉ-ⲛⲉϥⲛⲟⲃⲉ (two interpretations). o. ⲧⲡⲟⲗⲓⲥ ⲉⲛⲧ-ⲁϥ-
ⲛⲁⲩ ⲉⲣⲟ-ⲟⲩ ⲛ̄ϩⲏⲧ-ⲥ̄. p. ⲧⲡⲟⲗⲓⲥ ⲉⲛⲧ-ⲁϥ-ⲛⲁⲩ ⲉⲣⲟ-ⲥ ⲛ̄ϩⲏⲧ-ⲥ̄ (two
interpretations). q. ⲡⲉⲣⲡⲉ ⲉⲛⲧ-ⲁⲥ-ⲛⲁⲩ ⲉⲣⲟ-ⲟⲩ ⲛ̄ϩⲏⲧ-ϥ̄. r. ⲡⲉⲣⲡⲉ ⲉⲛⲧ-
ⲁⲥ-ⲛⲁⲩ ⲉⲣⲟ-ϥ ⲛ̄ϩⲏⲧ-ϥ̄ (two interpretations). s. ⲡⲁⲓ̈ ⲉⲛⲧ-ⲁϥ-ⲛⲁⲩ
ⲉⲣⲟ-ϥ ⲛ̄ϩⲏⲧ-ϥ̄ (three interpretations). t. ⲛⲁⲓ̈ ⲉⲧⲥ̄-ⲛⲁⲩ ⲉⲣⲟ-ⲥ ⲛ̄ϩⲏⲧ-ⲥ̄
(two interpretations). u. ⲡⲛⲟⲩⲧⲉ ⲉⲛⲧ-ⲁⲛ-ⲛⲁⲩ ⲉ-ⲛⲉϥⲣ̄ⲡⲏⲩⲉ. v. ⲛ̄ⲉⲣ-
ⲡⲏⲩⲉ ⲉⲛⲧ-ⲁⲛ-ⲛⲁⲩ ⲉ-ⲡⲉⲩⲛⲟⲩⲧⲉ.

D. Translate into Coptic, using the relative or circumstantial conversion, as appropriate.

Example: the angel who came from heaven = "the angel modified-by-the-complete-statement *he came from heaven*" = ⲡⲁⲅⲅⲉⲗⲟⲥ ⲉⲛⲧ-ⲁϥ-ⲉⲓ ⲉⲃⲟⲗ ϩⲛ̄-ⲧⲡⲉ

a. An angel who came from heaven

b. The woman who knew God

c. A woman who knew God

d. The apostles who loved their Lord

e. Apostles who loved their Lord

f. The things that I see, those which I see, the things that you (sing. masc.) see, those which you (sing. masc.) see, the things that you (sing. fem.) see, the things that he sees, the things that she sees, the things that we see, the things that you (pl.) see, the things that they see

g. Things that I see, some that I see, things that you (sing. masc.) see, some that you (sing. masc.) see, things that you (sing. fem.) see, things that he sees, things that she sees, things that we see, things that you (pl.) see, things that they see

h. The things that God sees, those which God sees

i. Things that God sees, some that God sees

j. The road on which I have travelled, the road on which you (sing. masc.) have travelled, the road on which you (sing. fem.) have travelled, the road on which he has travelled, the road on which she has travelled, the road on which we have travelled, the road on which you (pl.) have travelled, the road on which they have travelled, the road on which the man has travelled

k. A road on which I have travelled, a road on which you (sing. masc.) have travelled, a road on which you (sing. fem.) have travelled, a road on which he has travelled, a road on which she has travelled, a road on which we have travelled, a road on which you (pl.) have travelled, a road on which they have travelled, a road on which the man has travelled

l. The city whose king I saw, the city whose king you (sing. masc.) saw, the city whose king you (sing. fem.) saw, the city whose king he saw, the city whose king she saw, the city whose king we saw, the city whose king you (pl.) saw, the city whose king they saw

m. A city whose king I saw, a city whose king you (sing. masc.) saw, a city whose king you (sing. fem.) saw, a city whose king he saw, the city whose king she saw, a city whose king we saw, a city whose king you (pl.) saw, a city whose king they saw

LESSON 17

RELATIVE CONVERSION (CONTINUED).

130. *"Bare* ⲉⲧ.*"* [CG 405]

In present tense affirmative relative clauses, ⲉⲧϥ̄-, ⲉⲧⲥ̄-, and ⲉⲧⲟⲩ- are *always* replaced by simple ⲉⲧ- if their personal pronoun (-ϥ, -ⲥ, -ⲟⲩ) would refer to the antecedent. This will be notated as ⲉⲧ⁰-, and called "bare ⲉⲧ".

the man who listens	ⲡⲣⲱⲙⲉ ⲉⲧ⁰-ⲥⲱⲧⲙ̄ (*not* ⲉⲧϥ-)
the woman who listens	ⲧⲉⲥϩⲓⲙⲉ ⲉⲧ⁰-ⲥⲱⲧⲙ̄ (*not* ⲉⲧⲥ-)
the apostles who listen	ⲛ̄ⲁⲡⲟⲥⲧⲟⲗⲟⲥ ⲉⲧ⁰-ⲥⲱⲧⲙ̄ (*not* ⲉⲧⲟⲩ-)

Optionally, this construction can be negatived by ⲁⲛ after the predicate.

the man who does not listen	ⲡⲣⲱⲙⲉ ⲉⲧ⁰-ⲥⲱⲧⲙ̄ ⲁⲛ
the woman who does not listen	ⲧⲉⲥϩⲓⲙⲉ ⲉⲧ⁰-ⲥⲱⲧⲙ̄ ⲁⲛ
the apostles who do not listen	ⲛ̄ⲁⲡⲟⲥⲧⲟⲗⲟⲥ ⲉⲧ⁰-ⲥⲱⲧⲙ̄ ⲁⲛ

> The alternative negation is ⲡⲣⲱⲙⲉ ⲉⲧⲉ-ⲛ̄-ϥ-ⲥⲱⲧⲙ̄ ⲁⲛ, ⲧⲉⲥϩⲓⲙⲉ ⲉⲧⲉ-ⲛ̄-ⲥ-ⲥⲱⲧⲙ̄ ⲁⲛ, ⲛ̄ⲁⲡⲟⲥⲧⲟⲗⲟⲥ ⲉⲧⲉ-ⲛ̄-ⲥⲉ-ⲥⲱⲧⲙ̄ ⲁⲛ.

All the predicates of the durative sentence (**63**) can occur after ⲉⲧ⁰-: ⲡⲁⲓⲱⲛ ⲉⲧ⁰-ⲛⲏⲩ = the age to come, the age that is coming. ⲧⲟⲣⲅⲏ ⲉⲧ⁰-ⲛⲁ-6ⲱⲗⲡ ⲉⲃⲟⲗ = the wrath that is going to appear. ⲡⲉⲧⲛ̄ⲉⲓⲱⲧ ⲉⲧ⁰-ϩⲛ̄-ⲙ̄ⲡⲏⲩⲉ = your Father who is in the heavens.

The commonest occurrence of bare ⲉⲧ is found in the phrases ⲉⲧⲙ̄ⲙⲁⲩ (= that) and ⲡⲉⲧⲙ̄ⲙⲁⲩ, ⲧⲉⲧⲙ̄ⲙⲁⲩ, ⲛⲉⲧⲙ̄ⲙⲁⲩ (= that one, he, she, it, they) **60**. ⲧⲡⲟⲗⲓⲥ ⲉⲧⲙ̄ⲙⲁⲩ = that city. ⲛ̄ⲣ̄ⲣⲱⲟⲩ ⲉⲧⲙ̄ⲙⲁⲩ = those emperors. ⲡⲉⲧⲙ̄ⲙⲁⲩ = he, that one.

Adjectival meaning. When the predicate is a stative expressing a quality, such as ⲟⲩⲁⲁⲃ *is holy*, the meaning is like a modifying adjective: ⲧⲡⲟⲗⲓⲥ ⲉⲧ⁰-ⲟⲩⲁⲁⲃ = the holy city; ⲡ-ⲉⲧ⁰-ⲥⲏ6 = the lame man; ⲡⲛⲟⲩⲧⲉ ⲉⲧ⁰-ϫⲟⲥⲉ = the high(est) God; ⲛ-ⲉⲧ⁰-ⲙⲟⲟⲩⲧ = the dead. Cf. **70**.

LESSON SEVENTEEN

THE SENTENCE CONVERTER FOR RELATIVE CONVERSION

131. The relative sentence converter has four forms (identical in meaning), chosen to match the grammar of the relative clause. [CG 399] You've already learned one of these: ⲉⲛⲧ-, also spelled ⲛ̄ⲧ-. They are:

ⲉⲛⲧ- (also spelled ⲛ̄ⲧ-[82]) used only before ⲁ-, ⲁ⸗ (affirmative past)
ⲉⲧ- used before verboids when the subject pronoun refers to the antecedent[83]
ⲉⲧⲉ- used before all other sentence types
ⲉ- optionally used instead of ⲉⲧⲉ- before ϣⲁⲣⲉ-, ϣⲁ⸗, ⲛⲉⲣⲉ-, and ⲛⲉ⸗

Relative conversions are fairly easy to recognize, since almost every one begins with ⲉⲧ, ⲉⲧⲉ-, ⲉⲛⲧ, or ⲛ̄ⲧ.

Generally speaking, the relative is formed in the same way as the preterit (cf. **112**). [CG 396] (Note that there is a relative conversion of the preterit.)

ⲉⲧⲉ-ⲟⲩⲡⲣⲟⲫⲏⲧⲏⲥ ⲡⲉ
ⲉⲧⲉ-ⲟⲩⲡⲣⲟⲫⲏⲧⲏⲥ ⲁⲛ ⲡⲉ
ⲉⲧⲉ-ⲛ̄-ⲟⲩⲡⲣⲟⲫⲏⲧⲏⲥ ⲁⲛ ⲡⲉ
ⲉⲧⲉⲣⲉ-ⲡⲣⲱⲙⲉ ⲥⲱⲧⲡ̄
ⲉⲧⲉⲣⲉ-ⲡⲣⲱⲙⲉ ⲥⲱⲧⲡ̄ ⲁⲛ
ⲉⲧⲉ-ⲙ̄-ⲡⲣⲱⲙⲉ ⲥⲱⲧⲡ̄ ⲁⲛ
ⲉⲧϥ̄-ⲥⲱⲧⲡ̄
ⲉⲧϥ̄-ⲥⲱⲧⲡ̄ ⲁⲛ
ⲉⲧⲉ-ⲛ̄-ϥ-ⲥⲱⲧⲡ̄ ⲁⲛ
ⲉⲧ$^\emptyset$-ⲥⲱⲧⲡ̄ (**130**)
ⲉⲧ$^\emptyset$-ⲥⲱⲧⲡ̄ ⲁⲛ (optional) (**130**)
ⲉⲧⲉ-ⲛ̄-ϥ-ⲥⲱⲧⲡ̄ ⲁⲛ (optional) (**130**)
ⲉⲛⲧ-ⲁϥ-ⲥⲱⲧⲡ̄
ⲉⲧⲉ-ⲙ̄ⲡϥ̄-, ⲉⲧⲉ-ⲙ̄ⲡⲁⲧϥ̄-, ⲉⲧⲉ-ϣⲁϥ-, ⲉⲧⲉ-ⲙⲉϥ-, ⲉⲧⲉ-ⲛ̄ⲛⲉϥ-ⲥⲱⲧⲡ̄[84]
ⲉ-ϣⲁϥ-ⲥⲱⲧⲡ̄ (optional)
ⲉⲧⲉ-ⲛⲉϥ-ⲥⲱⲧⲡ̄
ⲉⲧⲉ-ⲛⲉϥ-ⲥⲱⲧⲡ̄ ⲁⲛ
ⲉ-ⲛⲉϥ-ⲥⲱⲧⲡ̄ (optional)
ⲉ-ⲛⲉϥ-ⲥⲱⲧⲡ̄ ⲁⲛ (optional)
ⲉⲧⲉ-ⲛⲁⲛⲟⲩ-ϥ
ⲉⲧⲉ-ⲛⲁⲛⲟⲩ-ϥ ⲁⲛ
ⲉⲧ-ⲛⲁⲛⲟⲩ-ϥ
ⲉⲧ-ⲛⲁⲛⲟⲩ-ϥ ⲁⲛ

---

[82] ⲛ̄ⲧ- is also the focalizing converter (lesson 18), and so it is ambiguous.

[83] ⲡⲕⲁϩ ⲉⲧ-ⲛⲁⲛⲟⲩ-ϥ "The good soil, the soil that is good" (Mark 4:8), where –ϥ refers to ⲡⲕⲁϩ.

[84] There is no relative conversion of the *affirmative* optative ⲉ⸗ⲉ-.

148

ⲉⲧⲉ-ⲟⲩⲛ̄-⁰ⲣⲱⲙⲉ ⲥⲱⲧⲡ̄
ⲉⲧⲉⲣⲉ-⁰ⲣⲱⲙⲉ ⲥⲱⲧⲡ̄ (optional, affirmative only)
ⲉⲧⲉ-ⲙⲛ̄-⁰ⲣⲱⲙⲉ ⲥⲱⲧⲡ̄
ⲉⲧⲉ-ⲡⲁⲓ̈ ⲡⲉ-ⲉⲧϥ̄-ⲥⲱⲧⲡ̄ ⲙ̄ⲙⲟ-ϥ[85]
Etc.

To convert a sentence formed with ⲟⲩⲛ̄-, it is possible to substitute the prenominal base ⲉⲧⲉⲣⲉ- in place of ⲟⲩⲛ̄-. [CG 324]

ⲟⲩⲛ̄-⁰ⲣⲱⲙⲉ ⲥⲱⲧⲡ̄   ⲉⲧⲉⲣⲉ-⁰ⲣⲱⲙⲉ-ⲥⲱⲧⲡ̄

OTHER USES OF THE RELATIVE

132. *The Articulated Relative.* [CG 411]

This construction has ⲡ-, ⲧ-, ⲛ- as its antecedent and means *he who . . . , that which . . . , someone who . . .*

ⲧ-ⲉⲛⲧ-ⲁ-ⲡⲣⲱⲙⲉ ⲕⲱⲧ ⲙ̄-ⲡⲉⲥⲏⲓ̈ = She whose house the man built
ⲛ-ⲉⲧ⁰-ⲛⲙ̄ⲙⲁ-ϥ = Those who are with him
ⲛ-ⲉⲧ⁰-ϣⲱⲛⲉ = The sick, those who are sick
ⲛ-ⲉⲛⲧ-ⲁ-ⲙⲱⲩⲥⲏⲥ ⲟⲩⲉϩ-ⲥⲁϩⲛⲉ ⲙ̄ⲙⲟ-ⲟⲩ = The things that Moses commanded

In the articulated relative construction, ⲛⲁ- usually expresses timeless generalization (ⲡ-ⲉⲧ⁰-ⲛⲁ- *whoever* or *whatever*) rather than futurity. That is, *whoever* and *whatever* can be formulated in Coptic with either the present or the ⲛⲁ- future.

ⲛ-ⲉⲧ⁰-ⲛⲏⲩ ⲉⲃⲟⲗ ϩⲙ̄-ⲡⲣⲱⲙⲉ = Whatever things come out of a person
ⲉⲃⲟⲗ ϩⲛ̄-ⲛ-ⲉⲧ⁰ⲙⲟⲟⲩⲧ = From the dead (whoever are dead)
ⲡ-ⲉⲧ⁰-ⲛⲁ-ⲥⲕⲁⲛⲇⲁⲗⲓⲍⲉ ⲛ̄-ⲟⲩⲁ ⲛ̄-ⲛⲉⲓ̈ⲕⲟⲩⲓ̈ ⲉⲧ⁰-ⲡⲓⲥⲧⲉⲩⲉ ⲉⲣⲟ-ⲓ̈ = Whoever puts a stumbling block before one of these little ones who believe in Me
ⲡ-ⲉⲧ⁰-ⲛⲁ-ϫⲓ-⁰ϣⲁϫⲉ = Whoever says a word

> Rarely, the articulated relative is formed with the pronouns ⲡⲁⲓ̈ or ⲡⲏ, or even ⲡⲁⲓ̈ + circumstantial.

133. *The Explanatory Relative.* [CG 410]

(*a*) ⲉⲧⲉ- . . . ⲡⲉ (etc.) *which is . . . , which means . . . , namely . . .*
(*b*) ⲉⲧⲉ-ⲡⲁⲓ̈ ⲡⲉ (etc.) *which is to say, . . .*

---

[85] Relative of a cleft sentence (see lesson 19).

ϩⲉⲛⲥⲁϩ ⲉⲧⲉ-ⲃⲁⲣⲛⲁⲃⲁⲥ ⲡⲉ ⲙⲛ̄-ⲥⲩⲙⲉⲱⲛ = Some teachers, namely, Barnabas and Simeon

ⲥⲁⲩⲗⲟⲥ ⲇⲉ ⲉⲧⲉ-ⲡⲁⲩⲗⲟⲥ ⲡⲉ = Saul, which means, Paul

ⲡⲉⲓⲙⲁ ⲛ̄-ⲟⲩⲱⲧ ⲉⲧ⁰-ⲙ̄ⲙⲁⲩ ⲉⲧⲉ-ⲧⲙⲛ̄ⲧ-ⲣ̄ⲣⲟ ⲛ̄-ⲙ̄ⲡⲏⲩⲉ ⲡⲉ = That very same place, which is, the kingdom of the heavens

ⲡⲉϥⲥⲱⲙⲁ ⲉⲧⲉ-ⲡⲁⲓ̈ ⲡⲉ ⲧⲉⲕⲕⲗⲏⲥⲓⲁ = His body, which is to say, the church

134. *The Appositive Relative.* [CG 408]

This relative construction relates loosely[86] to its antecedent and is introduced by ⲡ– or ⲡⲁⲓ̈, carrying on the number/gender of the antecedent. In English, this ⲡ– or ⲡⲁⲓ̈ *should not be translated* (or rather, it should be translated only by inserting a comma before the English relative pronoun).

ⲡⲉⲡⲛ̄ⲁ ⲛ̄-ⲧⲙⲉ ⲡ-ⲉⲧⲉ-ⲙ̄ⲙⲛ̄-⁰ϭⲟⲙ ⲙ̄-ⲡⲕⲟⲥⲙⲟⲥ ⲉ-⁰ϫⲓⲧ-ϥ̄
The Spirit of truth, whom the world cannot receive

ⲡⲉⲕⲟⲩϫⲁⲓ̈ ⲡⲁⲓ̈ ⲉⲛⲧ-ⲁⲕ-ⲥⲃ̄ⲧⲱⲧ-ϥ̄
Your salvation, which You have prepared

ⲡⲣⲓⲥⲕⲁ ⲙⲛ̄-ⲁⲕⲩⲗⲁ ⲛⲁⲓ̈ ⲉⲛⲧ-ⲁⲩ-ⲕⲱ ⲙ̄-ⲡⲉⲩⲙⲁⲕϩ̄
Prisca and Aquila, who laid down their necks

The circumstantial also appears in this construction after ⲡⲁⲓ̈.

ⲛⲉⲩⲟⲩⲏⲏⲃ ⲛⲁⲓ̈ ⲉⲣⲉ-ⲛⲉⲩⲁⲡⲏⲩⲉ ϭⲟⲗⲡ̄ ⲉⲃⲟⲗ
Their priests, whose heads are uncovered

> This is the normal way in which an attributive clause is attached to a personal name or a personal pronoun. ⲓ̄ⲥ ⲡ-ⲉ-ϣⲁⲩ-ⲙⲟⲩⲧⲉ ⲉⲣⲟ-ϥ ϫⲉ-ⲡⲉⲭ̄ⲥ̄ = Jesus, who is called the Christ.

135. *Relative Tense.* [CG 529–30]

The relative *present* expresses action *simultaneous* with the main verb.

ⲡⲏⲓ̈ ⲉⲧ-ⲕⲱⲧ ⲙ̄ⲙⲟ-ϥ ⲁϥ-ϩⲉ ⲉⲃⲟⲗ = The house that I was building perished
ⲡⲏⲓ̈ ⲉⲧ-ⲕⲱⲧ ⲙ̄ⲙⲟ-ϥ ϥ-ϩⲏⲩ ⲉⲃⲟⲗ = The house that I am building is perishing
ⲡⲏⲓ̈ ⲉⲧ-ⲕⲱⲧ ⲙ̄ⲙⲟ-ϥ ϥ-ⲛⲁ-ϩⲉ ⲉⲃⲟⲗ = The house that I am building will perish

[86] Like an English relative clause preceded by a comma ("London, which is the capital of England").

The relative *past* expresses action *before* the main verb.

ⲡⲏⲓ̈ ⲉⲛⲧ-ⲁⲓ̈-ⲕⲱⲧ ⲙ̄ⲙⲟ-ϥ ⲁϥ-ϩⲉ ⲉⲃⲟⲗ = The house that I had built perished

ⲡⲏⲓ̈ ⲉⲛⲧ-ⲁⲓ̈-ⲕⲱⲧ ⲙ̄ⲙⲟ-ϥ ϥ-ϩⲏⲩ ⲉⲃⲟⲗ = The house that I built is perishing

ⲡⲏⲓ̈ ⲉⲛⲧ-ⲁⲓ̈-ⲕⲱⲧ ⲙ̄ⲙⲟ-ϥ ϥ-ⲛⲁ-ϩⲉ ⲉⲃⲟⲗ = The house that I built will perish

And the relative *future* looks forward to action *after* the main verb.

ⲡⲏⲓ̈ ⲉϯ-ⲛⲁ-ⲕⲱⲧ ⲙ̄ⲙⲟ-ϥ ⲁϥ-ϩⲉ ⲉⲃⲟⲗ = The house that I was going to build perished

ⲡⲏⲓ̈ ⲉϯ-ⲛⲁ-ⲕⲱⲧ ⲙ̄ⲙⲟ-ϥ ϥ-ϩⲏⲩ ⲉⲃⲟⲗ = Any house that I build is perishing

ⲡⲏⲓ̈ ⲉϯ-ⲛⲁ-ⲕⲱⲧ ⲙ̄ⲙⲟ-ϥ ϥ-ⲛⲁ-ϩⲉ ⲉⲃⲟⲗ = The house that I am going to build will perish

EXERCISES 17

A. *Review vocabularies 5–7.*

B. *Reading selections from the New Testament.*

1. ⲡ–ⲉⲧ⁰–ⲱϣ ⲉⲃⲟⲗ ϩⲛ̄–ⲧⲉⲣⲏⲙⲟⲥ[87]. Mark 1:3
2. ⲡ–ⲉⲧ⁰–ⲟⲩⲁⲁⲃ ⲙ̄–ⲡⲛⲟⲩⲧⲉ. Mark 1:24
3. ⲥⲓⲙⲱⲛ ⲙⲛ̄–ⲛ–ⲉⲧ⁰–ⲛⲙ̄ⲙⲁ–ϥ. Mark 1:36
4. ⲡⲣⲱⲙⲉ ⲉⲧⲉⲣⲉ–ⲧⲉϥϭⲓ̈ϫ ⲙⲟⲟⲩⲧ. Mark 3:3
5. ⲛ–ⲉⲧϥ̄–ⲉⲓⲣⲉ ⲙ̄ⲙⲟ–ⲟⲩ. Mark 3:8
6. ⲛ–ⲉⲧϥ̄–ⲟⲩⲁϣ–ⲟⲩ. Mark 3:13
7. ⲓⲟⲩⲇⲁⲥ ⲡⲓⲥⲕⲁⲣⲓⲱⲧⲏⲥ ⲡ–ⲉⲛⲧ–ⲁϥ–ⲡⲁⲣⲁⲇⲓⲇⲟⲩ ⲙ̄ⲙⲟ–ϥ. Mark 3:19
8. ⲛⲉⲅⲣⲁⲙⲙⲁⲧⲉⲩⲥ ⲉⲛⲧ–ⲁⲩ–ⲉⲓ ⲉⲃⲟⲗ ϩⲛ̄–ⲑⲓⲉⲣⲟⲥⲟⲗⲩⲙⲁ. Mark 3:22
9. ⲛ–ⲉⲛⲧ–ⲁ–ⲡϫⲟⲉⲓⲥ ⲁⲁ–ⲩ ⲛⲁ–ⲕ. Mark 5:19
10. ⲛ–ⲉⲛⲧ–ⲁ–ⲓⲥ̄ ⲁⲁ–ⲩ ⲛⲁ–ϥ. Mark 5:20
11. ⲧ–ⲉⲛⲧ–ⲁⲥ–ⲣ̄–ⲡⲁⲓ̈. Mark 5:32
12. ⲡ–ⲙⲁ ⲉⲧⲉⲣⲉ–ⲧϣⲉⲉⲣⲉ ϣⲏⲙ ⲛ̄ϩⲏⲧ–ϥ̄. Mark 5:40
13. ⲡ–ⲉⲧⲉ–ⲟⲩⲁϣ–ϥ̄. Mark 6:22
14. ⲡ–ⲉⲧ⁰–ⲥⲏϩ ϩⲛ̄–ⲏⲥⲁⲓⲁⲥ ⲡⲉⲡⲣⲟⲫⲏⲧⲏⲥ. Mark 1:2
15. ϥ–ⲛⲁ–ⲃⲁⲡⲧⲓⲍⲉ ⲙ̄ⲙⲱ–ⲧⲛ ϩⲛ̄–ⲟⲩⲡⲛⲁ̄ ⲉϥ–ⲟⲩⲁⲁⲃ. Mark 1:8 alt.
16. ⲛⲉϥ–ϯ–⁰ⲥⲃⲱ ⲅⲁⲣ ⲛⲁ–ⲩ ⲛ̄–ⲑⲉ ⲁⲛ ⲉⲧⲟⲩ–ϯ–⁰ⲥⲃⲱ ⲛ̄ϭⲓ–ⲛⲉⲅⲣⲁⲙⲙⲁ–ⲧⲉⲩⲥ. Mark 1:22
17. ⲛⲉ–ⲩⲛ̄–ⲟⲩⲣⲱⲙⲉ ϩⲛ̄–ⲧⲥⲩⲛⲁⲅⲱⲅⲏ ⲉⲣⲉ–ⲟⲩⲡⲛⲁ̄ ⲛ̄–ⲁⲕⲁⲑⲁⲣⲧⲟⲛ[88] ⲛⲙ̄ⲙⲁ–ϥ. Mark 1:23
18. They removed the roof of ⲡⲙⲁ ⲉⲧϥ̄–ⲛ̄ϩⲏⲧ–ϥ̄. Mark 2:4
19. Another great crowd followed Him ⲉⲩ–ⲥⲱⲧⲙ̄ ⲉ–ⲛ–ⲉⲧϥ̄–ⲉⲓⲣⲉ ⲙ̄ⲙⲟ–ⲟⲩ. Mark 3:8
20. ⲛⲁϣⲉ–ⲛ–ⲉⲛⲧ–ⲁϥ–ⲧⲁⲗϭⲟ–ⲟⲩ[89]. Mark 3:10
21. ⲡⲛⲟⲩⲧⲉ ⲉⲧ⁰–ϫⲟⲥⲉ. Mark 5:7

---

[87] ⲉⲣⲏⲙⲟⲥ wilderness.
[88] ⲁⲕⲁⲑⲁⲣⲧⲟⲛ impure.
[89] ⲧⲁⲗϭⲟ heal.

22. ⲁⲩ-ⲉⲓ ⲉⲃⲟⲗ ⲉ-ᵠⲛⲁⲩ ⲉ-ⲡ-ⲉⲛⲧ-ⲁϥ-ϣⲱⲡⲉ. Mark 5:14

23. He said to them, ⲡⲏⲓ̈ ⲉⲧⲉⲧⲛⲁ-ⲃⲱⲕ ⲉϩⲟⲩⲛ ⲉⲣⲟ-ϥ ϭⲱ⁹⁰ ⲛ̄ϩⲏⲧ-ϥ̄. Mark 6:10

24. ⲁⲩ-ⲧⲁⲟⲩⲟ ⲉⲣⲟ-ϥ ⲛ̄-ⲛ-ⲉⲛⲧ-ⲁⲩ-ⲁⲁ-ⲩ ⲧⲏⲣ-ⲟⲩ. Mark 6:30

25. ⲡ-ⲉⲧᵠ-ⲛⲁ-ⲭⲓ-ᵠϣⲁⲭⲉ⁹¹ ⲉϥ-ϩⲟⲟⲩ ⲛ̄ⲥⲁ-ⲡⲉϥⲉⲓⲱⲧ ⲏ ⲧⲉϥⲙⲁⲁⲩ ϩⲛ̄-
ⲟⲩⲙⲟⲩ ⲙⲁⲣⲉϥ-ⲙⲟⲩ. Mark 7:10

26. ⲉⲡⲫⲁⲑⲁ ⲉⲧⲉ-ⲡⲁⲓ̈ ⲡⲉ ⲟⲩⲱⲛ. Mark 7:34

27. ⲙⲁⲣⲓⲁ ⲇⲉ ⲧⲙⲁⲅⲇⲁⲗⲏⲛⲏ ⲁⲩⲱ ⲙⲁⲣⲓⲁ ⲧⲁ-ⲓⲱⲥⲏⲥ ⲛⲉⲩ-ⲛⲁⲩ ⲉ-ⲡⲙⲁ
ⲛ̄ⲧ-ⲁⲩ-ⲕⲁⲁ-ϥ ⲛ̄ϩⲏⲧ-ϥ̄. Mark 15:47

28. ⲓ̄ⲥ̄ ⲡⲛⲁⲍⲁⲣⲏⲛⲟⲥ ⲡ-ⲉⲛⲧ-ⲁⲩ-ⲥⲧⲁⲩⲣⲟⲩ⁹² ⲙ̄ⲙⲟ-ϥ. Mark 16:6

---

⁹⁰ ϭⲱ Imperative.

⁹¹ ⲭⲓ- = ⲭⲉ- utter, say, speak about. The prenominal form ⲭⲓ- occurs before zero article;
otherwise ⲭⲉ- is used.

⁹² ⲥⲧⲁⲩⲣⲟⲩ crucify.

LESSON 18

FOCALIZING CONVERSION.

136. Like the preterit, the focalizing conversion forms a complete sentence. It tells the reader that the converted sentence contains (somewhere) a high point of interest that the reader should select and emphasize.

ⲘⲠⲤ–ⲘⲞⲨ ⲀⲖⲖⲀ ⲈⲤ–ⲚⲔⲞⲦⲔ̄
She has not died; *rather, she is sleeping*

Thus its use is a rhetorical strategy—it is a sort of not-very-specific stage direction to the reader—and so it typically occurs in literary writing but not in private letters and business documents. [CG 444–59]

137. *Focalizing Converters.* [CG 444]

Focalization is marked by the following converters:

conversion base	ⲈⲢⲈ–, Ⲉ⸗
sentence converter	Ⲛ̄Ⲧ– before past tense
	Ⲉ– before other sentence types
	ⲈⲦⲈ– forming some negations **139**

Note that ⲈⲢⲈ–, Ⲉ⸗, and Ⲉ– are also circumstantial converters, and Ⲛ̄Ⲧ– is also an optional spelling of the relative converter ⲈⲚⲦ– **131**.

The focalizing conversion is formed in the same way as the preterit. (Note that there is a focalizing conversion of the preterit.)

ⲈⲢⲈ–ⲠⲢⲰⲘⲈ ⲤⲰⲦⲠ̄
Ⲉϥ–ⲤⲰⲦⲠ̄
Ⲛ̄Ⲧ–Ⲁϥ–ⲤⲰⲦⲠ̄
Ⲉ–ϢⲀϥ–ⲤⲰⲦⲠ̄
Ⲉ–ⲚⲀⲚⲞⲨ–ϥ
Ⲉ–ⲞⲨⲚ̄–⁰ⲢⲰⲘⲈ ⲤⲰⲦⲠ̄
Ⲉ–ⲘⲚ̄–⁰ⲢⲰⲘⲈ ⲤⲰⲦⲠ̄
Ⲉ–ⲚⲈϥ–ⲤⲰⲦⲠ̄
Etc[93].

---

[93] There is no focalizing conversion of the nominal sentence. Of the non-durative conjugations,

Negation adds ⲁⲛ after the predicate (except for ⲟⲩⲛ̄-/ⲙⲛ̄-).

ⲉⲣⲉ-ⲡⲣⲱⲙⲉ ⲥⲱⲧⲛ̄ ⲁⲛ
ⲉϥ-ⲥⲱⲧⲛ̄ ⲁⲛ
ⲛ̄ⲧ-ⲁϥ-ⲥⲱⲧⲛ̄ ⲁⲛ (sic)
ⲉ-ϣⲁϥ-ⲥⲱⲧⲛ̄ ⲁⲛ

(Note the negation of ⲛ̄ⲧ-ⲁϥ- and ⲉ-ϣⲁϥ- with ⲁⲛ.)

Optionally the durative can be negatived by ⲛ̄- . . . ⲁⲛ and ⲛ̄ⲛ- . . . ⲁⲛ, with ⲛ̄- or ⲛ̄ⲛ- prefixed to the conversion base.

ⲉⲣⲉ-ⲡⲣⲱⲙⲉ ⲥⲱⲧⲛ̄ ⲁⲛ and ⲛ̄(ⲛ)-ⲉⲣⲉ-ⲡⲣⲱⲙⲉ ⲥⲱⲧⲛ̄ ⲁⲛ
ⲉϥ-ⲥⲱⲧⲛ̄ ⲁⲛ and ⲛ̄(ⲛ)-ⲉϥ-ⲥⲱⲧⲛ ⲁⲛ

For another kind of negation (formed with ⲉⲧⲉ-), cf. **139**.

To convert a sentence formed with ⲟⲩⲛ̄-, it is possible to substitute the prenominal base ⲉⲣⲉ- in place of ⲟⲩⲛ̄-:

ⲟⲩⲛ̄-ᵠⲣⲱⲙⲉ ⲥⲱⲧⲛ̄   ⲉⲣⲉ-ᵠⲣⲱⲙⲉ ⲥⲱⲧⲛ̄

Conjugation of the conversion base ⲉⲡⲉ-, ⲉ꞊.

ⲉⲓ̈-	ⲉⲛ-
ⲉⲕ-	ⲉⲧⲉⲧⲛ̄-
ⲉⲡⲉ-	
ⲉϥ-	ⲉⲩ-
ⲉⲥ-	
ⲉⲡⲉ-ⲡⲛⲟⲩⲧⲉ	

THE MEANING OF FOCALIZING CONVERSION

138. A focalizing converter signals that the reader should choose to understand some part of the converted sentence as a "focal point"—i.e. a point of special emphasis or attention. [CG 445–51]

But the conversion does not tell where the focal point is located. Almost any part of speech is eligible to be a focal point. And so, the selection of a focal point must be made by the reader, in view of the overall flow of the argument on that page of text. Even when the train of thought seems clear, several different performances of a focalizing conversion may seem justified.

only the past and the aorist have a focalizing conversion. Note also that in ancient manuscripts, the converter ⲛ̄ⲧ- is sometimes erroneously written ⲉⲛⲧ-.

Focalizing verbal constructions were used in earlier stages of the Egyptian language. In these much earlier stages, scholars have theorized that the location of the focal point is regular and predictable. But in any case, this is no longer true when we get to the Coptic stage of Egyptian.

Let's look at a few examples of focalizing conversions set in their context, in order to understand how the choice of focal point can be suggested by the surrounding text. In each example, my own choice of focal point is given in a footnote; but as a fellow reader you are entitled to choose some other place to put the focal point if it seems better. I have slightly condensed the passages.

i. Mary Magdalene came to the tomb (of Jesus) while it was dark and saw that the stone had been removed from its entrance. She ran to Simon Peter and the other disciple; they were coming to the tomb. The other disciple went in, looked, and had faith. Mary Magdalene was sitting outside the tomb weeping. Weeping, she turned and saw Jesus standing there. Jesus said to her, Mariam! She said, Rabbouni! Mary Magdalene went and told the disciples, I have seen the Lord! When it was evening and the doors were secured Jesus came and stood in their midst, and said to them, Peace be unto you! Jesus did many other miracles in the presence of His disciples. ⲙ̄ⲛ̄ⲛⲥⲁ-ⲛⲁⲓ̈ ⲟⲛ ⲁ-ⲓ̄ⲥ̄ ⲟⲩⲟⲛⲋ-ϥ̄ ⲉ-ⲛⲉϥⲙⲁⲑⲏⲧⲏⲥ ϩⲓⲭⲛ̄-ⲧⲉⲑⲁⲗⲁⲥⲥⲁ ⲛ̄-ⲧⲓⲃⲉⲣⲓⲁⲥ. ⲛ̄ⲧ-ⲁϥ-ⲟⲩⲟⲛⲋ-ϥ̄ ⲇⲉ ⲉⲃⲟⲗ ⲛ̄ⲧⲉⲓ̈ϩⲉ (Afterwards, again Jesus revealed Himself to His disciples—by Lake Tiberias. And He revealed Himself as follows[94]). They were gathered together, Simon Peter said to them, I'm going fishing. They came out and entered the boat. And after sunrise, Jesus stood on the bank. But the disciples did not know it was Jesus. Jesus said to them, You boys here, do you have any fish with you? (John 20:1–21:5)

ii. (From a letter that Paul is writing to the church in Corinth) One who "speaks in a tongue" (speaks ecstatic nonsense) speaks not to human beings but to God, for no person listens to him. The one who speaks in tongues edifies only himself. Speaking prophetic sayings is better than speaking in tongues. Listen, brethren, if I come to you speaking in tongues how will I be of any use to you? If a bugle makes a funny sound, who's going to get ready for battle? Likewise, if you don't produce clear speech, how will people understand what you're saying? Suppose the whole church gathers and they all speak in tongues, and then some simple folk or unbelievers come by. Wouldn't they say that ⲉⲧⲉⲧⲛ̄-ⲗⲟⲃⲉ† (You're crazy![95]). But if they are all uttering prophetic sayings and an

[94] My choice of focal point: *as follows.*
[95] My choice of focal point: *really crazy.*

156

unbeliever or a simple person comes by, they will be convinced by all. (1 Cor 14:2–24)

iii. John (the Baptist) replied, It is not I who am the Christ. He (the Christ) must rise, and I must sink: one who has come from heaven is superior to all; one who is from the earth is earthly ⲁⲩⲱ ⲉϥ-ϣⲁϫⲉ ⲉⲃⲟⲗ ϩⲙ-ⲡⲕⲁϩ (and speaks from the earth[96]). Now, the One who has come from heaven is testifying to what He has seen and heard. And no one accepts His testimony. Yet He has sealed the One who has accepted His testimony, for God is truthful. Indeed, the One whom God has sent ⲉϥ-ϫⲱ ⲛ̄-ⲛ̄ϣⲁϫⲉ ⲙ̄-ⲡⲛⲟⲩⲧⲉ (speaks the words of God[97]). ⲛ̄-ⲉⲣⲉ-ⲡⲛⲟⲩⲧⲉ ⲅⲁⲣ ϯ ⲁⲛ ⲙ̄-ⲡⲉⲡ̄ⲛ̄ⲁ ϩⲛ̄-ⲟⲩⲱϣⲓ (For, God does not give the spirit in a limited way[98]): the Father loves the Son and has put all things into His hands. (John 3:27–35)

iv. The kinsmen of the synagogue leader came and told him, Your daughter has died. But Jesus said, Fear not! Just have faith. And they went to the leader's house, and He saw that they were distraught and weeping. But when He had entered He said to them, Why are you distraught and weeping over the girl? ⲙ̄ⲡⲥ̄-ⲙⲟⲩ. ⲁⲗⲗⲁ ⲉⲥ-ⲛ̄ⲕⲟⲧⲕ̄ (She has not died; rather, she is sleeping[99]). They laughed at Him. But He took the girl's hand and said to her, Taleitha Koum. And immediately the girl got up and walked. (Mark 5:35–42)

v. They took Jesus from Kaiphas to the praetorium. And Pilate came out. Then Pilate went back into the praetorium, and summoned Jesus and said to Him, You are the King of the Jews? — Jesus answered, ⲉⲕ-ϫⲱ ⲙ̄-ⲡⲁⲓ̈ ϩⲁⲣⲟ-ⲕ ⲙⲁⲩⲁⲁ-ⲕ (Are you saying this as your own opinion[100]) or is it other people who have talked to you about Me? — Pilate replied, Excuse me, am I supposed to be a Jew? It's Your people and the high priests who put You into my custody. — Jesus responded: Personally speaking, My kingdom is not from this world. (John 18:28–36)

In form, the focalizing converters are identical with those of the circumstantial/relative (ⲉⲣⲉ-, ⲉ⸗, ⲉ-, ⲛ̄ⲧ-, ⲉⲛⲧ-, ⲉⲧⲉ-), and this is a potential source of confusion. However, because the focalizing conversion is by definition a complete sentence it can be distinguished from the circumstantial and relative (which are not)[101]. The focalizing is relatively rare compared to the circumstantial and relative.

---

[96] My choice of focal point: uncertain, maybe *from the earth* or *speaks*.

[97] My choice of focal point: uncertain, maybe *speaks,* or *God*.

[98] My choice of focal point: *in a limited way*.

[99] My choice of focal point: *is sleeping*.

[100] My choice of focal point: *as your own opinion*.

[101] A circumstantial conversion of the focalizing conversion exists, and it is rare, being mostly confined to the elaborate rhetoric of Shenoute: ⲉ-ⲉⲣⲉ-, ⲉ-ⲉ⸗, and ⲉ-ⲛ̄ⲧ- (unfortunately, sometimes simplified to ⲉⲣⲉ-, ⲉ⸗, ⲛ̄ⲧ-).

139. *Negations.* [CG 452–53]

In English we can sometimes translate the focalizing conversion by *It is/was . . . that . . .* , dividing the meaning into two parts. Thus: "It was in the following way | that He revealed Himself" — "It is the words of God | that He speaks"; etc.

This cumbersome English construction points to the existence of two logical forms of negation, depending on which part is negatived. Coptic carefully distinguishes these two forms. Form (i) is much more common.

   i. It was not in the following way | that He revealed Himself.
   ii. It was in the following way | that He did not reveal Himself.

   i. It is not the words of God | that He speaks.
   ii. It is the words of God | that He does not speak.

In Coptic, form (i) is expressed by the negations noted in **137**. Form (ii) is expressed by prefixing the sentence converter ⲉⲧⲉ– to an already negatived basic sentence pattern. Thus

   (i) ⲛ̄ⲧ–ⲁϥ–ⲟⲩⲟⲛ2̄–ϥ̄ ⲁⲛ ⲉⲃⲟⲗ ⲛ̄ⲧⲉⲓ2ⲉ
       It was not in the following way that He revealed Himself

   (ii) ⲉⲧⲉ–ⲙ̄ⲡϥ̄–ⲟⲩⲟⲛ2̄–ϥ̄ ⲉⲃⲟⲗ ⲛ̄ⲧⲉⲓ2ⲉ
       It was in the following way that He did not reveal Himself

   (i) ⲉϥ–ⲭⲱ ⲁⲛ ⲛ̄–ⲛ̄ϣⲁϫⲉ ⲙ̄–ⲡⲛⲟⲩⲧⲉ or ⲛ̄–ⲉϥ–ⲭⲱ ⲁⲛ ⲛ̄–ⲛ̄ϣⲁϫⲉ ⲙ̄–
       ⲡⲛⲟⲩⲧⲉ
       It is not the words of God that He speaks

   (ii) ⲉⲧⲉ–ⲛ̄–ϥ–ⲭⲱ ⲁⲛ ⲛ̄–ⲛ̄ϣⲁϫⲉ ⲙ̄–ⲡⲛⲟⲩⲧⲉ
       It is the words of God that He does not speak

When the negation ⲛ̄–ⲉϥ–ⲥⲱⲧⲛ̄ ⲁⲛ (or ⲛ̄ⲛ–ⲉϥ–ⲥⲱⲧⲛ̄ ⲁⲛ) occurs, it is focalizing; whereas, ⲉ–ⲛ̄–ϥ–ⲥⲱⲧⲛ̄ ⲁⲛ is circumstantial. But both conversions can be negated as ⲉϥ–ⲥⲱⲧⲛ̄ ⲁⲛ.

EXERCISES 18

A. Review vocabularies 8–11.

B. Reading selections from the New Testament.

The possible meaning(s) of any focalizing conversion can only be discovered by reading the text that surrounds it, in order to understand the overall train of thought. In these translation exercises, each example is accompanied by enough context to enable you to make a "reader's decision" about where to put the focus in the focalizing conversion. (If you can read Greek, you might also study the Greek originals from which these sentences were translated into Coptic. Is there something in the Greek original that led the Coptic translator to choose a focalizing conversion?)

Translate the Coptic passages. Where do you think the focal point should be?

1. As for me (John the Baptist), I have baptized you with water. ⲛ̄ⲧⲟϥ ⲇⲉ ⲉϥ–ⲛⲁ–ⲃⲁⲡⲧⲓⲍⲉ ⲙ̄ⲙⲱ–ⲧⲛ̄ ϩⲛ̄–ⲟⲩⲡ̅ⲛ̅ⲁ̅ ⲉϥ–ⲟⲩⲁⲁⲃ. Mark 1:8
2. And it (the demon) cried out, saying, What business do you have with us, O Jesus of Nazareth? ⲛ̄ⲧ–ⲁⲕ–ⲉⲓ ⲉ–$^{\emptyset}$ⲧⲁⲕⲟ–ⲛ Mark 1:24
3. Let us go elsewhere, to the nearby villages, so that I might preach in them also. ⲛ̄ⲧ–ⲁⲓ̈–ⲉⲓ ⲅⲁⲣ ⲉⲃⲟⲗ ⲉ–ⲡⲉⲓ̈ϩⲱⲃ. Mark 1:38
4. He said to the lame man, Arise. ⲉⲓ̈–ϫⲉⲣⲟ–ⲕ[102]. Take up your bedding and go home. Mark 2:10–11
5. Those who are well do not need a physician, but rather those who are ill. ⲛ̄ⲧ–ⲁⲓ̈–ⲉⲓ ⲁⲛ ⲉ–$^{\emptyset}$ⲧⲉϩⲙ̄–ⲛ̄ⲇⲓⲕⲁⲓⲟⲥ ⲁⲗⲗⲁ ⲛ̄ⲣⲉϥ–ⲣ̄–$^{\emptyset}$ⲛⲟⲃⲉ. Mark 2:17
6. No one puts new wine into old wineskins lest the wine break the wineskin and the wine spill out and the wineskin be ruined. ⲁⲗⲗⲁ ⲉ–ϣⲁⲩ–ⲛⲉϫ–$^{\emptyset}$ⲏⲣⲡ̄[103] ⲛ̄–ⲃⲣ̄ⲣⲉ ⲉ–$^{\emptyset}$ϩⲱⲧ[104] ⲛ̄–ⲃⲣ̄ⲣⲉ. Mark 2:22
7. And once He was walking in the ripe fields, and His disciples started to pluck ears of grain. And the Pharisees said to Him, Look at what they are doing on the Sabbath, which is forbidden to do. He said to them,

[102] ϫⲉⲣⲟ–ⲕ⸗ = ϫⲱ ⲉⲣⲟ–ⲕ.

[103] ⲏⲣⲡ̄ wine.

[104] ϩⲱⲧ wineskin.

Haven't you even read what David did when he and his companions were hungry? How he went into the house of God during Abiathar's priesthood and ate the sacred loaves, which it was forbidden for him to eat, and gave some to the others who were with him? He next said to them, ⲡⲥⲁⲃⲃⲁⲧⲟⲛ ⲛ̄ⲧ-ⲁϥ-ϣⲱⲡⲉ ⲉⲧⲃⲉ-ⲡⲣⲱⲙⲉ. ⲁⲩⲱ ⲛ̄ⲧ-ⲁ-ⲡⲣⲱⲙⲉ ϣⲱⲡⲉ ⲁⲛ ⲉⲧⲃⲉ-ⲡⲥⲁⲃⲃⲁⲧⲟⲛ. Mark 2:23–27

8. And He came home, and the crowd once again thronged to Him, so they could not eat their food. And when His relatives heard, they came out to sieze Him. For they were saying, His mind is deranged. And the Scribes who had come from Jerusalem were saying, ⲉⲣⲉ-ⲃⲉⲉⲗⲍⲉⲃⲟⲩⲗ[105] ⲛⲙ̄ⲙⲁ-ϥ. ⲁⲩⲱ ϩⲙ̄-ⲡⲁⲣⲭⲱⲛ[106] ⲛ̄-ⲛ̄ⲇⲁⲓⲙⲟⲛⲓⲟⲛ ⲉϥ-ⲛⲉⲝ-⁰ⲇⲁⲓⲙⲟ-ⲛⲓⲟⲛ ⲉⲃⲟⲗ[107]. Mark 3:20–22

9. When the Sabbath came, He began to teach in the synagogue. And the crowd, when they heard, were amazed, saying ⲛ̄ⲧ-ⲁ-ⲡⲁⲓ̈ ϭⲛ̄[108]-ⲛⲁⲓ̈ ⲧⲱⲛ. ⲁⲩⲱ ⲟⲩ ⲧⲉ ⲧⲉⲓ̈ⲥⲟⲫⲓⲁ[109] ⲛ̄ⲧ-ⲁⲩ-ⲧⲁⲁ-ⲥ ⲙ̄-ⲡⲁⲓ̈. Mark 6:2

10. He said to them, The prophet Isaiah spoke accurately about you, O you hypocrites, as it is written: This people honors Me with their lips, but their heart is far from Me; ⲉⲩ-ⲟⲩⲱϣⲧ ⲇⲉ ⲙ̄ⲙⲟ-ⲓ̈ ⲉ-ⲡϫⲓⲛϫⲏ[110] ⲉⲩ-ϯ-⁰ⲥⲃⲱ ⲛ̄-ϩⲉⲛⲥⲃⲟⲟⲩⲉ ⲛ̄-ⲉⲛⲧⲟⲗⲏ ⲛ̄-ⲣⲱⲙⲉ. Mark 7:6–7

11. He said to them, For your part you are ignorant, for you do not realize that no external thing that enters a person can pollute him, because ⲛ̄-ⲉϥ-ⲃⲏⲕ ⲁⲛ ⲉϩⲟⲩⲛ ⲉ-ⲡϩⲏⲧ[111] ⲁⲗⲗⲁ ⲉϩⲣⲁⲓ̈ ⲉ-ⲑⲏ. Mark 7:18–19

12. [A healing miracle] They brought Him a blind man and begged Him to touch him. And He took the hand of the blind man, led him outside the village, and after He had spat into his eyes He put His hand on him and asked him, ⲉⲕ-ⲛⲁⲩ ⲉ-ⲟⲩ Mark 8:22–23

13. He said to them, Whoever wants to follow Me, let him deny himself and take up his cross and follow Me. For whoever wants to save his life ⲉϥ-ⲛⲁ-ⲥⲟⲣⲙ-ⲉⲥ[112]. And whoever loses his life for My sake and for that of the Gospel ⲉϥ-ⲛⲁ-ⲧⲟⲩϫⲟ[113]-ⲥ. Mark 8:34–35

14. He said to them, What do you want Me to do for you? And they said to Him, Let one of us sit at Your right hand and another at Your left hand

---

[105] ⲃⲉⲉⲗⲍⲉⲃⲟⲩⲗ (personal name) Beelzebub, traditional name of a powerful demon.

[106] ⲁⲣⲭⲱⲛ leader.

[107] ⲛⲟⲩϫⲉ ⲉⲃⲟⲗ cast out (through exorcism).

[108] ϭⲓⲛⲉ find, discover.

[109] ⲥⲟⲫⲓⲁ wisdom.

[110] ⲉ-ⲡϫⲓⲛϫⲏ in vain, uselessly.

[111] ⲡϩⲏⲧ ... ⲑⲏ (ⲧϩⲏ) the heart ... the belly.

[112] ⲥⲱⲣⲙ̄ lose.

[113] ⲧⲟⲩϫⲟ vivify, cause to live, save.

in Your glory. But Jesus said to them, You do not know ⲉⲧⲉⲧⲛ̄-ⲁⲓⲧⲉⲓ ⲛ̄-ⲟⲩ. Mark 10:36–38

15. He said to them, You know that those who claim to be rulers of the people are their masters, and their superiors have authority over them. But this is not how it is among you. Rather, whoever among you wishes to be the greatest, ⲉϥ-ⲛⲁ-ⲁⲓⲁⲕⲟⲛⲉⲓ[114] ⲛⲏ-ⲧⲛ. And whoever wishes to be first among you, ⲉϥ-ⲛⲁ-ⲣ̄-⁰ϩⲙ̄ϩⲁⲗ ⲛⲏ-ⲧⲛ̄ ⲧⲏⲣ-ⲧⲛ̄. Mark 10:42–44

16. He was hungry. And when He saw a fig tree in the distance with leaves upon it, He went to it in case He might find anything (to eat) on it. And after He had come and had not found anything on it except leaves—for it was not the season for figs—He responded, saying to it, From hence-forth, no one shall eat fruit from you . . . . And when they passed it at dawn they saw that the fig tree was all dried up, roots and all. And when Peter remembered, he said to Him, Rabbi, look at the fig tree that You cursed. ⲛ̄ⲧ-ⲁⲥ-ϣⲟⲟⲩⲉ[115]. And Jesus answered them, saying, Have faith in God. Mark 11:13–22

17. And the Pharisees and Herodians sent some people to Him to trap Him by what He said. And when they encountered Him they said to Him, Teacher, we know that You are a truthful man and You are not worried about anything: for, You do not show favoritism to any people, ⲁⲗⲗⲁ ϩⲛ̄-ⲟⲩⲙⲉ ⲉⲕ-ϯ-⁰ⲥⲃⲱ ⲛ̄-ⲧⲉϩⲓⲏ ⲙ̄-ⲡⲛⲟⲩⲧⲉ. Is it proper to pay taxes to Caesar, or not? Mark 12:13–14

18. She poured the jar (of costly ointment) upon His head. And some people were annoyed and said to one another, Why was this ointment wasted? For it could have been sold for more than three hundred staters and given to the poor. And they were angry at her. But Jesus said to them, Leave her alone. Why do you bother her? It is a good deed that she has done to Me. For, the poor are with you always, and if you wish ⲉⲧⲉⲧⲛ̄-ⲉϣ[116]-ⲣ̄-⁰ⲡⲉⲧⲛⲁⲛⲟⲩϥ ⲛⲁ-ⲩ ⲛ̄-ⲟⲩⲟⲉⲓϣ ⲛⲓⲙ. ⲁⲛⲟⲕ ⲇⲉ ⲛ̄-ⲉⲓ̈-ⲛⲁ-ϭⲱ ⲁⲛ ⲛⲙ̄ⲙⲏ-ⲧⲛ̄ ⲛ̄-ⲟⲩⲟⲉⲓϣ ⲛⲓⲙ. Mark 14:3–7

19. And they came to a garden called Gethsemane. And He said to His disciples, Just sit down here until I have prayed. And He took Peter and James and John with Him . . . . And He prostrated Himself and prayed . . . Abba, Father, You have power over everything. Let this cup pass from Me. Yet—not as I wish it to be. And He came and found them

---

[114] ⲁⲓⲁⲕⲟⲛⲉⲓ ⲛ̄-/ⲛⲁ⸗ serve.

[115] ϣⲟⲟⲩⲉ dry up.

[116] ⲉϣ- or ϣ- be able to, can. Cf. vocabulary 15.

asleep. And He said to Peter, Simon, ек-ṅκοτκ[117]. Weren't you able to keep awake for a single moment? Mark 14:32–37

20. And early in the morning on the first day of the week they (Mary Magdalene, Mary the relative of Jose, and Salome) came out to the tomb, after the sun rose . . . And when they had gone into the tomb, they saw a young man sitting on the right side, wearing a white stole. And fear overcame them. But he said to them, Fear not. ετετṅ-κωτε ṅса[118]-ιс πναζαρηνος π-ент-аγ-стаγроγ ṁмо-ч. ач-тωо-γν-ч[119]. ṅ-ч-2ṁ-πεïма αν. Mark 16:2–6

21. There are some who have enough faith to eat every kind of food, while the weaker person eats vegetarian. Those who eat must not scorn those who refrain from eating. And those who refrain from eating must not pass judgment on those who eat . . . Let everyone be content in his heart. Whoever is mindful (мееγε) about the day's being a prescribed fast day, еч-мееγε ṁ-πχοεις. аγω π-ет[0]-оγωм еч-оγωм ṁ-πχοεις . . . аγω π-ете-ṅ-ч-оγωм αν ете-ṅ-ч-оγωм αν ṁ-πχοεις. Romans 14:2–6

C. Translate rapidly into Coptic, using the focalizing conversion.

I am revealing myself in this way
You (sing. masc.) are . . .
You (sing. fem.) are . . .
He is . . .
She is . . .
We are . . .
You (pl.) are . . .
They are . . .

D. Translate rapidly into Coptic, using the focalizing conversion and giving alternate forms where possible.

It is not in this way that I am revealing myself
 " " you (sing. masc.) are . . .
 " " you (sing. fem.) are . . .
 " " he is . . .
 " " she is . . .
 " " we are . . .
 " " you (pl.) are . . .
 " " they are . . .

[117] ṅκοτκ fall asleep, be asleep.
[118] κωτε ṅса- seach for, seek.
[119] тооγν cause to arise.

E. Translate rapidly into Coptic, using the focalizing conversion.

It is in this way that I am not revealing myself
      ,,   ,,   you (sing. masc.) are not . . .
      ,,   ,,   you (sing. fem.) are not . . .
      ,,   ,,   he is not . . .
      ,,   ,,   she is not . . .
      ,,   ,,   we are not . . .
      ,,   ,,   you (pl.) are not . . .
      ,,   ,,   they are not . . .

F. Translate rapidly into Coptic, using the focalizing conversion.

I revealed myself in this way
You (sg. masc.) revealed . . .
Etc. etc.

G. Translate rapidly into Coptic, using the focalizing conversion.

It was not in this way that I revealed myself
It was not in this way that you (masc. sing.) . . .
Etc. etc.

H. Translate rapidly into Coptic, using the focalizing conversion.

It was in this way that I did not reveal myself
It was in this way that you (masc. sing.) . . .
Etc. etc.

LESSON 19

CLEFT SENTENCE.
REPORTED DISCOURSE AND THOUGHT.

---

140. A more precise way to signal focalization is the cleft sentence construction. [CG 461–63]

ιнсоγс пε‒εнт‒ⲁq‒ⲧⲁλбо‒ï	= It is *Jesus* who healed me
ⲛⲧⲱⲧⲛ̄ ⲅⲁⲣ ⲁⲛ пε‒εⲧ⁰‒ϣⲁⲭε	= For, it is not *you* who speak
ⲁⲛоⲕ εⲧ⁰‒ⲛⲁ‒ⲕⲁⲧⲏⲅоⲣι ⲙ̄ⲙⲱ‒ⲧⲛ̄	= It is *I* who shall accuse you

The focal point always comes first, and it is always an article phrase, independent personal pronoun, or the like.

141. Cleft Sentence Pattern 1.

Pattern 1 [CG 464] has two parts.

i. A nominal sentence containing ⲡε "It is . . . ," in which either ⲡε/ⲧε/ⲛε agrees with the preceding focal point

ⲧεⲕⲡιⲥⲧιⲥ ⲧε . . . It is your faith . . .

(ⲛ̄‒)ⲧεⲕⲡιⲥⲧιⲥ ⲁⲛ ⲧε . . . It is not your faith . . .

or ⲡε is frozen in the singular masculine form

ⲧεⲕⲡιⲥⲧιⲥ ⲡε . . . It is your faith . . .

(ⲛ̄‒)ⲧεⲕⲡιⲥⲧιⲥ ⲁⲛ ⲡε . . . It is not your faith . . .

ii. An attached relative clause, in which a personal pronoun agrees in number/gender with the focal point (bare εⲧ **130** also occurs)

ⲧεⲕⲡιⲥⲧιⲥ ⲧε‒εⲛⲧ‒ⲁⲥ‒ⲛⲁ2ⲙ‒εⲕ
It is your faith that has saved you

(ⲛ̄‒)ⲧεⲕⲡιⲥⲧιⲥ ⲁⲛ ⲧε‒εⲛⲧ‒ⲁⲥ‒ⲛⲁ2ⲙ‒εⲕ
It is not your faith that has saved you

ⲧεⲕⲡιⲥⲧιⲥ ⲧε‒εⲛⲧ‒ⲁⲕ‒ⲛоⲩ2ⲙ̄ ⲛ̄2ⲏⲧ‒c̄
It is your faith through which you have become saved

(ⲛ̄-)ⲧⲉⲕⲡⲓⲥⲧⲓⲥ ⲁⲛ ⲧⲉ-ⲉⲛⲧ-ⲁⲕ-ⲛⲟⲩ2ⲙ̄ ⲛ̄2ⲏⲧ-ⲥ̄
It is not your faith through which you have become saved

ⲧⲉⲕⲡⲓⲥⲧⲓⲥ ⲧⲉ-ⲉⲧ⁰-ⲛⲟⲩ2ⲙ̄ ⲙ̄ⲙⲟ-ⲕ (with bare ⲉⲧ)
It is your faith that saves you

Note that ⲧⲉ (i.e. ⲡⲉ/ⲧⲉ/ⲛⲉ) and the relative converter (ⲉⲛⲧ-, ⲉⲧ⁰-) are attached to one another: ⲧⲉ-ⲉⲛⲧ-, ⲧⲉ-ⲉⲧ⁰-.

142. *Elided forms in Pattern 1.* Very often ⲡⲉ (ⲧⲉ, ⲛⲉ) and the attached relative converter elide (ⲉ-ⲉ written simply as ⲉ).

	Elided Form
ⲡⲉ-ⲉⲧϥ-	ⲡⲉⲧϥ-
ⲡⲉ-ⲉⲧⲉ-	ⲡⲉⲧⲉ-
ⲡⲉ-ⲉⲛⲧ-	ⲡⲉⲛⲧ-
ⲡⲉ-ⲉⲧ⁰-	ⲡⲉⲧ⁰-

The elided form is quite commonplace, and it looks misleadingly like an articulated relative **132** (i.e. ⲡ-ⲉⲧ⸗, ⲡ-ⲉⲧⲉ- ⲡ-ⲉⲛⲧ-, ⲡ-ⲉⲧ⁰-, etc. = the one who . . . ").

Thus, when you see a sequence of letters such as . . . ⲡⲉⲧ . . . or . . . ⲡⲉⲛⲧ . . . or . . . ⲡⲉⲧⲉ . . . or . . . ⲡⲉϣⲁϥ . . . or . . . ⲡⲉⲧϥ . . . , you must always remember to ask yourself whether this is an articulated relative or a part of an elided cleft sentence. Both are extremely common. For example

ⲓⲏⲥⲟⲩⲥ ⲡⲉⲛⲧⲁϥⲧⲁⲗϭⲟⲓ̈

means both (i) Jesus, who healed me (articulated relative, ⲓⲏⲥⲟⲩⲥ ⲡ-ⲉⲛⲧ-ⲁϥ-ⲧⲁⲗϭⲟ-ⲓ̈) and (ii) It is Jesus who healed me (cleft sentence pattern 1, elided ⲓⲏⲥⲟⲩⲥ ⲡ(ⲉ)-ⲉⲛⲧ-ⲁϥ-ⲧⲁⲗϭⲟ-ⲓ̈). By thinking about the context, you should be able to make the right choice between these two alternatives. And the choice is yours.

> Much more rarely, Pattern 1 contains a circumstantial clause instead of a relative. ⲛ̄ⲧⲟϥ ⲙⲁⲩⲁⲁ-ϥ ⲡⲉ ⲉϥ-ⲁⲛⲁⲭⲱⲣⲉⲓ 2ⲙ̄-ⲡⲙⲁ ⲉⲧ⁰-ⲙ̄ⲙⲁⲩ = It is *he alone* who is living as an anchorite in that place. [CG 470]

143. Pattern 1 can also be used as an opening formula at the beginning of a story, to introduce a character and circumstances: *There once was . . .* [CG 465]

ⲟⲩⲣⲱⲙⲉ ⲛ̄-ⲣⲙ̄ⲙⲁⲟ ⲡⲉⲛⲧ-ⲁϥ-ⲧⲱϭⲉ ⲛ̄-ⲟⲩⲙⲁ ⲛ̄-ⲉⲗⲟⲟⲗⲉ
There once was a rich man who planted a vineyard
("It is a rich man who . . . ")

144. Cleft Sentence Pattern 2.

Pattern 2 [CG 468] consists of

   i. An independent personal pronoun (ⲁⲛⲟⲕ, ⲛ̄ⲧⲟⲕ, etc.)

   ii. Either ⲉⲛⲧ- (relative conversion of past affirmative) or ⲉⲧ⁰- (bare ⲉⲧ **130**)

ⲛ̄ⲧⲟⲕ ⲉⲛⲧ-ⲁⲕ-ⲧⲁⲟⲩⲟ-ⲓ̈	= It is *you* who have sent me
ⲛ̄ⲧⲟⲕ ⲁⲛ ⲉⲛⲧ-ⲁⲓ̈-ⲧⲁⲟⲩⲟ-ⲕ	= It is not *you* whom I have sent
ⲛ̄ⲧⲟⲕ ⲉⲧ⁰-ⲭⲱ ⲙ̄ⲙⲟ-ⲥ	= It is *you* who say it (with bare ⲉⲧ)

After ⲉⲛⲧ-, a personal pronoun will agree in number/gender with the focal point (ⲛ̄ⲧⲟⲕ ⲉⲛⲧ-ⲁⲕ-; ⲛ̄ⲧⲟⲕ ⲉⲛⲧ-ⲁⲓ̈-ⲧⲁⲟⲩⲟ-ⲕ).

Note that pattern 2 does not contain ⲡⲉ. Nagation: ⲁⲛ following ⲁⲛⲟⲕ (etc.)

REPORTED DISCOURSE AND THOUGHT

145. Reported discourse is the content of speaking or thought quoted after a verb of speech or cognition. [CG 509] Reported discourse is mostly introduced by ⲭⲉ-.

The most common constructions are ⲭⲱ ⲙ̄ⲙⲟ-ⲥ ⲭⲉ-/ⲭⲟⲟ-ⲥ ⲭⲉ- *say* (say-it ⲭⲉ-) and ⲡⲉⲭⲁ-ϥ ⲭⲉ- *he said* (ⲡⲉⲭⲉ-, ⲡⲉⲭⲁ= **105**).

Verbs of speaking and cognition [CG 510] include ⲉⲓⲙⲉ ⲭⲉ- know, ⲙⲉⲉⲩⲉ ⲭⲉ- think, ⲛⲁⲩ ⲭⲉ- see, perceive, ⲡⲓⲥⲧⲉⲩⲉ ⲭⲉ- believe, ⲣ̄-⁰ⲙⲟⲉⲓϩⲉ ⲭⲉ- be amazed at the fact that, ⲣ̄-ⲡⲙⲉⲉⲩⲉ ⲭⲉ- remember, ⲥⲱⲧⲙ̄ ⲭⲉ- hear, learn, ⲥⲟⲟⲩⲛ ⲭⲉ- know, ⲧⲁⲙⲟ ⲭⲉ- tell, ⲟⲩⲱϣⲃ̄ ⲭⲉ- answer, ⲭⲱ ⲙ̄ⲙⲟ-ⲥ ⲭⲉ- say, ⲭⲛⲟⲩ ⲭⲉ- ask, ϭⲛ̄- find out, ⲡⲉⲭⲉ-/ⲡⲉⲭⲁ= ⲭⲉ- said, etc.

146. Formally speaking, most Coptic *questions* can't be distinguished from affirmations 4. [CG 511]

ⲛ̄ⲧⲟⲕ ⲡⲉ ⲡ̄ⲣ̄ⲣⲟ ⲛ̄-ⲓⲟⲩⲇⲁⲓ

= (1) You are the Jewish king, (2) Are You the Jewish king?

But some questions can be recognized because they begin with the interrogative initial morphs ⲁⲣⲁ, ⲉⲛⲉ- or ⲙⲏ; or contain an interrogative word (ⲛⲓⲙ = who?); or contain a verb meaning "ask" (ⲭⲛⲟⲩ).

ⲁⲣⲁ = so, . . . ; pray tell, . . .

ⲙⲏ = is it true that . . . ?

ⲙⲏ . . . ⲁⲛ (or ⲙⲏ + negated conjugation) = isn't it true that . . . ?

147. ⲭⲱ ⲙ̄ⲙⲟ-ⲥ ⲭⲉ- "say" in durative conjugation strictly alternates with ⲭⲟⲟ-ⲥ ⲭⲉ- in non-durative conjugation. [CG 514]

ϯ-ⲭⲱ ⲙ̄ⲙⲟ-ⲥ ⲭⲉ- *I say* versus ⲁⲓ̈-ⲭⲟⲟ-ⲥ ⲭⲉ- *I said*

In this construction, -ⲥ grammatically points ahead to the ⲭⲉ- clause. It should not be translated in English.

148. *Indirect and direct discourse* are two perspectives that an author can adopt when reporting a speaker's words or thoughts. [CG 519–24] *Indirect discourse* is a reporter's perspective, as though it were the report of an onlooker. Here is an example:

ⲁϥ-ⲥⲟⲟⲩⲛ ⲛ̄ϭⲓ-ⲓ̄ⲥ̄ ⲭⲉ-ⲁ-ⲧⲉϥⲟⲩⲛⲟⲩ ⲉⲓ
Jesus knew *that his hour had come*

If the author had chosen to report Jesus' words in *direct discourse* (as though the speaker's exact words) he would have written

ⲁϥ-ⲥⲟⲟⲩⲛ ⲛ̄ϭⲓ-ⲓ̄ⲥ̄ ⲭⲉ-ⲁ-ⲧⲁⲟⲩⲛⲟⲩ ⲉⲓ
Jesus knew, "My hour has come"

What are the signals of indirect discourse compared to direct discourse? How does the writer compose the speaker's own words (direct discourse) so as to create the effect of indirect discourse?

i. Indirect discourse can change the person (e.g. from first to third)

Direct: My hour ⲧⲁⲟⲩⲛⲟⲩ
Indirect: His hour ⲧⲉϥⲟⲩⲛⲟⲩ

ii. Indirect discourse can change the syntax of a command or request

Direct: He said, "Sit down" ⲁϥ-ⲭⲟⲟ-ⲥ ⲭⲉ-ϩⲙⲟⲟⲥ
Indirect: He commanded him to sit down, ⲁϥ-ⲟⲩⲉϩ-⁰ⲥⲁϩⲛⲉ ⲉ-⁰ⲧⲣⲉϥ-ϩⲙⲟⲟⲥ

iii. Indirect discourse can change the form of a question about place or manner

Direct: He asked, "Where is she staying?" ⲁϥ-ⲭⲛⲟⲩ ⲭⲉ-ⲉⲥ-ⲕⲏ ⲛ̄ⲁϣ ⲙ̄-ⲙⲁ
Indirect: He asked where she was staying ⲁϥ-ⲭⲛⲟⲩ ⲉ-ⲡⲙⲁ ⲉⲧⲥ-ⲕⲏ ⲙ̄ⲙⲁⲩ

Unlike English, Coptic does *not* shift the tense of indirect discourse. Instead, indirect discourse has the same tense as the equivalent direct discourse. Here English and Coptic diverge, when talking about the past.

Direct: ⲁϥ-ⲭⲟⲟ-ⲥ ⲭⲉ-ϯ-ϣⲱⲛⲉ He said, "I am sick"
Indirect: ⲁϥ-ⲭⲟⲟ-ⲥ ⲭⲉ-ϥ-ϣⲱⲛⲉ He said that he *was* sick (English signals indirect discourse by shifting the tense to *was*, but Coptic literally has "He said that he is sick")

Direct: ⲁϥ-ⲭⲟⲟ-ⲥ ⲭⲉ-ⲁⲓ̈-ϣⲱⲛⲉ He said, "I was sick"
Indirect: ⲁϥ-ⲭⲟⲟ-ⲥ ⲭⲉ-ⲁϥ-ϣⲱⲛⲉ He said that he *had been* sick

EXERCISES 19

A. Review vocabularies 12–13.

B. Take the following sentence as a basis:

He will give you a book. ϥ-ⲛⲁ-ϯ ⲛⲏ-ⲧⲛ̄ ⲛ̄-ⲟⲩϫⲱⲱⲙⲉ.

Translate into Coptic using the cleft sentence construction and giving alternate forms where possible.

1. It is he (ⲛ̄ⲧⲟϥ) who will give you a book.
2. It is you (pl. ⲛ̄ⲧⲱⲧⲛ̄) to whom he will give a book.
3. It is a book that he will give to you.
4. It is not he who will give you a book.
5. It is not you (pl.) to whom he will give a book.
6. It is not a book that he will give to you.

C. Reading selections from the New Testament.

1. ⲛⲓⲙ ⲡⲉⲧ$^{\emptyset}$-ⲛⲁ-ϣ-ⲕⲁ-$^{\emptyset}$ⲛⲟⲃⲉ ⲉⲃⲟⲗ ⲛ̄ⲥⲁ-ⲡⲛⲟⲩⲧⲉ ⲙⲁⲩⲁⲁ-ϥ. Mark 2:7

2. ⲁϣ ⲅⲁⲣ ⲡⲉⲧ$^{\emptyset}$-ⲙⲟⲧⲛ̄^{120} ⲉ-$^{\emptyset}$ϫⲟⲟ-ⲥ. Mark 2:9

3. ⲛⲁⲓ̈ ϩⲱ-ⲟⲩ ⲛⲉⲛⲧ-ⲁⲩ-ϫⲟ-ⲟⲩ^{121} ϩⲓϫⲛ̄-ⲙ̄ⲙⲁ ⲙ̄-ⲡⲉⲧⲣⲁ^{122}. Mark 4:16

4. ⲧⲁϣⲉⲉⲣⲉ ⲧⲟⲩⲡⲓⲥⲧⲓⲥ ⲧⲉⲛⲧ-ⲁⲥ-ⲛⲁϩⲙ-ⲉ^{123}. Mark 5:34

5. ⲟⲩ ⲡⲉⲧⲉⲣⲉ-ⲡⲣⲱⲙⲉ ⲛⲁ-ⲧⲁⲁ-ϥ ⲛ̄-$^{\emptyset}$ϣⲃⲃⲓⲱ^{124} ϩⲁ-ⲧⲉϥⲯⲩⲭⲏ. Mark 8:37

6. He rebuked the unclean spirit saying ⲡⲉⲡ̅ⲛ̅ⲁ̅ . . . ⲁⲛⲟⲕ ⲡⲉ-ⲉⲧ$^{\emptyset}$-ⲟⲩⲉϩ-$^{\emptyset}$ⲥⲁϩⲛⲉ ⲛⲁ-ⲕ ϫⲉ-ⲁⲙⲟⲩ (87 [box]) ⲉⲃⲟⲗ ⲙ̄ⲙⲟ-ϥ. Mark 9:25

7. ⲛⲓⲙ ⲡⲉ-ⲛ̄ⲧ-ⲁϥ-ϯ ⲛⲁ-ⲕ ⲛ̄-ⲧⲉⲓ̈ⲉϩⲟⲩⲥⲓⲁ ϫⲉⲕⲁⲥ ⲉⲕⲉ-ⲣ̄-ⲛⲁⲓ̈. Mark 11:28

---

^{120} ⲙⲟⲧⲛ̄ ⲉ- be easier than (ⲙ̄ⲧⲟⲛ to become rested, rest; stative ⲙⲟⲧⲛ̄ be easy, be peaceful).
^{121} ϫⲟ, ϫⲉ-, ϫⲟ= to sow (seed).
^{122} ⲡⲉⲧⲣⲁ rock.
^{123} ⲛⲟⲩϩⲙ̄ to save.
^{124} ⲛ̄-$^{\emptyset}$ϣⲃⲃⲓⲱ ϩⲁ- as payment for, in return for.

8. ογ πετερε-πχοεις ⲙ̅-πμα ⲛ̅-ελοολε[125] ⲛⲁ-ⲁⲁ-ϥ. Mark 12:9

9. ⲛ̅ⲧⲱⲧⲛ̅ ⲅⲁⲣ ⲁⲛ ⲛⲉⲧ[θ]-ϣⲁϫⲉ ⲁⲗⲗⲁ ⲡⲉⲡ̅ⲛ̅ⲁ̅ ⲡⲉ ⲉⲧ[θ]-ⲟⲩⲁⲁⲃ. Mark 13:11

10. ⲁⲩ-ⲣ̅-ⲡⲙⲉⲉⲩⲉ ⲛ̅ϭⲓ-ⲛⲉϥⲙⲁⲑⲏⲧⲏⲥ ϫⲉ-ⲡⲁⲓ̈ ⲡⲉⲛⲉϥ-ϫⲱ ⲙ̅ⲙⲟ-ϥ. John 2:22

11. ⲓ̅ⲥ̅ ⲁⲛ ⲡⲉⲛⲉϥ-ⲃⲁⲡⲧⲓⲍⲉ ⲁⲗⲗⲁ ⲛⲉϥⲙⲁⲑⲏⲧⲏⲥ ⲛⲉ. John 4:2

12. ⲁⲛⲟⲕ ⲉⲧ[θ]-ⲛⲁ-ⲕⲁⲧⲏⲅⲱⲣⲉⲓ[126] ⲙ̅ⲙⲱ-ⲧⲛ ⲛ̅ⲛⲁϩⲣⲙ̅-ⲡⲉⲓⲱⲧ. John 5:45

13. ⲉⲧⲃⲉ-ⲡⲁⲓ̈ ⲡⲁⲉⲓⲱⲧ ⲙⲉ ⲙ̅ⲙⲟ-ⲓ̈ ϫⲉ-ϯ-ⲛⲁ-ⲕⲱ ⲛ̅-ⲧⲁⲯⲩⲭⲏ ϫⲉⲕⲁⲥ
ⲟⲛ ⲉⲓ̈ⲉ-ϫⲓⲧ-ⲥ̅. ⲙ̅ⲛ̅-ⲗⲁⲁⲩ ϥⲓ ⲙ̅ⲙⲟ-ⲥ ⲛ̅ⲧⲟⲟⲧ-[θ]. ⲁⲗⲗⲁ ⲁⲛⲟⲕ ⲉⲧ[θ]-ⲕⲱ
ⲙ̅ⲙⲟ-ⲥ ϩⲁⲣⲟ-ⲓ̈ ⲙⲁⲩⲁⲁⲧ-[θ]. John 10:17–18

14. ⲁⲛⲟⲕ ⲉⲧ[θ]-ⲥⲟⲟⲩⲛ ⲛ̅-ⲛ-ⲉⲛⲧ-ⲁⲓ̈-ⲥⲟⲧⲡ-ⲟⲩ. John 13:18

15. ⲙⲏ ⲛ̅ⲧⲟⲕ ⲉ-ⲛⲁⲁ-ⲕ ⲉ-ⲡⲉⲛⲉⲓⲱⲧ ⲓⲁⲕⲱⲃ. John 4:12

16. ⲙⲏ ⲙ̅-ⲡⲁⲓ̈ ⲁⲛ ⲡⲉ ⲓ̅ⲥ̅ ⲡϣⲏⲣⲉ ⲛ̅-ⲓⲱⲥⲏⲫ. John 6:42

D. Cleft sentences that begin with an extraposited word or phrase (**98**).

1. ⲛ̅ⲁⲣⲭⲓⲉⲣⲉⲩⲥ, ⲛ̅ⲧⲟⲟⲩ ⲛⲉⲛⲧ-ⲁⲩ-ⲧⲁⲁ-ⲕ ⲉⲧⲟⲟⲧ-[θ]. ⲟⲩ ⲡⲉⲧ-ⲁⲕ-
ⲁⲁ-ϥ. John 18:35

2. ⲡϣⲁϫⲉ ⲉⲛⲧ-ⲁⲓ̈-ϫⲟⲟ-ϥ, ⲛ̅ⲧⲟϥ ⲡⲉⲧ[θ]-ⲛⲁ-ⲕⲣⲓⲛⲉ ⲙ̅ⲙⲟ-ϥ ϩⲙ̅-ⲡϩⲁⲉ
ⲛ̅-ϩⲟⲟⲩ. John 12:48

3. ⲛⲉϩⲃⲏⲩⲉ ⲁⲛⲟⲕ ⲉϯ-ⲉⲓⲣⲉ ⲙ̅ⲙⲟ-ⲟⲩ ϩⲙ̅-ⲡⲣⲁⲛ ⲙ̅-ⲡⲁⲉⲓⲱⲧ, ⲛⲁⲓ̈
ⲛⲉⲧ[θ]-ⲣ̅-[θ]ⲙⲛ̅ⲧⲣⲉ ⲉⲧⲃⲏⲏⲧ-[θ]. John 10:25

4. ⲛ-ⲉⲧ[θ]-ⲛⲏⲩ ⲉⲃⲟⲗ ϩⲙ̅-ⲡⲣⲱⲙⲉ, ⲛ̅ⲧⲟⲟⲩ ⲛⲉⲧ[θ]-ϫⲱϩⲙ̅[127] ⲙ̅-ⲡⲣⲱⲙⲉ.
Mark 7:15

5. ⲁⲛⲟⲕ, ⲛ-ⲉⲛⲧ-ⲁⲓ̈-ⲛⲁⲩ ⲉⲣⲟ-ⲟⲩ ⲛ̅ⲧⲙ̅-ⲡⲁⲉⲓⲱⲧ ⲛⲉϯ-ϫⲱ ⲙ̅ⲙⲟ-ⲟⲩ.
John 8:38

---

[125] ⲙⲁ ⲛ̅-ⲉⲗⲟⲟⲗⲉ vineyard (place of grapes).

[126] ⲕⲁⲧⲏⲅⲟⲣⲉⲓ accuse.

[127] ϫⲱϩⲙ̅ defile, pollute.

LESSON 20

CONDITIONAL SENTENCES.
PURPOSE AND RESULT.
CORRELATED COMPARISON.

149. Coptic conditional sentences (*if . . . then . . .*) talk about reality in three ways, which we shall study in turn. [CG 494–501]

> Presupposed or possible fact: *If* or *since X is* or *may be true, then Y is true.*
> Generalization: *If (or whenever) X is true, Y is (or will be) true.*
> Contrary to fact: *If X were true, then Y would be true.*

There are also past tense versions of these three (Since X was true, Whenever X was true, If X had been true).

The order of the *If* and *Then* clauses can be reversed at will (Y is true since X is true, Y is true if X is true, Y would be true if X were true).

150. (*a*) *Presupposed or Possible Fact.* [CG 495]

The *If* clause is introduced by

ⲉⲡⲉⲓ, ⲉⲡⲉⲓⲇⲏ, ⲉⲡⲉⲓⲇⲏⲡⲉⲣ *since, inasmuch as*
ⲉϣϫⲉ- or ⲉϣϫⲡⲉ- *since, if (as seems to be,* or *may be, the case)*
ⲕⲁⲛ, ⲕⲁⲛ ⲉϣϫⲉ- *even if*
ϫⲉ-, ϫⲉ-ⲉⲡⲉⲓⲇⲏ, ϫⲉ-. . . ⲅⲁⲣ, ⲉⲃⲟⲗ ϫⲉ-, ⲉⲧⲃⲉ-ϫⲉ- *because*

and the *Then* clause is a main clause or imperative.

ⲉϣϫⲉ-ⲁⲧⲉⲧⲛ̄-ⲥⲟⲩⲱⲛ-ⲧ̄, ⲧⲉⲧⲛⲁ-ⲥⲟⲩⲛ̄-ⲡⲁⲕⲉⲉⲓⲱⲧ
Since you have known Me, you will know My Father, too

ⲉϣϫⲉ-ⲛ̄ⲧⲟⲕ ⲡⲉ ⲡϣⲏⲣⲉ ⲙ̄-ⲡⲛⲟⲩⲧⲉ, ⲛⲟϫ-ⲕ̄ ⲉⲡⲉⲥⲏⲧ ϩⲓϫⲙ̄-ⲡⲉⲉⲓⲙⲁ
If (as You claim) You are the Son of God, throw Yourself down from here

ⲉⲡⲉⲓⲇⲏ ⲁⲕ-ϣⲱⲡⲉ ⲉⲕ-ⲛ̄ϩⲟⲧ ⲛ̄-ϩⲉⲛⲕⲟⲩⲓ̈, ϯ-ⲛⲁ-ⲕⲁⲑⲓⲥⲧⲁ ⲙ̄ⲙⲟ-ⲕ ⲉϫⲛ̄-
ϩⲁϩ
Since you have been faithful with a few things, I shall put you in charge of many

151. (b) *Generalization*. [CG 496]

The *If* clause is introduced by

ⲉϣⲱⲡⲉ *if ever, if* + main clause, circumstantial, or ⲉⲣϣⲁⲛ–
ⲕⲁⲛ *even if* + ⲛ̄ⲧⲉ– (conjunctive) or ⲉⲣϣⲁⲛ–

The *Then* clause is a main clause.

ⲉϣⲱⲡⲉ ⲇⲉ ⲡⲉⲕⲃⲁⲗ ⲟⲩⲡⲟⲛⲏⲣⲟⲥ ⲡⲉ, ⲡⲉⲕⲥⲱⲙⲁ ⲧⲏⲣ–ϥ ⲛⲁ–ϣⲱⲡⲉ ⲉϥ–ⲟ
ⲛ̄–ᶿⲕⲁⲕⲉ
And if your eye is bad then your whole body will be dark

ⲉϣⲱⲡⲉ ⲇⲉ ⲉⲣϣⲁⲛ–ⲡⲉⲕⲥⲟⲛ ⲣ̄–ᶿⲛⲟⲃⲉ, ⲃⲱⲕ ⲛⲅ̄–ϫⲡⲓⲟ–ϥ
And if ever your brother sins, go and censure him

ⲕⲁⲛ ⲉⲧⲉⲧⲛ̄ϣⲁⲛ–ϫⲟⲟ–ⲥ ⲙ̄–ⲡⲉⲓ̈ⲧⲟⲟⲩ ϫⲉ–ⲧⲱⲟⲩⲛ ⲛⲅ̄–ⲃⲱⲕ ⲉϩⲣⲁⲓ̈ ⲉ–ⲧⲉ–
ⲑⲁⲗⲁⲥⲥⲁ, ⲥ–ⲛⲁ–ϣⲱⲡⲉ ⲛⲏ–ⲧⲛ̄
Even if you say to this mountain, Arise and go into the sea, it will come to pass
for you

> When the *If* clause is simply ⲉϥϣⲁⲛ– or a circumstantial, not preceded by a
> conjunction, the distinction between types (1) and (2) is lost. ⲉⲧⲉⲧⲛ̄–ⲡⲓⲥⲧⲉⲩⲉ
> ⲧⲉⲧⲛⲁ–ϫⲓⲧ–ⲟⲩ = Since or If or Whenever you have faith, you will receive
> them. [CH 497]

152. (c) *Contrary to Fact*.

The *If* clause cannot be fulfilled or can no longer be fulfilled. [CG 498–99]

i. Present tense contrary to fact

If clause (*if . . . were . . .*): circumstantial preterit ⲉ–ⲛⲉⲣⲉ–, ⲉ–ⲛⲉ–

Then clause (. . . *would*)[128]:

ⲛⲉⲣⲉ–. . . ⲛⲁ– durative sentences
ⲛⲉ– other sentence types

ⲉ–ⲛⲉⲧⲉⲧⲛ̄–ⲡⲓⲥⲧⲉⲩⲉ ⲅⲁⲣ ⲉ–ⲙⲱⲩⲥⲏⲥ, ⲛⲉⲧⲉⲧⲛⲁ–ⲡⲓⲥⲧⲉⲩⲉ ⲉⲣⲟ–ⲓ̈ ⲡⲉ
For if you were believers in Moses, you would believe in Me

ⲉ–ⲛⲉ–ⲙ̄–ⲡⲁⲓ̈ ⲣ̄–ⲡⲉⲑⲟⲟⲩ ⲁⲛ, ⲛⲉⲛ–ⲛⲁ–ⲧⲁⲁ–ϥ ⲁⲛ ⲉⲧⲟⲟⲧ–ⲕ̄
If this Man were not an evildoer, we would not be handing Him over to you

ⲉ–ⲛⲉ–ⲡⲣ̄ⲣⲟ ⲡⲉⲕⲉⲓⲱⲧ ⲡⲉ, ⲛⲉ–ⲛ̄ⲧⲕ̄–ⲟⲩⲣⲙ̄ⲙⲁⲟ
If the emperor were your father, you would be rich

---

[128] Since the *Then* clause is a preterit conversion, the preterit particle ⲡⲉ (**116**) can occur optionally, as seen in the first example below.

ii. Past tense contrary to fact

If clause (*if . . . had . . .*):

    affirmative ⲉ–ⲛⲉ–ⲛ̄ⲧ–ⲁ–
    negative ⲉ–ⲛⲉ–ⲙ̄ⲡⲉ–

Then clause (*. . . would have*): ⲉϣⲭⲡⲉ, ⲉϣⲭⲉ, or ⲛⲉⲉⲓⲥⲡⲉ + past tense

ⲉ–ⲛⲉ–ⲙ̄ⲡⲉϥ–ⲉⲓ . . . ⲉϣⲭⲡⲉ ⲁⲥ–ϣⲱⲡⲉ ⲛ̄ϭⲓ–ⲑⲁⲏ ⲙ̄–ⲡⲕⲟⲥⲙⲟⲥ
If He had not come . . . , then the end of the world would have come to pass

---

Authors sometimes mix different types of *If* and *Then* clause in a single sentence. ⲉϣⲱⲡⲉ ⲁⲛⲅ̄–ⲟⲩⲥⲁⲃⲉ, ⲛⲉⲓ̈–ⲛⲁ–ⲙⲉⲣⲓⲧ–ϥ̄ = If ever I am wise, I would love him [mixture of generalization and contrary to fact]. [CG 500]

PURPOSE AND RESULT

153. Purpose (*to, in order to, so that . . . might . . .*) [CG 502] is expressed by

ⲉ–$^{\emptyset}$infinitive or ⲉⲧⲃⲉ–$^{\emptyset}$infinitive
ⲉ–$^{\emptyset}$ⲧⲣⲉ–
ⲭⲉ– or ⲭⲉⲕⲁⲥ + optative

For example

ⲛ̄ⲧ–ⲁⲕ–ⲉⲓ ⲉ–$^{\emptyset}$ⲧⲁⲕⲟ–ⲛ = You have come to destroy us

ⲁϥ–ⲉⲓ ⲛ̄ϭⲓ–ⲓ̄ⲥ̄ ⲉ–$^{\emptyset}$ⲧⲣⲉϥ–ⲭⲓ–$^{\emptyset}$ⲃⲁⲡⲧⲓⲥⲙⲁ = Jesus came so that he might be baptized

ⲁⲩ–ⲉⲓⲛⲉ ⲛⲁ–ϥ ⲛ̄–ϩⲉⲛϣⲏⲣⲉ ϣⲏⲙ ⲭⲉⲕⲁⲥ ⲉϥⲉ–ⲧⲁⲗⲉ–ⲛⲉϥϭⲓⲝ ⲉⲭⲱ–ⲟⲩ = They brought some children to Him so that He might lay His hands upon them

154. Result (*so as to, so that . . .*) [CG 503] is expressed by

ϩⲱⲥⲧⲉ ⲉ–$^{\emptyset}$infinitive
ϩⲱⲥⲧⲉ ⲉ–$^{\emptyset}$ⲧⲣⲉ–
ϩⲱⲥⲧⲉ + conjunctive

For example

ⲁⲩ–ⲙⲉϩ–ⲡϫⲟⲓ̈ ⲥⲛⲁⲩ ϩⲱⲥⲧⲉ ⲉ–$^{\emptyset}$ⲧⲣⲉⲩ–ⲱⲙⲥ̄ = They filled both boats, so that they sank

ⲥ–ⲁϣⲁⲓ̈ ⲛ̄ϭⲓ–ⲧⲁⲅⲁⲡⲏ ϩⲱⲥⲧⲉ ⲁⲛⲟⲛ ⲛ̄ⲧⲛ̄–ϣⲟⲩϣⲟⲩ ⲙ̄ⲙⲟ–ⲛ = Love is increasing so that we ourselves are boasting

As in Koine Greek, expressions of purpose and result are sometimes used interchangeably.

CORRELATED COMPARISON

155. Correlated comparisons *just as . . . so too . . .* [CG 505–6] are expressed by

ⲛ̄ⲑⲉ (ⲛ̄-ⲧ-ϩⲉ) or ⲕⲁⲧⲁ-ⲑⲉ *just as* + relative or circumstantial clause

answered by

ⲧⲁⲓ̈ ⲧⲉ ⲑⲉ *so, so too* + relative or circumstantial clause

For example

ⲕⲁⲧⲁ-ⲑⲉ ⲉⲛⲧ-ⲁⲛ-ⲥⲱⲧⲙ̄ ⲧⲁⲓ̈ ⲟⲛ ⲧⲉ ⲑⲉ ⲉⲛⲧ-ⲁⲛ-ⲛⲁⲩ = *Just as* we have heard, *so* have we also seen

ⲛ̄ⲑⲉ ⲉⲛⲧ-ⲁⲕ-ϫⲟⲟ-ⲥ ⲛⲁ-ⲛ ⲧⲁⲓ̈ ⲧⲉ ⲑⲉ ⲉⲛⲧ-ⲁⲛ-ⲥⲟⲧⲙ-ⲉⲥ = *Just as* you told us, *so* have we heard

The two elements can also occur in the opposite order: ⲧⲁⲓ̈ ⲧⲉ ⲑⲉ ⲉⲧϥ̄-ⲛⲏⲩ ⲙ̄ⲙⲟ-ⲥ ⲛ̄ⲑⲉ ⲉⲛⲧ-ⲁⲧⲉⲧⲛ̄-ⲛⲁⲩ ⲉⲣⲟ-ϥ ⲉϥ-ⲛⲁ-ⲃⲱⲕ ⲉϩⲣⲁⲓ̈ ⲉ-ⲧⲡⲉ = He will come just as you saw him going up into heaven (This is how he will come: just as you saw him going . . .)

Telling time [CG 133]

(1) The week (ⲡⲥⲁⲃⲃⲁⲧⲟⲛ or ⲛ̄ⲥⲁⲃⲃⲁⲧⲟⲛ or ⲧϩⲉⲃⲇⲟⲙⲁⲥ):

Sunday = ⲧⲕⲩⲣⲓⲁⲕⲏ or ⲡⲟⲩⲁ
Monday = ⲡⲉⲥⲛⲁⲩ or ⲡϣⲟⲣⲡ̄ ⲛ̄–ϩⲟⲟⲩ ⲛ̄–ⲟⲩⲱϣ
Tuesday = ⲡϣⲟⲙⲛ̄ⲧ or ⲡⲙⲉϩ–ⲥⲛⲁⲩ ⲛ̄–ϩⲟⲟⲩ ⲛ̄–ⲟⲩⲱϣ
Wednesday = ⲡⲉϥⲧⲟⲟⲩ or ⲧⲕⲟⲩⲓ̈ ⲛ̄–ⲛⲏⲥⲧⲉⲓⲁ or ⲧⲛⲏⲥⲧⲉⲓⲁ ϣⲏⲙ
Thursday = ⲡϯⲟⲩ or ⲡⲟⲩⲱϣ or ⲡⲟⲩⲱϣ ⲛ̄–ⲧⲙⲏⲧⲉ
Friday = ⲡⲥⲟⲟⲩ or ⲧⲡⲁⲣⲁⲥⲕⲉⲩⲏ or ⲧⲛⲟϭ ⲛ̄–ⲛⲏⲥⲧⲉⲓⲁ or ⲧⲛⲏⲥⲧⲉⲓⲁ–ⲱ
Saturday = ⲡⲥⲁⲃⲃⲁⲧⲟⲛ

(2) The twelve thirty-day months of the Egyptian calendar [CG 135]:

ⲑⲟⲟⲩⲧ begins near the end of August (in modern reckoning)
ⲡⲁⲟⲡⲉ begins near the end of September
ϩⲁⲑⲱⲣ begins near the end of October
ⲕⲟⲓⲁϩⲕ̄ begins near the end of November
ⲧⲱⲃⲉ begins near the end of December
ⲙ̄ϣⲓⲣ begins near the end of January
ⲡⲁⲣⲙ̄ϩⲟⲧⲡ̄ begins near the end of February
ⲡⲁⲣⲙⲟⲩⲧⲉ begins near the end of March
ⲡⲁϣⲟⲛⲥ̄ begins near the end of April
ⲡⲁⲱⲛⲉ begins near the end of May
ⲉⲡⲏⲡ begins near the end of June
ⲙⲉⲥⲟⲣⲏ begins near the end of July
plus five intercalary days, each called an ⲉⲡⲁⲅⲟⲙⲉⲛⲟⲛ.

(3) The hours of day and night [CG 131] are twelve from dawn to dusk (approximately 0600h to 1800h), and twelve from dusk to dawn. Their names are formed with the prefix ⲭⲛ̄– (= at hour number . . .) completed by a feminine cardinal number. Thus ⲭⲛ̄–ϣⲟⲙⲧⲉ (at hour number 3) = at 0900h/nine o'clock a.m., *and* = at 2100h/nine o'clock p.m.

Exercises 20

A. *Review vocabularies 14–15.*

B. *Translate.*

a. ⲉϣϫⲉ-ⲧⲉⲧⲛ̄-ϣⲓⲛⲉ ⲛ̄ⲥⲁ-ⲧⲙⲉ . . .

b. ⲉϣⲱⲡⲉ ⲉⲧⲉⲧⲛ̄ϣⲁⲛ-ϣⲓⲛⲉ ⲛ̄ⲥⲁ-ⲧⲙⲉ . . .

c. ⲕⲁⲛ ⲉϣϫⲉ-ⲧⲉⲧⲛ̄-ϣⲓⲛⲉ ⲛ̄ⲥⲁ-ⲧⲙⲉ . . .

d. ⲉⲡⲉⲓⲇⲏ ⲧⲉⲧⲛ̄-ϣⲓⲛⲉ ⲛ̄ⲥⲁ-ⲧⲙⲉ . . .

e. ⲉⲃⲟⲗ ϫⲉ-ⲧⲉⲧⲛ̄-ϣⲓⲛⲉ ⲛ̄ⲥⲁ-ⲧⲙⲉ . . .

f. ⲕⲁⲛ ⲛ̄ⲧⲉⲧⲛ̄-ϣⲓⲛⲉ ⲛ̄ⲥⲁ-ⲧⲙⲉ . . .

g. ⲉⲛⲉⲧⲉⲧⲛ̄-ϣⲓⲛⲉ ⲛ̄ⲥⲁ-ⲧⲙⲉ . . .

h. ⲉⲛⲉⲛ̄ⲧⲁⲧⲉⲧⲛ̄-ϣⲓⲛⲉ ⲛ̄ⲥⲁ-ⲧⲙⲉ . . .

i. ⲉⲛⲉⲙ̄ⲡⲉⲧⲛ̄-ϣⲓⲛⲉ ⲛ̄ⲥⲁ-ⲧⲙⲉ . . .

j. . . . ϫⲉⲕⲁⲁⲥ ⲉⲧⲉⲧⲛⲉ-ϣⲓⲛⲉ ⲛ̄ⲥⲁ-ⲧⲙⲉ

k. . . . ϩⲱⲥⲧⲉ ⲉⲧⲣⲉⲧⲛ̄-ϣⲓⲛⲉ ⲛ̄ⲥⲁ-ⲧⲙⲉ

l. ⲛ̄ⲑⲉ ⲉⲧⲉⲧⲛ̄-ϣⲓⲛⲉ ⲛ̄ⲥⲁ-ⲧⲙⲉ . . .

m. . . . ϩⲱⲥⲧⲉ ⲛ̄ⲧⲉⲧⲛ̄-ϣⲓⲛⲉ ⲛ̄ⲥⲁ-ⲧⲙⲉ

n. . . . ⲉ-⁰ϣⲓⲛⲉ ⲛ̄ⲥⲁ-ⲧⲙⲉ

C. *Translate into Coptic, giving alternate translations where possible.*
a. Since you love God, He will forgive you. *b.* Since you loved God, He forgave you. *c.* If you love God, pray to Him. *d.* Because you loved God, He forgave you. *e.* Whenever you pray to God, He forgives you. *f.* God forgives you whenever you pray to Him. *g.* If you loved God, He would forgive you. *h.* If you had loved God, He would have forgiven you. *i.* God came to forgive you. *j.* God loves you, and so He forgives you. *k.* Just as God loves you, so He forgives you.

THE GOSPEL OF MARK
Chapters One to Three¹

Turn back to lesson one and read the photograph of Mark 1:1–1:6 in a fifth-century manuscript.

ⲘⲀⲢⲔⲞⲤ

Chapter One²

1. ⲦⲀⲢⲬⲎ³ Ⲙ̄-ⲠⲈⲨⲀⲅⲅⲈⲖⲒⲞⲚ Ⲛ̄-ⲒⲤ̄ ⲠⲈⲬⲤ̄.
2. ⲔⲀⲦⲀ-Ⲡ-ⲈⲦᵠ-ⲤⲎⲢ Ⲣ̄Ⲛ̄-ⲚⲤⲀⲒⲀⲤ ⲠⲈⲠⲢⲞⲪⲎⲦⲎⲤ ⲬⲈ-ⲈⲒⲤⲢⲎⲚ̄ⲦⲈ Ⲧ̄-ⲚⲀ-ⲬⲈⲨ-ⲠⲀⲀⲅⲅⲈⲖⲞⲤ ⲢⲒⲢⲎ Ⲙ̄ⲘⲞ-Ⲕ⁴ Ⲛ̄Ϥ-ⲤⲂ̄ⲦⲈ-ⲦⲈⲔⲢⲒⲎ.
3. ⲠⲈⲢⲢⲞⲞⲨ⁵ Ⲙ̄-Ⲡ-ⲈⲦᵠ-ⲰϢ ⲈⲂⲞⲖ ⲢⲚ̄-ⲦⲈⲢⲎⲘⲞⲤ⁶ ⲬⲈ-ⲤⲞⲨⲦⲚ̄⁷-ⲦⲈⲢⲒⲎ Ⲙ̄-ⲠⲬⲞⲈⲒⲤ Ⲛ̄ⲦⲈⲦⲚ̄-ⲤⲞⲨⲦⲚ̄-ⲚⲈϤⲘⲞⲈⲒⲦ⁸.
4. ⲀϤ-ϢⲰⲠⲈ ⲆⲈ Ⲛ̄ϬⲒ-ⲒⲰⲢⲀⲚⲚⲎⲤ ⲈϤ-Ⲧ̄-ᵠⲂⲀⲠⲦⲒⲤⲘⲀ ⲢⲘ̄-ⲠⲬⲀⲈⲒⲈ⁹ ⲈϤ-ⲔⲎⲢⲨⲤⲤⲈ¹⁰ Ⲛ̄-ⲞⲨⲂⲀⲠⲦⲒⲤⲘⲀ Ⲙ̄-ᵠⲘⲈⲦⲀⲚⲞⲒⲀ¹¹ Ⲉ-ⲠⲔⲰ ⲈⲂⲞⲖ Ⲛ̄-Ⲛ̄ⲚⲞⲂⲈ.
5. ⲀⲨⲰ ⲀⲤ-ⲂⲰⲔ ⲚⲀ-Ϥ ⲈⲂⲞⲖ Ⲛ̄ϬⲒ-ⲦⲈⲬⲰⲢⲀ¹² ⲦⲎⲢ-Ⲥ̄ Ⲛ̄-ⲦⲞⲨⲆⲀⲒⲀ ⲘⲚ̄-ⲚⲀ-ⲐⲒⲈⲢⲞⲤⲞⲖⲨⲘⲀ ⲦⲎⲢ-ⲞⲨ. ⲀⲨ-ⲬⲒ-ᵠⲂⲀⲠⲦⲒⲤⲘⲀ Ⲛ̄ⲦⲞⲞⲦ-Ϥ̄ ⲢⲘ̄-ⲠⲒⲞⲢⲆⲀⲚⲎⲤ ⲠⲈⲒⲈⲢⲞ¹³ ⲈⲨ-ⲈⳜⲞⲘⲞⲖⲞⲅⲈⲒ¹⁴ Ⲛ̄-ⲚⲈⲨⲚⲞⲂⲈ.
6. ⲀⲨⲰ ⲒⲰⲢⲀⲚⲚⲎⲤ, ⲚⲈⲢⲈ-ⲢⲈⲚϤϢ¹⁵ Ⲛ̄-ϬⲀⲘⲞⲨⲖ ⲦⲞ¹⁶ ⲢⲒⲰⲰ-Ϥ ⲈⲢⲈ-

---

¹ According to Quecke's manuscript (but normalized): Hans Quecke, ed., *Das Markus-evangelium saïdisch:* (Barcelona: Papyrologia Castroctaviana, 1972), distributed by Biblical Institute Press (Rome).   ² New words (except for names of persons and places) are glossed in the footnotes.   ³ *Ⲧ-ⲀⲢⲬⲎ beginning.   ⁴ ⲢⲒⲢⲎ Ⲛ̄-, Ⲙ̄ⲘⲞ⸗ before (Compound preposition).   ⁵ ⲠⲈ-ⲢⲢⲞⲞⲨ voice, sound.   ⁶ *Ⲧ-ⲈⲢⲎⲘⲞⲤ wilderness, desert.   ⁷ ⲤⲞⲞⲨⲦⲚ̄ (ⲤⲞⲨⲦⲚ̄-, ⲤⲞⲨⲦⲰⲚ⸗) ⲤⲞⲨⲦⲰⲚ† straighten, stretch out.   ⁸ Ⲡ-ⲘⲞⲈⲒⲦ road, path.   ⁹ Ⲡ-ⲬⲀⲈⲒⲈ wilderness, desert.   ¹⁰ *ⲔⲎⲢⲨⲤⲤⲈ announce, proclaim.   ¹¹ *Ⲧ-ⲘⲈⲦⲀⲚⲞⲒⲀ repentance, change of heart.   ¹² *ⲦⲈ-ⲬⲰⲢⲀ region.   ¹³ Ⲡ-ⲈⲒⲈⲢⲞ river.   ¹⁴ *ⲈⳜⲞⲘⲞⲖⲞⲅⲈⲒ confess.   ¹⁵ Ⲡ-ϤϢ Ⲛ̄-ϬⲀⲘⲞⲨⲖ skin of camel, camel skin.   ¹⁶ ⲦⲞ† ⲢⲒⲰⲰ-Ϥ (was) put upon him, i.e. he was wearing it (Ⲧ̄, Ⲧ̄-, ⲦⲀⲀ⸗, ⲦⲞ†).

оүмохⲍ̄[17] ⲛ̄-ϣⲁⲁⲣ ⲙⲏⲣ ⲉ-ⲧⲉϥ†ⲡⲉ[18] ⲉϥ-ⲟⲩⲉⲙ-ⲟϣϫⲉ[19] ⲍ̣ⲓ-ⲟⲉⲃⲓⲱ[20] ⲛ̄-ⲍⲟⲟⲩⲧ.

7. ⲁⲩⲱ ⲛⲉϥ-ⲧⲁϣⲉ-ⲟⲟⲉⲓϣ ⲉϥ-ϫⲱ ⲙ̄ⲙⲟ-ⲥ ϫⲉ-ϥ-ⲛⲏⲩ ⲙ̄ⲛ̄ⲛ̄ⲥⲱ-ⲓ̈ ⲛ̄ϭⲓ-ⲡ-ⲉⲧⲟ-ϫⲟⲟⲣ[21] ⲉⲣⲟ-ⲓ̈ ⲉ-ⲁⲛⲅ̄-ⲟⲩⲍⲓⲕⲁⲛⲟⲥ[22] ⲁⲛ ⲉ-ⲟⲡⲁⲍ̄ⲧ̄-ⲟ[23] ⲉ-ⲟⲃⲱⲗ ⲉⲃⲟⲗ ⲙ̄-ⲡⲙⲟⲩⲥ[24] ⲙ̄-ⲡⲉϥⲧⲟⲟⲩⲉ.

8. ⲁⲛⲟⲕ, ⲁⲓ̈-†-ⲟⲃⲁⲡⲧⲓⲥⲙⲁ ⲛⲏ-ⲧⲛ̄ ⲍ̄ⲛ̄-ⲟⲩⲙⲟⲟⲩ. ⲛ̄ⲧⲟϥ ⲇⲉ, ⲉϥ-ⲛⲁ-ⲃⲁⲡⲧⲓⲍⲉ ⲙ̄ⲙⲱ-ⲧⲛ̄ ⲍ̄ⲛ̄-ⲟⲩⲡ̄ⲛ̄ⲁ ⲉϥ-ⲟⲩⲁⲁⲃ.

9. ⲁⲩⲱ ⲁⲥ-ϣⲱⲡⲉ ⲍ̄ⲛ̄-ⲛⲉⲍⲟⲟⲩ ⲉⲧⲟ-ⲙ̄ⲙⲁⲩ ⲁϥ-ⲉⲓ ⲛ̄ϭⲓ-ⲓ̄ⲥ ⲉⲃⲟⲗ ⲍ̄ⲛ̄-ⲛⲁⲍⲁⲣⲉⲧ ⲛ̄ⲧⲉ-ⲧⲅⲁⲗⲓⲗⲁⲓⲁ. ⲁⲩⲱ ⲁϥ-ϫⲓ-ⲟⲃⲁⲡⲧⲓⲥⲙⲁ ⲍ̄ⲙ̄-ⲡⲓⲟⲣ-ⲇⲁⲛⲏⲥ ⲛ̄ⲧⲛ̄-ⲓⲱⲍⲁⲛⲛⲏⲥ.

10. ⲛ̄ⲧⲉⲩⲛⲟⲩ ⲇⲉ ⲉϥ-ⲛⲏⲩ ⲉⲍⲣⲁⲓ̈ ⲍ̄ⲙ̄-ⲡⲙⲟⲟⲩ ⲁϥ-ⲛⲁⲩ ⲉ-ⲙ̄ⲡⲏⲩⲉ ⲉ-ⲁⲩ-ⲟⲩⲱⲛ ⲁⲩⲱ ⲡⲉⲡ̄ⲛ̄ⲁ ⲉϥ-ⲛⲏⲩ ⲉⲡⲉⲥⲏⲧ ⲉϫⲱ-ϥ ⲛ̄ⲑⲉ ⲛ̄-ⲟⲩ-ϭⲣⲟⲟⲙⲡⲉ[25].

11. ⲁⲩⲱ ⲟⲩⲥⲙⲏ, ⲁⲥ-ϣⲱⲡⲉ ⲉⲃⲟⲗ ⲍ̄ⲛ̄-ⲙ̄ⲡⲏⲩⲉ ϫⲉ-ⲛ̄ⲧⲟⲕ ⲡⲉ ⲡⲁϣⲏⲣⲉ ⲡⲁⲙⲉⲣⲓⲧ ⲉⲛⲧ-ⲁ-ⲡⲁⲟⲩⲱϣ ϣⲱⲡⲉ ⲛ̄ⲍⲏⲧ-ⲕ̄.

12. ⲁⲩⲱ ⲍ̄ⲛ̄-ⲧⲉⲩⲛⲟⲩ ⲡⲉⲡ̄ⲛ̄ⲁ, ⲁϥ-ϫⲓⲧ-ϥ̄ ⲉⲃⲟⲗ ⲉ-ⲧⲉⲣⲏⲙⲟⲥ.

13. ⲁⲩⲱ ⲛⲉϥ-ⲍ̄ⲛ̄-ⲧⲉⲣⲏⲙⲟⲥ ⲛ̄-ⲍ̄ⲙⲉ ⲛ̄-ⲍⲟⲟⲩ ⲉⲣⲉ-ⲡⲥⲁⲧⲁⲛⲁⲥ[26] ⲡⲉⲓ-ⲣⲁⲍⲉ[27] ⲙ̄ⲙⲟ-ϥ ⲉϥ-ϣⲟⲟⲡ ⲙⲛ̄-ⲛⲉⲑⲏⲣⲓⲟⲛ[28]. ⲁⲩⲱ ⲛ̄ⲁⲅⲅⲉⲗⲟⲥ, ⲛⲉⲩ-ⲇⲓⲁ-ⲕⲟⲛⲉⲓ[29] ⲛⲁ-ϥ.

14. ⲙ̄ⲛ̄ⲛ̄ⲥⲁ-ⲛ̄ⲥⲉ-ⲡⲁⲣⲁⲇⲓⲇⲟⲩ ⲛ̄-ⲓⲱⲍⲁⲛⲛⲏⲥ ⲁϥ-ⲉⲓ ⲛ̄ϭⲓ-ⲓ̄ⲥ ⲉⲍⲣⲁⲓ̈ ⲉ-ⲧⲅⲁⲗⲓⲗⲁⲓⲁ ⲉϥ-ⲕⲏⲣⲩⲥⲥⲉ ⲙ̄-ⲡⲉⲩⲁⲅⲅⲉⲗⲓⲟⲛ ⲙ̄-ⲡⲛⲟⲩⲧⲉ

15. ϫⲉ-ⲁ-ⲡⲉⲟⲩⲟⲉⲓϣ ϫⲱⲕ ⲉⲃⲟⲗ. ⲁⲩⲱ ⲁⲥ-ⲍⲱⲛ ⲉⲍⲟⲩⲛ ⲛ̄ϭⲓ-ⲧⲙ̄ⲛ̄ⲧ̄-ⲣ̄ⲣⲟ ⲙ̄-ⲡⲛⲟⲩⲧⲉ. ⲙⲉⲧⲁⲛⲟⲉⲓ ⲛ̄ⲧⲉⲧⲛ̄-ⲡⲓⲥⲧⲉⲩⲉ ⲍ̄ⲙ̄-ⲡⲉⲩⲁⲅⲅⲉ-ⲗⲓⲟⲛ.

16. ⲁⲩⲱ ⲉϥ-ⲙⲟⲟϣⲉ ⲍⲁⲧⲛ̄-ⲧⲉⲑⲁⲗⲁⲥⲥⲁ ⲛ̄-ⲧⲅⲁⲗⲓⲗⲁⲓⲁ ⲁϥ-ⲛⲁⲩ ⲉ-ⲥⲓ-ⲙⲱⲛ ⲙⲛ̄-ⲁⲛⲇⲣⲉⲁⲥ ⲡⲥⲟⲛ ⲛ̄-ⲥⲓⲙⲱⲛ ⲉⲩ-ⲛⲉϫ-ⲟϣⲛⲉ[30] ⲉ-ⲧⲉⲑⲁⲗⲁⲥⲥⲁ. ⲛⲉ-ⲍⲉⲛⲟⲩⲱⲍⲉ[31] ⲅⲁⲣ ⲛⲉ.

---

[17] ⲡ-ⲙⲟⲭⲍ̄ ⲛ̄-ϣⲁⲁⲣ girdle of leather, leathern girdle.   [18] ⲧ-†ⲡⲉ loins.   [19] ⲡⲉ-ⲱϫⲉ locust.   [20] ⲡ-ⲉⲃⲓⲱ ⲛ̄-ⲍⲟⲟⲩⲧ wild honey (ⲛ̄-ⲍⲟⲟⲩⲧ = wild).   [21] ⲭⲟⲟⲣ† is strong, ⲭⲟⲟⲣ ⲉ- stronger than.   [22] *ⲍⲓⲕⲁⲛⲟⲥ (Adjective) qualified, adequate.   [23] ⲡⲱϫⲧ (ⲡⲉⲍ̄ⲧ-, ⲡⲁⲍⲧⲍ) ⲡⲁⲍ̄ⲧ† bend.   [24] ⲡ-ⲙⲟⲩⲥ ⲙ̄-ⲡⲉϥⲧⲟⲟⲩⲉ strap of his sandel.   [25] ⲡⲉ- (and ⲧⲉ-) ϭⲣⲟⲟⲙⲡⲉ dove.   [26] ⲡ-ⲥⲁⲧⲁⲛⲁⲥ Satan.   [27] *ⲡⲉⲓ-ⲣⲁⲍⲉ put to the test, tempt.   [28] *ⲡⲉ-ⲑⲏⲣⲓⲟⲛ wild beast.   [29] *ⲇⲓⲁⲕⲟⲛⲉⲓ assist, serve.   [30] ⲡⲉ-ϣⲛⲉ, plural ϣⲛⲏⲩ net.   [31] ⲡ-ⲟⲩⲱⲍⲉ fisherman.

CHAPTER ONE

17. ⲡⲉϫⲁ-ϥ ⲛⲁ-ⲩ ⲛϭⲓ-ⲓⲥ ϫⲉ-ⲁⲙⲏⲉⲓⲛ³². ⲟⲩⲉϩ-ⲑⲏⲩⲧⲛ³³ ⲛⲥⲱ-ⲓ̈. ⲁⲩⲱ
ϯ-ⲛⲁ-ⲣ̄-ⲑⲏⲩⲧⲛ̄ ⲛ̄-⁰ⲟⲩⲱϩⲉ ⲛ̄-ⲣⲉϥ-ϭⲉⲡ-⁰ⲣⲱⲙⲉ³⁴.

18. ⲛ̄ⲧⲉⲩⲛⲟⲩ ⲇⲉ ⲁⲩ-ⲕⲁ-ⲛⲉⲩϣⲛⲏⲩ. ⲁⲩ-ⲟⲩⲁϩ-ⲟⲩ ⲛ̄ⲥⲱ-ϥ.

19. ⲁⲩⲱ ⲛ̄ⲧⲉⲣⲉϥ-ⲙⲟⲟϣⲉ ⲉⲑⲏ³⁵ ⲛ̄ⲟⲩⲕⲟⲩⲓ³⁶ ⲁϥ-ⲛⲁⲩ ⲉ-ⲓⲁⲕⲱⲃⲟⲥ
ⲡϣⲏⲣⲉ ⲛ̄-ⲍⲉⲃⲉⲇⲁⲓⲟⲥ ⲙⲛ̄-ⲓⲱϩⲁⲛⲛⲏⲥ ⲡⲉϥⲥⲟⲛ ⲛ̄ⲧⲟⲟⲩ ϩⲱ-ⲟⲩ ⲉⲩ-
ϩⲙ̄-ⲡϫⲟⲓ̈ ⲉⲩ-ⲥⲟⲃⲧⲉ ⲛ̄-ⲛⲉⲩϣⲛⲏⲩ.

20. ⲛ̄ⲧⲉⲩⲛⲟⲩ ⲁϥ-ⲙⲟⲩⲧⲉ ⲉⲣⲟ-ⲟⲩ. ⲁⲩⲱ ⲁⲩ-ⲕⲁ-ⲡⲉⲩⲉⲓⲱⲧ ⲍⲉⲃⲉⲇⲁⲓⲟⲥ
ϩⲙ̄-ⲡϫⲟⲓ̈ ⲙⲛ̄-ⲛ̄ϫⲁⲓ̈-⁰ⲃⲉⲕⲉ³⁷. ⲁⲩ-ⲃⲱⲕ. ⲁⲩ-ⲟⲩⲁϩ-ⲟⲩ ⲛ̄ⲥⲱ-ϥ.

21. ⲁⲩ-ⲃⲱⲕ ⲇⲉ ⲉϩⲟⲩⲛ ⲉ-ⲕⲁⲫⲁⲣⲛⲁⲟⲩⲙ. ⲁⲩⲱ ⲛ̄ⲧⲉⲩⲛⲟⲩ ϩⲛ̄-ⲛ̄ⲥⲁⲃ-
ⲃⲁⲧⲟⲛ³⁸ ⲁϥ-ϯ-⁰ⲥⲃⲱ ϩⲛ̄-ⲧⲥⲩⲛⲁⲅⲱⲅⲏ.

22. ⲁⲩⲱ ⲁⲩ-ⲣ̄-⁰ϣⲡⲏⲣⲉ ⲉϫⲛ̄-ⲧⲉϥⲥⲃⲱ. ⲛⲉϥ-ϯ-⁰ⲥⲃⲱ ⲅⲁⲣ ⲛⲁ-ⲩ ⲛ̄ⲑⲉ
ⲁⲛ ⲉⲧⲟⲩ-ϯ-⁰ⲥⲃⲱ ⲛ̄ϭⲓ-ⲛⲉⲅⲣⲁⲙⲙⲁⲧⲉⲩⲥ ⲁⲗⲗⲁ ϩⲱⲥ ⲉ-ⲩⲛⲧ-ϥ̄-ⲧⲉϩⲟⲩ-
ⲥⲓⲁ ⲙ̄ⲙⲁⲩ.

23. ⲁⲩⲱ ⲛ̄ⲧⲉⲩⲛⲟⲩ ⲛⲉ-ⲟⲩⲛ̄-ⲟⲩⲣⲱⲙⲉ ϩⲛ̄-ⲧⲥⲩⲛⲁⲅⲱⲅⲏ ⲉⲣⲉ-ⲟⲩⲡ̄ⲛ̄ⲁ̄
ⲛ̄-ⲁⲕⲁⲑⲁⲣⲧⲟⲛ³⁹ ⲛⲙ̄ⲙⲁ-ϥ. ⲁⲩⲱ ⲁϥ-ϫⲓ-⁰ϣⲕⲁⲕ⁴⁰ ⲉⲃⲟⲗ

24. ⲉϥ-ϫⲱ ⲙ̄ⲙⲟ-ⲥ ϫⲉ-ⲁϩⲣⲟ-ⲕ⁴¹ ⲛⲙ̄ⲙⲁ-ⲛ ⲓⲥ ⲡⲛⲁⲍⲱⲣⲁⲓⲟⲥ. ⲛ̄ⲧ-ⲁⲕ-ⲉⲓ
ⲉ-⁰ⲧⲁⲕⲟ-ⲛ. ϯ-ⲥⲟⲟⲩⲛ ⲙ̄ⲙⲟ-ⲕ ϫⲉ-ⲛ̄ⲧⲕ̄-ⲛⲓⲙ. ⲛ̄ⲧⲕ̄-ⲡⲡⲉⲧ-ⲟⲩⲁⲁⲃ
ⲙ̄-ⲡⲛⲟⲩⲧⲉ.

25. ⲁⲩⲱ ⲓⲥ, ⲁϥ-ⲉⲡⲓⲧⲓⲙⲁ⁴² ⲛⲁ-ϥ ⲉϥ-ϫⲱ ⲙ̄ⲙⲟ-ⲥ ϫⲉ-ⲧⲙ̄-ⲣⲱ-ⲕ⁴³
ⲛ̄ⲅ-ⲉⲓ ⲉⲃⲟⲗ ⲙ̄ⲙⲟ-ϥ.

26. ⲁⲩⲱ ⲛ̄ⲧⲉⲣⲉ-ⲡⲉⲡ̄ⲛ̄ⲁ̄ ⲛ̄-ⲁⲕⲁⲑⲁⲣⲧⲟⲛ ⲣⲁϩⲧ-ϥ̄⁴⁴ ⲉ-ⲡⲕⲁϩ ⲁⲩⲱ ⲁϥ-
ⲱϣ ⲉⲃⲟⲗ ϩⲛ̄-ⲟⲩⲛⲟϭ ⲛ̄-ϩⲣⲟⲟⲩ, ⲁϥ-ⲉⲓ ⲉⲃⲟⲗ ⲙ̄ⲙⲟ-ϥ.

27. ⲁⲩⲱ ⲁⲩ-ⲣ̄-⁰ϩⲟⲧⲉ ⲧⲏⲣ-ⲟⲩ ϩⲱⲥⲧⲉ ⲛ̄ⲥⲉ-ϣⲁϫⲉ ⲙⲛ̄-ⲛⲉⲩⲉⲣⲏⲩ
ⲉⲩ-ϫⲱ ⲙ̄ⲙⲟ-ⲥ ϫⲉ-ⲟⲩ ⲡⲉ ⲡⲁⲓ̈. ⲉⲓⲥ-ⲟⲩⲥⲃⲱ ⲙ̄-ⲃⲣ̄ⲣⲉ ϩⲛ̄-ⲟⲩⲉⲝⲟⲩⲥⲓⲁ.
ⲛ̄ⲕⲉⲡ̄ⲛ̄ⲁ̄ ⲛ̄-ⲁⲕⲁⲑⲁⲣⲧⲟⲛ, ϥ-ⲟⲩⲉϩⲥⲁϩⲛⲉ ⲛⲁ-ⲩ. ⲁⲩⲱ ⲥⲉ-ⲥⲱⲧⲙ̄ ⲛ̄ⲥⲱ-ϥ.

---

³² ⲁⲙⲏⲉⲓⲛ Special affirmative imperative of ⲉⲓ; cf. **87** (box).   ³³ ⲟⲩⲱϩ (ⲟⲩⲉϩ-,
ⲟⲩⲁϩ⁼) ⲟⲩⲏϩ† put, place; ⲟⲩⲉϩ-/ⲟⲩⲁϩ⁼ + reflexive personal object + ⲛ̄ⲥⲁ- = follow, be
a follower of (ⲁϥ-ⲟⲩⲁϩ-ϥ̄ ⲛ̄ⲥⲁ- = he followed, he 'put himself after').   ³⁴ ϭⲱⲡ
(ϭⲉⲡ-, ϭⲁⲡ⁼) ϭⲏⲡⲧ† seize, take, catch; ⲟⲩⲱϩⲉ ⲛ̄-ⲣⲉϥ-ϭⲉⲡ-⁰ⲣⲱⲙⲉ = human-catch-
ing fisherman.   ³⁵ ⲉⲑⲏ forward, onward.   ³⁶ ⲛ̄ⲟⲩⲕⲟⲩⲓ somewhat more.   ³⁷ ϫⲁⲓ̈-
⁰ⲃⲉⲕⲉ wage earning (Adjective) (ϫⲁⲓ̈- Construct Participle [lesson 9, box "Construct
Participles"] of ϫⲓ take + ⲡ-ⲃⲉⲕⲉ wages).   ³⁸ ⲛ̄ⲥⲁⲃⲃⲁⲧⲟⲛ = ⲡⲥⲁⲃⲃⲁⲧⲟⲛ as in
Koine Greek.   ³⁹ *ⲁⲕⲁⲑⲁⲣⲧⲟⲥ, ⲁⲕⲁⲑⲁⲣⲧⲟⲛ (Adjective) unclean, impure.   ⁴⁰ ϫⲓ-
⁰ϣⲕⲁⲕ cry out (ϫⲓ- before zero article = ϫⲉ- 'speak' + ⲡⲉ-ϣⲕⲁⲕ shout).
⁴¹ ⲁϩⲣⲟ⁼ ⲛⲙ̄ⲙⲁ⁼ what does . . . have to do with . . . ?.   ⁴² *ⲉⲡⲓⲧⲓⲙⲁ rebuke.
⁴³ ⲧⲱⲙ (ⲧⲙ̄-, ⲧⲟⲙ⁼) ⲧⲏⲙ† shut.   ⁴⁴ ⲣⲱϩⲧ (ⲣⲉϩⲧ-, ⲣⲁϩⲧ⁼) ⲣⲁϩⲧ† strike, cast.

28. ⲁ-ⲡⲉϥⲥⲟⲉⲓⲧ⁴⁵ ⲃⲱⲕ ⲉⲃⲟⲗ ⲛ̄ⲧⲉⲩⲛⲟⲩ ϩⲙ̄-ⲙⲁ ⲛⲓⲙ ⲙ̄-ⲡⲕⲱⲧⲉ ⲧⲏⲣ-ϥ̄
ⲛ̄-ⲧⲅⲁⲗⲓⲗⲁⲓⲁ.

29. ⲛ̄ⲧⲉⲩⲛⲟⲩ ⲇⲉ ⲛ̄ⲧⲉⲣⲟⲩ-ⲉⲓ ⲉⲃⲟⲗ ϩⲛ̄-ⲧⲥⲩⲛⲁⲅⲱⲅⲏ ⲁϥ-ⲃⲱⲕ ⲉϩⲟⲩⲛ
ⲉ-ⲡⲏⲓ̈ ⲛ̄-ⲥⲓⲙⲱⲛ ⲙⲛ̄-ⲁⲛⲇⲣⲉⲁⲥ ⲙⲛ̄-ⲓⲁⲕⲱⲃⲟⲥ ⲙⲛ̄-ⲓⲱϩⲁⲛⲛⲏⲥ.

30. ⲧϣⲱⲙⲉ⁴⁶ ⲇⲉ ⲛ̄-ⲥⲓⲙⲱⲛ, ⲛⲉⲥ-ⲛⲏⲭ⁴⁷ ⲉⲥ-ϩⲏⲙ⁴⁸. ⲁⲩⲱ ⲛ̄ⲧⲉⲩⲛⲟⲩ
ⲁⲩ-ϣⲁⲭⲉ ⲛⲙ̄ⲙⲁ-ϥ ⲉⲧⲃⲏⲏⲧ-ⲥ̄.

31. ⲁϥ-ϯ-ⲡⲉϥⲟⲩⲟⲉⲓ ⲇⲉ ⲉⲣⲟ-ⲥ. ⲁϥ-ⲧⲟⲩⲛⲟⲥ ⲉ-ⲁϥ-ⲁⲙⲁϩⲧⲉ ⲛ̄-ⲧⲉⲥ-
ⲃⲓⲭ. ⲁⲩⲱ ⲡⲉϩⲙⲟⲙ, ⲁϥ-ⲗⲟ ϩⲓⲱⲱ-ⲥ. ⲁⲥ-ⲇⲓⲁⲕⲟⲛⲉⲓ ⲛⲁ-ⲩ.

32. ⲣⲟⲩϩⲉ⁴⁹ ⲇⲉ, ⲛ̄ⲧⲉⲣⲉϥ-ϣⲱⲡⲉ ⲉⲣⲉ-ⲡⲣⲏ⁵⁰ ⲛⲁ-ϩⲱⲧⲡ̄̄⁵¹ ⲁⲩ-ⲉⲓⲛⲉ ⲛⲁ-ϥ
ⲛ̄-ⲛ-ⲉⲧ⁰-ⲙⲟⲕϩ̄⁵² ⲧⲏⲣ-ⲟⲩ ⲙⲛ̄-ⲛ-ⲉⲧⲉⲣⲉ-ⲛ̄ⲇⲁⲓⲙⲟⲛⲓⲟⲛ ⲛ̄ⲙⲙⲁ-ⲩ.

33. ⲁⲩⲱ ⲧⲡⲟⲗⲓⲥ ⲧⲏⲣ-ⲥ̄, ⲁⲥ-ⲥⲱⲟⲩϩ ϩⲓⲣⲙ̄-ⲡⲣⲟ⁵³ ⲙ̄-ⲡⲏⲓ̈.

34. ⲁϥ-ⲑⲉⲣⲁⲡⲉⲩⲉ⁵⁴ ⲛ̄-ⲟⲩⲙⲏⲏϣⲉ ⲉⲩ-ⲙⲟⲕϩ̄ ϩⲛ̄-⁰ϣⲱⲛⲉ ⲉⲩ-ϣⲟⲃⲉ⁵⁵.
ⲁⲩⲱ ⲟⲩⲙⲏⲏϣⲉ ⲛ̄-⁰ⲇⲁⲓⲙⲟⲛⲓⲟⲛ, ⲁϥ-ⲛⲟⲭ-ⲟⲩ ⲉⲃⲟⲗ ⲉ-ⲙⲉϥ-ⲕⲁ-
ⲛ̄ⲇⲁⲓⲙⲟⲛⲓⲟⲛ ⲉ-⁰ϣⲁⲭⲉ ⲉⲃⲟⲗ ⲭⲉ-ⲛⲉⲩ-ⲥⲟⲟⲩⲛ ⲙ̄ⲙⲟ-ϥ.

35. ⲁⲩⲱ ϩⲧⲟⲟⲩⲉ⁵⁶ ⲉⲙⲁⲧⲉ, ⲛ̄ⲧⲉⲣⲉϥ-ⲧⲱⲟⲩⲛ ⲁϥ-ⲃⲱⲕ ⲉⲃⲟⲗ ⲉ-ⲩⲙⲁ
ⲛ̄-ⲭⲁⲉⲓⲉ. ⲁϥ-ϣⲗⲏⲗ ⲙ̄-ⲡⲛⲁⲩ ⲉⲧ⁰-ⲙⲙⲁⲩ.

36. ⲁⲩⲱ ⲁⲩ-ⲡⲱⲧ ⲉⲃⲟⲗ ⲛ̄ⲥⲱ-ϥ ⲛ̄ⲃⲓ-ⲥⲓⲙⲱⲛ ⲙⲛ̄-ⲛ-ⲉⲧ⁰-ⲛⲙ̄ⲙⲁ-ϥ.

37. ⲁⲩ-ⲧⲁϩⲟ-ϥ. ⲁⲩⲱ ⲡⲉⲭⲁ-ⲩ ⲛⲁ-ϥ ⲭⲉ-ⲥⲉ-ⲕⲱⲧⲉ⁵⁷ ⲛ̄ⲥⲱ-ⲕ ⲧⲏⲣ-ⲟⲩ.

38. ⲡⲉⲭⲁ-ϥ ⲛⲁ-ⲩ ⲭⲉ-ⲙⲁⲣⲟⲛ⁵⁸ ⲉ-ⲕⲉⲙⲁ, ⲉ-ⲛ̄ⲕⲉⲧⲙ̄ⲙⲟ⁵⁹ ⲉⲧ⁰-ϩⲏⲛ
ⲉϩⲟⲩⲛ, ⲭⲉⲕⲁⲥ ⲉⲓ̈ⲉ-ⲕⲏⲣⲩⲥⲥⲉ ⲟⲛ ⲛ̄ϩⲏⲧ-ⲟⲩ. ⲛ̄ⲧ-ⲁⲓ-ⲉⲓ ⲅⲁⲣ ⲉⲃⲟⲗ
ⲉ-ⲡⲉⲓ̈ϩⲱⲃ.

39. ⲁⲩⲱ ⲁϥ-ⲃⲱⲕ ⲉϥ-ⲕⲏⲣⲩⲥⲥⲉ ϩⲛ̄-ⲛⲉⲩⲥⲩⲛⲁⲅⲱⲅⲏ ϩⲛ̄-ⲧⲅⲁⲗⲓⲗⲁⲓⲁ
ⲧⲏⲣ-ⲥ̄. ⲁⲩⲱ ⲛ̄ⲕⲉⲇⲁⲓⲙⲟⲛⲓⲟⲛ, ⲛⲉϥ-ⲛⲟⲩⲭⲉ ⲙ̄ⲙⲟ-ⲟⲩ ⲉⲃⲟⲗ.

40. ⲁⲩⲱ ⲁϥ-ⲉⲓ ϣⲁⲣⲟ-ϥ ⲛ̄ⲃⲓ-ⲟⲩⲣⲱⲙⲉ ⲉϥ-ⲥⲟⲃϩ̄⁶⁰ ⲉϥ-ⲡⲁⲣⲁⲕⲁⲗⲉⲓ⁶¹
ⲙ̄ⲙⲟ-ϥ ⲉϥ-ⲭⲱ ⲙ̄ⲙⲟ-ⲥ ⲛⲁ-ϥ ⲭⲉ-ⲉⲕϣⲁⲛ-ⲟⲩⲱϣ ⲕ-ⲛⲁ-ⲧⲃⲃⲟ-ⲓ̈.

---

⁴⁵ ⲡ-ⲥⲟⲉⲓⲧ reputation, fame.   ⁴⁶ ⲡ-ϣⲟⲙ father-in-law, ⲧ-ϣⲱⲙⲉ mother-in-law,
ⲛⲉ-ϣⲙⲟⲩⲓ̈ parents-in-law.   ⁴⁷ ⲛⲟⲩⲭⲉ = throw, cast; ⲛⲏⲭ† = lie.   ⁴⁸ ϩⲙⲟⲙ
become hot, ϩⲏⲙ† be hot, have a fever.   ⁴⁹ ⲡ-ⲣⲟⲩϩⲉ evening.   ⁵⁰ ⲡ-ⲣⲏ sun.
⁵¹ ϩⲱⲧⲡ̄ (ϩⲉⲧⲡ̄-, ϩⲟⲧⲡ=) ϩⲟⲧⲡ̄† join, reconcile; (sun or stars) set .   ⁵² ⲙ̄ⲕⲁϩ become
painful, grieved, ⲙⲟⲕϩ̄† be in pain, difficulty.   ⁵³ ϩⲓⲣⲙ̄-ⲡ-ⲣⲟ by the door.   ⁵⁴ *ⲑⲉⲣⲁ-
ⲡⲉⲩⲉ heal.   ⁵⁵ ϣⲓⲃⲉ (ϣⲃ̄-, ϣⲟⲃⲧ=) change; ϣⲟ(ⲟ)ⲃⲉ† be diverse, various.
⁵⁶ ϩⲧⲟⲟⲩⲉ ⲉⲙⲁⲧⲉ at dawn very early ("dawn very much").   ⁵⁷ ⲕⲱⲧⲉ ⲛ̄ⲥⲁ- (ⲕⲉⲧ-,
ⲕⲟⲧ=) ⲕⲏⲧ† seek.   ⁵⁸ ⲙⲁⲣⲟⲛ come on, let's go (fixed expression, cf. **81**).   ⁵⁹ ⲧⲙ̄ⲙⲟ
plural of ϯⲙⲉ village.   ⁶⁰ ⲥⲱⲃϩ̄ become leprous; ⲥⲟⲃϩ̄† be a leper, have leprosy.
⁶¹ *ⲡⲁⲣⲁⲕⲁⲗⲉⲓ appeal to, implore.

41. ⲁⲩⲱ ⲛ̄ⲧⲉⲣⲉϥ-ϣⲛ̄-ϩⲧⲏ-ϥ⁶² ⲁϥ-ⲥⲟⲩⲧⲛ̄-ⲧⲟⲟⲧ-ϥ̄ ⲉⲃⲟⲗ. ⲁⲩⲱ
ⲁϥ-ⲭⲱϩ⁶³ ⲉⲣⲟ-ϥ ⲉϥ-ⲭⲱ ⲙ̄ⲙⲟ-ⲥ ⲛⲁ-ϥ ⲭⲉ-ϯ-ⲟⲩⲱϣ. ⲧⲃ̄ⲃⲟ.

42. ⲁⲩⲱ ⲛ̄ⲧⲉⲩⲛⲟⲩ ⲁ-ⲡⲉϥⲥⲱⲃϩ̄ ⲗⲟ ϩⲓⲱⲱ-ϥ. ⲁϥ-ⲧⲃ̄ⲃⲟ.

43. ⲁⲩⲱ ⲛ̄ⲧⲉⲣⲉϥ-ϩⲱⲛ⁶⁴ ⲉⲧⲟⲟⲧ-ϥ̄ ⲛ̄ⲧⲉⲩⲛⲟⲩ ⲁϥ-ⲭⲟⲟⲩ-ϥ ⲉⲃⲟⲗ

44. ⲉϥ-ⲭⲱ ⲙ̄ⲙⲟ-ⲥ ⲛⲁ-ϥ ⲭⲉ-ϭⲱϣⲧ̄. ⲙ̄ⲡⲣ̄-ⲭⲟⲟ-ⲥ ⲛ̄-ⲗⲁⲁⲩ. ⲁⲗⲗⲁ
ⲃⲱⲕ ⲛ̄ⲅ-ⲧⲥⲁⲃⲟ-ⲕ⁶⁵ ⲉ-ⲡⲟⲩⲏⲏⲃ⁶⁶ ⲛ̄ⲅ-ⲭⲓ⁶⁷ ⲉϩⲣⲁⲓ̈ ⲉⲧⲃⲉ-ⲡⲉⲕⲧⲃ̄ⲃⲟ ⲛ̄-ⲛ-
ⲉⲛⲧ-ⲁ-ⲙⲱⲩⲥⲏⲥ ⲟⲩⲉϩ-ⲥⲁϩⲛⲉ ⲙ̄ⲙⲟ-ⲟⲩ ⲉ-ⲩⲙⲛ̄ⲧ-ⲙⲛ̄ⲧⲣⲉ ⲛⲁ-ⲩ.

45. ⲛ̄ⲧⲉⲣⲉϥ-ⲉⲓ ⲇⲉ ⲉⲃⲟⲗ ⲁϥ-ⲁⲣⲭⲉⲥⲑⲁⲓ⁶⁸ ⲛ̄-ᵠⲧⲁϣⲉ-ⲟⲉⲓϣ ⲛ̄-ϩⲁϩ ⲁⲩⲱ
ⲉ-ᵠⲥⲣ̄⁶⁹-ⲡϣⲁⲭⲉ ϩⲱⲥⲧⲉ ⲛ̄ϥ-ⲧⲙ̄-ϭⲙ̄-ᵠϭⲟⲙ ⲉ-ᵠⲃⲱⲕ ⲉϩⲟⲩⲛ ⲉ-ⲧⲡⲟⲗⲓⲥ
ⲛ̄ⲟⲩⲱⲛϩ⁷⁰. ⲁⲗⲗⲁ ⲛⲉϥ-ϩⲛ̄-ϩⲉⲛⲙⲁ ⲛ̄-ⲭⲁⲉⲓⲉ. ⲁⲩⲱ ⲛⲉⲩ-ⲛⲏⲩ ⲉⲣⲁⲧ-ϥ̄
ⲡⲉ ⲉⲃⲟⲗ ϩⲙ̄-ⲙⲁ ⲛⲓⲙ.

Chapter Two

1. ⲛ̄ⲧⲉⲣⲉϥ-ⲃⲱⲕ ⲇⲉ ⲉϩⲟⲩⲛ ⲉ-ⲕⲁⲫⲁⲣⲛⲁⲟⲩⲙ ϩⲓⲭⲛ̄-ϩⲉⲛϩⲟⲟⲩ ⲁⲩ-
ⲥⲱⲧⲙ ⲭⲉ-ϥ-ϩⲛ̄-ⲟⲩⲏⲓ̈.

2. ⲁⲩⲱ ⲁ-ⲩⲙⲏⲏϣⲉ ⲥⲱⲟⲩϩ ⲉⲙⲁⲩ ϩⲱⲥⲧⲉ ⲛ̄ⲧⲉ-ⲧⲙ̄-ⲉϣ-ᵠϩⲓⲣⲙ̄-ⲡⲣⲟ⁷¹
ϣⲟⲡ-ⲟⲩ. ⲁⲩⲱ ⲁϥ-ϣⲁⲭⲉ ⲛⲙ̄ⲙⲁ-ⲩ ϩⲙ̄-ⲡϣⲁⲭⲉ.

3. ⲁⲩ-ⲉⲓⲛⲉ ⲇⲉ ⲉⲣⲁⲧ-ϥ̄ ⲛ̄-ⲟⲩⲣⲱⲙⲉ ⲉϥ-ⲥⲏϭ ⲉⲣⲉ-ϥⲧⲟⲟⲩ ⲛ̄-ⲣⲱⲙⲉ ϥⲓ
ϩⲁⲣⲟ-ϥ.

4. ⲁⲩⲱ ⲙ̄ⲡⲟⲩ-ϣ-ⲃⲱⲕ ⲛⲁ-ϥ ⲉϩⲟⲩⲛ ⲉⲧⲃⲉ-ⲡⲙⲏⲏϣⲉ. ⲁⲩ-ϭⲉⲗⲡ̄-
ⲧⲟⲩⲉϩⲥⲟⲓ̈⁷² ⲉⲃⲟⲗ ⲙ̄-ⲡⲙⲁ ⲉⲧϥ̄-ⲛ̄ϩⲏⲧ-ϥ̄. ⲁⲩⲱ ⲛ̄ⲧⲉⲣⲟⲩ-ϣⲟⲧϣⲧ̄⁷³
ⲁⲩ-ⲭⲁⲗⲁ⁷⁴ ⲙ̄-ⲡⲉϭⲗⲟϭ⁷⁵ ⲉⲡⲉⲥⲏⲧ, ⲡ-ⲉⲧⲉⲣⲉ-ⲡ-ⲉⲧᵠ-ⲥⲏϭ ⲛⲏⲭ ϩⲓⲭⲱ-ϥ.

5. ⲁⲩⲱ ⲓ̅ⲥ̅, ⲛ̄ⲧⲉⲣⲉϥ-ⲛⲁⲩ ⲉ-ⲧⲉⲩⲡⲓⲥⲧⲓⲥ ⲡⲉⲭⲁ-ϥ ⲙ̄-ⲡ-ⲉⲧᵠ-ⲥⲏϭ ⲭⲉ-
ⲡⲁϣⲏⲣⲉ, ⲥⲉ-ⲛⲁ-ⲕⲁ-ⲛⲉⲕⲛⲟⲃⲉ ⲛⲁ-ⲕ ⲉⲃⲟⲗ.

6. ⲛⲉ-ⲩⲛ̄-ϩⲟⲉⲓⲛⲉ ⲇⲉ ⲛ̄-ⲛⲉⲅⲣⲁⲙⲙⲁⲧⲉⲩⲥ ϩⲙⲟⲟⲥ ⲙ̄-ⲡⲙⲁ ⲉⲧᵠ-ⲙ̄ⲙⲁⲩ
ⲉⲩ-ⲙⲟⲕⲙⲉⲕ⁷⁶ ϩⲛ̄-ⲛⲉⲩϩⲏⲧ

---

⁶² ϣⲛ̄-ϩⲏⲧ (ϣⲛ̄-ϩⲧⲏ= reflexive) have pity (ⲁⲥ-ϣⲛ̄-ϩⲧⲏ-ⲥ she had pity). ⁶³ ⲭⲱϩ
ⲉ-, ⲭⲏϩ† touch. ⁶⁴ ϩⲱⲛ ⲉⲧⲛ̄-, ⲉⲧⲟⲟⲧ= command. ⁶⁵ ⲧⲥⲁⲃⲟ (ⲧⲥⲁⲃⲉ-, ⲧⲥⲁ-
ⲃⲟ=) ⲧⲥⲁⲃⲏⲩ(ⲧ)† show, teach. ⁶⁶ ⲡ-ⲟⲩⲏⲏⲃ priest. ⁶⁷ ⲭⲓ ⲉϩⲣⲁⲓ̈ make an offer-
ing ("take up"). ⁶⁸ *ⲁⲣⲭⲉⲥⲑⲁⲓ begin. ⁶⁹ ⲥⲱⲣ (ⲥⲣ̄-, ⲥⲟⲟⲣ=) ⲥⲏⲣ† scatter,
spread. ⁷⁰ ⲛ̄ⲟⲩⲱⲛϩ openly, publicly. ⁷¹ ϩⲓⲣⲙ̄-ⲡⲣⲟ the place beside the door
(Prepositional phrase used as a noun, cf. 1:33). ⁷² ⲧ-ⲟⲩⲉϩⲥⲟⲓ̈ beams, roof (cf. ⲡ-
[and ⲧ-] ⲥⲟⲓ̈ beam). ⁷³ ϣⲟⲧϣⲧ̄ (ϣⲉⲧϣⲱⲧ=) ϣⲉⲧϣⲱⲧ† cut, carve. ⁷⁴ *ⲭⲁⲗⲁ
let down. ⁷⁵ ⲡⲉ-ϭⲗⲟϭ bed. ⁷⁶ ⲙⲟⲕⲙⲉⲕ (also ⲙⲉⲕⲙⲟⲩⲕ= reflexive) think,
ponder.

7. ϫⲉ-ⲉⲧⲃⲉ-ⲟⲩ ⲡⲁⲓ̈, ϥ-ϣⲁϫⲉ ϩⲓ-ⲛⲁⲓ̈[77]. ⲉϥ-ϫⲓ-^øⲟⲩⲁ[78]. ⲛⲓⲙ ⲡⲉⲧ^ø-
ⲛⲁ-ϣ-ⲕⲁ-^øⲛⲟⲃⲉ ⲉⲃⲟⲗ ⲛ̄ⲥⲁ-ⲡⲛⲟⲩⲧⲉ ⲙⲁⲩⲁⲁ-ϥ.

8. ⲁⲩⲱ ⲛ̄ⲧⲉⲩⲛⲟⲩ ⲛ̄ⲧⲉⲣⲉϥ-ⲉⲓⲙⲉ ϩⲙ̄-ⲡⲉϥⲡⲛⲁ̄ ϫⲉ-ⲥⲉ-ⲙⲟⲕⲙⲉⲕ ϩⲣⲁⲓ̈
ⲛ̄ϩⲏⲧ-ⲟⲩ ⲡⲉϫⲁ-ϥ ⲛⲁ-ⲩ ϫⲉ-ⲉⲧⲃⲉ-ⲟⲩ ⲧⲉⲧⲛ̄-ⲙⲉⲉⲩⲉ ⲉ-ⲛⲁⲓ̈ ϩⲛ̄-ⲛⲉ-
ⲧⲛ̄ϩⲏⲧ.

9. ⲁϣ ⲅⲁⲣ ⲡⲉⲧ^ø-ⲙⲟⲧⲛ̄[79] ⲉ-^øϫⲟⲟ-ⲥ ⲙ̄-ⲡ-ⲉⲧ^ø-ⲥⲏ6. ϫⲉ-ⲧⲱⲟⲩⲛ ⲛ̄ⲅ-
ϥⲓ-ⲡⲉⲕ6ⲗⲟ6 ⲛ̄ⲅ-ⲙⲟⲟϣⲉ. ϫⲛ̄-ⲉ-^øϫⲟⲟ-ⲥ ϫⲉ-ⲥⲉ-ⲛⲁ-ⲕⲁ-ⲛⲉⲕⲛⲟⲃⲉ
ⲛⲁ-ⲕ ⲉⲃⲟⲗ.

10. ϫⲉⲕⲁⲥ ⲇⲉ ⲉⲧⲉⲧⲛⲉ-ⲛⲁⲩ ϫⲉ-ⲟⲩⲛ̄ⲧ-ϥ̄-^øⲉϩⲟⲩⲥⲓⲁ ⲙ̄ⲙⲁⲩ ⲛ̄6ⲓ-
ⲡϣⲏⲣⲉ ⲙ̄-ⲡⲣⲱⲙⲉ ⲉ-^øⲕⲁ-^øⲛⲟⲃⲉ ⲉⲃⲟⲗ ϩⲓϫⲙ̄-ⲡⲕⲁϩ — ⲡⲉϫⲁ-ϥ ⲙ̄-ⲡ-
ⲉⲧ^ø-ⲥⲏ6

11. ϫⲉ-ⲧⲱⲟⲩⲛ. ⲉⲓ̈-ϫⲉⲣⲟ-ⲕ[80]. ϥⲓ ⲙ̄-ⲡⲉⲕ6ⲗⲟ6. ⲃⲱⲕ ⲉ-ⲡⲉⲕⲏⲓ.

12. ⲁⲩⲱ ⲁϥ-ⲧⲱⲟⲩⲛ. ⲛ̄ⲧⲉⲩⲛⲟⲩ ⲁϥ-ⲧⲁⲗⲉ-ⲡⲉϥ6ⲗⲟ6 ⲉϫⲱ-ϥ. ⲁϥ-ⲉⲓ
ⲉⲃⲟⲗ ϩⲓⲑⲏ[81] ⲙ̄ⲙⲟ-ⲟⲩ ⲧⲏⲣ-ⲟⲩ ϩⲱⲥⲧⲉ ⲛ̄ⲥⲉ-ⲣ̄-ϣⲡⲏⲣⲉ ⲧⲏⲣ-ⲟⲩ
ⲛ̄ⲥⲉ-ϯ-^øⲉⲟⲟⲩ ⲙ̄-ⲡⲛⲟⲩⲧⲉ ⲉⲩ-ϫⲱ ⲙ̄ⲙⲟ-ⲥ ϫⲉ-ⲙ̄ⲡⲛ̄-ⲛⲁⲩ ⲉ-ⲟⲩⲟⲛ
ⲉⲛⲉϩ ϩⲓ-ⲛⲁⲓ̈.

13. ⲁϥ-ⲉⲓ ⲟⲛ ⲉⲃⲟⲗ ϩⲁⲧⲛ̄-ⲧⲉⲑⲁⲗⲁⲥⲥⲁ. ⲁⲩⲱ ⲡⲙⲏⲏϣⲉ ⲧⲏⲣ-ϥ̄, ⲁⲩ-
ⲥⲱⲟⲩϩ ⲉⲣⲟ-ϥ. ⲁϥ-ϯ-^øⲥⲃⲱ ⲛⲁ-ⲩ.

14. ⲁⲩⲱ ⲉϥ-ⲡⲁⲣⲁⲅⲉ[82] ⲁϥ-ⲛⲁⲩ ⲉ-ⲗⲉⲟⲩⲉⲓ ⲡϣⲏⲣⲉ ⲛ̄-ⲁⲗⲫⲁⲓⲟⲥ ⲉϥ-
ϩⲙⲟⲟⲥ ϩⲓ-ⲡⲉϥⲧⲉⲗⲱⲛⲓⲟⲛ[83]. ⲡⲉϫⲁ-ϥ ⲛⲁ-ϥ ϫⲉ-ⲟⲩⲁϩ-ⲕ̄ ⲛ̄ⲥⲱ-ⲓ̈. ⲁⲩⲱ
ⲁϥ-ⲧⲱⲟⲩⲛ. ⲁϥ-ⲟⲩⲁϩ-ϥ̄ ⲛ̄ⲥⲱ-ϥ.

15. ⲁⲥ-ϣⲱⲡⲉ[84] ⲇⲉ ⲉϥ-ⲛⲏϫ[85] ϩⲙ̄-ⲡⲉϥⲏⲓ. ⲁ-ϩⲁϩ ⲛ̄-ⲧⲉⲗⲱⲛⲏⲥ[86] ϩⲓ-
ⲣⲉϥ-ⲣ̄-^øⲛⲟⲃⲉ ⲛⲟϫ-ⲟⲩ ⲙⲛ̄-ⲓ̄ⲥ̄ ⲙⲛ̄-ⲛⲉϥⲙⲁⲑⲏⲧⲏⲥ. ⲛⲉⲩ-ⲟϣ ⲅⲁⲣ. ⲁⲩⲱ
ⲁⲩ-ⲟⲩⲁϩⲟⲩ ⲛ̄ⲥⲱ-ϥ.

16. ⲛⲉⲅⲣⲁⲙⲙⲁⲧⲉⲩⲥ ⲙⲛ̄-ⲛⲉⲫⲁⲣⲓⲥⲁⲓⲟⲥ[87], ⲛ̄ⲧⲉⲣⲟⲩ-ⲛⲁⲩ ϫⲉ-ϥ-ⲟⲩⲱⲙ
ⲙⲛ̄-ⲛ̄ⲣⲉϥ-ⲣ̄-^øⲛⲟⲃⲉ ⲁⲩⲱ ⲛ̄ⲧⲉⲗⲱⲛⲏⲥ ⲡⲉϫⲁ-ⲩ ⲛ̄-ⲛⲉϥⲙⲁⲑⲏⲧⲏⲥ
ϫⲉ-ⲉⲧⲃⲉ-ⲟⲩ ϥ-ⲟⲩⲱⲙ ⲁⲩⲱ ϥ-ⲥⲱ ⲙⲛ̄-ⲛ̄ⲣⲉϥ-ⲣ̄-^øⲛⲟⲃⲉ ⲁⲩⲱ ⲛ̄ⲧⲉ-
ⲗⲱⲛⲏⲥ.

---

[77] ϩⲓ-ⲛⲁⲓ̈ thus, in this way. [78] ϫⲓ-^øⲟⲩⲁ utter blasphemy (ϫⲓ- before zero article = ϫⲉ- 'speak' + ⲡ-ⲟⲩⲁ blasphemy). [79] ⲙ̄ⲧⲟⲛ be at rest, at ease, relieved, ⲙⲟⲧⲛ̄† be easy, satisfied, hale; ⲙⲟⲧⲛ̄ ⲉ- easier. [80] ϫⲉⲣⲟ= i.e. ϫⲱ ⲉⲣⲟ=. [81] ϩⲓⲑⲏ ⲛ̄-/ⲙ̄ⲙⲟ= before, in front of (Compound preposition). [82] *ⲡⲁⲣⲁⲅⲉ pass by. [83] *ⲡ-ⲧⲉⲗⲱⲛⲓⲟⲛ tax office. [84] ⲁⲥ-ϣⲱⲡⲉ ⲇⲉ . . . and it happened that . . . . [85] ⲛⲏϫ† . . . ⲛⲟϫ-ⲟⲩ: ⲛⲟⲩϫⲉ ⲙ̄ⲙⲟ=, ⲛⲟϫ= (reflexive object) sit down, be seated ("cast oneself down"), ⲛⲏϫ† sit. [86] *ⲧⲉⲗⲱⲛⲏⲥ money changer. [87] ⲫⲁⲣⲓⲥⲁⲓⲟⲥ (Adjective) Pharisee, member of the Pharisee sect.

17. ⲁⲩⲱ ⲓⲥ̄, ⲛ̄ⲧⲉⲣⲉϥ-ⲥⲱⲧⲙ̄ ⲡⲉϫⲁ-ϥ ⲛⲁ-ⲩ ϫⲉ-ⲛ̄-ⲥⲉ-ⲣ̄-⁰ⲭⲣⲉⲓⲁ⁸⁸ ⲁⲛ
ⲛ̄ϭⲓ-ⲛ-ⲉⲧ⁰-ⲧⲏⲕ⁸⁹ ⲙ̄-ⲡⲥⲁⲉⲓⲛ⁹⁰ ⲁⲗⲗⲁ ⲛ-ⲉⲧ⁰-ϣⲟⲟⲡ⁹¹ ⲕⲁⲕⲱⲥ. ⲛ̄ⲧ-ⲁⲓ̈-
ⲉⲓ ⲁⲛ ⲉ-⁰ⲧⲉϩⲙ̄-ⲛ̄ⲇⲓⲕⲁⲓⲟⲥ ⲁⲗⲗⲁ ⲛ̄ⲣⲉϥ-ⲣ̄-⁰ⲛⲟⲃⲉ.

18. ⲁⲩⲱ ⲙ̄ⲙⲁⲑⲏⲧⲏⲥ ⲛ̄-ⲓⲱϩⲁⲛⲛⲏⲥ ⲙⲛ̄-ⲛⲁ-ⲛⲉⲫⲁⲣⲓⲥⲁⲓⲟⲥ, ⲛⲉⲩ-ⲛⲏ-
ⲥⲧⲉⲩⲉ. ⲁⲩ-ⲉⲓ ⲇⲉ ⲛⲁ-ϥ ⲉⲩ-ϫⲱ ⲙ̄ⲙⲟ-ⲥ ϫⲉ-ⲉⲧⲃⲉ-ⲟⲩ ⲙ̄ⲙⲁⲑⲏⲧⲏⲥ
ⲛ̄-ⲓⲱϩⲁⲛⲛⲏⲥ ⲁⲩⲱ ⲙ̄ⲙⲁⲑⲏⲧⲏⲥ ⲛ̄-ⲛⲉⲫⲁⲣⲓⲥⲁⲓⲟⲥ, ⲥⲉ-ⲛⲏⲥⲧⲉⲩⲉ. ⲛⲉⲕ-
ⲙⲁⲑⲏⲧⲏⲥ ⲇⲉ, ⲛ̄-ⲥⲉ-ⲛⲏⲥⲧⲉⲩⲉ ⲁⲛ.

19. ⲡⲉϫⲉ-ⲓⲥ̄ ⲛⲁ-ⲩ ϫⲉ-ⲙⲏ ⲟⲩⲛ̄-⁰ϭⲟⲙ ⲉ-⁰ⲧⲣⲉⲩ-ⲛⲏⲥⲧⲉⲩⲉ ⲛ̄ϭⲓ-
ⲛ̄ϣⲏⲣⲉ ⲙ̄-ⲡⲙⲁ-ⲛ̄-ϣⲉⲗⲉⲉⲧ⁹² ϩⲟⲥⲟⲛ ⲉⲣⲉ-ⲡⲁ-ⲧϣⲉⲗⲉⲉⲧ⁹³ ⲛⲙ̄ⲙⲁ-ⲩ.
ϩⲟⲥⲟⲛ ⲡⲁ-ⲧϣⲉⲗⲉⲉⲧ ⲛⲙ̄ⲙⲁ-ⲩ ⲛ̄-ⲥⲉ-ⲛⲁ-ϣ-ⲛⲏⲥⲧⲉⲩⲉ ⲁⲛ.

20. ⲟⲩⲛ̄-ϩⲉⲛϩⲟⲟⲩ ⲇⲉ ⲛⲏⲩ ϩⲟⲧⲁⲛ ⲉⲩϣⲁⲛ-ϥⲓ ⲛ̄ⲧⲟⲟⲧ-ⲟⲩ ⲙ̄ⲡⲁ-ⲧϣⲉ-
ⲗⲉⲉⲧ. ⲧⲟⲧⲉ ⲥⲉ-ⲛⲁ-ⲛⲏⲥⲧⲏⲩⲉ ϩⲛ̄-ⲛⲉϩⲟⲟⲩ ⲉⲧ⁰-ⲙ̄ⲙⲁⲩ.

21. ⲙⲉⲣⲉ-ⲗⲁⲁⲩ ⲛⲉϫ⁹⁴-⁰ⲧⲟⲉⲓⲥ⁹⁵ ⲛ̄-ϣⲁⲓ̈ ⲉⲣⲛ̄-⁰ϣⲧⲏⲛ⁹⁶ ⲙ̄-ⲡⲗ̄ϭⲉ⁹⁷.
ⲉϣⲱⲡⲉ⁹⁸ ⲙ̄ⲙⲟⲛ ⲧⲧⲟⲉⲓⲥ ⲛ̄-ϣⲁⲓ̈ ⲛⲁ-ϥⲓ-ⲡⲕⲱⲧⲉ⁹⁹ ⲙ̄ⲙⲁⲩ ⲛ̄-ⲧⲉϣⲧⲏⲛ
ⲙ̄-ⲡⲗ̄ϭⲉ ⲛ̄ⲥ-ⲡⲱϩ¹⁰⁰ ⲛ̄ϩⲟⲩⲟ.

22. ⲁⲩⲱ ⲙⲉⲣⲉ-ⲗⲁⲁⲩ ⲛⲉϫ-⁰ⲏⲣⲡ̄¹⁰¹ ⲛ̄-ⲃⲣ̄ⲣⲉ ⲉ-⁰ϩⲱⲧ¹⁰² ⲛ̄-ⲁⲥ¹⁰³.
ⲉϣⲱⲡⲉ ⲙ̄ⲙⲟⲛ ⲡⲏⲣⲡ̄ ⲛⲁ-ⲡⲉϩ-ⲛ̄ϩⲱⲧ ⲛ̄ⲧⲉ-ⲡⲏⲣⲡ̄ ⲡⲱⲛ¹⁰⁴ ⲉⲃⲟⲗ ⲛ̄ⲧⲉ-
ⲛ̄ϩⲱⲧ ⲧⲁⲕⲟ. ⲁⲗⲗⲁ ⲉ-ϣⲁⲩ-ⲛⲉϫ-⁰ⲏⲣⲡ̄ ⲛ̄-ⲃⲣ̄ⲣⲉ ⲉ-⁰ϩⲱⲧ ⲛ̄-ⲃⲣ̄ⲣⲉ.

23. ⲁⲩⲱ ⲁⲥ-ϣⲱⲡⲉ¹⁰⁵ ϩⲛ̄-ⲛ̄ⲥⲁⲃⲃⲁⲧⲟⲛ ⲉ-⁰ⲧⲣⲉⲩ-ⲙⲟⲟϣⲉ ⲉⲃⲟⲗ ϩⲛ̄-
ⲛ̄ⲉⲓⲱϩⲉ¹⁰⁶ ⲉⲧ⁰-ⲣⲏⲧ¹⁰⁷. ⲁⲩⲱ ⲛⲉϥⲙⲁⲑⲏⲧⲏⲥ, ⲉⲩ-ⲙⲟⲟϣⲉ ⲁⲩ-ⲁⲣⲭⲉⲓ
ⲛ̄-⁰ⲧⲗ̄ⲕ-⁰ϩⲙ̄ⲥ¹⁰⁸.

24. ⲛⲉⲫⲁⲣⲓⲥⲁⲓⲟⲥ ⲇⲉ, ⲡⲉϫⲁ-ⲩ ⲛⲁ-ϥ ϫⲉ-ⲁⲛⲁⲩ ϫⲉ-ⲉⲩ-ⲣ̄-ⲟⲩ ϩⲛ̄-
ⲛ̄ⲥⲁⲃⲃⲁⲧⲟⲛ ⲉ-ⲟⲩⲕⲉϩⲉⲥⲧⲓ ⲉ-⁰ⲁⲁ-ϥ.

25. ⲡⲉϫⲁ-ϥ ⲛⲁ-ⲩ ϫⲉ-ⲙ̄ⲡⲉⲧⲛ̄-ⲟϣ-ϥ ⲗⲁⲁⲩ ϫⲉ-ⲛ̄ⲧ-ⲁ-ⲇⲁⲩⲉⲓⲇ ⲣ̄-ⲟⲩ
ⲛ̄ⲧⲉⲣⲉϥ-ϩⲕⲟ¹⁰⁹ ⲛ̄ⲧⲟϥ ⲙⲛ̄-ⲛⲉⲧ⁰-ⲛⲙ̄ⲙⲁ-ϥ.

---

⁸⁸ ⲣ̄-*ⲭⲣⲉⲓⲁ need.   ⁸⁹ ⲧⲱⲕ (ⲧⲉⲕ-, ⲧⲟⲕ⸗) ⲧⲏⲕ† strengthen, confirm.   ⁹⁰ ⲡ- (and
ⲧ-) ⲥⲁⲉⲓⲛ physician.   ⁹¹ ϣⲱⲡⲉ/ϣⲟⲟⲡ† *ⲕⲁⲕⲱⲥ be in bad condition, do badly.
⁹² ⲧ-ϣⲉⲗⲉⲉⲧ bride, ⲡ-ⲙⲁ-ⲛ̄-ϣⲉⲗⲉⲉⲧ bridal hall, ⲡ-ϣⲏⲣⲉ ⲙ̄-ⲡⲙⲁ-ⲛ̄-ϣⲉⲗⲉⲉⲧ
wedding guest, ⲡⲁ-ⲧϣⲉⲗⲉⲉⲧ groom.   ⁹³ Cf. previous note.   ⁹⁴ ⲛⲟⲩϫⲉ put (patch
on garment, wine into wineskins).   ⁹⁵ ⲧ-ⲧⲟⲉⲓⲥ ⲛ̄-ϣⲁⲓ̈ new patch.   ⁹⁶ ⲧⲉ-ϣⲧⲏⲛ
garment, tunic.   ⁹⁷ ⲡ-ⲡⲗ̄ϭⲉ rag, ⲛ̄-ⲡⲗ̄ϭⲉ (Attributive construction) worn out.
⁹⁸ ⲉϣⲱⲡⲉ ⲙ̄ⲙⲟⲛ otherwise ("if No").   ⁹⁹ ϥⲓ-ⲡ-ⲕⲱⲧⲉ ⲙ̄ⲙⲁⲩ draw away the
edge (of the hole that was patched).   ¹⁰⁰ ⲡⲱϩ (ⲡⲉϩ-, ⲡⲁϩ⸗) ⲡⲏϩ† burst, tear.
¹⁰¹ ⲡ-ⲏⲣⲡ̄ wine.   ¹⁰² ⲡ-ϩⲱⲧ sack, bag, wineskin.   ¹⁰³ ⲁⲥ old (Adjective).   ¹⁰⁴ ⲡⲱⲛ
ⲉⲃⲟⲗ (ⲡⲉⲛ-, ⲡⲟⲛ⸗) ⲡⲏⲛ† pour out.   ¹⁰⁵ ⲁⲥ-ϣⲱⲡⲉ ⲉ-⁰ⲧⲣⲉⲩ- it once happened
that they . . . .   ¹⁰⁶ ⲡ-ⲉⲓⲱϩⲉ field.   ¹⁰⁷ ⲣⲱⲧ, ⲣⲏⲧ† grow, become covered with veg-
etation.   ¹⁰⁸ ⲧⲱⲗⲕ̄ (ⲧⲗ̄ⲕ- ⲧⲟⲗⲕ⸗) pluck out; ⲡ-ϩⲙ̄ⲥ ear of grain.   ¹⁰⁹ ϩⲕⲟ,
ϩⲕⲁⲉⲓⲧ† (or ϩⲕⲟⲉⲓⲧ† or ϩⲟⲕⲣ̄ⲡ̄†) be hungry.

26. ϫⲉ-ⲛ̄-ⲁϣ ⲛ̄-ⲅⲉ ⲁϥ-ⲃⲱⲕ ⲉϩⲟⲩⲛ ⲉ-ⲡⲏⲓ̈ ⲙ̄-ⲡⲛⲟⲩⲧⲉ ϩⲓ-ⲁⲃⲓⲁⲑⲁⲣ
ⲡⲁⲣⲭⲓⲉⲣⲉⲩⲥ. ⲁⲩⲱ ⲛ̄ⲟⲉⲓⲕ ⲛ̄-ⲧⲉⲡⲣⲟⲑⲉⲥⲓⲥ¹¹⁰, ⲁϥ-ⲟⲩⲟⲙ-ⲟⲩ ⲉ-ⲟⲩⲕⲉ-
ϣⲉⲥⲧⲓ ⲛⲁ-ϥ ⲉ-⁰ⲟⲩⲟⲙ-ⲟⲩ ⲛ̄ⲥⲁ-ⲛ̄ⲟⲩⲏⲏⲃ. ⲁⲩⲱ ⲁϥ-ϯ ⲛ̄-ⲛ̄ⲕⲟⲟⲩⲉ
ⲉⲧ⁰-ⲛⲙ̄ⲙⲁ-ϥ.
27. ⲡⲉϫⲁ-ϥ ⲟⲛ ⲛⲁ-ⲩ ϫⲉ-ⲡⲥⲁⲃⲃⲁⲧⲟⲛ, ⲛ̄ⲧ-ⲁϥ-ϣⲱⲡⲉ ⲉⲧⲃⲉ-ⲡⲣⲱⲙⲉ.
ⲁⲩⲱ ⲛ̄ⲧ-ⲁ-ⲡⲣⲱⲙⲉ ϣⲱⲡⲉ ⲁⲛ ⲉⲧⲃⲉ-ⲡⲥⲁⲃⲃⲁⲧⲟⲛ.
28. ϩⲱⲥⲧⲉ ⲡϣⲏⲣⲉ ⲙ̄-ⲡⲣⲱⲙⲉ ⲡϫⲟⲉⲓⲥ ⲡⲉ ⲙ̄-ⲡⲕⲉⲥⲁⲃⲃⲁⲧⲟⲛ.

Chapter Three

1. ⲁⲩⲱ ⲁϥ-ⲃⲱⲕ ⲟⲛ ⲉϩⲟⲩⲛ ⲉ-ⲧⲥⲩⲛⲁⲅⲱⲅⲏ. ⲛⲉ-ⲩⲛ̄-ⲟⲩⲣⲱⲙⲉ ⲇⲉ ⲙ̄ⲙⲁⲩ
ⲉⲣⲉ-ⲧⲉϥϭⲓϫ ⲙⲟⲟⲩⲧ.
2. ⲁⲩⲱ ⲛⲉⲩ-ⲡⲁⲣⲁⲧⲏⲣⲉⲓ¹¹¹ ⲉⲣⲟ-ϥ ϫⲉ-ⲉⲩⲉ-ⲕⲁⲧⲏⲅⲟⲣⲉⲓ¹¹² ⲙ̄ⲙⲟ-ϥ.
3. ⲁⲩⲱ ⲡⲉϫⲁ-ϥ ⲙ̄-ⲡⲣⲱⲙⲉ ⲉⲧⲉⲣⲉ-ⲧⲉϥϭⲓϫ ⲙⲟⲟⲩⲧ ϫⲉ-ⲧⲱⲟⲩⲛ-ⲅ̄.
ⲁⲙⲟⲩ ⲉ-ⲧⲙⲏⲧⲉ.
4. ⲁⲩⲱ ⲡⲉϫⲁ-ϥ ⲛⲁ-ⲩ ϫⲉ-ⲉϣⲉⲥⲧⲓ ϩⲛ̄-ⲛ̄ⲥⲁⲃⲃⲁⲧⲟⲛ ⲉ-⁰ⲣ̄-⁰ⲡⲉⲧ-
ⲛⲁⲛⲟⲩ-ϥ ⲭⲛ̄-⁰ⲣ̄-⁰ⲡⲉⲧ-ϩⲟⲟⲩ. ⲉ-⁰ⲧⲁⲛϩⲉ¹¹³-ⲟⲩⲯⲩⲭⲏ ⲭⲛ̄-ⲉ-⁰ⲙⲟⲟⲩⲧ-ⲥ̄.
ⲛ̄ⲧⲟⲟⲩ ⲇⲉ ⲁⲩ-ⲕⲁ-ⲣⲱ-ⲟⲩ̄¹¹⁴.
5. ⲁⲩⲱ ⲛ̄ⲧⲉⲣⲉϥ-ϭⲱϣⲧ̄ ⲉϩⲟⲩⲛ ⲉϩⲣⲁ-ⲩ ϩⲛ̄-ⲟⲩⲟⲣⲅⲏ ⲉϥ-ⲙⲟⲕϩ̄¹¹⁵ ⲛ̄ϩⲏⲧ
ⲉϫⲙ̄-ⲡⲧⲱⲙ¹¹⁶ ⲛ̄ϩⲏⲧ ⲙ̄-ⲡⲉⲩϩⲏⲧ ⲡⲉϫⲁ-ϥ ⲙ̄-ⲡⲣⲱⲙⲉ ϫⲉ-ⲥⲟⲩⲧⲛ̄-
ⲧⲉⲕϭⲓϫ ⲉⲃⲟⲗ. ⲁϥ-ⲥⲟⲩⲧⲱⲛ-ⲥ̄. ⲁⲩⲱ ⲁⲥ-ⲗⲟ¹¹⁷ ⲛ̄ϭⲓ-ⲧⲉϥϭⲓϫ.
6. ⲛ̄ⲧⲉⲣⲟⲩ-ⲉⲓ ⲇⲉ ⲉⲃⲟⲗ ⲛ̄ⲧⲉⲩⲛⲟⲩ ⲛ̄ϭⲓ-ⲛⲉⲫⲁⲣⲓⲥⲁⲓⲟⲥ ⲙⲛ̄-ⲛ̄ϩⲏⲣⲱⲇⲓ-
ⲁⲛⲟⲥ ⲁⲩ-ϫⲓ-⁰ϣⲟϫⲛⲉ¹¹⁸ ⲉⲣⲟ-ϥ ϫⲉⲕⲁⲥ ⲉⲩⲉ-ⲧⲁⲕⲟ-ϥ.
7. ⲁⲩⲱ ⲓⲥ̄, ⲁϥ-ⲁⲛⲁⲭⲱⲣⲉⲓ¹¹⁹ ⲙⲛ̄-ⲛⲉϥⲙⲁⲑⲏⲧⲏⲥ ⲉⲃⲟⲗ ⲉ-ⲧⲉⲑⲁⲗⲁⲥⲥⲁ.
ⲁⲩⲱ ⲟⲩⲛⲟϭ ⲙ̄-ⲙⲏⲏϣⲉ ⲉⲃⲟⲗ ϩⲛ̄-ⲧⲅⲁⲗⲓⲗⲁⲓⲁ, ⲁⲩ-ⲟⲩⲁϩ-ⲟⲩ ⲛ̄ⲥⲱ-ϥ
ⲙⲛ̄-ϯⲟⲩⲇⲁⲓⲁ
8. ⲙⲛ̄-ⲑⲓⲉⲣⲟⲥⲟⲗⲩⲙⲁ ⲁⲩⲱ ⲕⲉⲛⲟϭ ⲙ̄-ⲙⲏⲏϣⲉ ⲉⲃⲟⲗ ϩⲛ̄-ϯⲇⲟⲩⲙⲁⲓⲁ
ⲙⲛ̄-ⲡⲉⲕⲣⲟ ⲙ̄-ⲡⲓⲟⲣⲇⲁⲛⲏⲥ ⲙⲛ̄-ⲡⲕⲱⲧⲉ ⲛ̄-ⲧⲩⲣⲟⲥ ⲙⲛ̄-ⲥⲓⲇⲱⲛ ⲉⲩ-
ⲥⲱⲧⲙ̄ ⲉ-ⲛ-ⲉⲧϥ̄-ⲉⲓⲣⲉ ⲙ̄ⲙⲟ-ⲟⲩ.

---

¹¹⁰ *ⲧⲉ-ⲡⲣⲟⲥⲑⲉⲥⲓⲥ (i.e. πρόθεσις) presentation; the "loaves of presentation" were
sacred bread kept in the Jerusalem Temple. ¹¹¹ *ⲡⲁⲣⲁⲧⲏⲣⲉⲓ watch closely.
¹¹² *ⲕⲁⲧⲏⲅⲟⲣⲉⲓ accuse.   ¹¹³ ⲧⲁⲛϩⲟ (ⲧⲁⲛϩⲉ-, ⲧⲁⲛϩⲟ⸗) ⲧⲁⲛϩⲏⲩ† make alive.
¹¹⁴ ⲕⲁ-ⲣⲱ= (reflexive) fall silent.   ¹¹⁵ ⲙ̄ⲕⲁϩ ⲛ̄ϩⲏⲧ, ⲙⲟⲕϩ̄† ⲛ̄ϩⲏⲧ become distressed.
¹¹⁶ ⲧⲱⲙ (ⲧⲙ̄- ⲧⲟⲙ=) ⲧⲏⲙ† shut. Infinitive as noun, ⲡ-ⲧⲱⲙ ⲛ̄ϩⲏⲧ hard heartedness.
¹¹⁷ ⲗⲟ ("cease") also means "get well" (from disease or demonic infection).   ¹¹⁸ ϣⲟ-
ϫⲛⲉ take counsel. Infinitive as noun ⲡ-ϣⲟϫⲛⲉ counsel, design; ϫⲓ-⁰ϣⲟϫⲛⲉ take counsel, reflect, advise.   ¹¹⁹ *ⲁⲛⲁⲭⲱⲣⲉⲓ withdraw.

9. ⲁⲩⲱ ⲁϥ-ϫⲟⲟ-ⲥ ⲛ̄-ⲛⲉϥⲙⲁⲑⲏⲧⲏⲥ ϫⲉ-ⲉⲣⲉ-ϩⲉⲛⲉϫⲏⲩ ⲡⲣⲟⲥⲕⲁⲣⲧⲉⲣⲉⲓ[120] ⲉⲣⲟ-ϥ ⲉⲧⲃⲉ-ⲡⲙⲏⲏϣⲉ. ϫⲉ ⲛⲉⲩ-ⲑⲗⲓⲃⲉ[121] ⲙ̄ⲙⲟ-ϥ.

10. ⲛⲁϣⲉ-ⲛ-ⲉⲛⲧ-ⲁϥ-ⲧⲁⲗϭⲟ-ⲟⲩ[122] ⲅⲁⲣ ϩⲱⲥⲧⲉ ⲉ-ᵠⲧⲣⲉⲩ-ϯ-ⲡⲉⲩ-ⲟⲩⲟⲉⲓ ⲉⲣⲟ-ϥ. ⲁⲩⲱ ⲛ-ⲉⲧⲉ-ⲙ̄ⲙⲁⲥⲧⲓⲅ⳽[123] ϩⲓⲱ-ⲟⲩ

11. ⲙⲛ̄-ⲛⲉⲡ̄ⲛ̄ⲁ̄ ⲛ̄-ⲁⲕⲁⲑⲁⲣⲧⲟⲛ, ⲉⲩϣⲁⲛ-ⲛⲁⲩ ⲉⲣⲟ-ϥ ϣⲁⲩ-ⲡⲁϩⲧ-ⲟⲩ ϩⲁⲣⲁⲧ-ϥ̄[124] ⲛ̄ⲥⲉ-ϫⲓ-ᵠϣⲕⲁⲕ ⲉⲃⲟⲗ ⲉⲩ-ϫⲱ ⲙ̄ⲙⲟ-ⲥ ϫⲉ-ⲛ̄ⲧⲟⲕ ⲡⲉ ⲡϣⲏⲣⲉ ⲙ̄-ⲡⲛⲟⲩⲧⲉ.

12. ⲁⲩⲱ ⲛⲉϥ-ⲉⲡⲓⲧⲓⲙⲁ ⲛⲁ-ⲩ ⲉⲙⲁⲧⲉ ϫⲉ-ⲛ̄ⲛⲉⲩ-ⲟⲩⲟⲛϩ-ϥ̄ ⲉⲃⲟⲗ.

13. ⲁϥ-ⲃⲱⲕ ⲇⲉ ⲉϩⲣⲁ̈ⲓ ⲉ-ⲡⲧⲟⲟⲩ. ⲁⲩⲱ ⲁϥ-ⲙⲟⲩⲧⲉ ⲉ-ⲛ-ⲉⲧϥ̄-ⲟⲩⲁϣ-ⲟⲩ.

14. ⲁϥ-ⲛⲉϩ[125]-ⲙⲛ̄ⲧ-ⲥⲛⲟⲟⲩⲥ ⲉⲃⲟⲗ ϫⲉ-ⲉⲩⲉ-ϣⲱⲡⲉ ⲛⲙ̄ⲙⲁ-ϥ ⲁⲩⲱ ⲛ̄ϥ-ϫⲟⲟⲩ-ⲥⲉ ⲉⲃⲟⲗ ⲉ-ᵠⲧⲁϣⲉ-ⲟⲉⲓϣ

15. ⲛ̄ϥ-ϯ ⲛⲁ-ⲩ ⲛ̄-ⲧⲉⳤⲟⲩⲥⲓⲁ ⲉ-ᵠⲛⲉϫ-ᵠⲇⲁⲓⲙⲟⲛⲓⲟⲛ ⲉⲃⲟⲗ.

16. ⲁⲩⲱ ⲁϥ-ⲧⲁϩⲟ[126] ⲉⲣⲁⲧ-ⲟⲩ ⲙ̄-ⲡⲙⲛ̄ⲧ-ⲥⲛⲟⲟⲩⲥ. ⲁⲩⲱ ⲥⲓⲙⲱⲛ, ⲁϥ-ϯ-ⲟⲩⲣⲁⲛ ⲉⲣⲟ-ϥ ϫⲉ-ⲡⲉⲧⲣⲟⲥ.

17. ⲁⲩⲱ ⲓⲁⲕⲱⲃⲟⲥ ⲡϣⲏⲣⲉ ⲛ̄-ⲍⲉⲃⲉⲇⲁⲓⲟⲥ ⲙⲛ̄-ⲓⲱϩⲁⲛⲛⲏⲥ ⲡⲥⲟⲛ ⲛ̄-ⲓⲁⲕⲱⲃⲟⲥ — ⲁϥ-ϯ-ϩⲉⲛⲣⲁⲛ ⲉⲣⲟ-ⲟⲩ ϫⲉ ⲃⲟⲁⲛⲏⲣⲅⲉⲥ ⲉⲧⲉ-ⲡⲁⲓ̈ ⲡⲉ ⲡϣⲏⲣⲉ ⲙ̄-ⲡⲉϩⲣⲟⲩⲃ̄ⲃⲁⲓ̈[127] —

18. ⲁⲩⲱ ⲁⲛⲇⲣⲉⲁⲥ ⲙⲛ̄-ⲫⲓⲗⲓⲡⲡⲟⲥ ⲙⲛ̄-ⲃⲁⲣⲑⲟⲗⲟⲙⲁⲓⲟⲥ ⲙⲛ̄-ⲙⲁⲑ-ⲑⲁⲓⲟⲥ ⲙⲛ̄-ⲑⲱⲙⲁⲥ ⲁⲩⲱ ⲓⲁⲕⲱⲃⲟⲥ ⲡϣⲏⲣⲉ ⲛ̄-ⲁⲗⲫⲁⲓⲟⲥ ⲙⲛ̄-ⲑⲁⲇⲇⲁⲓⲟⲥ ⲁⲩⲱ ⲥⲓⲙⲱⲛ ⲡⲕⲁⲛⲁⲛⲁⲓⲟⲥ

19. ⲙⲛ̄-ⲓⲟⲩⲇⲁⲥ ⲡⲓⲥⲕⲁⲣⲓⲱⲧⲏⲥ, ⲡ-ⲉⲛⲧ-ⲁϥ-ⲡⲁⲣⲁⲇⲓⲇⲟⲩ ⲙ̄ⲙⲟ-ϥ.

20. ⲁⲩⲱ ⲁϥ-ⲉⲓ ⲉϩⲟⲩⲛ ⲉ-ⲡⲏⲓ̈. ⲁ-ⲡⲙⲏⲏϣⲉ ⲟⲛ ⲥⲱⲟⲩϩ ⲉⲣⲟ-ϥ ϩⲱⲥⲧⲉ ⲛ̄ⲥⲉ-ⲧⲙ̄-ⲥⲣ̄ϥⲉ[128] ⲉ-ᵠⲟⲩⲉⲙ-ⲡⲉⲩⲟⲉⲓⲕ.

21. ⲛ̄ⲧⲉⲣⲟⲩ-ⲥⲱⲧⲙ̄ ⲇⲉ ⲛ̄ϭⲓ-ⲛⲉϥⲣⲱⲙⲉ[129] ⲁⲩ-ⲉⲓ ⲉⲃⲟⲗ ⲉ-ᵠⲁⲙⲁϩⲧⲉ ⲙ̄ⲙⲟ-ϥ. ⲛⲉⲩ-ϫⲱ ⲅⲁⲣ ⲙ̄ⲙⲟ-ⲥ ϫⲉ-ⲁ-ⲡⲉϥϩⲏⲧ ⲡⲱϣⲥ̄[130].

22. ⲁⲩⲱ ⲛⲉⲅⲣⲁⲙⲙⲁⲧⲉⲩⲥ ⲉⲛⲧ-ⲁⲩ-ⲉⲓ ⲉⲃⲟⲗ ϩⲛ̄-ⲑⲓⲉⲣⲟⲥⲟⲗⲩⲙⲁ, ⲛⲉⲩ-ϫⲱ ⲙ̄ⲙⲟ-ⲥ ϫⲉ-ⲉⲣⲉ-ⲃⲉⲉⲗⲍⲉⲃⲟⲩⲗ ⲛⲙ̄ⲙⲁ-ϥ. ⲁⲩⲱ ϩⲙ̄-ⲡⲁⲣⲭⲱⲛ[131] ⲛ̄-ⲛ̄ⲇⲁⲓⲙⲟⲛⲓⲟⲛ ⲉϥ-ⲛⲉϫ-ᵠⲇⲁⲓⲙⲟⲛⲓⲟⲛ ⲉⲃⲟⲗ.

---

[120] *ⲡⲣⲟⲥⲕⲁⲣⲧⲉⲣⲉⲓ stand ready, await.   [121] *ⲑⲗⲓⲃⲉ press upon, oppress.   [122] ⲧⲁⲗϭⲟ (ⲧⲁⲗϭⲉ-, ⲧⲁⲗϭⲟ⸗) ⲧⲁⲗϭⲏⲩ† heal.   [123] *ⲧ-ⲙⲁⲥⲧⲓⲅ⳽ whip, suffering.   [124] ϩⲁⲣⲁⲧ-ϥ̄ ⲛ̄-, ϩⲁⲣⲁⲧ⸗ beneath (Compound preposition).   [125] ⲛⲟⲩϩⲉ ⲉⲃⲟⲗ (ⲛⲉϩ-, ⲛⲁϩ⸗) ⲛⲏϩ† separate, choose.   [126] ⲧⲁϩⲟ ⲉⲣⲁⲧ-ⲟⲩ ⲙ̄- established (made them stand upon feet of them).   [127] ⲡⲉ- (and ⲧⲉ-) ϩⲣⲟⲩⲃ̄ⲃⲁⲓ̈ thunder (cf. ϩⲣⲟⲟⲩ voice, sound).   [128] ⲥⲣ̄ϥⲉ, ⲥⲣⲟϥⲧ̄† be at leisure.   [129] ⲛⲉϥ-ⲣⲱⲙⲉ His family.   [130] ⲡⲱϣⲥ̄ (ⲡⲉϣⲥ̄-, ⲡⲟϣⲥ⸗) ⲡⲟϣⲥ̄† amaze, turn aside.   [131] *ⲡ-ⲁⲣⲭⲱⲛ leader.

23. ⲁϥ-ⲙⲟⲩⲧⲉ ⲇⲉ ⲉⲣⲟ-ⲟⲩ. ⲁϥ-ϣⲁϫⲉ ⲛⲙ̄ⲙⲁ-ⲩ ϩⲛ̄-ϩⲉⲛⲡⲁⲣⲁⲃⲟⲗⲏ¹³²
ⲉϥ-ϫⲱ ⲙ̄ⲙⲟ-ⲥ ϫⲉ-ⲛ̄-ⲁϣ ⲛ̄-ϩⲉ ⲡⲥⲁⲧⲁⲛⲁⲥ, ϥ-ⲛⲁ-ⲛⲉϫ-ⲡⲥⲁⲧⲁⲛⲁⲥ
ⲉⲃⲟⲗ.

24. ⲁⲩⲱ ⲉⲣϣⲁⲛ-ⲟⲩⲙⲛ̄ⲧ-ⲣ̄ⲣⲟ ⲡⲱⲣϫ̄¹³³ ⲉ-ⲛⲉⲥⲉⲣⲏⲩ ⲛ̄-ⲥ-ⲛⲁ-ϣ-ⲁϩⲉ
ⲁⲛ ⲉⲣⲁⲧ-ⲥ̄ ⲛ̄ϭⲓ-ⲧⲙⲛ̄ⲧ-ⲣ̄ⲣⲟ ⲉⲧ⁰-ⲙ̄ⲙⲁⲩ.

25. ⲁⲩⲱ ⲉⲣϣⲁⲛ-ⲟⲩⲏⲓ̈ ⲡⲱⲣϫ̄ ⲉ-ⲛⲉϥⲉⲣⲏⲩ ⲛ̄ⲛⲉ-ϣ-ⲡⲏⲓ̈ ⲉⲧ⁰-ⲙ̄ⲙⲁⲩ
ⲁϩⲉⲣⲁⲧ-ϥ̄.

26. ⲁⲩⲱ ⲉϣϫⲉ-ⲡⲥⲁⲧⲁⲛⲁⲥ, ⲁϥ-ⲧⲱⲟⲩⲛ ⲛ̄ⲧⲟϥ ⲉϫⲱ-ϥ ⲁⲩⲱ ⲁϥ-ⲡⲱⲣϫ̄
ⲛ̄ⲛⲉϥ-ⲉϣ-ⲁϩⲉⲣⲁⲧ-ϥ̄. ⲁⲗⲗⲁ ⲁ-ⲧⲉϥϩⲁⲏ ϣⲱⲡⲉ.

27. ⲁⲗⲗⲁ ⲙⲛ̄-ⲗⲁⲁⲩ ⲛⲁ-ϣ-ⲃⲱⲕ ⲉϩⲟⲩⲛ ⲉ-ⲡⲏⲓ̈ ⲙ̄-ⲡⲭⲱⲱⲣⲉ ⲛ̄ϥ-ⲧⲱⲣⲡ̄¹³⁴
ⲛ̄-ⲛⲉϥϩⲛⲁⲩ¹³⁵ ⲉϥ-ⲧⲙ̄-ⲙⲟⲩⲣ ⲛ̄ϣⲟⲣⲡ̄ ⲙ̄-ⲡⲭⲱⲱⲣⲉ ⲁⲩⲱ ⲧⲟⲧⲉ ⲛ̄ϥ-ⲧⲱⲣⲡ̄
ⲙ̄-ⲡⲉϥⲏⲓ̈.

28. ϩⲁⲙⲏⲛ ϯ-ϫⲱ ⲙ̄ⲙⲟ-ⲥ ⲛⲏ-ⲧⲛ̄ ϫⲉ-ⲛⲟⲃⲉ ⲛⲓⲙ ϩⲓ-ⲟⲩⲁ ⲛⲓⲙ ⲉⲧⲟⲩ-
ⲛⲁ-ϫⲟⲟ-ⲩ ⲛ̄ϭⲓ-ⲛ̄ϣⲏⲣⲉ ⲛ̄-ⲛ̄ⲣⲱⲙⲉ, ⲥⲉ-ⲛⲁ-ⲕⲁⲁ-ⲩ ⲛⲁ-ⲩ ⲉⲃⲟⲗ.

29. ⲡ-ⲉⲧ⁰-ⲛⲁ-ϫⲓ-⁰ⲟⲩⲁ ⲇⲉ ⲉ-ⲡⲉⲡⲛ̄ⲁ̄ ⲉⲧ⁰-ⲟⲩⲁⲁⲃ, ⲙⲛ̄ⲧ-ϥ̄-ⲕⲱ ⲉⲃⲟⲗ
ϣⲁ-ⲉⲛⲉϩ. ⲁⲗⲗⲁ ϥ-ϭⲏⲡ¹³⁶ ⲉ-ⲩⲛⲟⲃⲉ ϣⲁ-ⲉⲛⲉϩ

30. ⲉⲃⲟⲗ ϫⲉ-ⲥⲉ-ϫⲱ ⲙ̄ⲙⲟ-ⲥ ϫⲉ-ⲟⲩⲛ̄-ⲟⲩⲡⲛ̄ⲁ̄ ⲛ̄-ⲁⲕⲁⲑⲁⲣⲧⲟⲛ
ⲛⲙ̄ⲙⲁ-ϥ.

31. ⲁⲩⲱ ⲁⲩ-ⲉⲓ ⲛ̄ϭⲓ-ⲧⲉϥⲙⲁⲁⲩ ⲙⲛ̄-ⲛⲉϥⲥⲛⲏⲩ. ⲁⲩ-ⲁϩⲉⲣⲁⲧ-ⲟⲩ ϩⲓ-
ⲃⲟⲗ¹³⁷. ⲁⲩⲱ ⲁⲩ-ϫⲟⲟⲩ¹³⁸ ⲛⲁ-ϥ ⲉϩⲟⲩⲛ ⲉⲩ-ⲙⲟⲩⲧⲉ ⲉⲣⲟ-ϥ.

32. ⲁⲩⲱ ⲛⲉϥ-ϩⲙⲟⲟⲥ ϩⲙ̄-ⲡⲉϥⲕⲱⲧⲉ ⲛ̄ϭⲓ-ⲟⲩⲙⲏⲏϣⲉ. ⲡⲉϫⲁ-ⲩ ⲇⲉ
ⲛⲁ-ϥ ϫⲉ-ⲉⲓⲥ-ⲧⲉⲕⲙⲁⲁⲩ ⲙⲛ̄-ⲛⲉⲕⲥⲛⲏⲩ, ⲥⲉ-ⲕⲱⲧⲉ ⲛ̄ⲥⲱ-ⲕ ϩⲓⲃⲟⲗ.

33. ⲁϥ-ⲟⲩⲱϣⲃ̄ ⲇⲉ ⲉϥ-ϫⲱ ⲙ̄ⲙⲟ-ⲥ ⲛⲁ-ⲩ ϫⲉ-ⲛⲓⲙ ⲧⲉ ⲧⲁⲙⲁⲁⲩ. ⲁⲩⲱ
ⲛⲓⲙ ⲛⲉ ⲛⲁⲥⲛⲏⲩ.

34. ⲁϥ-ϭⲱϣⲧ̄ ⲉ-ⲛ-ⲉⲧ⁰-ⲙ̄ⲡⲉϥⲕⲱⲧⲉ ⲉⲧ⁰-ϩⲙⲟⲟⲥ ϩⲁϩⲧⲏ-ϥ. ⲡⲉϫⲁ-ϥ
ϫⲉ-ⲉⲓⲥ-ⲧⲁⲙⲁⲁⲩ ⲁⲩⲱ ⲛⲁⲥⲛⲏⲩ.

35. ⲡ-ⲉⲧ⁰-ⲛⲁ-ⲉⲓⲣⲉ ⲅⲁⲣ ⲙ̄-ⲡⲟⲩⲱϣ ⲙ̄-ⲡⲛⲟⲩⲧⲉ, ⲡⲁⲓ̈ ⲡⲉ ⲡⲁⲥⲟⲛ ⲁⲩⲱ
ⲧⲁⲥⲱⲛⲉ ⲁⲩⲱ ⲧⲁⲙⲁⲁⲩ.

---

¹³² *ⲧ-ⲡⲁⲣⲁⲃⲟⲗⲏ parable.   ¹³³ ⲡⲱⲣϫ̄ (ⲡⲣ̄ϫ-, ⲡⲟⲣϫ⸗) ⲡⲟⲣϫ̄† divide, separate.
¹³⁴ ⲧⲱⲣⲡ̄ (ⲧⲣ̄ⲡ-, ⲧⲟⲣⲡ⸗) ⲧⲟⲣⲡ̄† rob, seize.   ¹³⁵ ⲡⲉ-ϩⲛⲁ(ⲁ)ⲩ thing, vessel, foodstuff.
¹³⁶ Cf. note 34.   ¹³⁷ ϩⲓⲃⲟⲗ outside.   ¹³⁸ ϫⲟⲟⲩ ⲛⲁ-ϥ ⲉϩⲟⲩⲛ sent word into Him.

REFERENCE LIST
OF COPTIC FORMS

Numbers (e.g. 77) refer to paragraphs of the grammar except where "vocabulary" is specified.

Greek alphabetical order is followed, except that ⲑ, ⲫ, ⲭ, ⲯ are filed as ⲧⳛ, ⲡⳛ, ⲕⳛ, ⲡⲥ. The Greek letters are followed by ⲱ ⳛ ⲭ ⳝ. (ϯ is filed as ⲧⲓ; digrams ⲉⲓ and ⲟⲩ as ⲉ + ⲓ and ⲟ + ⲩ.)

ⲁ–, past tense affirmative 2d sing. fem., 77

ⲁ–, ⲁⳋ, past tense affirm. base, 76, 77

ⲁⲁ, instead of ⲁⲁⲁ, 15

ⲁⲗⲗⲁ ⲉⳋ (circumstantial), *though*, 122 box

ⲁⲗⲟⳋ, *cease* (imperative), 87 box

ⲁⲙⲏ, *come* (imperative), 87 box

ⲁⲙⲏⲉⲓⲛ, *come* (imperative), 87 box

ⲁⲙⲏⲉⲓⲧⲛ̄, *come* (imperative), 87 box

ⲁⲙⲟⲩ, *come* (imperative), 87 box

ⲁⲛ, *not* (negator)
of adverbs, 119
of cleft sentence, 141
of conversions, 120, 130, 131, 137, 139
of durative sentence, 64
of impersonal predicate, 107
of nominal sentences, 34, 41, 42
placement vis-a-vis direct object, 72
of verboid, 102

ⲁⲛ–, *we are*, 32

ⲁⲛⲁⳋ, *will of*, 56 box

ⲁⲛⲁ–ϥ ⲛ̄–, *will of*, 56 box

ⲁⲛⲁⲣⲕⲏ, *it is necessary*, 107

ⲁⲛⲁⲩ, *look* (imperative), 87 box

ⲁⲛⲅ̄–, *I am*, 32

ⲁⲛⲓ–, *bring* (imperative), 87 box

ⲁⲛⲓⳋ, *bring* (imperative), 87 box, 103 box

ⲁⲛⲓⲛⲉ, *bring* (imperative), 87 box

ⲁⲛⲟⲕ, *I/me*, 40

ⲁⲛⲟⲕ–, *I am*, 34 box

ⲁⲛⲟⲕ ⲉⲛⲧ–, cleft sentence, 144

ⲁⲛⲟⲕ ⲉⲧ–, cleft sentence, 144

ⲁⲛⲟⲛ, *we/us*, 40

ⲁⲛⲟⲛ–, *we are*, 32, 34 box

ⲁⲛⲟⲛ ⲉⲛⲧ–, cleft sentence, 144

ⲁⲛⲟⲛ ⲉⲧ–, cleft sentence, 144

ⲁⲛⲧⲓ–, *instead of* (preposition), 52 box

ⲁⲛⲧⲓ–ⲧⲣⲉ–, *instead of*, 100 box

ⲁⲟⲩⲱⲛ, *open* (imperative), 87 box

ⲁⲡ–, past tense affirmative 2d sing. fem., 77

ⲁⲡⲁ, *so* (marking question), 146

ⲁⲡⲉ–, past tense affirmative 2d sing. fem., 77

ⲁⲡⲏⲭ(ⲛ)ⳋ, *end of*, 56 box

ⲁⲡⲏⲭ(ⲛ)–ϥ ⲛ̄–, *end of*, 56 box

ⲁⲡⲓ–, *do* (imperative), 87 box

ⲁⲡⲓⳋ, *do* (imperative), 87 box, 103 box

ⲁⲡⲓⲡⲉ, *do* (imperative), 87 box

M̄–, in attributive construction, 36
M̄–, instead of N̄–, 11
M̄–, *not. See* N̄–, not.
M̄–, *of,* 29
M̄–, *the* (instead of N̄–), 22
MA–, forming imperative of infinitives in initial T, 87 box
MA–, *give* (imperative), 87 box
MA–N̄–, forming nouns, 21 box
MA–†–, *give* (imperative), 87 box
MAAB, *thirty,* 45
MAABE, *thirty,* 45
MAB–, *thirty* (forming cardinal numbers), 45
MAAICTA E⸗ (circumstantial), *especially if/since,* 122 box
MAPE–, MAP⸗, jussive affirmative base, 76, 81
MAYAA⸗, *alone,* 96
MAYAAT⸗, *alone,* 96
ME⸗, aorist negative base, 76, 79
MEN, *now*
  not answered by ΔE, vocabulary 5 (note b)
  position of, vocabulary 5 (note a)
MEPATE, *beloved,* 35
MEPE–, aorist negative prenominal, 75
MEPE–, aorist negative 2d sing. fem., 79
MEPE–, plus infinitive, 74 box
MEPE–, ME⸗, aorist negative base, 76, 79
MEPIT, *beloved,* 35
MEWA⸗, *not know,* 105
MEWWE, *it is not right,* 107
ME2–, forming ordinal numbers, 48
MH, marking question, 146
MHГENOITO, *may it not come to pass,* 107
MHT, *ten,* 45
MHTE, *ten,* 45
M̄MAY, untranslatable after OYN̄TE– and MN̄TE–, 103

M̄MINM̄MO, *yourself,* 96
M̄MINM̄MO⸗, *(my- etc.)self,* 96
M̄MN̄–, *not* (durative sentence), *there is no(t),* 63, 64
M̄MN̄TA⸗, *not have,* 103
M̄MN̄TE–, *you do not have* (2d sing. fem.), 103
M̄MN̄TE–, M̄MN̄TA⸗, *not have,* 103
M̄MO⸗, marking direct object, 72, 84
M̄MON, *no,* 88 box
MN̄–, *and,* 27
MN̄–, *not* (durative sentence), *there is no(t),* 63, 64
MN̄–6OM N̄–/M̄MO⸗, *is not able to,* vocabulary 15
MN̄N̄CA–E–TPE–, *after,* 100 box
MN̄N̄CA–TPE–, *after,* 100 box
MN̄T, instead of M̄T, 13
MN̄T–, forming nouns, 21 box
MN̄T–, *ten* (forming cardinal numbers), 45
MN̄T⸗, *not have* (with suffixed subject and direct object), 103
MN̄TA⸗, *not have,* 103
MN̄TE–, *you do not have* (2d sing. fem.), 103
MN̄TE–, MN̄TA⸗, *not have,* 103
MN̄TEPWOY, for MN̄T–P̄PWOY, vocabulary 2
MN̄T†– (for MN̄T–I–), *I do not have,* 103
MO, *take* (imperative), 87 box
MOY, instead of MW, 12
M̄ΠATE–, "not yet" prenominal, 78
M̄ΠATE–, "not yet" 2d sing. fem., 78
M̄ΠATE–, M̄ΠAT⸗, "not yet" conjugation base, 76, 78
  for E–M̄ΠATE–, E–M̄ΠAT⸗, 16
M̄ΠE, *no,* 88 box
M̄ΠE–, past tense negative prenominal, 77
M̄ΠE–, past tense negative 2d sing. fem., 77

oγ, instead of oγoγ, 15
oγ, *what?*, 43
oγ-, *a*, 18
-oγ, *they/them*, 52, 83
oγⲁ, *one*, 45
oγⲁ, *someone*, 18
oγⲁⲁ=, *only*, 96
oγⲁⲁⲧ=, *only*, 96
oγⲁⳛ, *which?*, 44
oγⲁⳛ=, *love*, direct object of, 84
oγⲁⲉ, *nor*, 28
-oγⲉ, *one* (forming cardinal numbers), 45
oγⲉⲃⲟⲗ, in nominal sentence predicate, 59
oγⲉⲓ, *one*, 45
oγⲉⲓ, *someone*, 18
-oγⲉⲓ, *one* (forming cardinal numbers), 45
oγⲉⲧ-, *is distinct*, 105
oγⲉⲧ- ... oγⲉⲧ-, ... *is one thing, but ... is quite another*, 105
oγⲉⳛ-, *want*
 direct object of, 84
 plus infinitive, 74 box
oγⲉⳓⲙ-, plus infinitive, 74 box
oγⲏⲣ, *how many?*, 43
oγⲕⲉϩⲉⲥⲧⲓ, *it is not permitted*, 107
oγⲗⲁⲁγ, *insignificant*, 44
oγⲛ-, forming arithmetical fractions, 21 box
oγⲛ̄-, *open* (imperative of oγⲱⲛ), 87 box
oγⲛ̄-, *there is*, 63
oγⲛ̄-ⲛ̄-, forming arithmetical fractions, 21 box
oγⲛ̄-ⳛϭⲟⲙ ⲛ̄-/ⲙⲙⲟ=, *is able to*, vocabulary 15
oγⲛ̄-ϭⲟⲙ ⲛ̄-/ⲙⲙⲟ=, *is able to*, vocabulary 15
oγⲛ̄- ... ⲙⲙⲟ-ϥ, *he has*, 104
oγⲛ̄- ... ⲛ̄ϩⲏⲧ-ϥ̄, *he has*, 104

oγⲛ̄- ... ϩⲓⲱⲱ-ϥ, *he has*, 104
oγⲛ̄ⲧ=, *have* (with both subject and direct object suffixed), 103
oγⲛ̄ⲧⲁ=, *have*, 103
oγⲛ̄ⲧⲉ-, *you have*, 103
oγⲛ̄ⲧⲉ-, oγⲛ̄ⲧⲁ=, *have* (verboid base), 103
oγⲛ̄ⲧ†- (for oγⲛ̄ⲧ-ⲓ-), *I have*, 103
oγⲟⲛ, untranslatable pronoun, 62
oγⲟⲛ, *yes*, 88 box
oγⲟⲛ ⲛⲓⲙ, *any*, 62
oγⲟγ, *what sort?*, 44
oγⲧⲉ, *neither/nor*, 28
oγⲱⲧ, *only*, vocabulary 13

ⲡ-, in place names, 23
ⲡ-, plus relative converter, 125, 132, 134, 142
ⲡ-, *the*, 18
ⲡ- ... ⲉⲧⲙ̄ⲙⲁγ, *that*, 60, 130
ⲡⲁ-, *my*, 30
ⲡⲁ-, *(the) one belonging to*, 57
ⲡⲁⲓ̈, plus circumstantial conversion, 132 box
ⲡⲁⲓ̈, plus relative conversion, 132 box, 134
ⲡⲁⲓ̈, *this*, 18
ⲡⲁⲗⲓⲛ ⲟⲛ ⲉ= (circumstantial), *moreover*, 122 box
ⲡⲁⲣⲁ-, ⲡⲁⲣⲁⲣⲟ=, *contrary to* (preposition), 52 box
ⲡⲉ, *(he/it) is*, 32, 42
ⲡⲉ (invariable), *it is*, 32
ⲡⲉ, preterit particle, 116
ⲡⲉ-, *the*, 22
ⲡ(ⲉ)-, with attached relative clause (forming cleft sentence), 141
ⲡⲉⲓ̈-, *this*, 18
ⲡⲉⲕ-, *your*, 30
ⲡⲉⲛ-, *our*, 30
ⲡⲉⲥ-, *her*, 30
ⲡⲉⲧ-, forming nouns, 21 box

ϣⲙⲛ̄ⲧ-ⲥⲱⲱⲡ, *three times*, vocabulary 14

ϣⲙⲛ̄ⲧ-ϣⲉ, *three hundred*, 45

ϣⲙ̄ⲛⲧ-ϣⲟ, *three thousand*, 45

ϣⲙⲟⲩⲛ, *eight*, 45

ϣⲙⲟⲩⲛⲉ, *eight*, 45

ϣⲟ, *one thousand*, 45

ϣⲟ, *yes*, 88 box

ϣⲟⲙⲛ̄ⲧ, *three*, 45

ϣⲟⲙⲧⲉ, *three*, 45

-ϣⲟⲙⲧⲉ, *three* (forming cardinal numbers), 45

ϣⲟⲟⲡ ⲛ̄-, *exists as*, 82

ϣⲟⲣⲡ̄, *first*, 35

ϣⲟⲣⲡⲉ, *first*, 35

ϣⲟⲩ-, *forming nouns*, 21 box

ϣϣⲉ, *it is right*, 107

ϣϥⲉ, *seventy*, 45

ϣϥⲉ-, *seventy* (forming cardinal numbers), 45

ϣϭⲙ̄-ϭⲟⲙ, *is able to*, vocabulary 15

ϥ-, *he/it (is)*, 63

-ϥ, *he/him*, 52, 83

-ϥ̄, *him*, 52, 83

ϥⲧⲉⲩ-ϣⲉ, *four hundred*, 45

ϥⲧⲉⲩ-ϣⲟ, *four thousand*, 45

ϥⲧⲟ, *four*, 45

ϥⲧⲟⲉ, *four*, 45

ϥⲧⲟⲟⲩ, *four*, 45

ϩ (initial), and Greek rough/smooth breathing, vocabulary 2 (note)

ϩⲁⲉ, *last*, 35

ϩⲁⲉⲉⲩ, *last*, 35

ϩⲁⲏ, *last*, 35

ϩⲁⲕ, *sober*, 35

ϩⲁⲙ-, *forming nouns*, 21 box

ϩⲁⲙ-ⲛ̄-, *forming nouns*, 21 box

ϩⲁⲙⲁ ⲉ= (circumstantial), *at the same time*, 122 box

ϩⲁⲙⲟⲓ̈, *how good it would be if*, 107

ϩⲁⲡⲥ̄, *it is necessary*, 107

ϩⲁⲑⲏ ⲉ-ⲙ̄ⲡⲁⲧ= (circumstantial), *before*, 122 box

ϩⲁⲑⲏ ⲉ-ⲧⲣⲉ-, *before*, 100 box

ϩⲁⲑⲏ ⲙ̄ⲡⲁⲧ=. *See* ϩⲁⲑⲏ ⲉ-ⲙ̄ⲡⲁⲧ= and 16

ϩⲁϩ, *many*, 43

ϩⲉ, ϩⲏⲩ, syntax of, 89

ϩⲉ ⲉ-, ϩⲏⲩ ⲉ-, syntax of, 89 note

ϩⲉ ⲉⲃⲟⲗ, ϩⲏⲩ ⲉⲃⲟⲗ, syntax of, 89 note

ϩⲉⲛ-, plural indefinite article, 18

ϩⲉⲛⲁϣ, *which?*, 44

ϩⲉⲛⲉⲃⲟⲗ, in nominal sentence predicate, 59

ϩⲉⲛⲕⲉ-, *other*, 61

ϩⲉⲛⲕⲟⲟⲩⲉ, *others*, 61

ϩⲉⲛⲗⲁⲁⲩ, *insignificant*, 44

ϩⲉⲛⲟⲩ, *what sort?*, 44

ϩⲏⲕⲉ, *poor*, 35

ϩⲏⲧ-ϥ ⲛ̄-, *belly of*, 54

ϩⲏⲧ-ϥ ⲛ̄-, *fore part(s) of*, 54

ϩⲏⲧ=, *belly of*, 54

ϩⲏⲧ=, *fore part(s) of*, 54

ϩⲓ-, *and*, 27

ϩⲓⲧⲙ̄-ⲡⲧⲣⲉ-, *because of*, 100 box

ϩⲓⲱⲧ-ⲧⲏⲩⲧⲛ̄, *on you*, 51

ϩⲓⲱⲱ-ⲧⲉ, *on you*, 51

ϩⲁⲗⲟ, *old*, 35

ϩⲁⲗⲟⲓ, *old*, 35

ϩⲁⲗⲱ, *old*, 35

ϩⲙ̄-, instead of ϩⲛ̄-, 11

ϩⲙ̄-ⲡⲧⲣⲉ-, *while*, 100 box

ϩⲙⲉ, *forty*, 45

ϩⲙⲉ-, *forty* (forming cardinal numbers), 45

ϩⲙⲉⲛⲉ, *eighty*, 45

ϩⲙⲉⲛⲉ-, *eighty* (forming cardinal numbers), 45

ϩⲙⲉⲛⲉⲧ-, *eighty* (forming cardinal numbers), 45

ϫⲱ=, *head of*, 54

ϫⲱⲱⲣⲉ, *strong*, 35

ϭⲉ, *another*, 61

ϭⲉ, *then* (position of), vocabulary 5
   (note a)

ϭⲓⲛ–, forming nouns, 21 box

ϭⲙ̄–ϭⲟⲙ, *is able to*, vocabulary 15

ϭⲟⲟⲩ= (*make narrow*), with personal
   second suffixes, 103 box

SUBJECT INDEX

Numbers (e.g. 17) refer to paragraphs of the grammar.

PRINTED ON PERMANENT PAPER • IMPRIME SUR PAPIER PERMANENT • GEDRUKT OP DUURZAAM PAPIER - ISO 9706

N.V. PEETERS S.A., WAROTSTRAAT 50, B-3020 HERENT